Tongnaab

Tongnaab

The History of a West African God

Jean Allman and John Parker

Indiana University Press
Bloomington and Indianapolis

Publication of this book is made possible in part with
the assistance of a Challenge Grant from the National
Endowment for the Humanities, a federal agency that
supports research, education, and public programming
in the humanities.

This book is a publication of

Indiana University Press
601 North Morton Street
Bloomington, IN 47404-3797 USA

http://iupress.indiana.edu

Telephone orders   800-842-6796
Fax orders   812-855-7931
Orders by e-mail   iuporder@indiana.edu

The paper used in this publication meets the minimum
requirements of American National Standard for Information Sciences—Permanence of Paper for Printed
Library Materials, ANSI Z39.48-1984.

Manufactured in the United States of America

Library of Congress Cataloging-in-Publication Data

Allman, Jean Marie.
     Tongnaab: the history of a West African god / Jean
Allman and John Parker.
          p.   cm.
     Includes bibliographical references and index.
     ISBN 0-253-34665-7 (cloth : alk. paper) — ISBN
0-253-21806-3 (pbk. : alk. paper)   1. Tallensi (African
people)—Religion.   2. Tongnaab (African deity)—
Cult—History—20th century.   3. Witchcraft—Africa,
West—History—20th century.   4. Witchcraft—
Africa, West—History—19th century.   I. Parker,
John, date   II. Title.
BL2480.T3A45   2005
299.6'835—dc22   2005010909

1 2 3 4 5 10 09 08 07 06 05

Contents

List of Maps

Acknowledgments

Our debts in the completion of this project are many. Jean Allman's research has been supported by the National Endowment for the Humanities and the United States Department of Education's Fulbright-Hays Program, the Institute of African Studies at the University of Ghana, the University of Minnesota, and the Research Board and Center for Advanced Studies at the University of Illinois. John Parker's research has been supported by the British Academy, the Arts and Humanities Research Board, and the School of Oriental and African Studies, University of London.

We would like to thank those who invited us to present seminar papers on aspects of our research as it developed and all who provided vital feedback, especially Alma Gottlieb and other members of the Social Anthropology Workshop at the University of Illinois; Takyiwaa Manuh, Kojo Amanor, and the faculty at the Institute of African Studies, University of Ghana; Richard Rathbone at the School of Oriental and African Studies; Murray Last at University College, London; Andrew Porter and David Killingray at the Imperial History Seminar of the Institute of Historical Research, University of London; and Patrick Harries at the University of Basel, Switzerland.

At many points along the way, we received crucial advice and encouragement from numerous colleagues: Sonia Abun-Nasr, Moses Anafu, Kwame Arhin, Gareth Austin, Lynne Brydon, Rijk van Dijk, Steve Feierman, Sandra Greene, Peter Haenger, John Hanson, Jennifer Hasty, Allen Isaacman, Jon Kirby, T. C. McCaskie, Carol Miles, David Owusu-Ansah, John Peel, Derek Peterson, Richard Rathbone, David Roediger, Anna Vinegrad, and Ivor Wilks. We are grateful to Susan Drucker-Brown, who facilitated access to the photograph collection of the late Meyer Fortes, to Sudeshna Guha at the Museum of Anthropology and Archaeology, University of Cambridge, to Chris Morton at the Pitt Rivers Museum, Oxford, and to Brad Boesdorfer, who drew the maps. Dee Mortensen, the wonderful staff at Indiana University Press, and Shoshanna Green, our copy editor, made sure this was the best book it could possibly be.

In Ghana, we are indebted to so many, who quite literally made our work possible: Takyiwaa Manuh, the Director of the Institute of African Studies, and her predecessors, especially Kwame Arhin and Irene Adotei; and Cletus Azangweo, Director of the Public Records and Archives Administration Department, and his staff at the National Archives of Ghana in Accra and its regional branches, who, with boundless patience, provided access to a wealth of archival documentation. We would especially like to mention Judith Botchway and A. K. Mensah (Accra), Dua Abrokwa, Zakari Mahama, Helen Aloba, Leila Issifu and Abdulai Abukari (Tamale), and Felix Ampong and Dorothy Armah (Cape Coast). We also wish to make special mention of Thomas Aning (Manhyia Record Office) and of A. W. K. Amoako-Atta (Akyem Abuakwa State Archives). Father Jon Kirby not only provided hospitality at the Tamale Institute of Cross-Cultural Studies, but over many breakfast "seminars" offered indispensable advice—including pointing us to Wiaga and Kadema, as we struggled to trace Tongnaab's network in the north. Robert Arbuckle, former U.S. Cultural Affairs Officer in Accra, provided generous financial support for the exhibition we launched with the Upper East Regional Museum, "The Cultural Landscape of the Tong Hills," in Bolgatanga in 2000. In Bolga, we owe far too many debts to count, but we would like especially to thank the staff at the Sacred Heart Social Center: Samson Aloko and Mathilda Aba Mbi, as well as Georgina, Michael, Francis, Clothilda, Pascalina, Vic, Dina, Luciana, and Rose; and the staff of the Regional Museum, especially Ben W. Kankpeyeng and R. H. Boateng. Baba "OK" was one of the first to introduce us to the ways and byways of the Upper East, and our dear friend Atechiman Awumbase Asumboya and his family helped make Bolga a second home. In Tongo and the Tong Hills, the *tongrana*, Golibdaana Malbazaa, and Assemblyman John Bawa Zuure provided invaluable support and guidance and were endlessly patient with our many questions. Our two research collaborators, Frederick Naab and William Namaani, guided us with skill and sensitivity into the culture of the Tong Hills, and worked long and hard providing translations and explanations in dozens of interviews. In Bole, we offer thanks to Esther Goody, Kate Hassan, and Hassan Mahama. Samson Sonfa Jimah provided skillful translation services in Senyon, as did Lawrence Jortnotey of the Wa Tourist Board in Kandiau and Owen Agoldem in Wiaga and surrounding towns in Builsaland. In Accra, we are hugely indebted to Emily Asiedu for years of wonderful hospitality, and to Albert Ahwireng, Eric Twum-Barimah, and Akua Karikari. Thanks also to

Bismark Enoch Larbi, who shared family stories of his grandfather, Kobina Assifu, with us. Our greatest debt, however, is to all those Ghanaians—most very old and some now sadly passed away—who generously gave their time to speak to us about their lives and the lives of their mothers, fathers, and ancestors.

Tongnaab

Introduction

$\mathcal{N}$either of us set out in 1992 to become enmeshed in the history of Tongnaab. We were both busy with our separate research projects based in Ghana's south—a social history of the capital, Accra, and a history of gender and colonialism in Asante—when we decided to take a break and together visit the northern savanna region of the country. Like too many of Ghana's historians, neither of us had spent much time in the north. After several days in Bolgatanga, the capital of the Upper East Region, we recollected that the renowned anthropologist Meyer Fortes had written in the 1940s about a powerful shrine located in the nearby Tong Hills. The hills, visible low on the horizon to the southwest from the balcony of our hotel, lay at the heart of the country inhabited by the Talensi. Inquiries in town revealed that they were still regarded as a sacred place and could be visited by interested travelers. We decided to have a look—two academic tourists with rather blurry ethnographic eyes. Because the day we chose to travel was not a market day and there was no public transport available, we chartered a taxi to Tongo, the principal Talensi settlement in the vicinity of the hills. The distance was only some eight miles, but due to the poor condition of the roads at the time the journey took over half an hour. As we reached the junction near the house of the chief of Tongo, we turned right on what resembled a footpath far more than a road. After a few hundred yards, the car could go no further. Our driver pointed to the

Figure I.1. Tengzugnaaba Dagban Zuure (died 2000; on the right), 1992.

granite outcrop rising steeply from the surrounding plains and said, "That's where you want to go."

It was September and getting toward the end of the rainy season, so the millet and sorghum stood tall on either side of the narrow track. As we approached the base of the hills, a small boy emerged from the crops and walked on ahead. After winding up the rocky outer slopes, the path dipped down into a bowl-shaped central valley planted with more millet and surrounded on all sides by steep walls of pink granite boulders. It was only after we came to a junction that we realized the boy was guiding us—but where, we were not quite sure, since we spoke no Talen and he spoke neither English nor Twi, the Akan language of the south. We followed. After nearly an hour's walk, he brought us to one of the largest compounds either of us had seen in the north of Ghana—one, we would later learn, that houses some three hundred people. We were told that it was the house of the "chief of Tengzug" and were taken to greet its owner.

After greeting the elderly chief, Tengzugnaaba Dagban Zuure, we explained that we had heard of a famous shrine in the vicinity and wished to visit it. Over the course of the next hour, male elders began to gather at the compound to accompany us to the sacred site. Once all had assembled and payment for the necessary mediation and sacrifices had been negotiated, we moved from the compound, single file along a winding footpath, toward the highest peak in the hills. As we began to ascend, a broad vista of the savanna grasslands opened up below us, stretching away in the south to the glint of the White Volta River and the Mamprugu escarpment. Continuing up the rocks, we finally reached a level space shaded by trees just below a cave. There, we were told, is where "the god is."

After lengthy discussions concerning the ritual requirements for entering the inner sanctum of the shrine, we finally climbed up and made our way, on hands and knees, through a narrow opening in the rocks. We were told that we had now entered the space inhabited by the most powerful of Talensi "gods"—Tongnaab (literally, "chief of the earth"). Tongnaab was attended by a young man sitting below us in the belly of the cave, gazing off distractedly into the middle distance. Before him lay the heaped remains of countless animal sacrifices, mostly fowls. We joined our guides in summoning Tongnaab with a burst of hand-clapping and were then asked to present our petitions to the god. What transpired after that point is, by proper Talensi protocol, best left with those who were present. What we can say is that the experience was unforgettable.

Perched amidst the granite boulders at the summit of the Tong Hills, we felt as though we had chanced upon one of the most remote and magical places on earth. Surely we must be among only a handful of foreign visitors who had ever journeyed to this secluded sacred place. As we picked our way down from the cave after our consultation with the oracle, a man whom we would come to know well, "Assemblyman" John Bawa Zuure, broke the silence. "Ah, you know, we have been very busy these days. This morning we had visitors from Asante and just yesterday six tourists came here from Japan to consult with Tongnaab." Tongnaab, Zuure informed us, attracted pilgrims from all over Ghana, from neighboring West African states, and from around the world. Far more adept at seeing the historical dynamics of the forests and coasts of Ghana's southern regions, we had mistakenly approached our visit to Tongnaab as a profoundly local, "traditional" experience in a remote corner of the West African savanna. We had no idea of the extent—both spatial and temporal—of the pilgrimage network we had joined when we climbed the hills that morning. We had no real sense that our profoundly "local" experience was, at one and the same time, global and historical. And so our project began.

Figure I.2. The entrance to the Yanii Tongnaab shrine, 1992.

Tongnaab: The History of an African God

While our blurred vision seems inexcusable from where we now sit, it is also the case that the sacred network centered on the Tong Hills has not occupied a particularly visible place in public, government, media, or scholarly discourse for nearly a half century. Indeed, the last widely disseminated account of Tongnaab that we have been able to locate appeared in a May 1956 issue of the London-based weekly *West Africa*.[1] The article, by Geoffrey Parrinder and entitled "The Prevalence of Witches," stands out amidst the welter of political stories dominating the magazine's coverage of events in Britain's four West African colonies. The Gold Coast, in particular, was in the grip of an election campaign, which two months later resulted in the return of Kwame Nkrumah's Convention People's Party to power and in the full independence of the new nation-state of Ghana in March 1957. "The Prevalence of Witches" was concerned with the shifting terrain of religion and popular belief underlying these dramatic political changes. A one-time Protestant missionary in the French colonies of Dahomey and Côte d'Ivoire, Parrinder was a pioneering figure in the study of African religion who became the first lecturer in religious studies at Nigeria's new University College of Ibadan in 1949. Confronted with the continuing belief in witchcraft as an explanation for misfortune throughout this part of West Africa, he sought to highlight the tenacity of indigenous religious movements in the battle against evil forces. One such cult, he argued, had an especially widespread impact in the region:

> In the last 30 years there spread a witch-finding movement across a great part of West Africa. It originated from the Tong Hills in the north of the Gold Coast, and in 1928 Dr R. S. Rattray described how people came long distances to obtain the power of the god Tong, of which one could buy a ritual clientship. As Nana Tongo the cult came down to the Gold Coast seaboard where Dr M. J. Field wrote of it in 1937. Thence it spread to the Ivory Coast and eastwards across Togoland and Dahomey. As Anatinga, abbreviated to Atinga, it became popular in western Nigeria until prohibited by an Order-in-Council in 1951.[2]

In the decades following Ghana's independence, the "god Tong" or "Nana Tongo," as it was known throughout southern Ghana, received little coverage in the national press and raised few concerns for the newly independent governments of the region. But that subsequent documentary silence should not be read as an end to the story. The ongoing ritual trajectory of indigenous gods like Tongnaab, we argue, remains central to the social history of West Africa. Indeed, Parrinder's 1956 description hints at a hidden story of cross-cultural religious exchange underlying the established narratives of twentieth-century West African history. It is a story that periodically forced its way onto the documentary record, only to subside again into relative obscurity.

With this book, we seek to bring historical light to bear on that obscurity. We aim to challenge the analytical distinction between tradition and modernity in the study of West African belief by reconstructing the movement and mutation of the indigenous religious complex centered on Tongnaab from the era of the slave trade to the era of the tourist trade. Tongnaab was and is a revered ancestor-deity of the Talensi, the people who inhabit the Tong Hills and their immediate surroundings in the Upper East Region of present-day Ghana. By the late nineteenth century, and arguably much earlier, Tongnaab was also the focus of what might be called a "regional cult," with well-established ritual constituencies among the surrounding peoples of the savannas of the middle Volta basin.[3] Its powers were closely linked to fertility, stability, and security—to bountiful harvests, to the production of numerous, healthy offspring, and to the maintenance of collective and personal safety. In the early colonial period, those powers underwent a striking expansion and transformation. By the 1920s, Tongnaab had spread beyond its established savanna heartland south to the

Akan forest and the trading towns of the Gold Coast, where it grew to extraordinary prominence as a powerful witch-finding deity.

In reconstructing the dynamic past of this West African god, our aim is not simply to write a religious history—to reconstruct a historical narrative of religious belief and practices. Rather, we use the story of Tongnaab as a prism through which to refract and then reflect upon a range of important themes in African history. We briefly introduce those themes here; in the sections that follow, we consider them in greater detail and in the context of debates within the broader scholarly literature. Our first and most fundamental point is that African religious belief and practice is profoundly historical. Too often scholars have privileged the processes of conversion to Islam and Christianity as the central historical dynamic of African religion, thereby consigning indigenous belief to the realm of unchanging tradition. Our concern here is to contribute to the ongoing project of reinserting African gods and their constituencies into history by showing how one deity underwent dramatic reconfiguration over time. Far from being an ancient "tribal" god swept aside by the coming of the so-called world religions, Tongnaab held its own in the increasingly competitive ritual marketplace of colonial West Africa. It remains today an integral part of the vibrant religious repertoire of modern Ghana.

Secondly, we demonstrate that the transformation of religious belief was not only temporal, it was spatial. As Parrinder noted in 1956, Tongnaab originated in the far north of the Gold Coast. From there it spread south through the Akan forest kingdom of Asante and on to the Atlantic seaboard before continuing its journey across colonial frontiers to the west and east. Tongnaab's passage from savanna to forest and the reciprocal movement of southern pilgrims to the Tong Hills cast in sharp relief the dynamics of trans-regional ritual dialogue in West African history. Those ongoing historical dynamics call into question the shape of much of Ghana's national history. While widely acknowledged as one of the most sophisticated in tropical Africa, the historiography of Ghana remains firmly focused on Asante and the other Akan states of the forest zone. The "stateless" peoples of the northern savanna—including the Talensi, the guardians and mediators of Tongnaab—have long been seen as peripheral to the main narratives of historical change. In the formulation of the early colonial ethnographer R. S. Rattray, these peoples formed the "tribes of the Ashanti hinterland."[4] The history of Tongnaab, we argue, complicates this vision of forest center and savanna periphery. The Talensi ancestor-deity possessed its own hinterland, centered on the shrines of the Tong Hills and by the 1930s extending outward through the Akan forest and beyond. The western schol-

arly focus on the "long conversation" between Africans and the world religions of Christianity and Islam should not obscure the ongoing talk among
indigenous African gods and their congregations.[5] Far from being a localized phenomenon rooted in a fixed ritual landscape, this talk often took
place across great distances and transcended a variety of political, cultural,
and ecological frontiers.

Thirdly, we aim to insert Tongnaab and the Tong Hills into the narrative of colonialism and anti-colonial resistance in Ghana—a narrative that
has focused largely on the south, especially on the great forest kingdom of
Asante. The resurgence and expansion of the Talensi shrine complex occurred despite sustained British efforts in the era of colonial conquest and
"pacification" to destroy Tongnaab and to suppress the ritual influence of
the Tong Hills. We reconstruct the encounter between Tongnaab on the
one hand and the range of forces subsumed under the rubric of "colonialism" on the other. In its initial stages, that encounter was characterized by
violent conflict, dispossession, and sustained resistance on the part of the
god's Talensi guardians to British efforts to assert control over the sacred
space of the Tong Hills. By the inter-war period, it included systematic attempts by colonial officials and pioneering anthropologists to make sense
of Tongnaab and its Talensi caretakers in order to construct a sustainable
system of colonial rule. Again, Parrinder alluded to this process in 1956
when he noted the roles of Rattray, the Gold Coast Government Anthropologist, and his successor, M. J. Field, in the production of knowledge
about Tongnaab's widening ritual network. The most significant figure in
the incorporation of the Talensi into western intellectual discourse, however, was the social anthropologist Meyer Fortes (1906–83), who conducted
fieldwork in and around the Tong Hills between 1934 and 1937. Our project
is not a "restudy" of Fortes's work on Talensi social structure, although it
shares a concern with Tongnaab and its Talensi custodians. *Pace* Fortes, our
central argument is that, far from being marooned in a state of timeless,
unchanging tradition, Talensi society in general and the ancestor cult of
Tongnaab in particular underwent profound change in the wake of colonial conquest.

Finally, we seek to insert the West African savanna into interdisciplinary analyses of witchcraft. Although the rise of anti-witchcraft movements
in Ghana, especially during the inter-war years, has attracted considerable
attention from both contemporary observers and subsequent scholars, the
focus of analysis has been almost exclusively on their southern manifestations. Little is known of the origins of the new cults in the savannas to the
north, much less of the trans-regional ritual dialogue out of which they

emerged. In its passage from the Tong Hills to Asante and the Gold Coast, the ancestor-deity of the Talensi became a god whose principal purpose was the identification and the healing of witches. In this respect Tongnaab—or Nana Tongo, as it was called by the Akan peoples and their immediate neighbors—was in no way unique. It was one of a whole range of gods that migrant workers, devoted pilgrims, and enterprising ritual entrepreneurs carried across the ecological and cultural divide between savanna and forest in the early twentieth century. In the southern forests, these savanna gods transmogrified into a range of heterodox religious cults. Tongnaab, for example, exploded into the purview of the colonial state as the witch-finding deity "Nana Tongo," initiating widespread debates within Gold Coast society on the meanings of good and evil, sickness and healing, "gods" and "fetishes." In recent years, there has been a wealth of cutting-edge scholarly inquiry into the nature of witchcraft, spirit possession cults, and other forms of ritual practice in contemporary Africa. The story of Tongnaab, we argue, demonstrates the importance of examining the idioms of witchcraft and anti-witchcraft as complex historical phenomena rather than as sets of inherent "structural" beliefs.

Gods, Shrines, and Religious Movements in African History

When R. S. Rattray (in the 1920s) and then Meyer Fortes (in the 1930s) encountered Tongnaab amidst the granite boulders of the Tong Hills, both men assumed they were dealing with an ancient tribal deity, part of a timeless ritual landscape that had emerged long before the coming of British rule and continued to exist in its primordial state beyond the reach of the modern world. Given the personal predilections and the theoretical models of these two pioneering ethnographers, this analysis is hardly surprising. Yet it is striking how persistent this emphasis on the timeless quality of African religion has been, even though the intellectual frameworks governing the practice of social anthropology in the first half of the twentieth century have long been abandoned. Indeed, the reflexive conclusions we drew during our first visit to Tongnaab are an obvious case in point. Despite a number of recent essays that critically examine the use of the concept "African traditional religion"—and even, in the African context, the term "religion" itself—the notion of a set of fundamental beliefs and practices, formulated sometime in the distant past and used as a precolonial baseline from which to measure the dynamics of conversion to Islam or Christianity, remains embedded within much of the literature on African history.[6]

There are two main problems here. First, and most obviously, "traditional religion" and its practitioners are by definition regarded as ahistoric. Second, the emphasis on the notion of "belief" in the form of homogeneous, systemized cosmologies has resulted in a striking neglect of ritual practice, or what the comparative theorist of religion Jonathan Z. Smith has called "religious work."[7] Yet beliefs "were linked to rituals and symbols," as Brenner has stressed, "and ritual was tied to specific [that is, historic and spatial] situations."[8] In the African context, the specificity of ritual has long been hinted at in an appreciation of the essentially eclectic nature of belief systems, and especially by the movement of religious ideas and practices across political, cultural, and ethnic boundaries. In West Africa, this movement is particularly well documented in the region encompassing present-day southwestern Nigeria, Benin, and Togo, where the Ifa divination cult and deities such as Ogun have long thrived across a broad swathe of Edo-, Yoruba-, Fon-, and Ewe-speaking peoples.[9] From there, Ogun and the other great *orisa*s traversed the Atlantic in the era of the slave trade, remaining alive today in the vibrant African American religions of the Caribbean and Brazil.

Yet it is to the range of case studies from central and southern Africa that we must turn for the richest comparative insights of relevance to the Tong Hills. Transformed in the colonial period by the combination of white settlement and mining capital, African labor migration, and rapid urbanization, central and southern Africa saw the emergence of a variety of innovative cultural forms that often transcended political and ethnic boundaries: voluntary associations, dance groups, and religious movements. Their study was pioneered from the late 1930s by anthropologists of the Rhodes-Livingstone Institute in Northern Rhodesia (present-day Zambia) and appeared in such classic statements as Gluckman's "Analysis of a Social Situation in Modern Zululand" and Mitchell's 'The Kalela Dance."[10] The most important insights on new religious forms came from Victor Turner, whose studies of Ndembu ritual action informed subsequent research into the interlocking realms of witchcraft, healing cults, and the topography of pilgrimage.[11] Particularly influential was Turner's analysis of "drums of affliction," his translation for the spiritual healing concept of *ngoma* (lit. "drum"). Taking a wide variety of forms throughout the Bantu-speaking regions of eastern, central, and southern Africa, *ngoma* alleviates misfortune by admitting the sufferer into a cult group that venerates the actual agent of misfortune.[12]

Despite Turner's efforts to demonstrate the role of the drums of affliction in the succession of "social dramas" that formed the micro-history of Ndembu villages, his work remained focused on healing cults as structural rather than historical phenomena. By the 1970s, however, some Africanist historians and a new generation of more historically sensitive anthropologists began to add a temporal dimension to earlier ethnographic insights. The result was a succession of ground-breaking publications exploring the roles of indigenous religious practice and Christianity in the history of central Africa.[13] For much of this part of the continent we now possess a highly nuanced analytical framework for understanding a diversity of ritual networks of varying magnitudes ("local cults," "regional cults"), organizational forms ("territorial cults," "shrine cults"), and animating powers ("prophetic cults," "High God cults"). Thanks to the sustained research of Terence Ranger, J. M. Schoffeleers, Wim van Binsbergen, and others, religious systems such as those of the High God, Mwari (in Zimbabwe), and Mbona and Chisumphi (in Malawi) have been shown to wax and wane over time and space, to take on new, innovative forms, and to be the dynamic products of forces of historical change.

Whether such new cults were the product of the social, economic, and political transformations engendered by colonial rule is a key question in the study of religious change in twentieth-century Africa. For central Africa, opinions remain divided. Whereas van Binsbergen regards colonial conquest as a watershed, others such as Karen Fields and John Janzen have identified an essential continuity in the structure and practice of ritual forms, despite the obvious twentieth-century innovations.[14] In a much-cited article, de Craemer, Vansina, and Fox also emphasize the underlying continuity of a widely shared cluster of "distinctive symbols, rites, beliefs and values" between the precolonial and colonial eras for the vast expanse of central Africa encompassed by the present-day Democratic Republic of Congo.[15]

More recently, two monographs from a distinctively West African perspective have begun the task of examining continuity and change in ritual forms and landscapes from the precolonial to the colonial and on to the postcolonial eras. Robert Baum's study of the Diola region of southern Senegambia and Rosalind Shaw's work on Sierra Leone explore not only how the trans-Atlantic slave trade reshaped ritual landscapes on the upper Guinea coast but how it is memorialized or "embodied" in present-day religious practice.[16] These two books constitute an important step in the task of freeing indigenous West African belief from the deadening grip of tradition and reinserting it into a broad narrative of historical change. The recognition of the impact of the slave trade on West African "religious work" has particularly important implications for our study of Tongnaab, for it was the eighteenth-century expansion of the Asante empire from its forest heartland into the savanna to the north that drew the Talensi into the periphery of the slave-based Atlantic economy. The ambivalent historical relationship between the Akan forest and the savanna world in turn shaped the twentieth-century transformation of Tongnaab into the renowned witch-finder "Nana Tongo."

Savanna, Forest, and Sacred Journeys in Ghanaian History

One scholar whose work touches on the problem of ritual exchange over time and space is the anthropologist Richard Werbner, who brought some of the insights garnered from studies of religious practice in central and southern Africa to the examination of ritual commerce in West Africa. In 1989, Werbner published a volume of essays entitled *Ritual Passage, Sacred Journey*, which set out to compare and contrast the "sacred journey" of deities and other consecrated commodities across cultural boundaries with the ritual passage by which individuals—typically through the act of being possessed—crossed boundaries in "cosmological space."[17] Werbner's book is noteworthy for a number of reasons, not least of which is his insistence on the central role of the body in ritual action.[18] More importantly from our perspective, he broadens his focus beyond the Bantu-speaking region by turning to Tongnaab as a key case study of "sacred journey." Drawing empirical data from Fortes's published work and from the literature describing the waves of anti-witchcraft cults in the forest region of the colonial Gold Coast, he uses an analysis of Tongnaab/Nana Tongo to advance an explanation for the rise and decline of such trans-regional religious movements.[19]

The appearance of *Ritual Passage, Sacred Journey* signaled a renewed interest on the part of West Africanist anthropologists in the interlocking issues of trans-regional ritual movements, boundary crossing, spirit possession, personhood, and cultural mimesis.[20] Fritz Kramer's comparative study *The Red Fez* is also animated by Fortes's description of Tongnaab in the 1930s, as well as by Jean Rouch's famous cinematic record of the Hauka possession cult in Ghana in the 1950s, *Les maîtres fous*.[21] Two recent studies based on extensive fieldwork in Ghana's immediate neighbor, Togo, have continued this theme. Judy Rosenthal's *Possession, Ecstasy, and Law in Ewe Voodoo* examines the absorption of Nana Tongo and other savanna gods into the present-day spiritual repertoire of the coastal Ewe people, while Charles Piot's *Remotely Global* stresses the modernity of trans-regional cultural dialogue by focusing on the Kabre region of Togo's northern savanna.

While we have benefited from the range of theoretical insights contained in Werbner's work and in subsequent anthropological studies of ritual dialogue between savanna and forest in West Africa, we have two main criticisms of this growing body of scholarship. First, despite the general acknowledgment of the importance of historical change and, in some cases, a nod toward archival research, its evidentiary base is often too fragile to sustain the sheer weight of its interpretative superstructure.[22] Second, a fuller understanding of the dynamics of trans-regional ritual movement has been hindered by a tendency to look at only one part of, or one "end" of, that movement—a weakness readily acknowledged by Werbner.[23] By mobilizing a wide variety of sources in our reconstruction of the history of Tongnaab, both in its savanna heartland and in its wider hinterland in the Akan forest and on the Gold Coast, we aim to situate the god's "sacred journeys" not only within the broad theoretical context of cross-cultural ritual exchange, but also within the specific historical relationship that developed from the early eighteenth century between the last and greatest of the Akan states, Asante, and the savanna peoples of the middle Volta basin.

The reconstruction of that relationship emerged as one of the main priorities of the first generation of Africanist historians working at the University of Ghana's Institute of African Studies, founded in 1960. The study of Arabic chronicles by Ivor Wilks, Nehemia Levtzion, and others generated an early interest in the role of Muslims in the conquest states of the middle Volta basin and in metropolitan Asante itself.[24] Wilks's opening statement, *The Northern Factor in Ashanti History*, was followed by further elaborations that argued for a central role for Muslims in Asante trade, popular belief, and statecraft.[25] Indeed, Wilks argues that following its military expansion into the northern grasslands in the first half of the eighteenth century, "Asante has to be regarded as being a savannah rather than a forest power."[26] Further research, especially that by David Owusu-Ansah, has focused specifically on the religious element of the "northern factor," highlighting the addition of Muslim prayer and talismanic charms to the spiritual armory of the expansionist state.[27]

That the role of Muslims, especially the far-flung diaspora of Mande-speaking Juula traders, has been of considerable importance in the history of the middle Volta basin and the Akan forest states is beyond question. As in other regions of West Africa, however, the role of state-building migrant warriors and Muslim traders has been emphasized at the expense of the vast majority of savanna dwellers: the "third estate" of non-centralized autochthonous agriculturalists. This neglect is due in large part to the dearth of written sources for the multitude of small-scale savanna societies, many of which remained beyond the frontiers of and implacably hostile to the Mossi and Gonja conquest states. But it is also due to a longstanding tendency to regard stateless peoples such as the Talensi as peripheral to the main thrusts of historical change—as residual "tribes" left behind in the processes of state formation and capital accumulation. Their historical role in the pre-colonial period has been seen as limited largely to supplying slave labor to the surrounding cavalry states, to the Asante imperial system, and beyond to the Atlantic economy. With the coming of colonial rule, the extraction of slaves was replaced by that of migrant labor to the capitalist enterprises of the south. Recent research has only just begun to qualify this picture of non-centralized savanna peoples as passive victims of predatory slave raiders and colonial labor systems. The story of Tongnaab contributes to this re-evaluation of the contours of West African history in general and of Ghana-ian history in particular. The circulation of Tongnaab and other savanna gods reveals that Muslim amulets were not the only sacred commodities flowing into Asante and beyond. Tongnaab's twentieth-century transfor-mation into Nana Tongo reveals a deep ambivalence in Akan perceptions of the "tribal" peoples of the north. Far from simply being primitive aliens beyond the norms of civilized order, the Talensi and others were also per-ceived as the guardians and mediators of the most potent ritual power. The notion of savanna peoples as the backward denizens of a distant "Ashanti hinterland," in other words, requires significant re-evaluation.

Colonial Encounter and Ethnographic Knowledge

Our desire to interrogate the idea of Ghana's northern savanna as "Ashanti hinterland" is intertwined with our third main objective: to reconstruct the encounter between Tongnaab and colonialism. Colonial rule—and espe-cially the period of British control over the sacred center of the Tong Hills, from 1911 to 1957—looms large in our narrative. This is in part because of the limited availability of sources for earlier periods. The isolation of the Talensi on a frontier between zones of indigenous state formation to the north and south means that few historical sources exist with which to reconstruct the earlier, precolonial history of Tongnaab. While that his-tory undoubtedly resonates with many of the themes we explore here, we have no way of adequately accessing it. For the twentieth century, in con-trast, we have ample material, written and oral, that allows us to explore the multi-dimensional processes by which an indigenous African god be-came imbricated with the forces of change.

The advent of colonial rule created the conditions for a dramatic ex-pansion in Tongnaab's ritual field, and that expansion occurred in the face of a sustained and often violent campaign to destroy the influence of the Tong Hills. Despite a recent wariness on the part of historians toward the

use of such terms as "resistance" and "collaboration," the story of Tongnaab is, at least in part, one of striking anti-colonial resistance. We are
concerned here to trace the changing contours and the inner contradic-
tions of that resistance. By the inter-war period, the terms of colonial rule
had shifted and British officials, finally aware of their inability to prohibit
access to the hilltop shrines, altered their policy from one of suppression
to one of guarded acquiescence. Paradoxically, the very isolation that obscured for outsiders the precolonial history of the Tong Hills acted as a
powerful catalyst for the Talensi's entry into widening networks of colonial knowledge. It was the ambivalent perception of Taleland as a primitive place, unsullied by witchcraft and the malign forces unleashed by colonial economic change, that drew pilgrims from the southern Gold Coast,
beginning in the 1920s, on arduous journeys north in search of exotic ritual power.

This same notion of isolation from the modern world also attracted Meyer
Fortes to the Tong Hills a decade later. Fortes's name became virtually synonymous with that of the Talensi, much as the names of other members of
the first generation of professional social anthropologists in colonial Africa
were identified with the peoples they studied—E. E. Evans-Pritchard and
the Nuer, Isaac Schapera and the Tswana, Marcel Griaule and the Dogon,
Audrey Richards and the Bemba, to cite some well-known examples. His famous monographs, *The Dynamics of Clanship among the Tallensi* (1945) and
The Web of Kinship among the Tallensi (1949), together with subsequent theoretical extrapolations make up, according to Jack Goody, "one of the most
important bodies of ethnographic work ever carried out by a single scholar
on a particular people."[28] This corpus has had a lasting impact on scholarly
interpretations not just of the Talensi, but of other non-centralized peoples
of the West African savanna and elsewhere.[29] Our reconstruction of the twentieth-century history of Tongnaab challenges some of these interpretations.
It also seeks to highlight Fortes's role as a historical actor rather than a dis-
passionate ethnographic observer. Fortes not only played a central role in
the "writing in"—the incorporation—of the Talensi into emerging networks of colonial knowledge and ethnographic discourse, he also, unwittingly
or not, wrote himself into the fabric of the Talensi past.[30]

Compared to that of his contemporaries, little has been written about
the local context or local impact of Fortes's fieldwork in the 1930s. This is
despite the fact that his discipline has undergone a period of intense self-
reflection.[31] Indeed, over the past two decades, there has been an outpouring
of articles and books that have sought variously to assess the intellectual
history of the discipline, to scrutinize the relationship between anthropol-

ogists and their subjects and the resulting production of ethnographic knowledge, and to develop new research paradigms that transcend the certainties of the past and embrace the fluid complexities of the postcolonial and postmodern world.[32] What this vast literature reveals is that the role of Fortes and other practitioners of the British school of functionalist social anthropology in colonial Africa was far from straight-forward and will continue to be the subject of considerable debate. On the one hand, these pioneering ethnographers have been subjected to a testing critique, with charges ranging from naiveté in the creation of the primitive "other" to active complicity with the project of colonial domination.[33] On the other hand, it has been countered that much of this re-evaluation has been polemical and baldly instrumentalist, serving only to over-privilege the role of western anthropologists in shaping the colonial encounter. In a recent response to the current fashion of "ancestorcide," Jack Goody has stoutly defended the achievements of British social anthropology in Africa in its classic phase from the 1920s to the 1960s, by asserting that, far from being complicit with colonialism, Evans-Pritchard, Fortes, and the rest (including himself, it should be noted) represented a positive "expansive moment" of intellectual engagement with African societies.[34] Because we are historians, our analysis of Meyer Fortes's encounter with Tongnaab has been shaped by the contours of this debate, but it is not our intention to enter into it, nor are we equipped to do so. We only wish to underscore one basic point: that the encounter between anthropology and the Talensi had an important *historical* impact on both.

Fortes's research agenda in the 1930s was not focused on Talensi religion. His aim was to piece together Talensi "social structure" at the domestic level (the "web of kinship") and in the political realm (the "dynamics of clanship") and to explore the links between the two. He termed the intricate network of rights and obligations that bound the entire society together in the absence of any centralized political power the "scheme of ritual collaboration," wherein he located the connections between the dual earth and ancestor cults. But in his efforts to portray a self-contained, highly elaborated social structure, Fortes marginalized the one aspect of the ancestor cult that reached beyond that structure and appeared to threaten its cohesion. That was Tongnaab in its role as trans-regional oracle, or what he called the cult of the "External *Boghar.*" He dismissed it as an illegitimate modern-day aberration, confining discussion of the resulting "disequilibrium" of the 1930s to a brief afterward in *The Dynamics of Clanship.*[35]

But Fortes ensured that the Talensi achieved a fame above and beyond their local reputation as the stubbornly independent mediators of a powerful oracle. In line with the dominant functionalist theoretical paradigm of the day, he did so by ignoring the struggles of the recent past and relegating the trans-regional expansion of Tongnaab to a minor aberration. Instead, Fortes constructed a picture of an intricately balanced tribal social structure that remained insulated from the main currents of social change under way elsewhere in the Gold Coast. The result was that the Talensi were enshrined in ethnographic discourse as the archetypal stateless society, marooned on the margins of a distant hinterland in a timeless ethnographic present. Our aim is to place the Talensi and their gods at the center of historical inquiry, to embed Fortes's "scheme of ritual collaboration," as it were, in broader narratives of political, social, and economic change that extend far beyond the Tong Hills.

Witchcraft and Anti-witchcraft

Several of those broader narratives take us to the southern fringes of Tongnaab's ritual field and into debates on the histories and meanings of witchcraft. There is some evidence that one aspect of Tongnaab's power in its established savanna hinterland was spiritual protection against the range of malevolent anti-social forces that have been translated loosely throughout sub-Saharan Africa as "witchcraft." However, its southern manifestation as Nana Tongo was described almost exclusively in the idioms of witchcraft. The common Akan perception that savanna peoples remained free from the ravages of maleficent witchcraft acted as the principal catalyst for the dramatic spread of northern gods throughout the forest region in the early twentieth century. Once established in the south, Nana Tongo and the other cults were focused overwhelmingly on finding and healing, or on securing protection from, individuals regarded as "witches."[36]

To a certain extent, these processes can be situated within debates over the nature of regional cults and other religious movements in Africa. Nevertheless, we have chosen to consider witchcraft as a distinct analytical theme for two main reasons. First, it was as a potentially subversive "witchfinder" that Tongnaab once again exploded into the purview of the colonial state in the 1930s, contributing directly to the first wave of writing on witchcraft in Africa. Second, in recent years the interest in witchcraft as a topic of academic research has undergone a quite extraordinary resurgence. Just as sorcery and witchcraft became standard concerns of functionalist anthropology in the late 1930s, so in the last decade "occult economies" have emerged at the very cutting edge of research for a new generation of Africanist social scientists.[37]

The impact of colonialism lies at the heart of a divide within the first generation of literature on the nature of Nana Tongo and other anti-witchcraft movements in Africa. As T. C. McCaskie pointed out twenty years ago in what remains one of the few analyses to deal with Akan anti-witchcraft cults from a historical perspective, the interpretative difference turns on the extent to which such movements can be regarded as "new."[38] The majority of early writers on the subject argued that witch-finding and -healing movements were indeed recent innovations—that is, were specifically twentieth-century responses to the mounting anxieties brought about by colonial conquest and rule. In line with the broader interpretation of religious innovation, others questioned the analytical utility of the notion of "anomie," arguing alternatively for an underlying continuity of belief rather than any abrupt change brought about by the coming of colonial rule.

We will examine these debates in more detail in chapter 3. However, it is important to note here that an analytical tension between continuity and change also characterizes the recent re-engagement of Africanists with the terrain of popular witchcraft belief. A central concern of much of this work has been to relocate the notion of witchcraft to the interstices between the local and the global and, in so doing, remove it from the realm of tradition to that of modernity.[39] The new research agenda therefore has much in common with earlier scholarship that stressed the link between colonial capitalism and witchcraft. Like its predecessor, it has been prompted, in part, by a perception that witchcraft and anti-witchcraft measures are very much on the increase and are taking striking new forms in contemporary Africa. Indeed, it is the idioms of witchcraft that are seen to provide the most fluent means by which many Africans perceive and articulate the ambivalent embrace of capitalist modernity, from issues of health and healing through to the tension between town and country and on to the rapacious "politics of the belly" practiced by the postcolonial state.[40] Yet despite claims to represent a new "historical anthropology," the methodological imperatives of this ever-expanding body of work have been firmly on "anthropology" at the expense of the "the historical." With few exceptions, recent analyses have been concerned with the various meanings of witchcraft in its late-twentieth-century guise rather than its reconstruction as a historical phenomenon.[41] This is hardly surprising given the often fragmented and recalcitrant nature of the historical data on issues concerning the supernatural realm. But the result has been a body of work that in its desire to demonstrate the contemporary salience of witchcraft beliefs stands detached from the colonial and precolonial past.

Method and Sources

In drawing Tongnaab and Nana Tongo together and then inserting them into broader historical narratives, we have relied on a vast range of documentary and oral sources. In addition to the rich interdisciplinary and comparative literature discussed here, we have gained valuable insights from the unpublished papers of R. S. Rattray and from the photograph collection of Meyer Fortes. Unfortunately, the latter's field-notes await cataloging in the library of the University of Cambridge and remain languishing outside the public arena. Because so little historical work has been conducted on the Talensi and their neighbors, government documentation—from the Public Record Office in London, as well as from the National Archives of Ghana in Accra and its regional branch in Tamale—was critical in helping us to develop a chronology of change for the region and to situate Taleland in the broader sweep of colonial, national, and West African regional histories. Moreover, especially for the earlier decades of colonial rule, the journals and record books of certain government officers, especially S. D. Nash, were enormously valuable. Despite the cultural baggage they carried with them, Nash and a handful of others were particularly keen social observers whose writing often captured some of the more nuanced and subtle changes in Talensi daily life in the first decades of the twentieth century. Unfortunately, there are no extensive mission record collections that provide similar insight for this period, as there are for many of the southern parts of Ghana. The White Fathers established an outstation in Bolgatanga in 1925, but the ethnographic correspondence they produced (some of which is available in the National Archives in Accra) makes it clear that they had little contact with and even less information on the Talensi area in general and Tongnaab in particular.[42]

In order to trace the expansion of Tongnaab's ritual network outside of the Upper East Region, we relied on the rich collections of colonial documentation housed in Ghana's regional archives—in Cape Coast, Koforidua, Kumasi, Sekondi, Sunyani, and Tamale. We also accessed important material in the archives of the kingdoms of Asante and Akyem Abuakwa: Manhyia Record Office in Kumasi and the Akyem Abuakwa State Archives in Kibi. Both collections include an extensive array of correspondence and customary court records from the colonial period. Along with a range of local newspapers, they provide extraordinary detail on daily life and lend access, sometimes unmediated, to community debates over power and authority, good and evil, health and healing, witchcraft and anti-witchcraft.

But by far the most significant source for reconstructing the history of

Tongnaab and the ritual network emanating from the Tong Hills was the memories of the women and men, north and south, who shared their time with us. In August 1999, we began to interview people who lived at the center of Tongnaab's ritual field—those who were within visual range of the shrine we had first visited in 1992. (We briefly visited again in 1996, but did not conduct formal interviews at that time.) Initially, we focused on those male elders who tended Tongnaab, especially the *tengdaana*s (earth priests) from the various clans in Tengzug, as well as from the Talensi villages surrounding the base of the hills. But we eventually cast our net more broadly, interviewing elderly men and women less formally connected to Tongnaab, in order to hear their perspectives on this powerful god. As our network of interviewees grew wider, so too did the range of stories shared with us. We were struck by the historical depth and precision of accounts of events which, although sometimes occurring a century or more ago, were remarkably fresh and alive—stories of mounted slave raiders, of British conquest, of forced labor and forced removal, of sustained resistance, of resettlement and ritual renewal. Those detailed recollections forced us to recognize that we were not embarking on a straight-forward religious history of one neglected West African shrine. The task before us was far more complex and far more expansive.

That recognition was powerfully reinforced in November 1999, during the Talensi harvest festival, when we met scores of southern pilgrims who had come to pay their annual respects to the god they called "Nana Tongo." We interviewed many of them in the hills and, in subsequent years, visited them in towns and villages throughout the south of Ghana, where we were privileged to witness, firsthand, the ways in which Tongnaab has been woven into the ritual landscapes of the Akan, Ewe, and Ga peoples. Among those who have shared their stories and recollections with us are the son and grandson of the first southerner to travel in the 1920s to the Tong Hills and bring Tongnaab back down with him, as well as several of Tongnaab's current priests and priestesses.

As we sought to understand processes of movement, transmutation, and translation between north and south, we realized that we needed to explore more carefully the broader regional context as well as the specific historical antecedents for Tongnaab's move into the forest. In 2000, we visited a number of the other sacred sites dotted around the frontiers of northern Ghana from which savanna gods had embarked on similar ritual journeys to the south. The following year, in addition to our ongoing interviews around the Tong Hills, we turned to Tongnaab's long-established network of supplicants in non-Talensi areas of the north. Our focus was primarily on the

Builsa-speaking region to the west, especially on the towns of Sandema, Wiaga, and Gbedemah, where connections to Tongnaab go back several generations, in some cases to the eighteenth century. From these contemporary supplicants we learned much about how, both literally and figuratively, Tongnaab first traveled and how separate and distinct communities, across time and space and generations, can engage in sustained ritual dialogue.

In sum, over the course of four years (1999–2003), we formally interviewed over sixty people, from the center of Tongnaab's ritual field to its fringes. Any new insight, any unexpected connections or fascinating turns that the reader might locate within these pages come from the stories and recollections those men and women generously shared with us. Indeed, one of our many regrets is that we were not always able to communicate directly with those whose narratives you will find here. While moving across regions, from savanna to forest and coast and back again, allowed us to decenter the Akan south in our narrative and to tell a more complex story, it did challenge our limited linguistic abilities, especially in the various northern languages. Unlike many of our hosts throughout the north, we are not fluent in five or more languages and were thus unable to converse with many of our Talensi and Builsa interlocutors without assistance. In and around the Tong Hills, we relied on the able linguistic abilities of Frederick Naab, William Namaani, and at times John Bawa Zuure. Owen Agoldem generously assisted us in Builsa-speaking towns to the west. The bulk of the interviews we conducted in the north were undertaken together, often with the aid of more than one translator and with the intermittent participation of local observers and onlookers. Thus, our sessions often resembled multi-participant, bi- or even trilingual conversations rather than the more typical one-on-one, or one-on-one plus translator, interview.[43] More importantly, our sessions in the Tong Hills always took place out of doors, amidst the granite boulders, hidden caverns, and sacred groves of Tongnaab's ritual epicenter. We soon learned that the dramatic landscape around us was powerfully mnemonic: that a nod toward this cave or that baobab tree often preceded a careful retelling of resistance to British conquest or to the incursions of slave raiders. We learned that history is not just stored in the memories of Talensi elders. It is inscribed in the landscape of the Tong Hills in ways that few from outside those hills have ever fully appreciated.

Chapter by Chapter

The chapters that follow are arranged chronologically, although there is also a thematic logic to the book's architecture. Chapter 1, "Tongnaab and the Talensi in the History of the Middle Volta Savanna," constitutes our first step toward returning the Talensi to history. It locates the Tong Hills in their regional and trans-regional context by considering the main forces that shaped the area's precolonial history. It then reconstructs the transition to colonial rule on the northeastern frontier of the Northern Territories Protectorate of the Gold Coast from the 1890s to 1911, the year British forces finally conquered the Talensi and mounted their first attempt to destroy the ritual power of Tongnaab. Chapter 2, "Gods and Guns, Rituals and Rule, 1911–1928," explores the early, faltering steps of British officials as they sought to make a colonial world in the Tong Hills and the ways in which the people of those hills negotiated the rough, uneven terrain of British rule. It begins with the aftermath of the conquest of the Tong Hills in March 1911 and ends with the arrival, in 1928, of Government Anthropologist R. S. Rattray, who came to study the customs, gods, and social systems of the "stateless" peoples in order to render them accessible to administrators still struggling to consolidate a system of rule on the northern frontier of their protectorate.

In chapter 3, "'Watch Over Me': Witchcraft and Anti-witchcraft Movements in Ghanaian History, 1870s–1920s," we set the stage for understanding Tongnaab's movement to the forests and coastal towns of the south. We consider witchcraft in Ghana not just as a structure of belief, but as a historical phenomenon that changed over time and acted as a catalyst for trans-regional religious transformation. It was precisely that kind of transformation which would render Tongnaab one of the southern Gold Coast's most dynamic anti-witchcraft gods—Nana Tongo. The following chapter, "From Savanna to Forest: Nana Tongo and Ritual Commerce in the World of Cash and Cocoa," reconstructs the rise of Nana Tongo as part and parcel of the dramatic efflorescence of organized witchcraft eradication detailed in chapter 3. Expanding physical mobility and ritual commerce in the inter-war period not only brought Talensi to the cocoa farms and mines of the south, but enabled Akan, Ga, and Ewe peoples of southern Ghana to draw upon the powers of the distant savanna shrine. The resulting movement had a profound impact on the lived experience of many people throughout Asante and the Gold Coast. Hitherto obscured by the ultimate triumph of Christianity in narratives of religious change, Tongnaab, in the form of Nana Tongo, is absolutely central, we argue, to the social history of twentieth-century Ghana.

In chapter 5, "Tongnaab, Meyer Fortes, and the Making of Colonial Taleland, 1928–1945," we leave the forests and coastlines of the south and return once again to the north—to the epicenter of Tongnaab's ritual network—in order to explore the centrality of Tongnaab and its lucrative pilgrim trade to struggles over the implementation of indirect rule in and around the Tong Hills. Woven prominently throughout our narrative is the British anthropologist Meyer Fortes. If Tongnaab has been excluded from historical accounts of twentieth-century Ghana, so too has been this renowned scholar who, in many ways, authored the terms of colonial control for the Tong Hills in the 1930s.

In our concluding chapter, "Tongnaab and the Dynamics of History among the Talensi," we argue that Tongnaab's resilience was rooted not in the timeless, localized "dynamics of clanship" set out by Fortes in the 1930s, but in the historically constructed network of ritual commerce that reached far beyond the boundaries of Taleland. That network has persisted and expanded to the present day, as subsequent generations of Tongnaab's keepers continue to reinforce and cultivate connections throughout the region and, indeed, throughout the globe. In these final pages, we contemplate the ongoing significance of ritual commerce in contemporary Ghana—especially with the rise of eco-tourism in an increasingly globalized political economy. We also consider what Fortes unfortunately did not do, at least in his published writings. We contemplate our own historical agency, our own roles as historical actors in the ongoing story of Tongnaab. In what ways, we wonder, have we now become part of the historical narratives that continue to unfold from the Tong Hills?

1

Tongnaab and the Talensi in the History of the Middle Volta Savanna

*T*he history of Tongnaab and its Talensi guardians before the colonial conquest of 1911 remains beyond the reach of detailed reconstruction. While British documents and the oral testimonies of elderly informants provide enough evidence to piece together the opening phase of colonial encounter, the precolonial Tong Hills emerge only in the vaguest of outlines. The earliest written accounts date only to the end of the nineteenth century, with the arrival of the agents of European imperial expansion. With the exception of oral traditions of origin and migration recorded by colonial ethnographers in subsequent decades, there is an almost complete absence of historical sources for what had long been a remote frontier zone bisecting the regions of Mossi state-building to the north and south. Even when we move into the twentieth century, recovering the historical trajectory of something as intangible and omnipresent as a "god" presents a whole raft of evidential and interpretative problems. Violently suppressed during the era of British conquest, Tongnaab's ritual network was reforged largely beyond the purview of the hostile colonial state. While the colonial archive has much to tell us about many aspects of African life, it is stubbornly recalcitrant concerning issues of religion and belief in general and the dynamics of savanna deities like Tongnaab in particular.

Of course, this lament can be made with regard to many African societies. It has prefaced numerous historical studies that open with an introductory chapter serving as a precolonial backdrop to recuperable narratives of twentieth-century change.[1] In restating the problem here, our aim is not to engage in the usual hand-wringing over the difficulties in writing a fully realized African history. The issue is not simply that geographical isolation has conspired to place the Talensi past beyond our reach. Indeed, the very isolation that prevented the Talensi from emerging onto the historical record before the 1890s is an integral part of our story. It was the perceived remoteness and mysterious other-worldliness of the Tong Hills that in the twentieth century drew southern pilgrims into their ritual field. External perceptions of the Talensi and their gods as timeless, "traditional," and outside the realm of history, therefore, were not necessary inimical to the interests of Tongnaab's guardians. Rather, our concern is that an essentialized version of the Talensi past has been constructed from the ethnographic present of the early twentieth century. The elevation of the Talensi to the status of the archetypal stateless society has resulted in a tendency to extrapolate the notion of their "statelessness"—with the attendant implication that such societies have existed outside the realm of history—backward through time. And if Talensi society as a whole has been consigned to the deadening embrace of tradition, so too have the great Tongnaab oracle shrines atop the Tong Hills.

Much of what we argue in this chapter is therefore tentative, speculative, and hedged with qualification and uncertainty. But what we hope to achieve is to suggest some new ways of looking at the small-scale, fiercely independent savanna societies that hitherto have been swept to the margins of Ghanaian and West African history. The aim is to begin the task of relocating Tongnaab and its Talensi custodians from the realm of static tradition to that of historical change. We begin with an overview of the savanna grasslands of the middle Volta basin and suggest that Talensi society was shaped by the same processes as those that gave rise to surrounding conquest states. We then focus on the rise of the Asante imperial system in the eighteenth and nineteenth centuries, which drew the Talensi and their neighbors into the periphery of the slave-based Atlantic economy. The resulting dialogue between forest and savanna would set the scene for the dramatic expansion of Tongnaab's ritual network into the Akan forests in the twentieth century. Next, we consider the place of Tongnaab in the sacred landscape of precolonial Taleland and its wider savanna hinterland. The chapter ends with an account of the Talensi collision with European colonial expansion from the 1890s to 1911—the years in which the Tong Hills first begin to emerge in the historical record. It was in 1911 that British forces finally conquered the hills, forcibly incorporated their inhabitants into the Northern Territories Protectorate of the Gold Coast, and mounted the first attempt to destroy the ritual power of Tongnaab.

Societies and States in the Middle Volta Basin

Historical accounts of that part of the West African Sudanic zone lying between the Akan forests to the south and the great bend in the Niger River to the north have been dominated by the emergence of the so-called Mossi (or Mossi-Dagomba) complex of kingdoms.[2] In contrast to the powerful agricultural and gold-mining entrepreneurs who from the fifteenth century began to forge the Akan forest kingdoms, the savanna state-builders appear to have been alien intruders. Analysis of royal traditions suggests that Mossi migrants had begun to enter the Voltaic region from the northeast by the early fifteenth century. Whether they arrived as mounted warriors or acquired horses later is unclear, although cavalry technology was certainly crucial to the consolidation of rule over the autochthonous agriculturalists.[3] A separate population movement toward the Niger Bend brought Mossi forces into conflict with the rulers of the emergent Songhay empire in the 1480s, initiating a century of recurrent warfare that is well documented in the Timbuktu chronicles. Traditions of origin identify the pioneer of the southern migration as one Na Gbewa, who established himself at Pusiga in the northeastern corner of present-day Ghana. Na Gbewa's descendants are said to have branched out to found the historic kingdoms of Mamprugu and Dagbon to the south and Wagadugu (or Ouagadougou) and Yatenga to the north. Dynastic quarrels and kinship divisions were said in turn to have resulted in the emergence of further, smaller kingdoms, such as Wa on the northwestern frontier and Nunumba on the eastern frontier of Ghana. In addition to these Mossi conquest states, a distinct group of mounted warriors of Mande origin also pushed into the region from the mid-sixteenth century, laying the foundation of the kingdom of Gonja on the Black Volta to the southwest of Dagbon.

Oral traditions suggest that the dynamics of conquest varied from region to region. In some cases, the process of state formation was marked by violent conflict and the displacement of earlier settlers.[4] The more common pattern seems to have been one of mutual accommodation between imported political power vested in the person of the secular ruler (*na* or *naaba*, as in Na Gbewa) and established ritual authority as retained by the indigenous "earth priest," known in much of the southern Mossi region as the *tengdaana* (lit. "custodian of the land").[5] This at least is the perspective

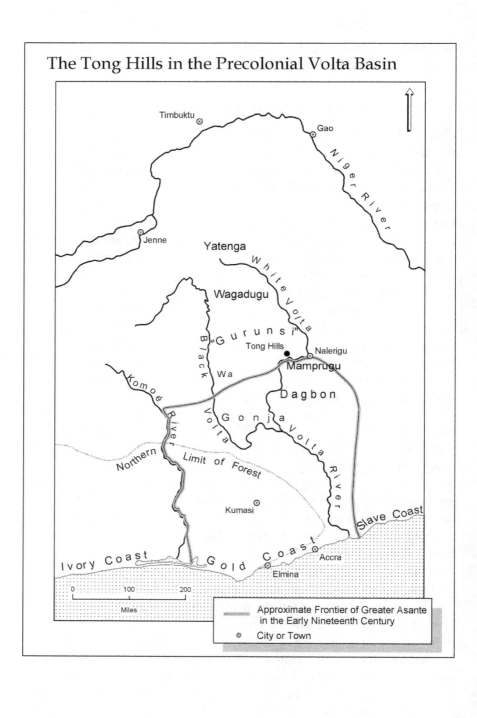

The Tong Hills in the Precolonial Volta Basin

Timbuktu

Gao

Niger River

Jenne

Yatenga

White Volta

Wagadugu

Black Volta

"Gurunsi"

Tong Hills

Nalerigu

Mamprugu

Wa

Komoé River

Dagbon

Gonja

Volta River

Northern Limit of Forest

Kumasi

Slave Coast

Ivory Coast

Gold Coast

Accra

Elmina

| 0 | 100 | 200 |

Miles

Approximate Frontier of Greater Asante
in the Early Nineteenth Century

⊚ City or Town

from the political center, where a history of conflict followed by accommodation between the incoming ruling classes and indigenous "commoners" is symbolically re-enacted in the yearly *Damba* festival staged by the Mossi-Dagomba kingdoms. The view from the periphery is less easy to discern. As Wilks concedes, the kingdoms themselves emerge only dimly from oral histories and Arabic chronicles. Lacking specialized court historians of the type that produced the famous Dagomba drum histories and invariably reduced by Muslim chroniclers to a homogeneous mass of primitive "pagans," the small-scale societies lying beyond the reach of state authority are barely discernible in either.[6]

Neither has the linguistic history of the middle Volta basin been subjected to the sort of intensive analysis that has resulted in the recent transformation of our view of the precolonial past of Bantu-speaking Equatorial Africa.[7] It can simply be noted that in northern Ghana there is no clear distinction between the languages spoken by the Mossi state-builders on the one hand and the non-centralized peoples on the other. All speak languages of the so-called Gur family, specifically of the Grusi and Oti-Volta branches.[8] Thus, within the western cluster of Oti-Volta, the language of the Talensi (Talen, or Talni) is extremely close to that of both the Mamprusi (Mampruli) and the Dagomba (Dagbani), while the tongues of two other non-centralized peoples, Nankani and Dagara, are equally close to that of the northern Mossi of Burkina Faso (Mooré). As in Equatorial Africa, the linguistic evidence can be interpreted in different ways, but the most likely scenario is that incoming warrior groups established military and political dominance, but adopted the languages and other cultural and religious elements of the existing populations.

As we will see, the first European accounts of the region in the 1880s–90s drew a sharp distinction between centralized kingdoms on the one hand and dispersed, stateless "tribes" on the other. This dichotomy anticipated the tenor of much subsequent ethnographic inquiry. The Talensi have featured prominently in various scholarly constructions of the savanna world, due in large part to the sustained ethnographic research of Meyer Fortes from the 1930s onward.[9] Yet this bifurcated vision of the social terrain of the savannas is too flat and too static, missing the interpenetration of social forces over space and time. On the one hand, despite their superior military technology, the authority of the cavalry states was far from even and many peoples within their orbits remained outside sustained political control. On the other hand, the influence of state systems often reached beyond their recognized frontiers.[10] The latter was certainly the case with regard to the relationship between the Talensi and the nearby kingdom of Mamprugu. The Talensi were among the non-centralized societies that cut across the zone of Mossi state formation to the north and south, but their country lay only some twenty miles beyond the center of Mamprusi royal power. As Rattray and Fortes discovered, Talensi society was characterized by a fundamental split between the immigrant Namoo and the indigenous Tale.[11] The Namoo (a term cognate with Mossi) comprised clans who traced their origins to the Mamprugu kingdom across the White Volta river and from whose ranks were drawn titular chiefs such as the *tongrana*. On the grounds of their status as "first comers," the Tale clans provided the *tengdaana*s, who retained ritual custody of the land. The sacred epicenter of the Talensi world, the Tong Hills, were inhabited mainly by indigenous Tale (Fortes's "Hill Talis") whose ritual functionaries co-ordinated the cycle of great festivals and managed the earth shrines and ancestor shrines.[12] They also controlled access to the ancestor-deity, Tongnaab, whose fame as an oracle extended beyond Taleland and deep into the zones of Mossi state-building. In his defining statement on the nature of stateless societies in West Africa, Horton identified the Voltaic savannas as the *locus classicus* of such "disjunctive migration" into frontier zones. One result was the emergence of societies divided between "landowners" and "latecomers" whose solidarity was defined in terms of territory rather than genealogy. Another was the tendency for ideas about the spiritual force of the earth to come to the forefront of social organization, giving rise to powerful shrines, such as those dedicated to Tongnaab, around which group relations turned.[13]

Despite some evidence pointing to a broad pattern of accommodation between Mossi and Gonja migrants and the earlier inhabitants of the middle Volta basin, there is little doubt that the relationship between the warrior elites and those peoples who remained outside the frontiers of state formation was also characterized—in particular localities at specific historical junctures—by predation and violence. It generally has been accepted that militarized states in the western and central Sudan were sustained in part by the enslavement of surrounding non-centralized peoples, who were drawn by regular cycles of predation into local servitude, the Saharan trade, and, increasingly from the eighteenth century, the Atlantic slave trade.[14] However, recent reinterpretations have begun to qualify what has been described as the "predatory state thesis," especially the resulting picture of a dichotomized political landscape comprising dynamic, rapacious states on the one hand and passive labor reservoirs on the other.[15] Arguing for a more nuanced analysis of the impact of the slave trade on savanna societies, these contributions suggest not only that many stateless peoples were remarkably successful in defending themselves against the incursions of slave raiders, but that slaves were also procured by a wide range of mechanisms often involving the active participation of communities hitherto portrayed simply as victims. Despite the paucity of evidence, there is every indication that precolonial Talensi history followed the pattern outlined in the revisionist analysis of the impact of the slave trade on non-centralized peoples in West Africa.

The Slave Trade in the "Asante Hinterland"

Unfortunately, very little can be said about the dynamics of enslavement in the savannas of the Volta basin before the mid-eighteenth century. One fugitive source, a list of enslavable non-Muslims compiled by the Timbuktu jurist Ahmad Baba in 1615, suggests that captives from as far south as Dagbon may well have been drawn into the middle Niger valley slave system and beyond into the Saharan trade.[16] However, in terms of the wider circulation of both human and non-human commodities, Wilks argues that until the eighteenth century the region lay between the great Juula and Hausa trading networks linking the savanna and forest zones to the west and east and appears to have remained largely isolated from the outside world.[17] One measure of this isolation is the limited impact of Islam. Small Muslim communities composed of migrants from the middle Niger did emerge in the Gonja and Mossi-Dagomba kingdoms, and by the eighteenth century some ruling elites began to express some attachment to Islam. But the quietist, "Suwarian" approach adopted by Muslim settlers, combined with the stubborn ancestral piety of local communities, meant that the religion had little or no impact beyond the region's few commercial centers. With the partial exception of Gonja and Wa, the kingdoms remained firmly outside the *dar al-Islam* and were regarded by Muslim chroniclers as bastions of paganism.[18] The vast majority of the population remained—and remains to this day—devoted to local ancestors and the gods of the earth.[19]

The relative isolation of the middle Volta basin would end in the eighteenth century, when the rise of Asante power drew the diverse peoples of the region into more intensive contact with the Akan forest zone and the broader Atlantic economy beyond. The consolidation of the metropolitan Asante kingdom by 1700 was followed by a half century of military expansion that extended the imperial system from its forest heartland into the savannas to the north and to the Gold Coast to the south.[20] Using European muskets acquired from the coast, Asante gunmen (*kambonse*, sing. *kambona*, a term still used in northern Ghana today for the Asante) asserted

their superiority over savanna cavalry forces with relative ease. The first Asante campaign across the Volta River (in 1732–33) overran western Gonja,
the second (in 1744–45) was directed against Dagbon and the eastern Gonja
chiefdom of Kpembe, while the third (in 1751–52) effected the reoccupation
of Kpembe and the regularization of its tributary status. A similar settlement
with the Dagomba followed in about 1772, when an Asante force marched
north and arrested the paramount chief, Ya Na 'Abdallah Gariba. Reputedly
ransomed for a thousand slaves, the *ya na* agreed to the creation of a local
corps of *kambonse* and to the payment of a yearly tribute to Kumasi. Tribute
from the north was paid mainly in people. The extraction, composition, and
size of payments waxed and waned over the decades, but it is likely that between the 1770s and the 1870s, Gonja and Dagbon each delivered somewhere
between one thousand and two thousand slaves per year to their Asante overlords. There can be little doubt that the bulk of these captives were raided
or purchased (this crucial distinction will be returned to shortly) from the
non-centralized societies in the interstices of the kingdoms.[21]

Although Mamprugu remained outside the Asante imperial frontier, the
farming communities beyond the bend in the White Volta were soon being targeted by mounted slavers. As early as 1777, slaves in the Danish West
Indies sold through Christiansborg Castle in Accra are recorded as originating from the realms of King Atabad of "Gambaak" (i.e., the Mamprusi
commercial center of Gambaga).[22] This is clearly a reference to Nayiri
Atabia (c. 1690–1741/2), who is remembered in Mamprusi oral traditions
as making a determined effort to extend his rule over the so-called Gurunsi peoples. By the early nineteenth century, the term "Gurunsi" itself
begins to appear in the historical record. In 1817, Bowdich was informed
in Kumasi that "Gooroosie" lay two days' journey north of Gambaga, and
by 1854 the missionary Koelle was able to compile short lexicons of a variety of Gurunsi languages garnered from resettled ex-slaves in Freetown,
Sierra Leone.[23] For both the warrior elites of the savanna states and their
Asante overlords—and ultimately for the agents of European conquest—
the term carried particular implications of primitive isolation and barbar-
ity. Attempts to define its exact boundaries and constituent "tribal" identities would be hotly debated amongst early colonial administrators and
ethnographers on both sides of the Anglo-French imperial frontier.[24] Unfortunately, sources contain few details on the magnitude of slaving in the
different areas of this broad ethnic constellation before the very end of the
nineteenth century. Yet there can be no doubt that precolonial Talensi society in general and the ritual power of the Tong Hills in particular were
shaped by the deepening involvement of the region in the Asante imperial

system. Moreover, the identification by outsiders of the Talensi as primitive "Gurunsi" would have a profound impact on the role of Tongnaab in twentieth-century ritual commerce between the savanna and the forest.

Asante perceptions of the northern savanna, or Sarem (from the Twi *seremu*, "the grasslands"; cf. *kwaem*, "the forest"), were characterized by a wide variation in the degree of civilization accorded to its inhabitants.[25] The Gonja (Twi: *Ntafo*) and the Dagomba (*Anwafo*) were certainly seen as alien outsiders, but like other non-Akan peoples, such as the coastal Ga, they possessed recognizable political hierarchies and by the mid-eighteenth century were tied to the empire by formal treaty arrangements. From these and other more distant savanna polities came Muslim traders, scholars, and diviners, who were given special leave to settle in Kumasi and who provided crucial services to the Golden Stool.[26] In contrast, the non-centralized peoples were regarded as uncivilized barbarians who were fit only to be exploited as slaves. In Asante and the other Akan states they were called *nnonkofoo* (sing. *odonko*), a term probably of Mande derivation that suggested an identity outside of jural corporateness and indeed on the fringe of perceptions of humanity. As Asantehene Kwaku Dua famously explained to the Methodist missionary T. B. Freeman in 1841, "The small tribes in the interior fight with each other, take prisoners and sell them for slaves; and as I know nothing about them, I allow my people to buy them as they please: they are of no use for any thing but slaves; they are stupid, and little better than beasts."[27] Kwaku Dua's view may be extreme; he stood, after all, at the apex of an urban ruling elite whose social distance from the *nnonkofoo* population was far greater than that of the average Asante subject. Yet it is clear that the Gurunsi and other *nnonkofoo* stood on the very lowest rung of the Akan scale of civilization and that their numbers were growing rapidly in the mid-nineteenth century.[28] Both these factors help to explain the increasing allure that northern anti-witchcraft gods such as Tongnaab held for the peoples of the forest and coast by the early colonial period. *Nnonkofoo* may have been seen as "little better than beasts," but as denizens of the world of nature rather than the world of culture they were also perceived to have intimate access to an array of potent ritual powers "out there" beyond the reach of civilized Akan society.

Although the overseas slave trade from the Gold Coast was in rapid decline from the 1820s, the second half of the nineteenth century witnessed an escalation of violence and insecurity in Asante's savanna hinterland. A revised tribute settlement imposed on Ya Na 'Abdullah (c. 1864–76) by Asantehene Kofi Kakari after the latter's succession in 1867 resulted in an intensification of slave raiding into Gurunsi country and elsewhere. The

Dagomba cavalry were aided in this enterprise by the so-called Zabarima—Songhay and Zerma warriors who from the 1860s began to arrive in the kingdom from their home country in the west of present-day Niger.[29] Within a decade, Asante had lost control of its northern provinces in the wake of a humiliating military defeat at the hands of the British in 1874. Yet the internal slave trade continued, as Zabarima armies under the leadership of Babatu turned from mercenary work to the independent conquest of a swathe of territory between Wagadugu and Wa. Babatu's destructive campaigns together with incursions by the forces of the Juula militarist Samori Toure generated a final surge of south-bound Gurunsi captives through the great slave market at Salaga, until both state-building enterprises were terminated in the 1890s by the advent of European colonial conquest.[30] Even British officials engaged in the laborious "pacification" of the Talensi and other fiercely independent communities on the frontiers of the Northern Territories Protectorate explained the resistance they encountered as due in part to the rapacity of the centralized states. "The whole of the Grunshi towns formed, in former times, the happy hunting ground for the Moshi, Mamprussi and Dagomba when in search of slaves," wrote S. D. Nash, the most informed of the early district commissioners in the north, "and so fresh is this in the memory of the people . . . that they run away on the approach of strangers."[31]

Demographic patterns in the Voltaic savanna provide some clues as to how this history of slave raiding affected the Tong Hills. In response to an established theoretical model that posits a link between high population density and the emergence of states, the anthropologist Jack Goody has argued that the opposite appeared to be the case in northern Ghana, where the twentieth-century population density of the Mossi-Dagomba and Gonja kingdoms was very low compared to much of the stateless belt of the northern frontier.[32] The very uneven spread of human settlement noted by early colonial officials was confirmed by the census of 1931, which recorded average densities of about 172 inhabitants per square mile in the Zuarungu District (comprising the Talensi, Nabdam, and Nankani peoples) and 124 per square mile in the neighboring Kusasi District, compared to 23 in Mamprugu and 16 in Dagbon.[33] Meyer Fortes sought an explanation for this demographic imbalance in ecological factors, contrasting the relatively well drained and healthy watersheds of the Talensi region with the less fertile, disease-ridden flatlands of the plains to the south.[34] Goody, while acknowledging the importance of ecology, pointed instead to the impact of predatory state-building and slave raiding. According to his hypothesis, the densely inhabited countryside of the present-day Upper East Region of Ghana can

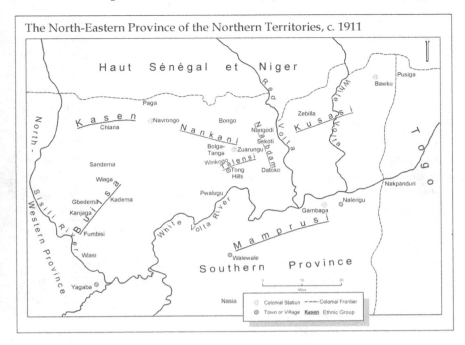

The North-Eastern Province of the Northern Territories, c. 1911

be seen as an archetypal "deep rural" society: one that has long attracted migrants, refugees, and independent agricultural colonizers at the expense of zones of established state-formation and merchant capital.[35] In this respect the broken terrain of the Talensi countryside, with its landscape of defensible rocky outcrops dominated by the natural citadel of the Tong Hills, can be compared to other deep rural zones of refuge in West Africa such as the Bandiagara escarpment in Mali, the Atakora massif of northern Togo, and the plateaux of the Nigerian Middle-Belt. Like that of the Chamba, a Middle-Belt people straddling the present-day Nigerian-Cameroonian border studied by Richard Fardon, Talensi society can be seen as being built from accretions of "raiders and refugees."[36] In other words, rather than being a residual, timeless formation, it was a product of the same historical forces that shaped the emergence of neighboring states.

The problem remains, however, of fleshing out this general model of change in a region for which there is no documentary evidence before the 1890s. Talensi traditions of origin and migration are therefore of considerable importance. But these, as recorded in the early colonial period, are sketchy at best, as well as being fraught with interpretative difficulties. Fortes rejected the historicity of oral traditions altogether, maintaining the strictly functionalist line that they were "nothing more than formulations of the contemporary scheme of political and ceremonial relationships."[37] This seems overstated. Accounts of lineage and clan origins recorded by Rattray in 1928 do contain fragments of historical memory that link the settlement of the Tong Hills and the construction of a distinct Talensi identity to the broader dynamics of the slave trade. There are indications, moreover, that these processes continued well into the nineteenth century, to the time of the escalation of Dagomba and Zabarima slave raiding from the 1860s to the 1890s. Rattray's informant in Wakii, the settlement on the northern flank of the Tong Hills, said that his ancestors were Gurunsi from around Navrongo who "were driven away by Kanbuse [i.e., *kambonse*, translated here as 'fighters']."[38] "We like now to be called Talense not Grunsi. We used to speak Gurne now we talk Talene." Evidence of ongoing linguistic change in the neighboring Talensi community of Gorogo further suggests nineteenth-century population movements: "Our ancestors came from Tchama [i.e., Chiana in the Kasena or "Yulise" region], from there they went to Po. . . . We no longer talk Yule (except the old people) we talk Talene."[39] District Commissioner Nash also noted the impact of slave raiding on settlement patterns following an interview with Talensi elders on the subject in 1913.[40] Nash's impression from the conversation was that the Tong Hills "seem to have been left in comparative peace for generations" and had as a result long attracted Kasena, Builsa, and other "Gurunsi" peoples from the west seeking sanctuary from the threat of mounted slavers.

Yet there is no doubt that for the Talensi and other Gurunsi peoples, the late nineteenth century was a time of acute insecurity. As in other savanna regions, kidnapping and raiding (Talen: *ngok*) were often highly localized affairs, with local "strongmen" preying on neighbors and forging links with expanding regional slave networks.[41] "'No Chief could fine any man one penny' or seize his fowls or compel any man to farm for him. 'Men would have seized their quivers had he attempted to do so,'" Rattray was informed. But "a Chief's profit in olden days lay in his right to seize and sell strangers."[42] Here we get a glimpse of the emergence of informal leadership from the ranks of Talensi society, based not on ascription but on the manipulation of scarce resources and kinship relations. This in turn created a tendency toward small-scale warfare over resources (or, in the eyes of colonial officials, "raiding"), especially women and honor. It also placed a great emphasis on shrines as key agents of local mediation and on the mobilization of ritual networks in the definition of who was and who was not a "stranger."

Present-day informants recall tales of the danger their parents faced in moving about the countryside due to the constant threat of kidnapping and sale to passing slave caravans. "People were afraid to move from house to

Figure 1.1. Inside the central basin of the Tong Hills, with the protective heights of the outer walls rising in the background. Unpublished photograph by Meyer Fortes captioned "Carrying water for housebuilding Tenzugu Dec. 1934."

house," explained the late Ba'an of Sipaat, one of the communities on the western flank of the Tong Hills. "You would have to be well armed with bows, arrows and cutlasses, in case you met people stealing human beings."[43] Personal security was further endangered during periods of severe food shortage, when poorer households resorted to the selective pawning and even outright sale of kin in order to fend off collapse. In the mid-1890s, prolonged drought—certainly exacerbated by the escalating insecurity of the period—resulted in the most devastating famine in Talensi historical memory. Many died of starvation and disease, and so many children were pawned or sold that fifteen years later colonial courts were still dealing with disputes over the ownership of those exchanged locally for food.[44] Again, Ba'an provides illuminating detail:

At that time, people were eating grass and they were dying. The only solution they could find was to sell some of their children in order to cater for others. There was

Figure 1.2. Ba'an (c. 1910–2000).

a slave trade at that time. Then they had to sell some of their children to people who, in turn, would send them across the White Volta. They would tie them under a tree and the children would stand there and those who buy the slaves would come and look at them and get the ones they preferred and then buy them and send them far away to sell. . . . If you wanted food and didn't have money, you would bring your children out.[45]

The sale of kin was a traumatic experience for all concerned. Ritually, it was seen as defiling the land, which, in turn, needed to be purified by a series of rites and sacrifices.[46] One unfortunate child thus sold was Victor Aboya, Rattray's research assistant and collaborator, who was born in Winkogo, five miles to the west of the Tong Hills on the frontier between the Talensi and Nankani countrysides. During the 1890s famine, Aboya "had been exchanged by his uncle for a few baskets of grain which were to help in keeping the remainder of his family from actual starvation."[47] Sold down to Asante, he was later freed and educated by Basel missionaries in Kumasi before returning home to play a key role in the colonial "discovery" of Tongnaab.

Sacred Landscapes and Ritual Networks:
Tongnaab in Historical Perspective

If the rocky heights of the Tong Hills served as a natural fortress against the predations of state-builders and slave raiders, they were also a hallowed ritual sanctuary—a repository of the most potent sacred power. In the absence of precolonial sources, the temptation is to portray this power as part of a timeless terrain of mysterious holy places. This is certainly how British officials tended to view the ritual landscape of the northern frontier. "The Fetish Shrine in the Tong Hills," ran a typical early report, "has been in existence from time immemorial."[48] The earliest detailed account of a Tongnaab shrine (Talen: *bo'ar*) was written in 1913 by Captain S. D. Nash, the first district commissioner of the Zuarungu District. For his time, Nash was an articulate and thoughtful observer of local African society. In a diary entry that could have come from the pages of Sir James Frazer's *The Golden Bough*, Nash makes sense of indigenous religious belief and practice by locating the "abode of the Tonzugu fetish"—probably the particular Tongnaab *bo'ar* called Bonaab—in the context of classical antiquity:

A pen of a Vergil would be required to describe it. So nearly does it assimilate to the grottoes he describes and in which the Sibyl utters her injunctions and awful mysterious oracles. A grove of nice shade trees surrounds the Tonzugu shrine. A stream of clear water flows through and suddenly disappears under two immense rocks. Between these rocks there is a hole, hardly large enough to admit a man, which seems to communicate with the stream far below. On the rocks there are beads, cloth, cowries, some hair shaved from men's heads . . . , left by consultants of the oracle. Childless women were particularly prone to visit this place . . . , and prospective mothers would also come to hear their fate and to bring good luck on their offspring. It was tapu for anyone to wear clothes on entering the hills. . . . Skins however might be worn. The fetish man's *ipse dixit* [dogmatic assertion or statement] was regarded as a kind of nostrum to cure every ill of mind and body. He can bring rain and he can stop it. The crops will not be good unless he is consulted. Mothers to be and childless women were especially faithful to him. Such beliefs would seem childless [*sic*; here Nash means "childlike"] were it not a fact that exactly the same idea is carried out at home when a Cardinal leads 3 or 4 thousand pilgrims to the sacred Grotto at Lourdes.[49]

Present-day Talensi informants also regard the sacred places of the hills as having existed since the dawn of time. "Our ancestors, our grandfathers, our fathers—all met Tongnaab here," we were told by the late Yiran Boare, who until his death in 2002 was the ultimate custodian of the Tongnaab *bo'ar* called Yanii. "He was here before they came. We don't know where he came from—he is just there."[50] This is also the implication of Meyer Fortes's anthropological vision of Talensi society in the 1930s, bound together by an intricate, unchanging "scheme of ritual collaboration" focused on the rites of the dual earth and ancestor cults. There is no doubt that the shrines atop the Tong Hills are indeed very old: one British official noted in 1925 that the granite boulders around the Yanii *bo'ar* were "worn away, polished glass smooth, evidence of Tongnab's considerable age and popularity," and the erosion can still be seen today.[51] The problem with all of this, however, is that it reinforces the established image of African traditional religion as existing outside of history. The origins of Tongnaab will of course always be shrouded in obscurity. But just as the evolution of Talensi society as a whole must be located in a broader precolonial history shaped by the slave-raiding economy of the Asante hinterland, so too must be the evolution of Talensi religious belief and practice, in particular the elaborate pilgrimage network linking the Tong Hills with their own ritual hinterland. Indeed, it is likely that the two main historical functions of the hills reinforced each other, with their status as a physical sanctuary in an insecure world lending weight to their ritual power and vice versa. This connection emerges in what Goody describes as "the opposition of the horse and the earth": that is, the well-documented prohibition throughout the Voltaic savanna region on horses entering the precincts of earth and ancestor shrines.[52]

That the forms of Talensi religion and belief evolved in a particular historical juncture rather than a timeless void is further suggested by an account given to Fortes in the 1930s by an (unnamed) elder of Sawaleg of the origins of his clan's totemic animals:

> Bows were in conflict (*tap ndaa ŋme*), ("Perhaps," he added as an afterthought, "there was a fight with Mamprusi who came to raid for slaves") and our ancestor fled, seeking refuge in an animal's burrow. The enemy was about to break open the burrow when a squirrel (*sinsɛreg*) darted past. They turned to pursue it, and left our ancestor. Thereupon, he vowed never to eat the squirrel again, neither he nor his descendants.[53]

Such myths, of course, are composed of narrative clichés and unlikely to be related to specific historical incidents. Yet the fact that Fortes's informant located the origin of something as fundamental to his own identity and to Talensi ritual thought as an animal totem in the context of resistance to Mamprusi slave raiders—even as an afterthought—speaks volumes. Different totemic avoidances (*kih*) clearly mark the boundary between indigenous Tale and immigrant Namoo: for the latter, the crucial social definition of the former is "those who gird their dead with a sheepskin cover (*ba suona pehug*) and taboo (*kih*) the tortoise (*pakur*) and the water-tortoise (*mieŋ*)."[54] Totemic animals are in turn intimately associated with particular Tongnaab congregations, symbolizing a set of common sanctions and practices that bind members into the ritual community of the ancestor cult.

There is every indication that the imposing edifice of the Tong Hills dominated the sacred landscape of the region long before the coming of British rule. Rising steeply to a height of over six hundred feet from the surrounding plain and with great stacks of pink granite boulders piled one on the other as if by some mighty supernatural hand, the hills stood out in a landscape where any striking feature tended to be invested with cosmological significance.[55] Quite simply, the complex mechanisms linking clients from surrounding regions to Tongnaab were too well organized to have sprung up during or just previous to the era of colonial conquest. The antiquity of Tongnaab's far-flung ritual field was confirmed by Meyer Fortes in the 1930s. Despite his emphasis on the bounded unity of Talensi society, he readily acknowledged the importance of the ancestor shrines in what he called the "external relations" of its constituent clans and lineages. "This aspect of the cult is by no means a mere side-line," he wrote. "It is an intrinsic and obviously old-established feature of it."[56] Indeed, Fortes's discussion of ritual commerce is one of the few points in his two famous monographs where he not only locates Talensi society in a broader regional perspective but also considers the past as something rather different from the ethnographic present. He lays particular emphasis on the economic aspects of the precolonial pilgrim traffic, which involved the exchange of ritual goods and services for commodities such as salt, cloth, and iron hoe blades. "Nowadays these gifts are of small, though by no means negligible, worth, for all these commodities can be bought in any market far more cheaply than in the past. But in the past they represented a valuable source of supply of scarce and highly prized goods."[57] Concerned with piecing together the intricate ritual bonds that he saw as cementing individual households, lineages, and clans into a unitary Talensi "social structure," Fortes failed to explore the full implications of the historical role of this commerce in forging links outside of that bounded ethnic entity. Yet his detailed anthropological analysis of religious belief and practice in the 1930s has much to tell us about the broader history of Tongnaab. It can, with caution, be extrapolated in its fundamentals back to the period before the colonial conquest, as well as forward to the present day.

Fortes identified a basic distinction in the organization of Talensi belief between the cult of the earth (*teng*) and the cult of the ancestors (*bo'ar*). At the most fundamental level of understanding, the two sets of rites can be seen as encapsulating the myriad tensions and interactions between the world of nature on the one hand and the world of human culture on the other. "The natives sum up the relationship between *Bɔɣar* and *Tɛŋ* in the following formula," Fortes explained. "The *Bɔɣar*, they say, rests on the Earth and cannot act without it; but the Earth would be derelict without men, the children of the ancestors whose spiritual abode is the *Bɔɣar*. The sacredness of the Earth is due to the fact that men live on its surface, tend it, and worship it."[58] A further set of spiritual forces were seen to inhabit the wilderness (Talen: *mo'o* or *moog*) beyond the cultivated *teng*. These were the *kolkpaari*s (sing. *kolkpareeg*), malicious "bush sprites" whose occasional eruption into human affairs was manifested most clearly in the case of twin births.[59] None of these powers were represented or invoked with the use of masks, as they were among many other Gur-speaking savanna peoples. Talensi artistic achievement was limited largely to architecture—which, like that of neighboring peoples, was often stunning in design and conception.

The dual earth and ancestor cults were localized at a range of sacred spots that served principally as sites of sacrifice, or *kaab*. The term *kaab*, Fortes stressed, "embraces every kind of ritual offering or libation" and can be further glossed as "worship" or "prayer."[60] An earth shrine or *tongban* (pl. *tongbana*), he observed, "may be a grove of trees, a pool, a stream, a pile of boulders, a single tree, or merely a small patch in the midst of cultivated fields. In the settled parts of Taleland half a mile's walk along any footpath

The Tong Hills

Baare

Winkogo

Gbeog

Tongo

Wakii

Gorogo

Sipaat

Shia

Tengzug

Yinduri

Santeng

White Volta River

over 750 feet

over 1000 feet

0   1   2 miles

takes one past two or three *tongbana*, so numerous are they."[61] The single most important Talensi *tongban* was—and remains today—Ngoo, the sacred grove at Tengzug that serves as the focus for *Gologo* (or *Golib*), the great sowing festival held at the end of each dry season in March. "Ngoo is the palladium of all the Talis," Fortes wrote, "the centre about which the equilibrium of all their corporate relations with one another swings."[62]

The broad band of linguistic reference of the term *teng* reflects the intimate relationship between the earth and human culture in Talensi perceptions of the world. As Fortes points out, *teng* and its cognate *tong* (as in *tong-ban*) are used not only to denote the earth in all its physical and mystical aspects, but also to describe elements of the man-made world that sits upon it.[63] Thus, *teng* (pl. *tes*) also means a particular settlement or community (such as Baari, Wakii, or Shia, for example). In this form it is broadly synonymous with what the newly arrived British conquerors, confronted with an absence of any nucleated villages, called a "countryside." It obviously forms the name of the principal Namoo settlement, Tongo; that of the community occupying the central valley of the hills, Tengzug (lit. "the head [or top] of the earth"); and of course that of the hills themselves. Finally, it appears again in the name of the great ancestor-deity Tongnaab, literally "Chief of the Earth" or, in Fortes's evocative gloss, "Lord of the Country."

Like *tongbana* or earth shrines, Talensi ancestor shrines appeared in a variety of different manifestations, from small household altars up to the famous sites of trans-cultural pilgrimage. Fortes placed great emphasis throughout his work on the absolute centrality of the ancestors to Talensi religious belief and practice. "[T]heir religion consists, essentially, of an elaborate system of ancestor worship," he reflected in a 1966 paper. "It so dominates their thought that the other occult agencies postulated by them, the mystically powerful Earth or the magically efficacious medicines, for instance, are all conceived of as being under the ultimate control of the ancestors."[64] Horton and Goody have questioned in passing this tendency to subordinate all aspects of the Talensi worldview to the concept of "ancestor worship," particularly as it was manifested in Fortes's later and more overtly Freudian analyses of the psychological relationship between the individual and society.[65] Be that as it may—and without entering into debates over the usefulness or otherwise of Freud in formulating anthropological theory—there can be no doubt that Talensi cosmology and ritual practice were very much focused on the influence of the ancestors over the world of the living. It was the ancestors (*kpeem*, "the dead," but usually referred to with the kinship terms *banam*, fathers, or more commonly *yaanam* [sing. *yaab*], grandfathers), rather than "God," who controlled quotidian human existence and toward whom *kaab*, sacrifice or "prayer," was directed.

Like many other African cosmologies, however, that of the Talensi recognized the existence of a distant, ill-defined deity (variously, Naayin or Naawun) who, after creating the world, had withdrawn from direct contact with humans. Naawun, Fortes suggests, is better translated as the more nebulous concept of "heaven," although the use of the prefix *naa* (as in a chief's title, but broadly suggesting authority over, or custody of) perhaps implies a greater degree of personification than he allows for.[66] More importantly, Naawun or Naayin is also cognate with *yin*, personal destiny, the mystical concept at the heart of Fortes's famous essay on Talensi belief, "Oedipus and Job in West African Religion." *Yin* was seen to have two main aspects: predestiny or "fate" (*nuor yin*, "*yin* of the mouth"), which the unborn child of both sexes receives from Naayin before coming into the world, and a *yin* for men alone, associated with his ancestors and commonly "revealed" (*naam*) to him in childhood or early manhood through an unusual chain of events, a strange coincidence, a hunting incident, or the like. Following consultation with a specialized diviner (*bakoldaana*), the young man would then construct an ancestor shrine, which remained the focus of his individual ritual practice throughout his life. "A man's *Yin*," Fortes stressed, "is both the chart of his life and the helm with which he steers his way through life."[67]

The generic Talen term for all types of ancestor shrines is *ba'er* (pl. *ba'a*). As in much of the Gur cultural zone, those devoted by an individual to his or her own forebears typically take the form of conical clay structures ranging from about one to six feet in height, often capped with a broken pot and incorporating hoe blades, stones, and other ritually significant objects. Sometimes free-standing and sometimes built seamlessly into the polished outer walls, rooms, or grain stores of compounds, they remain a ubiquitous feature of Talensi vernacular architecture to the present day.[68] Within the broad designation of *ba'a* was the *bo'ar* (pl. *bo'a*), a shrine specifically dedicated by or to the founding ancestor of a lineage or clan. One well-known *bo'ar* was that associated with Musuor, the demiurgic figure revered by the Namoo as the first migrant from Mamprugu and the founder of Tongo. Fortes identified a third and even more specialized type of *ba'er* that was particularly associated with the autochthonous "Hill Talis" rather than the immigrant Namoo. It was described as *yengha bo'a*, but throughout his published work Fortes used the translation "External *Bɔɣar*" or *"Boghar"*—capitalized to distinguish it from ordinary *bo'a*. It is unclear exactly why Fortes chose this construction, especially as he notes in passing that the term actually used by the Talensi for these shrines was Tongnaab.[69] The *yengha* or Tongnaab *bo'a* served as common shrines for all the ancestors of the autochthonous Tale clans. It was "external," Fortes argued, in two senses. First, it was physically located out in the open, as opposed to within a compound like the *dugni bo'ar* or *"bo'ar* of the room." "A [external] *boyar*," he noted, "may be a grove of trees, a cave in the hillside, or a small enclosure made by trees and boulders. It is truly sacred, for it may be entered only for ritual purposes, and in the company of all ritual officiants."[70] Second, it was "outside" in the social sense of not being associated with any one particular lineage.[71] Fortes could have added a third sense: that Tongnaab was also external in that it acted as a focus of devotion and pilgrimage for a diverse range of peoples from outside of Talensi society.

Opinion differs as to whether Tongnaab was a primordial ancestor who underwent apotheosis or an existing deity encountered by the first Talensi. According to Fortes, Tongnaab was the "Primordial Ancestor, who is believed to manifest himself in the oracular voice."[72] The present-day *yikpemdaan* of Gorogo, Wakbazaa, provided a similar interpretation: "The original man, Taleng . . . was called Tongnaab."[73] In contrast, an unnamed informant (likely to have been Victor Aboya) told Rattray in 1928 that "Its power is from God (*Na Yin*)," a statement echoed by Yiran Boare seventy years later: "Tongnaab is not our ancestor, even though it is a *ba'er*. It came from God [*Naawun*]—God created it. Tongnaab made the people come here. When our ancestors migrated to this area he made the people settle around here."[74] The implication here is that the spiritual power called "Tongnaab" was embedded in the rocky heights of the Tong Hills before the emergence of mankind and before the land was converted from *mo'o* to *teng*. Either way, it is clear that Tongnaab—like the ancestors—is generally perceived as a readily accessible refraction of the withdrawn High God, Naawun.

Not all Tongnaab *bo'a* were located amidst the granite boulders atop the heights of the Tong Hills. Down on the flat in Tongo, for example, the ritual life of the Zubiung clan was focused on the Duunkpaleg *bo'ar*, "a sacred grove whose mystical powers are renowned and respected far beyond the borders of Taleland."[75] But it was amongst the hill folk that this aspect of the ancestor cult was most fully elaborated. Fortes estimated in the 1930s that the Tong Hills contained about a dozen Tongnaab *bo'a*. Each site was managed by a group of what he called "ritual collaborators," that is, a particular combination of autochthonous lineages and clans. The ritual functionaries with direct responsibilities for the shrines were male elders who held either a *tengdaana*-ship or a more specialist office such as *yikpemdaan* ("the custodian of the lineage ancestors") or *bo'arana* ("the custodian of the *bo'ar*"). Historically, all of these shrines shared an ideological capacity to incorporate constituencies from beyond the frontiers of Talensi settlement. At various times in the distant past, one or the other may well have risen to a position of prominence in the regional ritual landscape. By the early twentieth century, two Tongnaab shrines in particular emerge from the sources as forming the main focus of the external pilgrim trade. The fame of Duunkpaleg notwithstanding, these were Bonaab and Yanii, both of

Figure 1.3. A typical *dugni bo'ar* or household ancestor shrine, photographed by R. S. Rattray in 1928–29. This one belonged to an (unnamed) soothsayer (*bakoldaana*) of Winkogo, a settlement on the frontier of the Talensi and Nankani countrysides. Pitt Rivers Museum, University of Oxford 1998.312.1025.1; published as figure 5 of *Tribes of the Ashanti Hinterland*, facing 218, captioned "Soothsayer's shrine, showing hole by which the spirit goes in and out."

Figure 1.4. Meyer Fortes's caption on the back of this unpublished photograph reads "Inside a *Tongnaab Bɔyar*. A heap of gifts brought by pilgrims from client villages in Mampurugu, bottom right. Cowrie shells, small packets of salt in white wrappings, hoe blades & dried meat of animals sacrificed on their affiliated shrines by pilgrims, can be seen." 1934–37.

which were located at the top of the hills in the ritual stronghold of Tengzug. Bonaab means literally "Chief of Things," a name glossed by Fortes as "Great Benefactor."[76] The etymology of Yanii (or, according to Fortes, Wannii) is less clear, although there are indications that the name is another of the range of cognates associated with *yin* and Naayin/Naawun.[77]

As we will see in the next chapter, British officials gradually became aware of the full extent of the pilgrimage routes radiating out from the Tong Hills only from about 1920 onward. Yet early documentary sources together with the testimonies of present-day informants suggest that the hilltop shrines had long attracted supplicants not only from contiguous non-centralized peoples, the Kusasi to the east and the various Gurunsi groups such as the Nankani, Builsa, and Kasena to the west, but also from the zones of state formation beyond: Mossi to the north, Mamprugu, Dagbon, and Nunumba to the south, and unidentified peoples from the north of what became German Togoland.[78] These various groups of ethnically designated "strangers" tended to be associated with particular Tongnaab shrines. The influence of the Degal *bo'ar*, for example, was reported as being especially strong in the southeast of Mamprugu, that of Bonaab in the southwest of Mamprugu and amongst the autochthonous *Dagbon-sabelig* or "Black Dagombas," while Yanii seems to have attracted pilgrims from other Dagomba communities and from throughout the Gurunsi region. Amongst the Dagomba, the Yanii shine is known as *Yabyili*, "Grandfather's house," and is widely known as a longstanding site of pilgrimage where the god "is strong for every tribe."[79] Individual intermediaries of each *bo'ar* also maintained links with particular constituencies. Thus, Builsa peoples tended to approach Yanii through the Shia *bo'arana*, the Dagomba through either the *golibdaana* of Bukiuk or the Kambangire *tengdaana* of Yinduri, and the Gurunsi through the *yikpemdaan* of Gorogo.[80]

Of all these lines of ritual communication, the one that crops up most frequently in documentary sources is that between Shia and the Builsa peoples. The Builsa (known in early colonial sources as Kanjarga, after one part of their territory) occupy a belt of open country some thirty to forty miles west and southwest of the Talensi. It was the Builsa who bore the brunt of the eastward advance of the Zabarima raiding frontier and who in the 1890s gained a reputation for military prowess when they combined to turn back Babatu's horsemen. We have already touched on the difficulties in interpreting the close Builsa connection with the Tong Hills: should claims of Builsa origins amongst communities on the western flanks of the hills be read literally as accounts of actual population movement, or as a charter for longstanding ritual bonds? Perhaps the best answer to this question is to suggest that there is no reason why these two interpretations should be mutually incompatible. If we accept, *pace* Fortes, that there is some indication that groups of Builsa origin did in fact settle in the Tong Hills, then whether this movement was facilitated by existing ritual links or whether it was the ritual links that arose from existing kinship ties must remain a moot point. In 1928, the then Shia *bo'arana* told Rattray that the ancestors of the Shia people came from Chiana and Nakong in the Kasena region and from Kadema, Sandema, and Wiaga in Builsa.[81] It is striking that Kadema, Sandema, and Wiaga remain, together with Gbedema, Wiasi, and Fumbisi, present-day outposts of the Tongnaab cult in the Builsa region. All of these communities lie on or very near to one of the main precolonial trade routes traversing the Gurunsi region, linking the Mossi center of Wagadugu in the north with the Gonja trading town of Daboya to the south. Just south of Builsa country it passed through the town of

Figure 1.5. Tongnaab in its savanna hinterland. In Yagaba, some fifty miles from the Tong Hills, a *tengdaana* sacrifices a fowl to Tongnaab. The god lies before him in the portable "shrine" or *bo'artyii*. Unpublished photograph by Meyer Fortes, 1935.

Yagaba, a long-established staging post in the slave trade located in the vague borderlands between Mamprugu, Dagbon, and Gonja. As Fortes discovered in the 1930s, Yagaba also had a strong connection to Tongnaab.[82] Along with other commodities—including slaves—Tongnaab appears to have traversed this major artery through Builsa country in precolonial times to Yagaba and perhaps beyond.

Ideological flexibility and physical mobility were the two key characteristics that facilitated the spread of Tongnaab. In contrast with *tongbana*, which were rooted in particular sacred locations, the power of *bo'a* could be moved with ease from place to place. One vessel of this power was the *bo'artyii*, a portable "shrine" in the form of a large leather bag stuffed with sacred earth and other ritual elements. As Fortes noted, the *bo'artyii* "draws the ancestors themselves along to the scene of [a] ritual."[83] Another common vessel was an animal horn, again containing lumps of red laterite clay referred to as *Tongnaab teng* ("Tongnaab earth"), taken from an established shrine. The process of investing ritual power in soil was touched on by one Talensi in 1928 as he attempted to explain to Rattray the essential difference between the *ba'ar* and the more specific *bo'ar*: "A *bogere* [i.e., *bo'ar*] . . . you fetch from your mother's country after she is dead. You go to your mother's father's compound, and take some earth from the *bagere* [i.e., *ba'ar*] of your mother's father and put this in a calabash, which your wife will carry home. . . . This soil will be put in a horn and is called my mother's *bogere*. . . . a *bogere* is like a shade to a *bagere*."[84] The key concept here is the "shade" or the "shadow" of an existing source of ritual power, in Talen the *yihiyii* (or, as rendered by Fortes, *yilenyilug*). Not only could supplicants visit a *bo'ar* atop the Tong Hills, but the *yihiyii* of Tongnaab could be granted to them by the god's custodians in order that they might carry it back to their homes. Some even became intermediaries of Tongnaab themselves, attracting supplicants to their own "satellite" shrines. This was a complex transaction, involving a high degree of incorporation into the ritual congregation and in some cases full initiation into the *bo'ar* cult. The result was a blurring of the ethnic distinction between "Talensi" and "stranger." After all, Talensi belonging to Namoo clans had nothing directly to do with the management of Tongnaab and were never initiated into the cult. "The fetish is for all people, Dagombas, Mamprusi, Kanjarga etc.," the Shia *bo'arana* testified to British investigators in 1925. Despite this ideology of inclusiveness, however, access to Tongnaab was closely regulated. "Tongnab spirit is in the cave in the hill," the *bo'arana* continued. "I have to go to the place of Tongnab every 2 months to fetch fresh supplies of Tongnab earth. . . . I can only visit the fetish place every 2 months. The fetish would be tired and get angry if I visit too often."[85]

Members of present-day Tongnaab congregations amongst the Builsa have provided crucial evidence of both the historical depth and the operation of the cult in its precolonial savanna setting. Anyaam is the current guardian of one of the oldest satellite shrines in the region, in the Kpikpaluk section of Kadema. He told us that his ancestor Akpagin journeyed to the Tong Hills and returned with a *bo'artyii* containing Tongnaab "before the slave trade even started"—possibly a reference to the period before the Zabarima campaigns, but perhaps much earlier.[86] Ben Atongnaab Akanisoam of Gbedema was more specific, reporting that his family had acquired Tongnaab four generations before, while Asiidem Akanguli of Wiaga stated emphatically that the god had been in his house for six generations—which gives a date somewhere in the middle to late eighteenth century.[87] A number of informants reported that it was a particularly intractable problem that had prompted their ancestors to seek out a ritual solution beyond their own community and to embark on the long and potentially hazardous journey to the Tong Hills. That many sought children underlines the historic connection between Tongnaab and the issue of fertility, first reported by Nash in 1913.

The overwhelming importance of childbirth for local communities cannot be overestimated as a factor in explaining Tongnaab's rise to preeminence in the regional sacred landscape. Of course, human fertility has long been identified as a central concern of religious belief and practice among people throughout sub-Saharan Africa. But in the precarious environment of the middle Volta savanna, with its capricious rainfall patterns leading to regular droughts, crop failures, and hunger, and thus high infant mortality, plus the loss of people through slave raiding and other forms of organized violence, the imperative to maximize rates of reproduction was all the stronger. We have already noted the impact of the great famine of the 1890s and in chapter 5 will examine the role of Tongnaab during another period of recurring drought and hunger in the late 1920s and early 1930s. Further indications of the historical struggle to maintain numbers can be found in the oral traditions recorded by Rattray, in which famines, the large-scale sale of kin, local raiding in times of hardship, and outbreaks of disease (especially smallpox, called *naba*, "the chief") are employed as mnemonics to reconstruct family genealogies.[88] It is also embedded in the fundamental Talensi belief—emphasized repeatedly by Fortes throughout his work—that the transformation of the dead into ancestors was solely dependent on their having left children behind in order to ritually negotiate that apotheosis.

It was such a crisis of reproduction that faced Asiidem Akanguli's ancestor, who undertook a pioneering journey from Wiaga to Tongnaab after his wife suffered repeated miscarriages. It was also the grim situation facing Atulum and Gariba Angiaknab's grandfather, Abang, who set out from Fumbisi sometime before the coming of Babatu:

> Our grandfather . . . had nothing, no son, no child at all and he . . . heard from someone that you could go there and Tongnaab would help you, so he also went there. When he went there, he promised that when he comes and he gets children, he will build a house and it will mean that the house and the children all belong to Tongnaab. And when he came back from there, he actually had children and he put up the house and now . . . the house and the family all . . . belong to Tongnaab.[89]

Successive generations of this thriving house, the Abang-yire, thus became, in Buli, Tongnaab-*biik*, "sons of Tongnaab." In Talensi terminology, Tongnaab became their *seyer* or "spirit-guardian."[90] Tongnaab-*biik* were required to keep the totemic avoidances of their particular shrine community and to make the pilgrimage to Tengzug up to three times each year during the run-up to the great *Bo'araam* harvest festival in order to renew their allegiance to the god and to secure prophetic advice on the coming year. In return, ritual intermediaries from the hills—and in Builsaland this usually meant representatives of the Shia *bo'arana*—would make one journey out to those who possessed the *yihiyii* to ensure that all was correct. As Fortes observed in the 1930s, "These visitors, coming as emissaries of the *Bɔyar*, are received with the hospitality due to honoured kinsmen and travel long distances in hostile country under the safe conduct of their client associates without danger."[91] Thus the bond linking the Tong Hills to their widely scattered ritual constituencies would be secured for another season. The yearly renewal of bonds was especially important for those who became intermediaries of Tongnaab in their own right. Two such satellite shrines that continue to function in Builsaland today are those operated by Anyaam in Kadema and by Ben Atongnaab Akanisoam in Gbedema. Both houses have long functioned as the central place of their own smaller ritual hinterlands, attracting supplicants who wish to consult locally with Tongnaab rather than make what would in the past have been an arduous journey to Tengzug.

It is the second of the two great annual festivals celebrated by the hill Tales, *Bo'araam*, that has long acted as the principal collective sacrament of the ancestors. Falling at the end of the agricultural cycle in the lunar month of the same name (roughly November), after the harvest has been gathered and at the onset of the dry season, *Bo'araam* is focused on the great Tongnaab shrines of the Tong Hills. Together with *Gologo*, it serves as a decisive marker of *Talis menga*, "real Tale," identity. The hill settlements of Tengzug, Santeng, Yinduri, Sia, Gorogo, and Wakii, together with Gbeog and Soog, a Tengzug elder informed Fortes, "perform the works of Talis, our *Gɔlib* and *Bɔyaraam*." Tongo and the other settlements down on the flat, he continued, "celebrate (lit. work) after the Namoo fashion, the *Giŋgaaŋ* and *Da'a* festivals."[92] As Fortes noted in 1936, "The Namoos know the dates of Bɔyaraam, and the dances . . . [but] of the rituals they had, despite centuries of intimate contact, absolutely no knowledge. Indeed they refuse to hear of it, for they regard the cults of the Talis with fear and aversion."[93] *Bo'araam* is the time when young men of the hill clans undergo ritual induction into the *bo'ar* cult—the only formalized rite of passage practiced by the Talensi. Crucially, it is also when spiritual wards (*seyeraan*) and other devotees from outside the Talensi area journey to Tengzug in order to reaffirm their allegiance to Tongnaab. A key gender distinction is apparent between these two categories of supplicants. Among the Tale themselves, only men may become members of the ancestor cult. Although bound by the same totemic taboos as the menfolk of their lineages, women are not admitted. According to the patrilineal rules of Talensi society, women marry outside of the lineage, are not responsible for its continuation, and, according to many of our present-day (male) informants, are not to be trusted with the esoteric knowledge of Tongnaab. In contrast, supplicants from the outer reaches of the cult's ritual field include—and appear to have included in the past—many women, who unlike their Tale sisters were permitted to enter the inner sanctum of Tongnaab shrines and present their petitions directly to the deity.

As we will see, the great festivals make a first, fleeting appearance in the historical record in the opening decade of the twentieth century, when twice they intersected with British advances in the process of colonial pacification. But a brief description of some of the key ritual and performative aspects of *Bo'araam* at this stage will serve to convey a sense of the aura of potent spiritual power surrounding the Tong Hills and the Tongnaab cult. The ritual cycle devoted to the ancestors begins down among the Namoo on the plains with the *Da'a* or *Gingaang* festival. On the first day of the last month of the rainy season, *Kuom ngmarig*, the "Moon of Waters" (September), the Baari *tengdaana* announces the start of the festival season. That night the people of Baari, on the northern frontier of Taleland, begin their celebrations. Five days later, the focus switches to Tongo, where, following a succession of sacrifices and divinations, the sacred *Gingaang* drum is brought out and used to propel the first of a fortnight of nocturnal dances. Following a two-week lull while the guinea-corn and late millet is harvested, festivities recommence at the start of *Da'a ngmarig*. More nightly *Gingaang* dances follow, climaxing in an episode in the second week of the moon when late in the night a dozen or so solemn figures take the center of the dancing ground. "They wear faded red caps [i.e., the red fez, *mung*]," observed Fortes in 1934, "and gorgeous, though sometimes tarnished, gowns—the garbs of chiefs—and carry spears."[94] These dancers represent ancestors who had been chiefs and men of rank, encapsulating one side of the balance between imported *naam* and the ritual power of the indigenous Tale *tengdaana*s.

The following month, *Bo'araam ngmarig*, a corresponding set of rites, dances, and festivities, takes place in the Tong Hills. Unlike *Gologo*, during which all the lineages and clans come together in a sequence of communal dances and ritual activities, *Bo'araam* is celebrated separately by the congregations of each Tongnaab *bo'ar*. Beginning on successive days, the male elders of the various congregations gather outside the compound of their ranking *tengdaana*, where—with women and children confined indoors and out of sight—fowls are sacrificed on the ancestral altars. The parties then move off in designated order, each man carrying a newly harvested millet stalk, to the inner sanctums of the Tongnaab *bo'ar*, where further sacrifices are made. This ritual process culminates in the induction of young men into membership in the *bo'ar* cult. Fortes is deliberately vague concerning these esoteric rites of passage—following his own initiation into the cult in 1935, he was sworn to secrecy regarding their details.[95] But in outline, the proceedings are clear enough: the initiands are seized late at night, dressed in antelope skins, and escorted in conditions of great secrecy into the *bo'ar* high in the rocks at the summit of the hills. There, in a ritual described by Fortes as "sensationally dramatic," Tongnaab is invoked. In the terrifying presence of the ancestor-deity, the young men swear the most solemn oath of the hill folk: *Nyaab Tongnaab ni u za zom kuom*, "By my ancestor Tongnaab and his late-millet water"—flour-water made from late millet being the strictest of Tongnaab's totemic taboos—to uphold the secrets of the cult as well as the entire social order bequeathed to the living by the ancestors.[96] The initiation rites continue into the next day, and over the ensuing week the various ritual congregations busy themselves with dancing, feasting, and hosting members who have journeyed from outside Taleland.

The extent and operation of Tongnaab's ritual field suggests that some reconsideration is needed of the established view of the stateless frontier as characterized by discrete ethnic groups defined in an insecure precolonial world by mutual hostility. British officials regarded the non-centralized "tribal" peoples of the Northern Territories as immobilized by a combination of primitive insularity and a fear of warlike strangers. In reality, the social landscape of the precolonial savanna appears to have been characterized by a considerable degree of physical mobility and interaction between different groups. The *yihiyii* or "shadow" of Tongnaab emerges as a crucial tool in negotiating cultural boundaries and crossing frontiers. It offered protection against the myriad spiritual dangers of the wilderness as well as against the physical dangers posed by potentially hostile neighbors. According to Yiran Boare, "if you had to travel somewhere you used the name of Tongnaab or [carried] something that held the shadow of Tongnaab, and nobody would touch you."[97] In this respect, allegiance to a recognized source of ritual power—and it is recognition that is crucial here—served to overlay and to some extent blur the distinctions that separated, say, the Talensi from the Nankani, the Nankani from the Kasena, the Kasena from the Builsa, and so on.[98] "Each small community lived apart from, and was in constant dread of being raided by, its neighbours," Nash

was informed by the *tongrana* and other Talensi elders in 1913. "A Zoua-
rangu man would not visit Tongo and vice versa, nor would a Sekoti warrior pass through the Zanlerigu range, unless he had a permit to do so in
the form of a relation at Zanlerigu."[99] Nash had earlier noted that this "permit" was often shaped by ritual links: "A chief of one countryside will often
have a connection with another countryside owing to his grandfather or
other ancestor having a fetish there and the appointment of the fetishman
[i.e., *tengdaana*] rests with him."[100] In the increasingly insecure environment
of the nineteenth-century middle Volta basin, that could mean the difference between freedom and enslavement.

Despite—and perhaps to some extent because of—that rising insecurity, Tongnaab's ritual network by the late nineteenth century radiated out
from Taleland to embrace diverse communities throughout much of the
middle Volta region. This did not, of course, mean that those supplicants
who journeyed to Tengzug in order to receive oracular advice, to ensure
fertility, or to solve spiritual crises can be described as "Tongnaab worshippers" *per se*, to the exclusion of local gods or their own ancestors. Rather,
Tongnaab acquired fame as a provider of specialized spiritual services that
could not be provided locally and that were certainly reinforced by the performative ritual of pilgrimage itself. As such, Tongnaab emerged as one of
a number of famous oracle shrines dotted across the savannas characterized by the possession of a trans-regional cult. We will see in chapter 3 how
some of those shrines that fell within the orbit of "Greater Asante" were
in the nineteenth century already attracting supplicants from the Akan
peoples of the forest to the south. Yet there is no evidence whatsoever that
Tongnaab's precolonial ritual field breached the ecological and cultural divide between the savanna and forest worlds. Located beyond the frontier
of Asante overrule and in the heart of the belt of fiercely independent "Gurunsi" peoples, the Tong Hills were well off-limits for Akan strangers and
would remain so until the imposition of colonial peace in the second decade
of the twentieth century.

"Organized Governments" and "Barbarous Tribes": Colonial Encounter in the 1890s

As the scramble for African territory entered its decisive phase in the 1890s,
the middle Volta region became the focus of a race for power involving rival European forces, local rulers, and the ephemeral Zabarima and Samo-
rian conquest states. That the British managed to secure a substantial savanna hinterland to the north of Asante in the face of French and German

advances was due largely to the efforts of the Gold Coast government agent, George Ekem Ferguson, whose four treaty-making expeditions between 1890 and his death near Wa in 1897 laid the groundwork for military occupation in the closing years of the century. After years of complex diplomatic maneuvering and in the wake of the British subjugation of Asante in 1896, the 1898 Anglo-French Convention and the 1899 Anglo-German Agreement fixed the colonial frontiers of the region. The 11th parallel was established as the border between French and British territory and the Talensi people found themselves twenty miles inside the Northern Territories Protectorate of the Gold Coast.[101]

The first European to traverse the Gurunsi belt was the German explorer Adolph Krause, who in 1886 traveled from Accra to Wagadugu via Salaga. He was followed in 1888 by another German, Von François, who passed through the Mamprusi commercial center of Gambaga, and, later the same year, by the French army officer Louis Binger. Binger passed within a few miles of the Tong Hills as he followed the main trade route south from the Mossi capital of Wagadugu to Salaga. Traveling through the Talensi settlements of Balungu and Pwalugu before crossing the White Volta, he identified their inhabitants—his text suggests partly on the basis of facial scarification—as "Mampourga," (i.e., Mamprusi). He then qualified this, observing that as these people are "nearer to the Dagomba Muslims of Nabari and Walewale, to whom they often sell livestock, they are less inclined to evil than the Gourounga [i.e., Gurunsi] of the region to the north; like these, however, they have all the attributes of a wild people ['un peuple sauvage']."[102] The Volta River, Binger makes clear, formed the effective boundary between the lawless expanses of Gurunsi territory and the Mamprugu kingdom. Later in his account he makes the first specific reference in European sources to "the Talensi," mistakenly noting their presence to the west of the Youlsi (i.e., Kasena) and observing that they are to be distinguished from neighboring Gurunsi peoples by their distinctive facial markings.[103]

Alarmed by forward moves on the part of the French and Germans in the wake of Binger's journey, the Gold Coast government in 1890 despatched George Ekem Ferguson on the first of his missions to secure British influence over the hinterland beyond Asante. The reports of this resourceful Euro-African surveyor from the Fante coastal town of Anomabu are extraordinary documents that have yet to receive the detailed historical interpretation they deserve.[104] The main point to make here about Ferguson's writings—the first recension of British colonial knowledge of the ethnic and political configuration of the "North"—is that, like those of Binger and other Victorian travelers, they are shaped by an overriding concern with relative degrees of African "civilization" and "barbarism." Charged with the task of signing treaties with native rulers, it is unsurprising that Ferguson should divide the peoples of the region into two basic groups: "Countries with organized government" on the one hand and "Barbarous tribes" on the other.[105] Amongst the latter, Ferguson was particularly struck by the ferocity of the various Gurunsi peoples, whose raiding activities had forced him in 1892 to abort his planned journey to Wagadugu. Again in 1894, he found the main trade route from Gambaga to Wagadugu closed by Talensi, Kusasi, and Bussanga attacks on passing caravans.[106] These Gurunsis, Ferguson observed,

> live mostly in family communities, and resist intercourse, even amongst their own selves, with showers of arrows. These people . . . move about in perfect nudity, their lips, noses, and ears, are pierced, into which straws and beads are inserted as ornaments. Some of them, principally those through which caravans fight their way, live in village communities with a strong man (who has arrogated to himself the position of a chief) as the head of the community. He demands transit dues and makes various extortions which are often the cause of a fight. As a tribe or a district, none of them is capable of negotiating with a European Power, and can only be civilized by force of arms.[107]

Later British reports confirm Ferguson's assertion that banditry provided an avenue for the accumulation of political power by local "strong men" even in the most highly decentralized of "barbarous tribes." One such figure was the chief of Bolgatanga, a Nankani settlement eight miles northwest of the Tong Hills, who was reported in 1896 to have "established himself on the main road to Wagadugu . . . [and] collected all the criminals and refugees from the surrounding countries" in order to pillage passing caravans.[108]

In May 1894, Ferguson arrived at the twin centers of the Mamprugu kingdom: the trading town of Gambaga, with its heterogenous community of merchants and Muslim clerics, and the nearby royal capital of Nalerigu, the seat of the paramount chief or *nayiri*. There he secured a treaty of friendship between Britain and Nayiri Yamusa, who explained that his territory "includes portions only of Grunshi, Talensi, Kusasi and Pampamba [i.e., Konkomba] but is coterminous with Dagomba on the South."[109] The ambiguity of the historical relationship between Mamprugu and surrounding stateless peoples would have a direct bearing on the dynamics of colonial conquest in Gurunsi country. In short, British imperial claims north of the bend in the White Volta came to rest on the notion of a "Greater Mamprusi," an ideological construct that had little reality on the ground and, moreover, was not recognized by French and German forces operating in the region. The result was an increase in the spiral of violence, as British, French, and German columns criss-crossed the disputed frontier between their respective spheres of influence, mounting punitive raids on communities seen to be conspiring with rival powers.[110]

By the late 1890s, British military intelligence had begun to identify the "Frafra" as an especially recalcitrant section of the Gurunsi tribes. Derived from a local form of greeting and exhortation ("*furra furra*," lit. "suffering, suffering"), the term "Frafra," like "Gurunsi," was probably coined by Mossi-Dagomba intruders and had clear pejorative connotations. Indeed, British commander Colonel Northcott was led to understand by his chief informant, the *imam* of Gambaga, that the name implied "a concentration of all evil characteristics."[111] "They are under Gambaga," reported one British officer, "but they are a very lawless people, wear no clothes, are armed with poisoned arrows and spears, and are constantly blocking the road for traders."[112] The Frafra in fact comprised three distinct ethno-linguistic groups: the Talensi; their neighbors to the east, the Nabdam; and the Nankani (or "Frafra-Gurunsi"), straddling the new colonial frontier to the north.[113] What set these communities apart in the eyes of outsiders—both African and European—was their particular "primitiveness" and a reputation for aggression and insularity. The most visible indicator of the former was the Frafra's perceived nakedness. Echoing Ferguson's earlier reading, the first Annual Report on the Northern Territories, for the year 1898–99, noted that the Frafras were "composed of men whose naked savagedom was a by-word of contempt among the more civilised inhabitants of the Mamprussi towns."[114] Primitiveness was seen in turn to breed a fear and loathing of all contact with outsiders. By the turn of the century, many Gurunsi and Builsa to the west had already been recruited as colonial soldiers, but the fiercely independent Frafras could not be persuaded to abandon their well-defended hill country and submit to European rule. In the terminology of officials, they refused to "come in." The British responded with a series of punitive expeditions, which, beginning in 1899 and continuing throughout the 1900s, periodically swept through the Talensi, Nabdam, and Nankani countrysides, burning crops, seizing cattle, and destroying compounds.

The colonial "ethnicization" of the Frafra—and especially that of the Talensi of the Tong Hills—was also shaped by African and colonial perceptions of religious authority and belief. In the opening phase of their occupation of the north, the British drew heavily on information gleaned from Muslim interlocutors in established urban centers: Gambaga in the northeast, Wa in the northwest, plus the various trading towns scattered across the vast expanses of Gonja.[115] Although Islam had made only partial in-roads into the ruling structures of the savanna kingdoms, the Muslim cul-tural influence was enough that the independent communities beyond their frontiers were branded as essentially "pagan."[116] British authorities soon picked up and developed this concept of uncivilized "pagan tribes," whose lawlessness was seen to stem not simply from an absence of kings and clothes but from the malign influence of so-called "fetish priests." "I have been well received in Mahomedan towns," reported one officer in 1898, "whereas, whenever I have gone to a bush village of fetish people in Mamprusi, the people have always turned out against me."[117] The kings and chiefs of the savanna states were themselves rarely more than nominally Muslim. Yet as secular rulers they were seen as having a certain legitimacy as well as po-tential utility, while fetish priests tended to be regarded as illegitimate and implacably hostile to the new colonial order. As in the country of the so-called Lobi and Dagarti peoples to the west, ongoing Frafra intransigence was put down in part to the pernicious influence of pagan priests and their control over a hostile landscape dotted with shrines and other sacred places.[118]

This perception began to emerge from the very beginning of the colo-nial encounter with the Talensi. Sometime between 1896 and early in 1898, a passing British column had secured the allegiance of Tongrana Pilibazaa, the leading Namoo chief in the countryside immediately to the north of the Tong Hills. In February 1899, however, a second military expedition found Tongo deserted, the inhabitants having fled to the safety of the rocks. Emerging from the hills, Pilibazaa explained that the British troops had been mistaken for French, who the previous year had exacted a brutal re-venge on the Tongo people for treating with the British: shooting dead a hundred men and carrying off livestock and grain supplies. "Now we have very little food," reported the old chief, "and my people fear to come out of the hills."[119] Six months later, it would be the turn of the British to wreak havoc among the Talensi. In response to reports of Frafra banditry, a heav-ily armed column under Captain Stewart consisting of over two hundred "Hausa" infantrymen supported by Mossi cavalry was despatched from Gambaga. On 19 July 1899, Stewart's force fought its way through the Tong Hills in the face of fierce resistance from Talensi warriors armed with bows and poisoned arrows. According to Adongo, the chief of Bolgatanga—who since 1896 had worked hard to transform himself from a dangerous ban-dit into the chief ally of the British—this resistance was orchestrated by the *tongrana*, in his role as "the chief fetish priest of all the Fra Fra."[120] Stew-art was misinformed: the *tongrana* was not a *tengdaana*, but a titular Namoo chief. Nevertheless, the misperception represents the first vague reference to the ritual importance of the Tong Hills throughout the region. Again, crops were burnt and livestock confiscated, the settlement of Tongo was destroyed, and Tongrana Pilibazaa was arrested and imprisoned at Gambaga. "The carrying of the Sapari [i.e., Tong] hills has done an enormous amount of good," Stewart reported, "[as] the natives of the country now realise their hills are not impregnable."[121] Pilibazaa would die in exile, and it was perhaps a sign of the times that his successor as *tongrana* took the name Kunbanbeo—"Cannot-know-tomorrow."[122]

"A Great Fetish Place":
Resistance and Ritual Power in the 1900s

Despite Stewart's optimistic assessment of the psychological impact of his punitive expedition, the reality was that while a well-armed force could shoot their way through the Tong Hills, the British were quite unable to maintain any kind of hold on the hostile Frafra countryside. When in 1900 imperial energies were diverted to quelling the Yaa Asantewaa rebellion in Asante, British military presence in the frontier zones of the Northern Territories virtually disappeared. As late as 1905, the chief commissioner had to admit that "in the most densely populated part of these Territories, namely:—the districts known as Fra-Fra, Grunshi, Dagarti, and Lobi-Dagarti, . . . many parts . . . have never even been visited by a Government Officer while the remaining parts have only been visited by . . . Punitive Expeditions."[123] The result in the northeastern corner of the Protectorate was ongoing insecurity, as freebooters claiming association with the British added to the crude violence of official punitive raids.[124]

It was not until 1905 that the British moved to construct a rudimentary administration in the frontier region north of Mamprugu. As would so often be the case in an impoverished hinterland Protectorate regarded as a drain on the Gold Coast exchequer, the primary motive was financial. Following an announcement that the Imperial Grant-in-Aid for the Northern Territories would be slashed to £10,000 for the year 1906 and terminated altogether in 1908, stations were established astride the main north-south trade routes at Bawku, Navrongo, and Tumu in an attempt to increase revenue from the newly imposed caravan tax.[125] Navrongo (or Navarro), a Kasena community some twenty-five miles to the northwest of the Tong Hills, became the headquarters of the so-called Frafra District.[126] The problem facing the inchoate Northern Territories administration was how to first pacify the densely populated Frafra countryside and then mobilize its manpower.

Neither willing nor able to impose direct taxation, the British instead chose
to extend the ambiguously labeled "free labor" system already in operation
in the centralized states to the tribes of the frontier. "Free labor," of course,
meant forced labor. In the dry, non-farming season between December and
March, designated chiefs were required to supply labor for the building and
maintenance of roads and stations and the head-loading of goods. Nevertheless, despite the beginning of the bureaucratization of conquest with the
creation of the Navrongo station, British contact with many Frafra communities remained fleeting. "The people . . . are very wild," ran the report
of a typical encounter, "and when visited . . . ran away and followed the column through the bush whistling and shouting and coming within 100 yards
of the carriers although they did not actually fire any arrows."[127]

In September 1907, Navrongo district commissioner Captain O'Kinealy
made a bold attempt to extend British influence amongst the Frafra. Ignoring standing instructions to stay well away from the recalcitrant "hill
tribes," he decided to mount a visit into the heart of the Tong Hills. Aware
of their "great reputation as a big fetish place," O'Kinealy suspected that
to control the hills was to control the entire region.[128] Accompanied by an
escort of only eighteen soldiers of the Northern Territories Constabulary,
he passed through Bolgatanga and on the twenty-first arrived on the northern flank of the hills at the settlement of Wakii. The people of Wakii fled
into the rocks, but O'Kinealy managed to call them back and to convince
one man to guide his force up to Tengzug, the settlement nestled in the
central valley of the range. Ignoring the prevarication of his guide and the
pleas of several Tengzug men who implored him to turn back, O'Kinealy
pushed on—"and we were already at the chief's compound, before they
had decided what to do." His gamble of abandoning the tactic of moving
through the countryside only in heavily armed columns appeared to have
paid off. The people of Tengzug were clearly startled, but the next day gathered to meet with their visitors. They explained that their refusal to deal
with the British was due to ongoing raiding and extortion by Mossi horsemen, who they believed—with some justification—to have been "sent by
the white man." After years of vague rumors, O'Kinealy was able to confirm that the hills indeed contained a powerful shrine that attracted pilgrims from as far away as Dagomba. "No one," he recorded, "not even the
Chief of Tong, may come to Tinzugu with his clothes on, under penalty
of paying a fine of a cow to the headman and fetishman, failing which he
will certainly die within the year."[129] Following a week-long stay during
which he also toured the main settlements around the base of the hills, Sipaat,
Shia, Gorogo, Yinduri, Wakii, and Tongo, O'Kinealy recommended that

the military campaign against the Talensi being planned for the coming dry season be canceled in the hope that their leaders would now voluntarily "come in" and submit to British rule.

O'Kinealy's emphasis on the prohibition against the wearing of cloth in Tengzug should be noted here, as it returns to the important theme of clothing, bodily adornment, and identity in the colonial encounter.[130] If nakedness and a predilection for fetishism were the cultural attributes that for the early colonial mind most clearly defined the essence of "primitiveness" on the frontiers of the Northern Territories, then the two came together in the Tong Hills in a way that posed a direct challenge to British authority. The rate at which local garments made of animal skins and plant fibers were replaced with those of woven cotton became a key indicator of the progress of the colonial civilizing mission as early as 1898, when the British opened a Government Store at their new headquarters of Gambaga in an attempt to encourage trade by "familiarising the natives" with imported cloth."[131] This initiative was extended in 1905 to the new station at Navrongo, from where the district commissioner reported an "extraordinary demand for clothes amongst a people who up to then wore nothing, neither men nor women."[132] This is misleading, as it is quite likely that both the Frafra and Gurunsi areas had long had access to the distinctive white-and-indigo striped "Mossi cloth," one of the staple trade commodities circulating throughout the region.[133] In the Tong Hills, however, all cloth was regarded as ritually impure. *Tengdaanas* could wear only animal skin (Talen: *gbung*) and were forbidden even to touch cloth, which was barred from the precincts of the great earth and ancestor shrines. Neither were they permitted ever to fire a gun. "The Tong people are of a lower type of savage than many about them," reported Captain Wheeler following a visit to the hills in 1909. "I found it impossible to get a boy for the Navarro school, the very idea of letting their boys run the risk of wearing clothes filled the assembly with horror."[134]

For the Talensi, it was the wearing of cloth—associated with predatory Mossi horsemen—that historically had signified the hostile and uncivilized "other." This reading was enshrined in the founding myth of the encounter between the first Namoo migrant, Musuor, and the primordial Gbezug *tengdaana*, Genet. In a version recorded by Fortes in Tongo, Musuor asks the *tengdaana* why he fled into the hills on his approach. "Genet replied that he had seen him wearing a gown and that there was something on his head all red [i.e., the red fez, *mung*], and fear took hold of him."[135] Early descriptions of Tongnaab all note the shreds of Mossi and European cloth hanging from trees on the approaches to the shrine—a powerful image of the encounter between local ritual power and the wider world of commodity circulation. Yet cultural differences embedded in the symbolism of bodily adornment were far more ambivalent than the simplistic colonial equation of nakedness with primitiveness. Just as the Talensi absorbed the immigrant Namoo on their own terms, so too would they appropriate exotic commodities. By the early twentieth century, if not before, Mossi cloth was being sewn into the long, triangular loin-piece (*kpalang*) worn by Talensi men at key points in the ritual cycle.[136] In another version of the founding charter told to Fortes by the elders of Gbezug, it was not Musuor's gown and fez but his horse and guns that had startled Genet. Horses too were prohibited from entering the sacred hills, and the use of horse-tail whisks in ritual dances represented an explicit and pithy commentary on the historical success of the Talensi in resisting mounted raiders. It was in these terms that Yiran Boare described the defiance of the inhabitants of Tengzug in the face of the final British assault on their hilltop sanctuary: "The British were using horses, and the people said that they would use the tails of their horses to dance the *Golib*."[137] The central event of the yearly *Gologo* festival, the massed *Golib* dance served to release community tensions through a combination of performative collaboration and ritualized satire. Unfortunately for the people of the Tong Hills, in 1911 even *Golib* was incapable of defusing the pent-up military aggression of the inchoate colonial state.

"Setting Fire to the Hills": March 1911

The British failed to take advantage of O'Kinealy's dramatic visit to Tengzug in 1907. The enterprising Irishman was posted elsewhere, direct contact with the hills lapsed, and many communities in the eastern, Frafra part of the Navarro District still refused to submit to colonial rule. By the end of the decade, the administration of the Northern Territories had shifted from a military to a civil basis, a new headquarters had been laid out at Tamale, and migrant laborers were beginning to be recruited for the gold mines and other capitalist enterprises in the south. Yet the Tong Hills remained an all too visible symbol of the inability of the British to impose their will on the recalcitrant "pagan tribes" on the northeastern frontier. Officials tended to cast the problem in terms of the essential criminality of the Talensi and their renowned fetish:

> The general feeling of insecurity culminated in the terror of the Tong Hills and of the rabble who had made it their strong hold. No better spot could have been chosen from which to work on the superstitious fears of the natives. Rising sheer out of the flat country, and strewn with immense slabs and boulders of granite, piled

up in the most fantastic heaps, as though tumbled from some huge sack, the hills were an ideal abode for a powerful "Fetish," which was used as a cloak to conceal the real object of its occupation, namely to serve as a strong hold and base for a gang of raiders. Every outlaw or desperade in the country took refuge in the Tong Hills, where he was welcomed by his brothers in crime.[138]

Written by Chief Commissioner Armitage four months after the final military assault on the Talensi, this account of the "terror of the Tong Hills" has an air of exaggeration and self-justification about it. The description of the Tongnaab shrine as little more than a cunning guise for raiding activities is clearly one-dimensional and there is little corroborating evidence that the farming communities of the hills were especially orientated toward the systematic looting of passing trade caravans. Yet the image of a stubbornly independent montagnard community, surviving in an insecure world by the mobilization of ritual power and attracting malcontents fleeing the demands of militarized state-formation, broadly accords with our sketch of the precolonial history of the Tong Hills.

Whether or not the hills were in fact filling up with raiders and refugees as a result of the gradual consolidation of colonial rule in the region is unclear. What is certain is that by the end of the 1900s, British exactions began for the first time to directly affect the Talensi. The proximate cause was the murder in January 1910 of the leading British ally in the neighboring Nabdam area, the chief of Nangodi.[139] Following the usual punitive expedition directed against the supposed culprits, the forward base of conquest was extended with the opening of a post at the Nankani settlement of Zuarungu (or "Zouaragu") just four miles to the north of the Tong Hills. Building materials were required for the construction of the new station, and labor for a road that was to run from Zuarungu past the western flank of the hills and on to the White Volta river crossing at Pwalugu. There are indications that these demands came at a time of real hardship. The 1910 harvest was a poor one in many parts of the Navarro and Zuarungu districts and by early the following year food shortages were becoming acute.[140] This coincided with an outbreak of bovine pleuro-pneumonia, which raged through local herds, causing widespread impoverishment.[141] Yet Talensi responses to the deepening crisis were far from uniform. Despite the retribution inflicted on the unfortunate *nangodinaaba* by his disgruntled neighbors, the Namoo chief of Tongo, Yirisano, chose to cooperate with the British. But the *tongrana* had little or no sway over the hill folk. Ensconced in their rocky fortress, they chose to resist—and in the situation of scarcity may well have escalated raids on neighbors, traders, and nearby markets. In February 1911, the acting chief commissioner at Tamale,

Major Festing, decided to act. While admitting that the demand for labor and supplies was too heavy for the local population, Festing requested reinforcements to be marched north from Kumasi in order to effect the occupation of the Tong Hills.[142] Fifteen years after British forces had conquered the mighty Asante kingdom by marching unopposed into Kumasi, they prepared to reduce the last stubborn outpost of resistance to colonial rule in the Gold Coast.

Kpalbil Mebogire, a man in his mid-sixties with a detailed knowledge of local history, gave us an account of the gradual progress of the colonial advance as seen from Wakii, the community lying between Tongo and the northern flank of the hills:

> When we heard the British were coming they were at Nalerigu. The Nalerigu chief sent a message to Kurugunaab that the British were coming and that they were friendly, but had certain principals. Receive them well and let them enjoy their stay. They then intended to continue to the Tongo area, so the *kurugunaab* sent a message to Tongrana telling him that the British came in good faith. Tongrana then sent messages to the Wakii people and the Gbeog people, telling them that the British would soon be coming round to them. Receive them well—they are good visitors. Messages were also sent to the Tengzug people, but they said *no*, they would not receive the British. "We will fight them," [they said]—"why should they come and destroy our gods?"[143]

Kpalbil's narrative is interesting on two levels. First, it is a graphic description of the finely wrought chains of linkages that enabled people, commodities, information, and ideas to circulate through the fragmented and fiercely localized precolonial landscape. Second, it explains the resistance of the Tong Hills to British overtures in a way that is strikingly similar to how British themselves explained it. For colonial officers, the underlying reason for the particular hostility of the hill people was the existence of a powerful and malevolent "fetish." Despite the difference in tone, Kpalbil, too, points to the role of Tengzug as the sacral epicenter of the Talensi world: "why should they come and destroy our gods?" Now, the subsequent British obsession with destroying Tongnaab may well have colored historical memory on this point. Other informants stressed that it was forced labor on the road rather than defense of the great hilltop shrines that was the main reason for resistance.[144] Nevertheless, Kpalbil's thoughtful interpretation of events accords with that given by Yiran Boare of Tengzug. Indeed, Yiran brings the two factors together in a highly suggestive way: "The British wanted to build a road through here. Our people were afraid that this would destroy our *ba'ar* and *tongban*, so we did not agree. This caused the problem."[145]

On 2 March 1911, a 260–strong force comprising Northern Territories Constabulary and two companies of the Gold Coast Regiment under the military command of Captain Furnell (18th Royal Irish) and the political direction of Acting Chief Commissioner Festing moved into camp at Tongo.[146] The following morning, the force—equipped with two Maxim guns and two seven-pound field guns—divided into two, one column proceeding along the western slope and the other the eastern slope of the hills. At 7:15 am, the western column reached Gorogo, where it was met with a hail of poisoned arrows from the caves and boulders of the hillside that killed one soldier and wounded two. The eastern column met with similar determined resistance from the inhabitants of Santeng. It managed to withdraw without casualties only thanks to the timely arrival of twenty mounted constabulary from Tamale under Sergeant-Major Egala Grunshi, a veteran of Stewart's march through the hills in 1899. The next day, 4 March, the two columns again moved out from Tongo, "visiting and punishing" all the "unruly villages in the plains and outer slopes of the hills": Gorogo, Sipaat, Shia, Yinduri, and Santeng.[147] A number of our elderly informants recalled details of the fighting on the western flank of the hills, laying particular stress on the privation suffered in the caves due to the severe lack of water at what was the very end of the dry season. According to Ba'an, as the warriors held off colonial troops ("some of the soldiers were even Africans!") with bow and arrow, "the women had to creep down to collect water for the people to drink."[148]

On 5 March, Furnell and Festing rested their infantry while Sergeant-Major Egala Grunshi and thirty-four cavalrymen circuited the hills. Egala returned to camp with two prisoners, who after questioning were released with instructions to deliver an ultimatum to Talensi leaders: surrender within twenty-four hours or operations would continue. Festing's bare report of this attempt at dialogue is echoed in rather more interesting detail in the oral accounts of Ba'an and Pahinooni. Both name the key interlocutors as one Dengoo of Sipaat and his brother-in-law Yigare, a Gurunsi and one of the colonial soldiers, who did succeed in negotiating the end of fighting at Sipaat.[149] When by the following afternoon the British had received no response from Tengzug, Furnell ordered the artillery pieces to be hauled to the rim of the hills in preparation for the final assault. That assault began at dawn the next day, 7 March, with troops advancing up the rocky pass under cover of an artillery barrage. A total of thirty-two shells rained down into the central valley, with considerable loss of life. "As the natives expressed it," reported Festing, "'we began setting fire to the hills themselves.'"[150] By the end of the day, the stronghold of Tengzug had

Figure 1.6. A Talensi hunter equipped with distinctive calabash helmet, bow, and arm-quiver, photographed by R. S. Rattray in Tongo in 1928. British records noted that arm-quivers allowed the defenders of the Tong Hills in 1911 to fire poisoned arrows with great rapidity. Pitt Rivers Museum, University of Oxford 1998.312.1048.1; published as figure 7 of *Tribes of the Ashanti Hinterland*, facing 224.

been occupied and its demoralized defenders were melting away into the surrounding heights. British casualties amounted to only two men killed and three wounded, against unknown numbers of Talensi. In stark military terms, the repeating rifle, machine gun, and high-explosive artillery shell had won out against the bow and poisoned arrow.

The late Yiran Boare was aged about six in 1911 and vividly remembered being carried away by his mother during the attack on Tengzug. While Yiran confirmed the destruction wreaked by the superior firepower of the colonial forces, he offered a quite different interpretation of the fall of the Tong Hills. The crucial factor in explaining the catastrophe, he stated emphatically in 1999, was that the British campaign coincided with *Gologo*, the great annual sowing festival staged just before the onset of the rains:

> It was around the *Gologo* festival time. At this time people never fight—even if someone wrongs you, you must exercise patience. You must not fight the person—it is forbidden by custom. Our elders were fully aware of this, but they still decided to fight the British. . . . Because our elders decided to fight, our *bo'a* and *tongbana* decided to favor the British. The ancestors were annoyed, and they turned away from us and towards the British. We were conquered and we ran away. . . . We caused the fight in the month we were forbidden to fight.[151]

Almost a century later, Yiran offers a fleeting glimpse of what was happening inside the Tong Hills in the first week of March 1911. The collective Talensi leadership, the *tengdaana*s and clan elders, faced an agonizing decision on whether or not to defy ritual sanctions and fight. The power of these sanctions cannot be overestimated. Fortes's analysis of *Gologo* as the single most important ritual mechanism binding together Talensi society and as a "powerful counterweight to war" underscores Yiran's account: "Bloodshed during *Gɔlib* is a dreadful sacrilege; bloodshed on Tɛnzugu on the day of the most important ceremonies and during the dancing is a religious enormity that cannot be compared to anything else in the Tale calendar of sins."[152] It should be noted that similar sanctions against conflict and bloodshed also governed *Bo'araam* at the opposite end of the ritual cycle. This fact may well explain O'Kinealy's success in arriving at Tengzug unmolested in late September 1907. Some indication of the intensity of the debate that must have been raging amongst Talensi elders—and of the recriminations following defeat—can be gleaned from Fortes's passing reference to the death of one Siiyelib in 1936. "When Siiyɛlib died, the diviner consulted to find out the cause of his death revealed an unexampled story of misfortune going back twenty-five years. One after another, Siiyɛlib's wives and children had died; rinderpest had wiped out his cattle; and at last

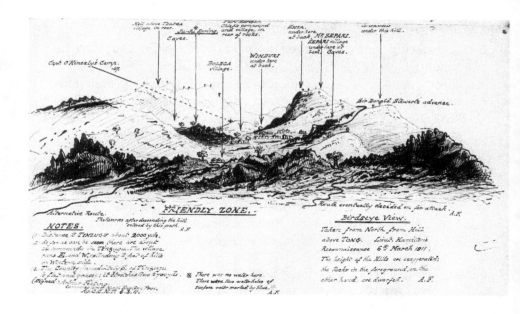

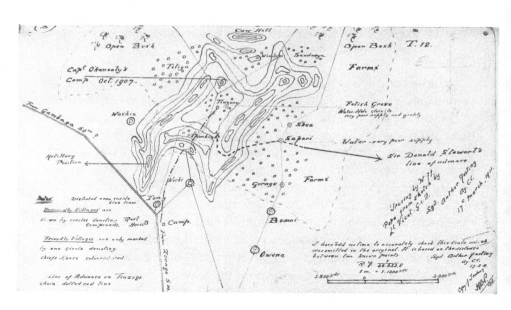

Figures 1.7a and 1.7b. Two sketch maps outlining the British advance into the Tong Hills in March 1911. Note the division of settlements into "Friendlies" and "Unfriendlies." From Public Record Office, London, CO 96/506.

Figure 1.8. Yiran Boare (c. 1905–2002), the representative of the Shia
bo'arana at Tengzug responsible for overseeing access to the Yanii site
of Tongnaab, photographed in 1999 wearing the red fez of office.

Figure 1.9. Gologo dancers at Tengzug, 2000.

he himself had died without a son to mourn him and in extreme poverty."[153] The reason for all this, Fortes was told, was that the unfortunate Siiyelib was one of the leading proponents of war with the British in 1911, and "the most heinous sin of all was to instigate (*sa*) a war."[154]

Once the fighting had ended and Talensi warriors began turning themselves in to the occupying forces, Festing turned his attention to eliminating what he regarded as the underlying cause of resistance: "As in the case of Benin, AroChuko and numerous other places, the fetish was worked for all it was worth to enable a community of scoundrels to carry on their raids and robberies with impunity."[155] An elderly *tengdaana*, Fuohibazaa, mistakenly identified as the "chief fetish priest," and four other elders were arrested and detained at the new Northern Territories headquarters at Tamale. The chief commissioner ordered that Tengzug be "completely demolished and obliterated and the Fetish grove destroyed," and those inhabitants who had not already fled were forcibly removed from their ancestral homes.[156] In the following months a stone boundary marker was constructed around the base of the hills, within which it was forbidden to rebuild. Pilgrimages to the hills were prohibited and no one was allowed even to approach the site of the destroyed sacred grove. Although the British did not yet know the name of the great ancestor-deity, it appeared that Tongnaab's ritual paramountcy had been abruptly terminated by colonial conquest.

Conclusions

Despite the settlements between rival colonial powers and the capitulation of the Mossi-Dagomba and Gonja kingdoms to European "protection," the military conquest of the non-centralized peoples on either side of the Anglo-French boundary dragged on into the second decade of the twentieth century. For the Talensi and their "Gurunsi" and "Frafra" neighbors on the frontiers of the Northern Territories Protectorate of the Gold Coast, the coming of colonial rule represented not so much a break with the past as a continuation of the heightened insecurity and violence of the late nineteenth century. Unfortunately for the historian, the lineaments of that past emerge only in hazy outline. Yet from the few sources that are available, it is possible to discern a cluster of peoples whose isolation was a result not of being left behind by the forces of history, but of active resistance to the predations of state-builders and slave raiders to the north and south. Also visible is the ritual power of Tongnaab, the Talensi ancestor-deity whose cult radiated out from the sacred center of the Tong Hills to encompass a broad swathe of the middle Volta savanna. The extent of Tongnaab's established network suggests that the lingering anthropological vision of the region as one characterized by self-contained, fiercely parochial "tribal" groups must finally be abandoned. At the same time, the perception held by the Asante and other Akan peoples to the south that the Talensi and their neighbors were primitive "pagan tribes" inhabiting a distant and mystically potent netherworld is crucial in understanding the spread of Tongnaab in the twentieth century. With the imposition of colonial order and the expansion of migration and mobility, knowledge of the great oracle began to filter across the savanna-forest frontier, drawing Akan pilgrims in search of new ritual solutions to the problems of the modern world to the shrines of the Tong Hills. It is to these processes that we now turn.

2

Gods and Guns,
Rituals and Rule, 1911–1928

When the Whiteman first came to your country you were
backward and primitive, a prey to slave raiders from the north
and south. You had no cohesion and in many cases no constitution
to speak of which was really the root of your troubles.[1]

We were once the owners of this land; since the scorpion Europeans came we have entered into holes. You have burned our bows
and arrows; we once were keepers of the moons.[2]

*F*or the British, the conquest of the Tong Hills in March 1911
represented the final act in the pacification of the warlike "pagan tribes"
on the frontiers of the Northern Territories. Official correspondence in the
aftermath of the military operation was filled with self-congratulations and
an unbridled optimism regarding the future stability of the colonial state
in the Protectorate. As Major Festing reported, "With little loss of life on
our side and I hope comparatively little on the side of an ignorant enemy
we have been able in one week to vindicate our rule. This rule has been
defied in this particular district ever since we proclaimed a Protectorate."[3]
He and others moved quickly to take advantage of the dramatic defeat of
the sacred stronghold in the hills and to end the truculence that its independence was believed to have inspired throughout the region. It was time
to make the people of the Tong Hills "come in."[4] In addition to ordering
the "obliteration" of Tengzug and the destruction of the "fetish grove," Festing instructed Lieutenant Elkan to have one road immediately cut through
the hills and another cut around its base. The latter was to serve as a clearly
marked boundary; no crops were to be cultivated between the road and the
hills. Meanwhile, the "unfriendly villages" encircling the base of the hills—

Gorogo, Sipaat, Yinduri, Tiliga, and Shia—were allowed to rebuild their compounds, but only on the far side of the road.[5] The inhabitants of Tengzug were ordered off and away from the hills; they were to "divide up among the other villages [and] to never come back."[6] In short, the former "stronghold of terror" was to be rendered a clearly demarcated no-man's-land in a now fully pacified Protectorate.

But the conclusiveness of the campaign, of which Festing was so certain, would soon prove illusory. Anyone who has plowed through the stacks of official documentation on the institution of colonial rule in this part of the Northern Territories cannot help but be struck by the degree of confusion, division, and ineffectiveness which characterized British rule in the area right into the 1930s. One could argue that the Talensi and their gods were not, in fact, "ruled" in any meaningful ways during this period. Rather, the crises they posed for the colonial state were at best ineffectually "managed." Granted, chiefs were made, unmade, and remade in what seemed a vain, never-ending attempt to invent a system of rule capable of drawing the Talensi into a reconstituted Mamprugu state. But most Talensi, especially those from the hills, still did not "come in" and continued to operate well outside the purview of the colonial state as it labored to impose order.

This chapter explores the early, faltering steps of British officials as they sought to make a colonial world in the Tong Hills and the ways in which the people of those hills, some with far greater success than others, negotiated the rough, uneven terrain of British colonialism. It begins with the defeat of the Talensi in 1911 and ends with the arrival of Government Anthropologist R. S. Rattray in 1928. Rattray was commissioned to study the customs of the "stateless" peoples of the Northern Territories in order to render them accessible to administrators still struggling to consolidate a system of rule on the northern frontier of the Protectorate. Yet by the time he got down to business, there had already been substantial shifts in local power in Taleland—ritual, generational, and economic—that would further frustrate efforts to impose colonial rule in the area. The extant colonial blueprints, with their static vision of a subordinate Taleland in a revested Mamprugu state, were incapable of factoring contemporary social change into their equations of rule. There was no place in the colonial script for reconfigurations of power and ritual within Tale society. Of these processes of change, administrators remained largely ignorant, as they did of the ongoing, dynamic, and central role of Tongnaab. Indeed, by the close of the First World War, some Talensi were in positions to broker political relationships with the colonial order largely on their own terms, to author, in other words, their own scripts for colonial rule in Taleland. And they could accomplish this with the powerful and decisive assistance of Tongnaab.

"The Most Tractable and Amiable People Imaginable"?

Even before the last Tengzug resident was forced down from the Tong Hills in 1911, the attitude of local administrators toward the people of the area had softened dramatically. No longer were hill folk depicted as a ferocious "community of scoundrels." In his initial field report on the military operations, Festing emphasized "the wisdom of dealing leniently with these primitive people in the way of collective labour or labour outside their own district. They are a conservative agricultural race and industrious so long as they are left in their own districts and only called upon to do labour for which they are fitted viz. road making, building etc."[7]

From the official perspective, any threat the Talensi might have posed to British authority seemed to have dissipated entirely in less than a year. District Commissioner Nash reported at the end of the year that local trade showed signs of expansion and that some "Frafra" had even begun to drive cattle down to Asante—long associated with predation and slavery—rather than sell to passing Mossi and Hausa merchants.[8] In reward for their good behavior, Nash permitted the Talensi once again to plant crops and graze cattle in the Tong Hills, although permanent settlement remained restricted to the surrounding plains.[9]

By July 1912, Chief Commissioner Armitage had agreed to allow the three surviving men who had been exiled to Tamale after the 1911 operations to return to the area, as long as they resided off the hills in Tiliga and reported periodically to local officials.[10] At the close of 1912, Armitage began a two-month tour of inspection of the Northern Territories. One of the highlights of his trip was a visit to the Tong Hills,

> where I held a palaver with the local chiefs and people, with whom the local administration is now on the best terms. The Fra-Fras have proved to be the most tractable and amiable people imaginable and I have more than a suspicion that it was simply due to an overwhelming fear of the whiteman and his methods that made them in the past resist every expedition . . . and gained them their reputation—to me unjustified—of being truculent and warlike. . . . the Tong Hills people exhibited a simple gratitude and affection toward me that was quite touching, if somewhat embarrassing.[11]

Even the "great fetish place," which, according to Festing in 1911, had been "worked for all it was worth" by that "community of scoundrels," was treated with some respect in the reports of District Commissioner Nash. Admittedly, Nash was not the most typical of British officers in the area at the time—his accounts often being rich in detail and insight and not consistently scarred by racist condescension. Still, his 1913 description of a Tongnaab *bo'ar*, quoted at length in chapter 1, is notable not simply because it is an empathetic portrayal, but because an empathetic portrayal was now possible in the climate of calm immediately following the Tong Hills operations. Nash even went on to commend the tolerance and inclusiveness of local belief systems in comparison with Christianity:

> The only difference appears to be that we gnash our teeth at anyone who does not respect our Tapu, whereas the native is more liberal in these matters. He would certainly never try and force a man to agree with his beliefs. Different people have different gods, is what he says, and let each believe in his own fetish.[12]

Nash's account would have been unthinkable three years before, but by 1913 seemed perfectly in tune with official reports that extolled the "remarkable advance in every direction" taking place throughout the district.[13] Only brief reports of the odd highway robbery—"the victims said the robbers were naked, that is to say either disguised as or actually Frafras"—or of (predictable) cattle theft by disgruntled in-laws belied the calm on the northeastern frontier.[14] But British officials were soon to learn, for the first of many times, that nothing in the Tong Hills was as it seemed to be.

A Tenacious "Fetish"

On the morning of 2 January 1915, the chief commissioner walked through the ruins of Tengzug on his way from Yinduri to Tongo. Noticing that "the household 'Fetishes', which are to be found outside every compound, had been replaced and were being tended," he decided to return to the area on horseback that afternoon in order to investigate "the old Fetish Grove" he had last seen three years before. "I found that the whole thing had been restarted," he wrote, "apparently for some time—as there were signs of long continued careful attention."[15] Armitage was not pleased with his discovery and ordered District Commissioner Ievers to launch an immediate investigation. Ievers forwarded his report to Navrongo on January 28.[16] In it, he noted that the shrine had been in existence "from time immemorial" and was important not only to the "Frafra Natives," but also to the "Dagomba, Kanjarga, Manprussi [*sic*] and even the Moshi Tribes." Its powers included "conferring Fecundity on barren women . . . granting a good Rainfall . . . determining whether an individual accused of Magic is guilty or whether a man has sworn falsely." Ievers insisted, however, that the fetish had been in progressive decline since 1911 and that it was of little "political significance." Still, "it must be noted that the local inhabitants have never ceased to frequent the Shrine either openly or secretly. This is the more remarkable as they have so often been ordered not to do so by the responsible Commissioners." In Ievers's view, the only way to prevent people from visiting the shrine was to destroy it, as people's "Natural inclinations are being repeatedly aroused by the visits of Dagomba and other Pilgrims."

Based on Ievers's findings, Armitage returned to Zuarungu in early February and launched a full inquiry into the "renewal of the Fetish." The "chiefs" of Yinduri, Shia, and Tengzug, the son of the aging *tongrana*, and the Mamprusi chief of Kurugu (the *kunaaba*) were ordered to give testimony. So too was the *kpatarnaaba*, the head of the Kpatar section of Tengzug and one of those arrested and exiled in 1911. The Yinduri chief testified that the shrine had been reopened by Kpatarnaaba Wonsaba, who had served as "Chief in Tingzugu before the Hills were taken." He was assisted by his *tengdaana* ("Chief of the Fetish"), a man called Nawa, also arrested in 1911. For his part, Wonsaba admitted that he had reopened the shrine with the help of Nawa, but sought to defend his decision by arguing that when he returned from Tamale and "saw people farming in the Hills . . . [I] thought I could reopen the Fetish." Although there is no record in the notes of evidence, Nawa was also brought forward to testify. Armitage noted in his diary that the priest denied having had anything to do with the fetish since he returned from Tamale. "He is a short wiry man of middle age," the chief commissioner wrote,

> and is dressed in nothing beyond a kilt of skin with another skin slung over his shoulders. He has given out that he cannot wear any other costume and that he would die if he donned a cover-cloth or robe of any kind. I learnt that the natives have implicit belief in this absurd assertion.[17]

After Nawa's statement, a man referred to in the notes as "Tingwa," who identified himself as "Chief of Tinzugu," claimed that his people were now off of the hills and down on the plains. He had heard that the shrine was reactivated but never went to it and did not know when the reopening had occurred. Finally, the chiefs of Shia and Yinduri "admitted that the Fetish was bad and said that they and their people would like to see it done away with, and would assist in its destruction." At the end of the inquiry, Armitage reached his decision: "Fetish to be destroyed."[18]

In the absence of military resistance, the second assault on Talensi sacred space, in February 1915, was less violent but in many ways more psychologically aggressive than that of four years earlier. Once again, the cultural meanings of cloth and clothing were central to the Talensi encounter with British rule. On the morning following the inquiry, all of the chiefs and *tengdaana*s, together with their followers, gathered at Zuarungu, from where they were to march into the hills and destroy the "fetish." But before departing, the chief commissioner spotted Nawa in the crowd. Knowing that it was believed "he would die if he donned a cover-cloth or robe of any kind," Armitage forced the elderly *tengdaana* to take off his skins and put on a woven smock. Nawa tried to explain "that he wore the skins because they belonged to his ancestors," but eventually acquiesced, "though he was badly frightened." When he reappeared, wearing a smock and cover cloth supplied by the *kunaaba*, "his appearance so clad caused a sensation among the natives present," as it did when the group reached Tongo. There, Armitage wrote, "the arrival of the Fetish Priest robed in cloth . . . was succeeded by shrieks of laughter from the natives who flocked from their compounds to see the discomfited Priest, who, however, showed no signs of dying."[19] Nawa was not made to accompany the party up to Tengzug, but was left under guard at Tongo on the grounds that he "might feign one of those seizures, simulated by Fetish-men to overawe the laity." The rest of the party continued to Tengzug, where they were joined by some three hundred men who began their work by destroying the grove of trees surrounding the shrine. The headmen of Yinduri and Shia were given machetes to assist with the work and set an example.

The following morning, the chief commissioner returned to the hills and was joined again by "bands of natives armed with matchets and axes." They gathered underbrush and branches to construct a great pile on top of the shrine, which was then set on fire. "Soon the flames fanned by a strong wind," Armitage wrote, "were shooting up round the home of the 'Fetish', reminding one of the circle of magic flame placed by Wotan, for her protection, round the sleeping Brunhild." As the fire burned, many were set the task of destroying one large, stubborn tree whose trunk withstood the assault of local axes. Finally, by early afternoon, the tree had fallen and the chiefs were led back to Tongo, where they were each given £3 to be distributed to the drummers who had played during the exercise. Armitage concluded his diary entry by contemplating the significance of what he had witnessed over the previous two days:

> I cannot recollect a previous instance of the natives of a number of villages in the Colony or its Dependencies combining, without compulsion of any kind, to destroy a "Fetish," so powerful, well-known and with such a sinister reputation, as was that of the Tong Hills. It was consulted by natives who came from all parts of

the Northern Territories, and from French and German Territory, and the news of it's [*sic*] end will, I think, spread like wild-fire throughout the country and will have a most beneficial effect. I am endeavouring to ascertain how it was that the "Fetish" was allowed to be revived and will report officially when I have gained this information.[20]

It would be a further decade before the British began to gain some appreciation of the complexity of forces at work in the Tong Hills in February 1915.

But for the time being, officials contented themselves with the belief that they had finally defeated the fetish in the hills. Armitage issued another set of orders forbidding ritual activity of any kind in the hills and the erection of any structures. Farming and the grazing of cattle were permitted, but the district commissioner was ordered to tour the area at least once per quarter to be sure that these remained the only activities. Meanwhile, Kpatarnaaba Wonsaba and his *tengdaana*, Nawa, were detained in Navrongo.[21] From the British perspective, then, the "Tong Hill Fetish" had been relegated to the dustbin of history, one official at the Colonial Office in London even lamenting that "the ancient fetish is in ashes instead of the British Museum."[22] Still, the chief commissioner was not entirely complacent. In order to be absolutely sure that activities at the former shrine could never be renewed, he sent two explosives experts to the hills at the end of May with orders to blow up the remaining "Fetish Rocks." Not without poetic justice, their efforts came to nought. The drills were too soft to make any impression on the granite boulders, and when the workers attempted to set the dynamite in the cracks between the rocks they only blew dust from the cracks. The provincial commissioner tried to reassure Armitage that it really made no difference that the rocks were not physically destroyed, as the Fetish was "thoroughly 'dead'." "The first bad knock out to the fetish was when the Tindana wore cloth with no harm coming to him. Its death blow came . . . when the very worshippers of the Fetish themselves in clothes, walked backwards and forwards over the rocks without harm."[23]

Defeat or Delusion?

Colonial officials may have considered Tongnaab destroyed in 1915, but what did the Talensi make of these extraordinary public spectacles? As we shall see, local people exiled to the plains as well as pilgrims from Tongnaab's ritual network continued to visit the sacred sites throughout the period when the Tong Hills were off-limits. As Tengzug resident Naoh recently remembered, "We could not leave our ancestors, so we would come secretly in the night to do our sacrifices."[24] But how then do we explain the official accounts of 1915—of people continually defying British orders not to visit the shrine, but then agreeing to destroy, as the chief commissioner phrased it with great puzzlement, their own "fetish"? Testimony collected by officials in the 1920s, by Fortes in the 1930s, and by us in recent interviews sheds some light on this question. It is a question whose answer is essential for understanding not only the historicity and tenacity of Tongnaab, but the shifting configurations of power and authority among the Talensi over the course of the twentieth century.

The British misunderstood much of what they saw in the Tong Hills, but there were two fundamental misapprehensions that rendered it difficult for them to implement even a rudimentary system of colonial rule in the area. First, officials continued to operate with a very simple binary view of savanna societies inherited from the era of colonial conquest. Either people lived under "organized governments" or they constituted "primitive tribes." The Talensi were considered to be the latter—one "tribe" of the "Frafra" peoples who at some point in the distant past paid allegiance to the king of Mamprugu, the *nayiri*. In the next section, we will explore the political implications of that binary vision. Here we need to consider its ritual implications, especially as we deconstruct these spectacles of colonial subjugation. By and large, those in and around the hills constituted for the British an undifferentiated mass of "Frafras" who, in the period of colonial pacification, could meaningfully be distinguished only as "friendlies" or "unfriendlies." Officials had very little idea of the diverse migration histories of people in the area, much less of the fact that only some Talensi clans— the Namoo—traced their ancestry back to Mamprugu. Yet that division was and is of profound ritual significance. Namoo do not share *bo'a* or *tongbana* with the hill Tales and have never been a part of Tongnaab's ritual network. Thus, when the Tongo chief repeatedly spoke out against the "great fetish in the hills," advocated its destruction in 1915, and sent workers to assist in that task, he was not participating in the destruction of his "own fetish" at all. Indeed, he might even be seen as advocating the demolition of a competing ritual power and thereby enhancing his own political authority as a Namoo chief, vis-à-vis the clans of the hills. And when the predominantly Namoo residents of Tongo reportedly laughed at the old Kpatar *tengdaana* Nawa as he was paraded through the countryside in cloth, they were not mocking one of their own. From their perspective, we suspect, they were witnessing the shattering of jealously guarded ritual sanctions and esoteric knowledge associated with a cult from which they themselves were explicitly barred.

Second, the British had no idea in 1911 or in 1915 that the Tong Hills contained not one "fetish place" but a number of powerful shrines that served as the foci of the dual earth and ancestor (*teng* and *bo'ar*) cults. The most important earth shrine (*tongban*) was Ngoo, described by Fortes as "the palladium of all the Talis, the centre about which the equilibrium of all their corporate relations with one another swings."[25] But the shrines that attracted outside pilgrims and therefore the suspicion of the British were the great ancestor shrines devoted to Tongnaab. "To the Hill Talis," Fortes stressed, "their [*bo'ar*] cult is the most important religious phenomenon in the world."[26] Numerous *bo'a* congregations in the hills—perhaps as many as a dozen when Fortes was there in the 1930s—were operating in a complex network of overlapping rights, responsibilities, and collaboration. Each of these congregations, comprising several distinct clans, referred to the great *bo'a* Tongnaab by a different name—for example, Bonaab, Yanii, or Samoo. "Tongnaab," however, was the generic name for the *bo'a*, or as Fortes referred to it, the "External *Bɔɣar*." What British officials never fully understood about this web of ritual collaboration was that in 1911 and, again, in 1915 they had attacked only one of the many sacred sites in the hills. From archival descriptions of the site, as well as the accounts of present-day informants, it is clear that the shrine desecrated in 1911 and then deforested, burnt, and unsuccessfully dynamited in 1915 was Bonaab—the *bo'a* tended by the Kpatar, Gundaat, Samiit, and Sakpee clans of Tengzug and overseen by the *kpatarnaaba* as senior custodian.[27] It was thus no coincidence, given the number of *tengdaana*s in the hills, that it was Kpatarnaaba Wonsaba and his *tengdaana*, Nawa, who were exiled to Tamale in 1911 and then to Navrongo in 1915.[28] It was their specific shrine to Tongnaab that had been mistakenly identified by the British as the one "great fetish."

That Tongnaab had multiple sites and was tended by distinct congregations goes some way toward explaining the complex reality behind Armitage's superficial perception of local "natives . . . without compulsion" participating in the destruction of their own shrine. Clearly, many of those who took part in the 1915 attack were not, in fact, subject to any of the *bo'a* in the hills—they were Namoo from Tongo or Nankani from the Zuarungu area who had no direct ritual connection to Tongnaab. As far as we can ascertain, those hill folk who did participate in the spectacle of destruction, though members of the *bo'ar* cult, were not members of the specific congregation that tended Bonaab. But is that the decisive factor explaining their complicity in the destruction of a shrine whose power they knew and respected? Although it is impossible to know what went through the minds of the Talensi men present on that critical day, the extent of British military coercion may well have left them with no other choice. Perhaps those who wielded their machetes were resigned in their belief that Bonaab had been defiled and defeated by the British and they were simply finishing off a site of sacred power that had failed to serve them well. It is also likely that the destruction of the rocks and trees surrounding the shrine had little if any ritual significance for those involved. Omnipresent and without physical manifestation, Tongnaab defied early colonial notions of a primitive "fetish" that could be eliminated by machetes and dynamite. Unfortunately, we have no evidence with regard to motivation which can point us in one direction or the other. We are simply left with the incontrovertible fact that some from among those who participated in the destruction of Bonaab were Hill Tales of a different *bo'ar* congregation—a congregation that called Tongnaab "Yanni" and whose site of devotion, a half mile away near the very summit of the Tong Hills, would not be discovered by the British for another decade.

What was understood by the British, then, as a powerful colonizing moment in which the Talensi were made to acknowledge their subjugation by participating in a public spectacle that entailed destroying their own gods was nothing of the sort. Admittedly, those devoted to Bonaab were dealt a heavy blow. Yet Tongnaab, as "chief of the earth," was virtually unscathed. Even Kpatar *tengdaana* Nawa, who had been ritually disarmed by being forced into cloth, probably did not suffer serious ritual consequences. It is certainly of some significance that, once clothed, he was not allowed back in the hills or anywhere near Bonaab, thanks to the chief commissioner's orders, and therefore was never made to violate that most strict of prohibitions (which continues to this day)—approaching a *bo'ar* in cloth. Of course, we can only speculate as to how various Talensi viewed these strange spectacles, but we suspect that none among those who jeered at Nawa in Tongo were from up in the hills. And we can only guess what went through the minds of local bystanders as they witnessed the stubborn granite boulders surrounding Bonaab's abode defy the mechanical drills of the dynamiters.

Inventing Chiefs

British officials could believe they had effected the resounding defeat of the Talensi only because they so misapprehended the political and ritual landscape of the Tong Hills. From very early on they decided, with few dissenting voices, that the most effective way to rule the Frafra and Gurunsi "tribes" of the northern frontier was to ignore the ritual power of local *tengdaana*s, bolster the waning authority of the paramount chief of Mamprugu, the *nayiri*, and extend that authority through local hierarchies of chiefs. In what Jack Goody has described as a "Law of Colonial Reversal," British policy was aimed at "centralizing acephalous societies and decapitating strongly centralized ones."[29] Following a tour of the North-Eastern Province in the aftermath of the 1911 operations, Chief Commissioner Armitage wrote that "the breaking of the Tong Hills 'Fetish' power . . . gives us an excellent opportunity to revive the authority of the Chiefs . . . and this should be seized at once."[30] The problem remained that most communities had no chiefs, and those that did considered them of little consequence. This reality, however, had little impact on official policy, despite the fact that several key individuals argued against "reviving" the chiefs. One such dissenting voice was the conqueror of the Tong Hills, Major Festing, who argued that he "could see no benefit to be derived from electing paramount chiefs. . . . To expect these independent warlike people to obey so called paramount chiefs holding the ludicrous positions of say Mamprussi or Dagomba is I submit with the greatest respect, too much."[31] But such dissent rapidly dissipated and Armitage's vision of "bolstering Mamprugu" became the order of the day. When the commissioner for the North-Eastern Province toured his newly pacified domain in June 1911, he found it "regrettable that the authority of the King [i.e., the *nayiri*] has not been upheld . . . with the result that a state of anarchy has existed in the Province until quite recently. . . . every effort must be made to rehabilitate the lost prestige of the King and his Chiefs."[32] As Armitage would later put it, the chiefs, under the British colonial government, must become "rulers of their people in fact, and not in name."[33]

The immediate problem was to establish a viable connection between the Tong Hills and the Mamprugu kingdom. In 1910, a solution seemed imminent when the newly installed Mamprusi chief of Kurugu, Kunaab Sulsiba, appeared in Zuarungu, claiming suzerainty over the Talensi. Some officials believed that the *kunaab* "might be of some assistance in getting in touch with the people."[34] Nash, however, was dubious when he learned that Sulsiba had never before ventured across the White Volta and that in the past the hill folk had "disclaimed his [predecessor's] suzerainty—in fact [had] crossed the river, destroyed [the] greater part of the Town, besides killing a good many people."[35] After the 1911 conquest, however, the *kunaab* would play a central role in colonial visions of the incorporation of the Talensi into a reconstituted Mamprugu. Although Nash remained pessimistic—"it is impossible to introduce the 'Pax Britannica' into a comparatively thickly-populated country when each little village Headman remains a law unto himself"[36]—he reported that during a visit to the hills

Figure 2.1. Nangodinaaba Azure, the officially sanctioned "head chief" of the Nabdam, photographed by R. S. Rattray in 1928 sporting the key accoutrements of a Mamprusi-style ruler: horse, woven smock, red fez, and the "four inch" chief's medal. Azure was elected in 1910 following the murder of his brother Tii, the event that triggered the British assault on the nearby Tong Hills. Pitt Rivers Museum, University of Oxford 1998.312.1174.1; published as figure 79 of *Tribes of the Ashanti Hinterland*, facing 368.

later in 1911 accompanied by Sulsiba, the people "expressed their willingness to follow him [the *kunaab*] in the future." Nash began to urge the chief to "come out here and live among the Talansi."[37] This he eventually agreed to do, although he located his house nearer to the British headquarters at Zuarungu than to the Tong Hills.[38] A month later, in April 1912, a structure for colonial rule was roughly framed when the colonial government officially declared Nayiri Mahama to be "Paramount Chief of all lands situated within the North Eastern Province."[39] In 1913, the *kunaab*—on the strength that he served as the elector of the leading Namoo chief, the *tongrana*—was appointed "chief in general charge of the Tong Hill People."[40]

And so it was—via the Namoo *tongrana*, who was elected by the Mamprusi *kunaab*, who in turn was appointed by the *nayiri* in distant Nalerigu—that the people of the hills were brought into a colonial hierarchy. The connections were ephemeral at best. As Moses Anafu explained in an important article thirty years ago,

> the Kunab, as an executive authority, had no *locus standi* in Tale social and political life. True, he was an elector to the Tongo and most other chiefships. But . . . he was not an overlord and the position gave him no right to levy tribute on these settlements. . . . If the Kunab's ties with the Namoos via the office of chiefship were tenuous, they were practically non-existent . . . with the "real" Talis.[41]

Nonetheless, British officials saw few alternatives to Armitage's vision of centralization and the bolstering of chiefs' authority in the Northern Territories.[42] They remained wedded to his overall course of action, despite almost immediate evidence that in Taleland the arrangement was far from satisfactory. Less than a year after extending the *kunaab*'s authority, the provincial commissioner admitted that "bringing Kurugu out has not been altogether a success, as he is not popular in the District, and I am not sure that eventually it will be found expedient to get him to retire once more to the seclusion of his own village on the South side of the Volta and there resume his shadowy claims to paramountcy over the people on the other side."[43] Nash's entry in the district diary for 15 October 1913 bluntly described the experiment of using the *kunaab* as head chief as "the reverse to success": "For any practical ends of chieftancy, a ragdoll . . . [would be] equally as efficient as Kurugu at the present moment."[44]

Yet the *kunaab* remained a key figurehead in the British system of rule in Taleland from 1912 until 1937. Under him sat the *tongrana* and beneath him was arrayed a set of chiefs and headmen more or less created by the British. Called by the Talensi and others "*kambonaaba*s," after the Asante-style offices in Mamprugu and Dagbon, many of these men had no claims to local legitimacy whatsoever—"their authority [resting] solely on the threats of retaliation by the administration if their peoples showed any disinclination to obey them."[45] Some of these men had simply put themselves forward or were put forward because of their age, their status, or their willingness to collaborate.[46] In other cases, indigenous positions were subsumed by the category "*kambonaaba*." As Anafu points out, the Shia *bo'arana* was named a *kambonaaba* in 1916, but was "one of the most important and senior ritual dignitaries in Taleland," his office long preceding colonial rule. In other instances, *tengdaana*s were made into chiefs, as was the case with Abinbini of Yinduri, who was recognized as a chief after he had gotten "people to make the road, build the Rest House etc."[47] But no matter what their origins, all Talensi *kambonaaba*s served Nalerigu and the British colonial administration through the chief of Kurugu.

Complaints against the *kunaab* were constant, but the problem was not simply personal incapacity, despite ongoing British complaints that he was inept, a "fool," a "ragdoll," or a "'thorn-in-the-side'" of the administration.[48] The fundamental problem was systemic. *Kambonaaba* chiefships were bought and sold, bolstered and undermined as the central dynamic of rule in the North-Eastern Province.[49] The administration's bankruptcy is well captured in one of Nash's 1913 diary entries:

> Chiefs have never wielded any power except during a temporary clash of arms or an obscure raid. The people therefore, far from having any deification of rulers, are most individualistic in their ideas, and for a very good reason too. As far as I can make out no dominating intellect has ever risen amongst them. An obscure raider or a pro-tem conqueror certainly has occasionally appeared on the horizon. But what did he almost always do? He certainly did not make any attempts to form even the crudest foundation of settled government. No it was always easier for him to live by slave raiding than to foster trade and industries and promote agriculture. The people have not forgotten this and they now look with suspicion on anyone who prospers and becomes the owner of property, or any of their so called "chiefs," who backed up by us "put on airs" and try to assume control over their people. The Chiefs have no prestige, no historical names to quote as their predecessors, and these considerations count far more amongst an uncivilised than a civilised people.[50]

Armitage considered Nash to be "unduly pessimistic" but, like him, approved of the *kunaab*'s continuing in his capacity with the hope that "he may be brought eventually to realize his responsibilities."[51] In so doing, he endorsed a system of colonial rule which had as its core components 1) bestowing unprecedented powers on Mamprusi chiefs like the *kunaab*; 2) transforming elders, former slaves, or even outcasts into headmen and chiefs (who often then had to pay dearly for that recognition); 3) privileging Namoo (originally Mamprusi migrants to Taleland) over the original inhabitants; and 4) severely undermining the authority of the *tengdaana*s, whose ritual work was woven throughout the social fabric of the hills. All of this was done in the name of reinforcing what the British imagined to be the fragmented hegemony of Mamprugu. It does not take a vivid imagination to envision how this system of rule looked to the exiled inhabitants of the Tong Hills or why those inhabitants would continue to refuse to "come in." It is also not difficult to see that it was a system that had to ultimately rely, as many have written, on coercion and compulsion.[52]

"Leaders of Gang Labourers"?

The fortunes of chiefs within the new colonial dispensation depended primarily on their ability to mobilize compulsory labor, or what the British referred to—with no apparent sense of irony—as "free labor." Indeed, as was the case with Abinbini of Yinduri, some men were recognized as chiefs precisely because of their ability to mobilize labor. These "new men of Tallensi politics," as Anafu calls them, "were, strictly speaking, leaders of gang labourers."[53] For the people of the hills, the association was eminently clear: the British recruited chiefs and the chiefs recruited labor. Some Talensi today explain the original call to arms in 1911 precisely in terms of a widespread fear that they were going to be forced to work for the British: "They were afraid because, as they [the British] have come, they would be working the way the British wanted them to be working. That's why they didn't want to accept their rule."[54] Because many from in and around the hills had witnessed the use of "free labor" in the building of a rest-house at Tongo in 1909 and some, especially from Shia, had even been ordered to participate by bringing grass and sticks (they refused), it is clear that such fears were not without justification.[55]

It was "as an administrative convenience," Thomas explains in his article on forced labor in the Northern Territories, "and in line with the policy of supporting chiefly power, [that] labour for government work was usually recruited through the chiefs by political officers."[56] Such labor was mobilized to construct and maintain the roads both through and around the Tong Hills after 1911, an onerous task that is well preserved in local memories of colonial rule:

> The British forced the people to work, using the chiefs to organize the labor. They made the chiefs very powerful, and the chiefs instructed their sons to go around the houses to get workers. If you refused, you would be punished. We had to build bridges, culverts, and roads for the British to run their cars on. We had to beat down the roads with wood to make them compact. Certain stretches of road were allocated and, if you didn't complete the work, you could be punished.[57]

While some British officials cautioned that it was important to keep free labor to a minimum during the two most labor-intensive months of farming, such concern did not always shape policy.[58] For the family of Lambazaa Naoh, the burden of free labor was so heavy they fled their home and farm and traveled south. Lambazaa's father was the senior man in the household and, with the exception of the young Lambazaa, his children were all girls. He was forced to go to Pwalugu to build the bridge and, at the same time, there was other work at Kurugu where we were forced to work. My father was forced to work at Kurugu and the next day would be forced to the Pwalugu bridge. What time would he get to farm in order to feed his family? He decided to run far away to escape the British demands, so he could farm. That was the main reason why he took us to Dagbon.[59]

As Pahinooni recalls, the burdens of free labor did not fall just on men. "They would demarcate this area," she recalled.

> Up to this end belongs to this particular clan. And they were not only men who were doing the work. Women were also doing it because the women were using that wood [for compacting the road], fetching gravel and then using the wood to press it. And children were also working. Everybody was doing the work—not only the men at that time. . . . They would say, "Yinduri people should take from this area up to this; Shia will continue theirs to this; Balungu people up to this; Separ, Gorogo . . . going to Winkogo."[60]

British officials argued that free labor was justified because it was a way for residents to pay for their area's upkeep, especially after the abolition of the caravan tax in 1908.[61] But those who actually did the work did so reluctantly. In 1914, the district commissioner at Gambaga admitted that the demand for labor is "met by a more or less forced exaction of a supply from the chiefs." His point is an important one, for it underscores both the central role of chiefs as "leaders of gang labourers" and the essential, ever-present role of coercion in the day to day functioning of chiefs within the colonial state. As Iliasu so succinctly put it, the British presence in Taleland "depended, in the final analysis, upon force or the threat of its use." The creation of chiefs and the use of chiefs as labor recruiters imparted little legitimacy to the colonial state on the northern frontier. In the final analysis, "the fabric on which the chiefs' power rests," Nash admitted in 1913, "is the whiteman."[62]

"The White Man Has Gone"?

That British colonial rule on the newly conquered frontiers of the Northern Territories was extremely fragile, lacked any degree of legitimacy, and rested ultimately on the continued threat of force was made abundantly clear with the onset of the First World War in August 1914. Less than a week after the declaration of war, the Gold Coast Regiment was decamped from Zuarungu and Navrongo for the campaign against German forces in neighboring Togo. At first, official reports downplayed the impact of the troops' departure.[63] Yet as district diaries for the first weeks of the war reveal, and as Thomas describes, the local response was "virtually immediate," and it was aimed directly at British-installed chiefs.[64] The district commissioner at Zuarungu was faced with numerous complaints from chiefs who said "their people won't obey as everybody has gone away."[65] But the problem was not just that troops had decamped. The entire administrative apparatus was pared down to a minimum. The district commissioner was put in charge of both the Zuarungu and Navrongo stations, and the station at Bawku to the east was closed completely. It is clear that this vacuum in rule—the sudden disappearance of the coercive apparatus of the state—was not lost on the local residents. Even calls for contributions to the Imperial War Fund were interpreted by some as evidence that "the Germans had beaten 'the English' and they had no money to feed themselves and their people."[66]

Simmering tensions throughout the region escalated in 1916 into a full-scale and bloody uprising against colonial rule in Bongo, a densely populated Nankani region some ten miles to the north of the Tong Hills.[67] Although the violence remained confined to the neighborhood of Bongo, the events surrounding the revolt reveal much about the nature of British rule throughout the North-Eastern Province and local perceptions of that rule. As Thomas correctly argues, what happened in Bongo was neither an aberration nor a unique response to a unique circumstance—the departure of British troops. "Between 1897 and 1911 in eastern upper Ghana," he argues,

> There had been a virtually continuous armed resistance by one group of people or another to British demands—demands made more vexatious by the depredations of extortionate and largely puppet chiefs, constabulary, soldiers, petty officials, chiefs' sons and messengers and a variety of freebooters claiming the sanction of the British.[68]

The Tong Hills resistance, both in 1911 and in 1915, was very much a part of that opposition to British rule. Moreover, testimony given during the inquiry into the Bongo uprising provides insight into how residents of the district perceived the British presence and understood the connections between chiefs, coercion, and the colonial state. "Previous to the riot, people were always saying 'now the White man has gone,'" explained the chief of Nangodi.

> It was a common saying. It commenced shortly after the Company was withdrawn from Zouaragu. It became much more acute when Zouaragu was closed and the Commissioner went to Navarro. They used to say that the Commissioner was only a trader, walking about the Country. The meaning of that is, that there was no resident Commissioner but that the Commissioner from Navarro came over and saw them as a trader would coming occasionally to the Country.[69]

But perhaps the most telling testimony came from the *kunaab*, the "chief" of the Talensi. Like the many of the other chiefs who testified, he explained that everyone thought the British had left. But he also described his treatment by his "followers" long before the outbreak of hostilities at Bongo:

> Shortly after the Chief Commissioner Northern Territories had been here and the Tong Fetish was destroyed a threat was made by the people against my life. This was the Talansi people. They said that the White man made me a Chief, and that now the White man was gone they would kill me and have no Chief. Information on this subject used to filter to me through various sources. Small children and old people, but I was never actually threatened to my face. . . . When the Company Gold Coast Regiment was taken away from Zouaragu the people began to say "the White man has gone." When we—the chiefs—called upon them to work on roads etc. they refused to turn out. It always was the same reply—"the White man has gone."[70]

How did the British respond to this testimony? Despite all that was laid bare in the wake of the Bongo revolt, very little changed in their administrative policy. With the country at war, it was no time for reflection and reconsideration. The approach to rule on the northern frontier remained essentially intact: administrators would rule through chiefs and chiefs would provide labor. If any lesson was learned, it was that coercion was not an insignificant component in the equation of rule. For those who might have been lulled into a sense of security or complacency, believing that the pyramidical system of rule based on chiefly authority lent legitimacy and self-sustainability to the colonial presence, the events of 1916 were a dramatic reminder that "consent" and "free labor" only really came through the barrel of a gun.

Still, in May 1917 the government tried to launch a recruitment drive for soldiers in the Northern Territories. Elderly Talensi informants who recall this recruitment inevitably speak about the time during which young men were hunted down and captured by the colonial state. "When the British came and were forcing them to fight in the World War," recalled Tengdaana Pehibazaa of Tongo, "the young men ran away and hid. Others escaped. At that time they were forcing people to join and they didn't like it."[71] Government sources tell a very similar story. "Arrested some boys around Tong," wrote the district commissioner. "They threatened with arrows the Chief of Kurugu's messengers. It is becoming increasingly evident to me the difficulty the Zouaragu chiefs will have to collect the recruits. . . . The crops are now getting high and the boys just hide in the corn."[72] As soon as the recruiting drive began, young men began to flee the area. In Tongo, the district commissioner had to issue an order that "all stranger Talansi boys . . . be told to return to their houses," because so many had fled, some south of the Volta. "I can see by the chiefs' faces, that they think the task set them is impossible."[73] Indeed, by all accounts, the recruitment drive operated very much like a high-stakes game of hide-and-seek. "Chiefs tell me now," wrote the district commissioner in his diary,

> that if they don't surround compounds at dawn, the recruits have flown into the corn. Travelled around the place to see where the incidents occurred and made some arrests. The country is undulating round here and many boys are seen on the hills. On my approach they descended into the valleys and mounted the next hills. I sent them word that I was not going to catch them.[74]

In the event that young men were "captured," recruitment did not necessarily follow. When the chief commissioner arrived in Tongo on 5 August 1917, he met officers with 119 recruits. He spoke at length to the recruits "and they all assured me that desertion was the last act they contemplated. Shortly afterwards 25 of these boys ran away at Winduri."[75] So unsuccessful were these early efforts that the district commissioner recommended "the closing down of recruiting among the FraFra . . . for the present."[76] The situation seemed impossible. In September, Armitage tried to hold a meeting in Zanlerigu, a Nabdam area to the northeast of the Tong Hills also known for its truculent "hill people." Almost no one attended the meeting, and 240 compound owners were summarily fined. In nearby Nangodi, the situation was repeated, with another 300 compound owners fined. Shortly thereafter, recruiting in the area was terminated for several months.

The difficulty of military recruiting in the area was just one specific manifestation of the continued impossibility of ruling the "truculent" sections of the North-Eastern Province. If the years since British troops stormed into the hills in 1911 had demonstrated anything, it was that resistance was continuous, coercion indispensable, and "rule" easily evaded by all but the elderly and infirm. This is not to minimize or discount the devastation of military aggression and punitive expeditions, the brutality of "free labor," or the horror of being "captured" to fight a war. But it is to underscore how British attempts at rule were experienced by the ordinary farmers from in and around the hills up to the close of the First World War. British administration, as we have seen, was experienced as brutal, illegitimate, and unpredictable, but it was also encountered unevenly, episodically, and in ways that were often marginal to the rituals and work of daily life. For long stretches of time, it must have seemed to a good many people from the hills as if the whiteman really had gone, after only a brief sojourn in their midst.

Accidental Colonialism: Labor Migration, Travel, and Cash

But to contend that British colonialism was highly unsuccessful at imposing itself as a coherent system of rule in the years before and during the First World War is not to claim that the British presence had no impact on the people and the ritual landscape in and around the Tong Hills. Rather, it is to argue that the most profound effects of colonial rule were often unintended—what might best be described as "accidental colonialism." Outside of moments of direct coercion, the British presence only made a difference in people's daily lives when it was allotted a role in local narratives, that is, when it intersected with local configurations of power—be they ritual or political or gendered. We have seen how some men, aspiring to chiefly authority, used the British presence to bolster their positions locally by becoming *kambonaaba*s. But the colonial government was unwittingly implicated in other local narratives—particularly around travel, money, and migration—that would have profound repercussions for Tongnaab and its ritual field.

Thanks to Roger Thomas's work, we know much about the colonial state's involvement in the forced recruitment of labor in the Northern Territories for privately owned mines and for government projects in Asante and the Gold Coast Colony.[77] Those recruitment efforts were vigorously resisted throughout much of the northern frontier, including Taleland. In a not atypical 1922 case, two gangs of Talensi laborers deserted en masse even before reaching Kumasi.[78] What we know far less about is the story of migrant workers who struck out for the south on their own initiative in a process that emerged as a counter-narrative to forced recruitment campaigns. While British officers were busy managing labor resources and dealing with mass desertions, alternative, locally authored scripts of travel and migration were being written, and they were not in sync with the pace of recruitment drives. They unfolded according to the rhythms of agricultural work and the ritual calendar, often encompassing personal desires for adventure, social advancement, or escape from patriarchal authority. The very same man who might flee the recruiter, or desert on his way south, might show up on a southern cocoa farm a month later, but as a voluntary migrant who had gone for his own reasons, on his own time.[79] As early as 1913, Nash wondered just how many young men from his district were heading south in any given year:

I should very much like to know the number of NTs [Northern Territories] boys now working in Ashanti and the Colony on roads, cocoa farms and other employment. I am sure the figures would astonish some people. Like Scotsmen however they seem to say "Fair these board meads these hoary woods are grand, But we are exiles from our father's land." They always return at seed time, and will leave again as soon as the crops are cut. Rarely do they become permanent exiles.[80]

By the 1920s, the government still had no clear idea of how many men went south every year, although in 1923 a checkpoint at one ferry crossing recorded the passage of 16,816 "itinerant" workers (that is, men not mobilized by recruiters). A good percentage of these men were from French territory to the north.[81] Yet voluntary migration from Taleland and elsewhere in the Northern Territories had become such a predictable event that it was described as the "usual exodus" of "young men going south."[82]

Some of the migrant men traveled outside of their local areas for the same reasons their fathers and grandfathers did—to obtain food in times of hunger, perhaps from a neighboring community a few miles away, or perhaps from as far as Dagbon.[83] But for the vast majority, traveling voluntarily out of the north and into the forests of the south was a very new experience—an accidental consequence of the British colonial presence and the dramatic expansion of the economy of Asante and the Gold Coast Colony.[84] We saw in chapter 1 that the "Frafra" and "Gurunsi" peoples had long been subjected to slave raiding by horsemen from the surrounding cavalry states. As insecurity grew in the second half of the nineteenth century, culminating in the drought, military violence, and famine of the 1890s, it is likely that many Talensi were sold or sent in tribute to Asante and the other Akan forest states of the south. Vivid community memories of this forced migration obviously prevented all but the most adventuresome from making their way into the forest zone in the first years of the twentieth century. Atuli Asamane, who was about a hundred years old when we spoke to him, described how apprehensive he was when he made his first journey to Kumasi as a young man:

In fact, there was danger on the way! . . . We didn't want to have a rest on the way until we reached Kumasi. . . . when we got to Kumasi, we were informed of just how dangerous Prempeh House was. That if anybody should walk into that house, the person will be killed, the person would not return. So, we were afraid of going to the Prempeh House in Kumasi. We heard that anybody who entered that house would be killed. . . . When we were children we heard that when they killed you they would cut your head off and put it into a calabash form and then would drink pito. The Ashantis, that's what they were doing. We heard that![85]

Clearly, memories of the trade in slaves and stories of ritual killings in Kumasi were ever-present in the minds of these early voluntary migrants. A British official stationed in the area in 1911 noted the fear of traveling south, particularly among older people. They "have a long and tenacious memory," he wrote. "Wedged as they are between the Moshis, Mamprusi and Ashanti they have a lively recollection of former bad times and the uncertainty of the road."[86] But well-founded fear notwithstanding, young Talensi men could readily access the colonial cash economy by migrating to the south—a feat not easily accomplished anywhere in the northern savanna. By working for some time on public works or on cocoa farms in Asante and the Gold Coast, men could earn enough to purchase a few luxury items or, more importantly, to expedite their marriage, since they would not be solely reliant on their fathers and uncles to provide cattle and other necessities.

Fortunately, the recollections of those early days of voluntary travel are still alive in the memories of some of the oldest residents of Taleland and neighboring areas.[87] As Azabu of Tengzug remembered,

> In those days, we were around here and we were always hearing rumors from people who had traveled down south. And they would say, "Oh, that place is better. When you go there you get a job, everything is available and you can get enough food to eat." So, we decided to leave our parents here and to hide and then run and go there. . . . I went with my friends.[88]

Like Azabu, Atuli Asamane ran away to the south as a young man in search of adventure and the things that money could buy in the south. He also hoped to earn enough to perform his own marriage rites, rather than having to rely on his elders:

> In fact, I had to really walk. There was no road at the time. . . . We used to just dodge. I could not have gotten [my parents'] permission to go. . . . So, we did not tell our parents. I went with my friends. . . . We took nothing with us! Even our shirts were very torn. . . . We had only the Mossi dress at that time and it was even difficult to get. But anytime you had it, whether torn or not, you just put it on your body and, provided the seniors would allow you to follow them, you just moved with them. . . .
>
> Our main objective was to get clothes to wear, because we were working without wearing anything too much. . . . And always we were referred to go to Kumasi and work. That was the only place to work, get money and buy these things . . . but also to get some money to come home and perform marriage rites.[89]

Neither Azabu nor Atuli ran to Asante because they were forced. Their memories of travel and migration capture locally authored scripts that de-

Figure 2.2. Migration to the south. This unpublished photograph appeared in an exhibition called "Exploring the Gold Coast: Photographic Report by Dr. M. Fortes" with the caption "Farafara youths and men in Kumasi. These young men come here raw and mostly naked from the bush. Here in the big town they obtain work as sanitary labourers, railway labourers, etc. their first earnings they invest in clothes—flashy cloths from Manchester which they wear like togas [i.e. Akan style], or European clothes. The youth in the centre is wearing a Moshi gown of which large numbers, made by the Moshi people [of Upper Volta] are imported into the Gold Coast. Note the youth with his new clock—very proud of it!"

veloped in opposition to sustained British efforts to recruit labor in gangs for work in the south.[90] Most Talensi workers who migrated south (an estimated 10 percent of the adult male population, according to Fortes's estimate in the 1930s) did so of their own accord.[91] Many "dodged" fathers and uncles to make their way to Kumasi and beyond, some for only a few months, others for many years, in order to purchase some clothes, save a bit of cash to use toward a marriage, or simply experience the wider world. And of those captured and forcibly recruited, a good number never made

Figure 2.3. Azabu (born c. 1910), who spent many years in the south as a migrant worker.

it to their destinations—desertion and flight being typical responses to British efforts to organize labor to meet southern demands.

Political efforts to construct a legitimate and legitimizing system of rule, centered on Mamprugu and linking Taleland with the *nayiri* through specious connections via Kurugu, had been an unmitigated failure. Time and again, the government had to rely on coercion to preserve its rule, as it did during labor recruitment, in military mobilization, when dealing with the crisis at Bongo, and when controlling the ritual space of the Tong Hills. And when the British presence did appear to have a meaningful impact, outside of those coercive moments, it was seldom the impact intended: migrant laborers, many of whom were very young men, made their own way south, many of them, as we shall see, carrying the "shadow" of Tongnaab with them, while the government fumed over desertions from recruited gangs. A decade and a half after the conquest and depopulation of the Tong Hills, it was probably still fair to wonder whether the colonial state had made any headway at all in cajoling the Talensi to "come in."

Forbidden Gods?
Ritual Continuities in and around the Tong Hills

Perhaps the most striking confirmation of the ongoing incapacity of the British to "bring the Talensi in" was evidenced right atop the Tong Hills. Despite the assaults of 1911 and 1915 and the total prohibition on any ritual activity, exiled hill folk and long-distance pilgrims continued to steal up to Tengzug in order to "sacrifice" (*kaab*) to the great *bo'a* and *tongbana*. "During the time we were sacked by the British," recalled the *sipaatnaaba*, "people were still coming and anytime the people wanted to sacrifice to Tongnaab, we would hide in the night and then send the stranger there. For Ngoo, during the Gologo festival, we would hide in the night and then go and do the sacrifices."[92] Bo'arnaab Dilimit of the Gundaat section of Tengzug had similar tales to tell: "In those days, the people knew the area very well. They are native here. They knew the area far better than the British. What they could do was to come secretly at night. They would hide, go secretly to the gods, then return."[93] Of this ongoing continuity in Talensi ritual practice the British knew very little, despite monthly constabulary patrols and quarterly treks through the hills by the district commissioner.[94] Now and again they would discover that someone had built a compound within the exclusion zone around the hills or had removed the stone markers. For these infractions, compound owners were fined and houses razed to the ground.[95] But generally, reports were brief and simple: "The fetish place does not seem to have been visited."[96]

However, in December 1918, District Commissioner George Freeman made note of recent footprints that "lead only to the fetish place." "From the direction of the footsteps I should gather that they came from the direction of Tiliga up the central pass on the east side of the hill."[97] And then in October 1920, fresh and seemingly incontrovertible evidence came to light that the "fetish" had indeed been reactivated. Chief Commissioner Armitage, noting his "displeasure and surprise," ordered a further inquiry.[98] In early November, Freeman sent for the chiefs of Tongo, Gorogo, Tiliga, and Tengzug with the intent of fining each of them £5 and warning them "that they will be far more severely punished if the practice is not stopped instantly."[99] The "Tongo chiefs," as they were described, subsequently produced someone they called the "Tendana of Tiliga"—in fact, the Kpatar *tengdaana*, Dubazaa, who like many exiled hill folk now resided down on the plains in Tiliga. Dubazaa had succeeded his brother, Fuohibazaa, the *tengdaana* who had been arrested in 1911. Along with four other men from Tiliga, he was brought before Louis Castellain, now promoted to commissioner for the North-Eastern Province, who sentenced him to one year's detention at Tamale as a political prisoner. The four others were to be detained at Gambaga for six months. Castellain also proposed that one "Tengoli of Tiliga," who had been "put in charge of Tongzugu people by Capt Nash," be fined £5 and made to report monthly to the district office.[100] Finally, Castellain announced that he would soon visit the "fetish grove" himself "and have the hole filled in with stones and later, when there is time, . . . blow it up with dynamite."[101]

At the close of 1920, Castellain launched an inquiry into the "alleged reopening of the Tong Hills Fetish." Freeman testified that he had seen evidence that the grove had been visited toward the end of October and then learned from his court interpreter that a man named "Tingoli, a former resident of Tonzugu," had made "further fetish." When he visited the site the next day, he found a "small tunnel in a cleft of the rocks. . . . At the end of this small tunnel . . . I saw a mass of feather and muck, but how long it had been there I could not say." The interpreter provided a similar account, adding that the man who had led them to the spot, an ex-private from the Gold Coast Regiment, told them that Kanjargas (i.e., Builsas), Dagombas, and Gurunsis came to visit the place and that "Tingoli was to keep all the things that the Dagomba people brought." "Tingoli" himself— that is, Tengol—acknowledged that Nash had instructed him years before to "look after the Tinzugu people," but denied knowing anything about the shrine being reopened. "I do not go into the hills," he claimed. "If I did I should not wear any clothes again." Tengol testified that he had learned that Dubazaa had "made fetish" in the hills, but reported that "he made his sacrifice at a different place and not at the old shrine."[102] The day before the inquiry, Castellain had visited the shrine and "could find no trace of it having been used recently."[103] Based on what he had seen, coupled with the testimony heard at the inquiry, he ruled that the "fetish grove" which was destroyed in 1915 had not been reopened and that the "feathers etc found by Mr. Freeman were those used to make fetish for the farms, which are allowed in the hills."[104]

It took another four and a half years for colonial officials to realize just how thoroughly their orders continued to be ignored. In July 1925, the nephew of the Yinduri chief was awaiting an escort to the Tamale prison, having been sentenced on assault charges. Angered by the *kunaab's* attempts to remove his uncle from office and hoping to get the former in trouble with the British, the nephew told officials that the "Tong Fetish" had consistently been tended for the last six years.[105] The resulting inquiry marked a watershed in colonial understanding of the sacred landscape of the Tong Hills. What the British finally were able to discern in 1925 was that there was not just one "fetish," but a multiplicity of sites tended by diverse constituencies extending well beyond the hills themselves. Under questioning from Provincial Commissioner Cuffield, local leaders for the first time revealed the existence of Tongnaab in a cave at the summit of the granite peak rising above the settlement of Tengzug. Yet it is clear that sacred knowledge was offered up in a highly selective manner. Witnesses assured Cuffield that the Bonaab shrine destroyed in 1915 (one name/place for Tongnaab, as we have seen) was very different from Tongnaab. It was a "bad fetish," they insisted, but Tongnaab (and here they used the generic name rather than the shrine's specific name, "Yanii") did only good, providing the farmers with bountiful harvests and women with healthy children.[106] They maintained that they had not understood that Tongnaab was forbidden, only Bonaab. British officials began to appreciate for the first time the futility of past efforts to physically destroy the sacred sites. "If a man wants to worship Tongnaab," explained the Shia *bo'arana*, one of the senior guardians of the *bo'ar*, "he can come to my compound in Shia [and] I can give the man a bit of earth in a horn and he can take it away and get all the good of Tongnaab, it is not necessary for me or for the man who solicits the fetish to go to the fetish place."[107]

While the British learned much on this crucial day, there was also much that remained unsaid or unheard. In essence, they had learned precisely what certain Talensi wanted them to learn. It is of enduring importance that two of those who testified that day, the leading Namoo chief (the *ton-grana*) and the Mamprusi chief (the *kunaab*), had no connections to any of the *bo'a* in the hills. The other two (Bantanga, the nephew of the Yinduri chief, and the Shia *bo'arana*) were both members of the *bo'ar* congregation that referred to Tongnaab as "Yanii." Critically, no one from Kpatar or any of the other clans who tended the Bonaab site were present. On 14 September, therefore, the British did not learn that there was one god, tended by various ritual congregations at different sites, but that there were two different gods—one good and one bad. As luck would have it, the god they had destroyed in 1915 was the malign one, while that which had gone un-noticed for so many years was entirely benevolent.[108] The British were told about the "good" fetish by those who tended it, but those who tended the "bad" one were not present to voice their stories. Tongnaab had never been place-specific, but at this critical juncture in the history of the Tong Hills it became inscribed in colonial knowledge as bound to one sacred site. One congregation was able to appropriate the generic name "Tongnaab" as *the* name of its *bo'ar*, Yanni. One congregation's story was told to colonial au-thorities in 1925 and that congregation—from the Bukiok lineage of Tengzug as well as Zandoya, Yinduri, Shia, and Gorogo—was able to ap-ply the labels and name the names.

The day after the inquiry, Provincial Commissioner Cuffield visited the newly discovered Tongnaab shrine, describing it as a "cave or hole between granite boulders at the summit of a very high conglomeration of stones about 3/4s mile to the South West of Bongnab." It was actually not nec-essary to go into the hills to worship Tongnaab, he reported, as "the fetish priests have merely to visit the shrine periodically to replenish their stock of sacred earth."[109] For this reason, he concluded, the "cult cannot be pre-vented, did Government wish to prohibit it." But in Cuffield's view, it re-ally was not necessary to ban Tongnaab. The bad fetish, Bonaab, he argued, was virtually dead or "so weak that it has been of no inconvenience what-soever." Meanwhile, the Talensi had proven to be "perfectly loyal helpful citizens." Many had served in the Gold Coast Regiment and the Constab-ulary and had "readily supplied labour when called upon to do so." Initi-ating a striking turn-around in colonial policy, Cuffield recommended that "with some pomp and show permission be given for the open practice of the Tongnab fetish in its stronghold of the Tong Hills."[110] Since the officials could not prevent its use, he argued, they "may as well pretend to be gen-erous."[111] In November 1925, Chief Commissioner A. H. Walker-Leigh approved the "Tong Fetish" being "openly practised as long as the people behave themselves."[112]

Tongnaab and the Rise of Tengol

The official recognition of Tongnaab in 1925 constituted a moment not just of great ritual magnitude, but of profound political consequence. To the British it may not have seemed particularly significant at the time: a "good fetish" was now allowed to operate where previously a neighboring "bad fetish" had been banned. But Walker-Leigh's decision to sanction the Yanii shrine alone effectively upset the balance of ritual power surrounding Tongnaab. Yanii—now believed by the British to be the one and only Tongnaab "fetish"—thus achieved what can be described as ritual paramountcy over the other sacred sites in the hills. The process by which the guardians of the Yanii shrine were able to accumulate ritual power with the support of the colonial state was not unlike that which brought paramount chieftaincy to peoples who had never before known chiefs. Indeed, for the Talensi, the rise of Yanii was inextricably linked to chiefly paramountcy—though not the paramountcy that the British had tried to construct via Tongo, Kurugu, and Mamprugu. Rather, key figures from within the hills offered up an alternative to the British model of colonial rule—one informed by the past, but driven by profound shifts in economic, political, and ritual power over the past two decades. Positing themselves as the legitimate rulers of the Tong Hills, they brokered an accommodation between the Talensi and colonial rule. The recalcitrant hill folk may finally have "come in," but they did so on terms scripted, in large part, by their own leaders.

The key actor in the development of this alternative to the British model was Tengol (a.k.a. Tingoli or Tingwa), the man whom Nash had "placed in charge" of the Tengzug people who had been forced off the hills in 1911. Despite his position as a colonial *kambonaaba*, we know very little about Tengol's activities before 1925. Like many other local "chiefs," he operated for the most part well below the radar of British rule and thus left few traces in the archival record. In 1915, he testified before the chief commissioner during the first investigation into the "fetish." Identifying himself as "Chief of Tinzugu," he explained that he had heard that the shrine was open but denied ever visiting it.[113] The following year, when the British released Nawa (the leading guardian of Bonaab), they handed him over to Tengol who, as head of the Tengzug people living at Tiliga, was held responsible for the old *tengdaana*'s behavior.[114] In 1917, Tengol resurfaces briefly in the archival record as a rather overzealous labor recruiter, who complained to the British when the Tiliga chief refused his order to bring in sticks for roofing the new constabulary lines. At that time, Tengol had no authority over the Tiliga chief and, in fact, was a guest on Tiliga land. But as the British official recorded, "Tingoli is a much stronger man than Segrana [the Tiliga chief] and is trying it on."[115] A few months later, Tengol apparently tried to reassemble all of the Tengzug people in Tiliga, including those who ran to the other side of the Volta river, and to convince the British that all should follow him.[116] Although Tengol was encouraged at the time to leave things as they were, by 1920 he was again pressing District Commissioner Freeman to allow the Tengzug people to leave Tiliga and "set up separately" under his authority. In that year, he was again brought before the British during the second inquiry into the reopening of the shrine.

Who was this man Tengol and how was he able to posit himself as "Chief of Tengzug"? Because of the paucity of archival documentation and the difficulty in accessing specific memories of this period, we can answer this only with conjecture and circumstantial evidence. We do know that by the 1930s, Tengol was recognized as the *golibdaana*—the keeper of the sacred drums brought out every year for *Golib* (or *Gologo*), the sowing festival that takes place before the first rains in late March or early April and is centered on the great *tongban* Ngoo.[117] But we have no specific evidence that he had acquired any recognized position within Talensi society by the time of the British conquest and there was almost certainly no recognized chief of Tengzug before the colonial conquest of 1911.[118] If any one person had more ritual authority than others it was probably the *kpatarnaaba*, the senior custodian of both the *tongban* Ngoo and the Bonaab *bo'ar*. Indeed, it was the *kpatarnaaba* who was identified by the British as the leader of the resistance in Tengzug in 1911. As we have seen, Kpatar bore the brunt of the British assaults in 1911 and 1915 and Kpatarnaaba Fuohibazaa and his *tengdaana* were jailed. Meanwhile, Tengol and his ritual collaborators, centered on the *bo'ar* Yanii, suffered exile to the plains below, but little else. Their *bo'ar* remained hidden from British officials until 1925. Settled at Tiliga, Tengol emerged as a Tengzug leader and, eventually, as *the* Tengzug chief—the obvious successor to the truculent *kpatarnaaba*. Like those of other *kambonaaba*s, his claims were facilitated by the fact that he was an able labor recruiter. But he was also amazingly adept at playing the powers that be—from British officials to the *tongrana* to the local Mamprusi overlord, the *kunaab*.

Yet there was more to Tengol's story than being in the right place at the right time or having keen political savvy. His recognition as chief of Tengzug was also built upon the rising fortunes of the Yanii *bo'ar*, which after 1925 was known increasingly as simply "Tongnaab." During the very years that the hills were supposed to be off-limits to supplicants, especially in the decade after 1915, there was, if anything, a dramatic expansion in the number of pilgrims coming to consult the oracle. With Bonaab largely out of the picture thanks to colonial surveillance, Yanii was able to garner a greater and greater proportion of the growing long-distance pilgrim trade.[119] A ritual entrepreneur *par excellence*, Tengol parlayed that trade, and the wealth it brought into the hills, into increased authority and political recognition by the British.

While Tongnaab had long attracted supplicants from surrounding savanna peoples, it was the expansion of the pilgrim trade south to Asante and the Gold Coast that was the key transformative moment in the god's twentieth-century history. Tengol was at the very center of that historical change. We can only speculate as to how and when Tongnaab's ritual network first breached the ecological and cultural frontier between savanna and forest. Fortes dated the expansion of Tongnaab's ritual field into the Akan forest to the 1910s, and it is possible that the first trickle of pilgrims made the three- or four-hundred-mile journey on foot and were smuggled up into Tengzug in this decade, unbeknownst to the British.

How did word get to the south? It seems likely that Talensi, as well as members of other northern groups who historically had accessed Tongnaab's power, took it with them as they made their trek south as migrant workers and colonial soldiers (both forced and voluntary) from the first years of the twentieth century. Barbara Ward, writing of the 1940s, described a process probably typical of how news spread: "[One pilgrim] had had a series of mysterious illnesses and a general run of bad luck which had culminated . . . in an accident with his lorry—an expensive as well as a painful experience. On the advice of a Northern Territories man who was labouring for him on his cocoa-farm he had set out for the Northern Territories to try to gain spiritual protection and salvation from his bad fortune from this man's local Earth spirit, Kune [i.e., Kunde]."[120] Fortes speculated that the process may have been rather more deliberate:

Men from the Hills, with a mixture of inborn business acumen and sincere faith in the magical powers of the oracle cult, advertised the cult quietly. A trickle of pilgrims from these wealthy and comparatively sophisticated areas began to flow northwards. And the trickle soon became a broad stream. Rich and poor, farmers, traders, chiefs, commoners, literate and illiterate, pagans and Christians joined the stream."[121]

An important facilitating factor was certainly the expansion in physical mobility which came with the completion of the motor road from Accra via the Zuarungu District to the northern frontier in 1922.[122] By 1926, the southern transport contractor Tette Blankson was operating a regular service from Tamale to Bolgantanga and Navrongo.[123] The following year, it was reported that there had been a "marked increase in the number of Fanti and Ashanti women and men who have made the pilgrimage to the legitimized Tong Fetish—which is supposed to have the power of making women pregnant. These people however soon return back to the Colony and Ashanti. The increase may no doubt be due to the increasing number of lorries that are coming up here from the South."[124] A. W. Cardinall, an astute official with wide experience of the north, was certain that this was the case. "Worship at all the great shrines of the Northern Territories have [*sic*] received a very marked impetus since the opening of that Country by motor traffic," he observed in 1930, "and Ashantis and Gold Coast visitors to Bruku, Dente, Senyonkipo, Tongzugu, and even smaller shrines are very frequent."[125]

What were the immediate implications of this expanding trade for those living around the Tong Hills? As Fortes was well aware, from the outset the new southern pilgrim traffic was monopolized by the lineage of Golibdaana Tengol, a "shrewd and resolute man of unbounded ambition . . . recognized by the Government as the headman of the Hills clans."[126] In other words, the expanding trade and the wealth it generated created new forms of political authority. That authority, particularly in the hands of Tengol and his associates, posited itself as the answer to the longstanding British problem of how to rule the hills, while it assured the concentration of the southern pilgrim traffic in the hands of one Tongnaab congregation. The dynamic of ritual and rule, in other words, was self-perpetuating.

Even so, Tengol felt bound to legitimate his authority on terms the British appeared more able to understand. Thus, when Government Anthropologist R. S. Rattray visited Tengzug in 1928, Tengol regaled him with a long account of his royal Mamprusi forebears, claiming that his ancestor Sumri was the son of a *nayiri* who after a dynastic dispute had migrated to the Tong Hills from Nalerigu. He claimed to be the grandson of the first *golibdaana* to go to Mamprugu to get his chieftaincy, but admitted that he, himself, had not yet been confirmed by the *nayiri*; he was "made Chief by the Europeans."[127] Less than a decade later, Fortes discounted Tengol's story, arguing that "fabrication or distortion of myths of origin" was occasioned in the hills both by struggles for power among rival clans and by the fact that the administration only recognized as chiefs those who could claim a connection to Mamprugu:

Hence we find the Golibdaana of Tenzugu justifying his pretensions to recognized chiefship by concocting, for the benefit of a white inquirer, a story of how the founder of his lineage migrated thither from Mampurugu—a story which his enemies scoff at. . . . These new myths are part of the defensive ideologies engendered by social conflict, but they follow the axioms of Tale thought.[128]

Myth-making was not the only way by which new political authority was legitimated and articulated. Fortes reported that on one occasion, Tengol, "in his overwhelming conceit," attempted to attend the court of the *tongrana* dressed as a Mamprugu chief, with a full gown and a red fez. Apparently, in this instance, Tengol went too far and he was censured by the *tongrana*, who also reported his inappropriate behavior to the district commissioner.[129] The officer ordered Tengol to "stop his new practices."[130]

Conclusions

But "new practices" would continue to be at the very center of economy, ritual, and rule in the Tong Hills. When the British conquered the hills in 1911, they thought they had broken the final stronghold of the unclothed raiders who used the hills and their malevolent fetish as a virtual refuge from modernity. The Talensi had to be brought into—forced into—a colonial modernity through markets, labor recruitment, and the creation of a political infrastructure based on chiefly authority.[131] Yet at every turn, Talensi refused to "come in" on British terms, and coercion remained the central feature of colonial rule in this area well into the 1920s. But Talensi did not refuse to come in because they were clinging to the refuge of an unchanging past, but because the terms offered by the British bore absolutely no legitimate connections to their real, lived history—to their gods and their ancestors—and took no account of contemporary change. Colonial officials, with the partial exception of the astute S. D. Nash, could not see in front of their own eyes an unfolding Talensi history of both continuity and change. By the end of the 1920s, when the Talensi were finally brought into the colonial state, it was via a script largely authored by Tengol and his supporters. The answer to the problem of colonial rule, in other words, was provided by key sections of Tale society who could posit an alternative political system grounded in the past, but speaking to the expanding world of migrants, ritual entrepreneurs, cash, and commodities. In so doing, Tengol and others worked out an accommodation with British colonial rule which preserved some degree of local autonomy in the face of ongoing efforts to "bring the Talensis in" under Mamprugu.

And central to that accommodation was Tongnaab—a god as old as the hills and yet very much a part of the ongoing construction of Talensi modernity. For centuries, Tongnaab had worked to ensure the fertility of the land and of women in the Tong Hills and its broader savanna hinterland. But it was also profoundly historical. Tongnaab was central to lived experiences of the slave trade and how the Talensi protected themselves from the worst of its ravages. It stood at the heart of Tale resistance to British incursions from the late nineteenth century to the 1920s. And it was then imbricated in complex struggles for power and authority among its own congregations. These were struggles at the very heart of ritual and rule—Tengol's rise and the sacred paramountcy of the Yanii shrine. Colonial rule in Taleland, in other words, had to be brokered through Tongnaab. Yet if it is clear that the great ancestor-deity is fundamental to Talensi history, it is not at all self-evident why Akans and other southern pilgrims made their way to the Tong Hills. What did Tongnaab offer to those men and women—many of whom came from societies that historically had disparaged the primitive wilderness of the savanna hinterland? Why did they come, and in such numbers? Southern pilgrims and the wealth they brought reshaped the political and ritual landscape of the Tong Hills from the 1910s. But how could Tongnaab speak to the specific spiritual concerns of Akans, Ewes, or Gas? How could the Talensi god be incorporated into the very different ritual landscapes of the forest and coast? It is to those questions that we next turn.

3

"Watch Over Me": Witchcraft and Anti-witchcraft Movements in Ghanaian History, 1870s–1920s

*B*y the 1920s, the pilgrimage network focused on the Tong Hills began to expand beyond its established heartland to Asante and the Gold Coast. Tongnaab's passage across the savanna-forest divide represents the key shift in the twentieth-century history of the *bo'ar* cult—a shift that occurred in three overlapping phases. First, the imposition of colonial rule and the refashioning of the slave-raiding economy into one based on migrant wage labor served to spread knowledge of the Talensi god to the cocoa farms and trading towns of the south. Second, Asante and other southern peoples, as they learned of Tongnaab, began to make long-distance pilgrimages to the hills. Third, favored southern pilgrims were granted the right to carry the *yihiyii* or "shadow" of Tongnaab away with them and to establish their own satellite shrines in the south. The final phase of this ritual movement involved a transformation not just in the organization but also in the ideology of the cult. In its savanna heartland, Tongnaab participated in the identification of witches, both from Talensi communities and from those forming its ritual hinterland, but such ritual work was tangential to central concerns with fertility and the successful reproduction of the generations.[1] Once it was established in the southern forests in the late 1920s, however, Tongnaab became something quite different— a new religious movement known by the Akanized name of "Nana Tongo."[2] While retaining many of the tutelary powers recognized by the Talensi and their savanna clients, Tongnaab in its southern manifestation of

Nana Tongo was focused almost exclusively on the detection and the eradication of "witchcraft."

In this chapter, our focus shifts from the Talensi world south to Asante
and the Gold Coast and to the wider search for solutions to the problem
of witchcraft in Ghanaian societies. In exploring the ambivalence, the mobility, and the transformation of ritual power, the chapter provides a broad
historical context for understanding two cross-cultural journeys: the movement of southern pilgrims to the Tong Hills and the subsequent passage
of Tongnaab to the Akan forest and beyond. It opens with a first-person
account of a visit to the Yanii shrine of Tongnaab in 1928 by the ethnographer R. S. Rattray and his local assistant Victor Aboya. Rattray's narrative
contains the first detailed evidence for the working of the long-distance
pilgrimage trade from the Akan forest. It also represents a key moment in
the construction of colonial knowledge about Tongnaab. We then turn to
the question of witchcraft amongst the Akan and their neighbors, focusing on the impact of colonial conquest on indigenous perceptions of misfortune and evil. Finally, we explore the wider context for the transformation
of Tongnaab into Nana Tongo by charting the history of anti-witchcraft
cults from the emergence of the Domankama movement in Asante in 1879
to the proliferation of exotic savanna gods throughout the forest zone in
the 1920s.

R. S. Rattray and Victor Aboya Visit Tongnaab, 6 May 1928

After many years of ethnographic research in Asante, R. S. Rattray journeyed north from the forest kingdom at the start of 1928 to begin fieldwork for what would be his last great work, *The Tribes of the Ashanti Hinterland* (1932). Rattray had recently completed the final volume of his trio of
works on Asante and his move into the Northern Territories represented
the culmination of his tenure as the first director of the Gold Coast Government's Anthropology Department (1920–30). "I crossed the boundary
on January 8th," he wrote of his passage from the forest to the savanna.

> After some score of years spent, in the forest zone, among the Akan-speaking
> peoples, the contrast presented by this Hinterland and its inhabitants is indeed very
> striking. The traveller appears to pass in a few hours into a country where climate,
> physical features, peoples, customs and problems present as striking divergences as
> those which would exist, for example, between East and West Africa.[3]

Rattray decided to motor straight through Dagbon in order to focus his
attention on the non-centralized "tribal" peoples occupying the northern

extremities of the Protectorate. "This decision was reached, partly because this is one of the most thickly populated areas, partly because it was the most remote from civilization, and partly because it was the only portion of the country concerning which there existed any previous literature."[4] Four days after his "crossing," Rattray arrived in Navrongo, where he spent a month drawing on the local knowledge of Monsignor Morin and the other French-Canadian missionaries at the White Fathers' station. He initially planned to base himself at Tumu in Sisala country to the west, but then changed his mind in favor of the Zuarungu District. Rattray's decision to concentrate his efforts on the "Frafra" peoples may also have been due to one more factor: his good fortune in securing the services of Victor Aboya, "a Nankani, who, once sold as a slave to the Ashanti, had acquired a very sound colloquial knowledge of this language and also of Hausa, with both of which . . . I am familiar."[5]

Victor Aboya's contribution to Rattray's research should not be underestimated. Born in about 1888, Aboya fell victim to the famine that gripped the region during the era of colonial conquest in the mid-1890s. Exchanged by an uncle for a few baskets of grain, he was eventually sold into slavery at Kumasi around 1900. He was subsequently released into the care of the Basel Mission, where he attended school, converted to Christianity, and for three years trained as a catechist. In 1917, however, Aboya severed his relationship with the Presbyterian Church in Kumasi and returned home to Winkogo, five miles west of the Tong Hills. By 1925, he was assisting the Catholic White Fathers at their newly opened Frafra outstation, walking into Bolgatanga each Sunday to work on a vernacular translation of the English Catechism and to teach the Fathers Guruni.[6] It was no doubt they who recommended his services to Rattray in 1928. Yet like so many other unsung (and all too often unnamed) indigenous intermediaries in the history of ethnography in colonial Africa, Victor Aboya was far more than merely a translator. Not only was he Rattray's host and principal informant in the Zuarungu District, he wrote an extensive treatise on Nankani social life in the vernacular that in his own English translation was incorporated verbatim into *Tribes of the Ashanti Hinterland.*[7] Rattray's earlier writing on Asante is characterized by a scrupulous avoidance of any modern, urban influence that might contaminate the world of pristine custom and tradition that he sought to reconstruct.[8] If the ethnographer was concerned by his reliance on the young, mission-educated Aboya, however, he was soon relieved by the latter's apparently seamless reinsertion into local culture. "He was persuaded to record various events in the village life," Rattray wrote. "He has done so faithfully and without any attempt to impress us by airing or dragging in his later acquired European knowledge."[9]

On leaving Navrongo, Rattray based himself in Aboya's own homestead in Winkogo, where he launched into a study of Nankani society before turning his attention, in April 1928, to the neighboring Talensi. "Had the Talense [*sic*] not been labelled with a separate appellation," he wrote, "I doubt if the anthropologist . . . would have considered it necessary to deal with them as a group distinct from the Namnam [i.e., Nabdam] and the Nankanse."[10] Yet it soon became apparent to Rattray that at least one aspect of Talensi "rites and customs" was strikingly different from those of the surrounding peoples, and that was the functioning of the great ancestor shrines of the Tong Hills. Indeed, Rattray devoted an entire chapter of *Tribes of the Ashanti Hinterland* to an account of his visit to what by the late 1920s was emerging as the most renowned of the Tongnaab *bo'a*. There, he witnessed what he described as "the most interesting and extraordinary of many curious rites which it has been my privilege to attend in the course of many years of anthropological field-work." Employing the sort of startling juxtapositions that recently have become the staple of anthropological exegesis of the interconnections between the global and the local, Rattray goes on:

> I use the word "extraordinary" advisedly, on account of the almost grotesque blending of the ultra-new with the things which are very old. Flying-machines, motorcars, and the cultivation of cocoa—these seem out of place with pagan gods and naked humanity, but in this ceremony all were mingled, and staged in a setting which must have been familiar to troglodyte man.[11]

On the morning of 6 May 1928, Rattray and Aboya were escorted into the Tong Hills, through the abandoned environs of Tengzug and up into the granite rocks housing the Yanii *bo'ar*.[12] Arriving at 8 A.M. at the ledge below the cavern that formed the shrine, the two men and their guides sat down to wait for the presiding ritual intermediaries. Expecting to encounter pristine "pagan gods and naked humanity," Rattray was astounded at what he saw:

> From then onwards, until about 9 A.M., groups of pilgrims began to arrive. To my wonder and astonishment I saw well-dressed Africans, men and women who I later discovered had motored hundreds of miles from Kumasi, Kwahu, and Mampon. Among these were several of my Ashanti friends of old days, and never shall I forget the look of amazement on their faces at meeting me again in such a place.[13]

The group (which Rattray's notebooks reveal also included several Dagomba pilgrims) was then joined by an unnamed *tengdaana* and the "Chief of

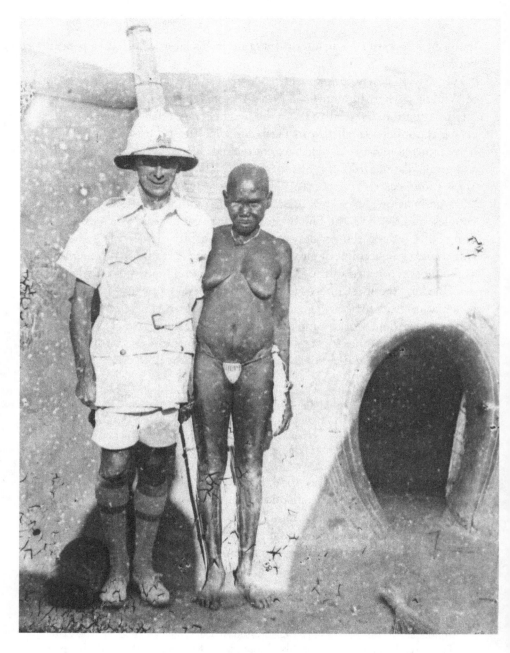

Figure 3.1. R. S. Rattray posing with Victor Aboya's mother in the latter's house at Winkogo in 1928. Photograph by Aboya. Pitt Rivers Museum, University of Oxford, 1998.312.1015.1; published as figure 60 of *Tribes of the Ashanti Hinterland*, facing 336.

Tenzuk." The former may well have been the then-*yiran*, Naoh, while the latter was certainly Tengol—"a magnificent-looking man, standing well over six feet and very finely proportioned." These two then climbed up into the cave, from where Rattray and the others could hear Tongnaab being summoned by the clapping of hands. "All the pilgrims now began to undress. The Coast women disrobed and put on shorts; hats, shoes, white pith helmets, and clothes were piled up and scattered over the boulders."[14] Once they had removed their garments, the supplicants were summoned to make the final ascent and to enter the inner sanctum.

Rattray was the first to approach Tongnaab with his petition. "I asked Aboya . . . to state the nature of my work; how I was trying to record their ancient customs, that the best of them might be retained, and that I would like a blessing on this task. I also said I hoped some day to fly over this spot, and I ended with the promise of a cow if these requests were granted."[15] The *tengdaana* then called on the ancestor-deity, as later recalled and translated from Talen by Aboya:

> My father, I call your father that he may call Takuru-nab,[16] that they may come and sit before Tong-naba's face and receive the white man favourably; permit him to work at the work which he wishes to do. He says that if he sees all, he will give you a cow. Permit his name to mount up more than all his neighbours and let Chieftainship be added to Chieftainship. Do not allow fever to catch him any day; let him go and return (like) a hawk, that you may be able to receive your cow. Keep his children who will follow him, that they may receive and give us [*sic*].[17]

"At the end of this speech," Rattray writes, "a long wail came from somewhere in the back of the cave. Every one then clapped their hands with a kind of masonic rhythm for the space of at least a minute."

As the Asantes and other pilgrims in turn pressed forward, Rattray jotted down a selection of their petitions in his notebook in the original Twi. Some wished for health and children, others for bountiful cocoa harvests, increased profits from trading ventures, and the recovery of debts. One man even pleaded for help from Tongnaab in his efforts to stop drinking. "Their petitions were then translated into Talene, in which language they were finally recited by the *Ten'dan'*."[18] Kwaku Opon's appeal was quite typical:

> I was at my town of Mampon, and I heard about grandfather (*nana*, here a term of respect), so I came to lean upon him, that he might give me health, which I once had. I keep a store and I have two motor-cars. From that store I derive no profit whatever. As for my two motor-cars, when I ply them for hire and people enter them, I only incur debts and there is no profit in them. Because of that, and because I have heard of grandfather, I have come to ask him if he will show me the way to make profit. Again, I have four wives and they have either not borne children,

Figure 3.2. Tengol (standing on left) with the officiating *tengdaana* (probably
Yiran Naoh), photographed by R. S. Rattray on the rocks below the cave
housing the Yanii shrine of Tòngnaab on 6 May 1928. Pitt Rivers Museum,
University of Oxford 1998.312.1058.1; published as figure 74 of *Tribes of the
Ashanti Hinterland*, facing 363.

or, if they have, the children die. Therefore help me, and permit my wives to bear children, and give my relations health and long life.

Other supplicants were more explicit in identifying the probable cause of their misfortune as the maleficence of others. "I have heard about this god," said another pilgrim from the Mampon party. "I have a sickness in my belly; it never ceases; it cries out *ko! ko!* Look to my sickness that it may cease. If any one is doing this to me, catch him for me, or kill him and let me get health and strength."

"When the service was ended," Rattray writes, "we all backed out again into the sunlight and were led, complete silence being enjoined upon us, to the entrance of the second cave." There, the gifts of livestock brought by each person were sacrificed, Rattray himself offering up a fowl and a sheep. "They were promised nothing. If their prayers were answered, they would bring back an offering. Nearly every one asked for 'money' or 'profit.'" The pilgrims then picked their way back down the rock face to the ledge where earlier they had undressed. Before collecting their clothes and descending the hill, each was marked with a line of red clay on the cheeks, arms, and legs as well as on the back and between the breasts. "When I state that these supplicants were educated men and women, some of who owned large businesses, well-furnished European houses, and not a few of them their own cars, in which they had come hundreds of miles to visit this pagan god, the power and influence of the old beliefs may readily be imagined."[19]

Rattray's evocative account resonates with many of the intellectual and personal predilections that shaped his overall ethnographic project in Asante and in the Northern Territories. In order to understand why he appeared to be so irresistibly drawn toward Tongnaab, one point in particular should be stressed. Despite a stated lack of interest in grand theories, his view of African society was strongly influenced by nineteenth-century evolutionist ideas that posited a linear historical progression from an original "primitive" society to increasingly more sophisticated forms of social and political organization. In short, he came to perceive the stateless peoples of the Northern Territories as representing the purest, oldest form of social organization, based on "totemic clans" governed only by the ritual authority of *tengdaanas*.[20] At the opposite end of the African evolutionary spectrum stood the Asante kingdom, the most sophisticated development of the "highly elaborated Akan organization, military and civil, with its wonderful system of decentralization."[21] It was this fascination with "a people in a very primitive state, as primitive as anywhere in Africa," that drew Rattray to the Frafra region and explains why so much of *Tribes of the Ashanti Hinterland* was focused on the

Nankani and their neighbors.[22] It also helps to explain Rattray's shock at discovering the existence of pilgrimage routes leading from the heart of Asante to the far extremities of the Northern Territories. He took this to be a graphic indication of the resilience of "the old primitive religious institution" that underpinned autochthonous social forms—of the "power and influence of the old beliefs" to which he was so strongly attracted.[23]

While Rattray's account provides the first insights into the dynamics of north-south ritual dialogue three years after the shrine finally received British sanction, his portrayal of the Tongnaab cult as "old" and "primitive" is of course misleading. The ancestor shrines of the Tong Hills may well have been very old, but the extension of their influence to the Akan forest was something quite new and innovative. Far from being a "traditional" deity worshipped since the dawn of time by a primitive, isolated tribe, Tongnaab possessed the ideological flexibility to provide a range of solutions for the pressing spiritual problems of the modern world. That said, Rattray's obsession with origins, with untouched, primitive peoples, and with mysterious, faraway holy places may inadvertently have captured the essence of Tongnaab's appeal to southern pilgrims. At the very climax of their sacred journey, these pilgrims temporarily abandoned the hard-won accoutrements of colonial modernity ("hats, shoes, white pith helmets, and clothes were piled up and scattered over the boulders") before crossing the final threshold into the ritual epicenter of a quite different world.[24]

Why was this? What drew Asantes and other Gold Coasters on arduous, expensive journeys to the isolated savanna country far to the north? Why were they so eager to tap into the ritual resources of a people historically viewed as backward and subservient "Gurunsis" or *nnonkofoo*? As we have argued in chapter 2, newfound mobility certainly provided the means for the expansion of ritual networks. By the early 1920s, wage laborers from the Northern Territories and beyond were migrating in increasing numbers to the cocoa farms and trading towns of the south, leading to a sudden expansion of cultural contacts between forest and savanna. The same roads that carried migrant workers south in turn carried Akan pilgrims north. Yet colonial mobility was only an enabling factor in religious change. For the underlying motives, we must consider the impact of colonialism and capitalism in Asante and the Gold Coast and in particular the ways in which perceptions of health, wealth, and misfortune were being reshaped by rapid social and economic change. These changes must in turn be located within established Akan perceptions of the ritual landscape of the northern savanna. Like other savanna gods, Tongnaab in its southern manifestation as Nana Tongo was specifically dedicated to the eradication of witchcraft or, in Twi, *bayi.* To what extent was colonial rule responsible for a perception that *bayi* was on the increase or taking new and more dangerous forms?

The Modernity of the "New Cults": The Debate

As noted in the introduction, the impact of colonialism emerged as a central issue in the first wave of writing on Nana Tongo and other anti-witchcraft movements in the Akan region. Most observers argued that the witch-finding cults were innovative religious responses to a range of new anxieties and problems brought about by colonial conquest and rule.[25] The keenest contemporary observer of the so-called "new cults" was M. J. Field, Rattray's successor as Government Anthropologist, whose research focused on the eastern areas of the Gold Coast Colony. "In the last twenty years there has been in the forest country an enormous increase in preoccupation with witchcraft," Field reported in 1940.[26] She identified two main reasons for this: the rising incidence of sexually transmitted disease, and—more generally—the social and economic changes wrought by the booming cocoa industry:

> The chief crimes attributed to witches are the killing of children, the causing of sterility and the conversion of other people into witches (i.e., neurotics) against their knowledge; it was therefore inevitable that witchcraft should be blamed when these ills unmistakably increased. The secondary activities attributed to witches include the power to spoil crops, to spoil cocoa fermentation and to become rich by "sucking away" the invisible essence of money so that the victim meets financial losses and the spoiler financial windfalls.[27]

The long-serving Basel missionary Reverend Hans Debrunner also regarded witchcraft as a "neurotic reaction" to modern change. Comparing the waves of twentieth-century anti-witchcraft cults to the lack of evidence for such movements in European accounts of the Gold Coast in the era of the slave trade, Debrunner concluded that before about 1850 witches were believed to be few in number and to pose no major danger to society.[28] New and complex problems, the argument ran, demanded radically new solutions. Taking advantage of the imposition of colonial peace and the resulting increase in physical mobility, troubled individuals and ambitious ritual entrepreneurs alike sought to tap into the sacred landscape of the newly accessible Northern Territories. Fueling this process was the widespread perception amongst the Akan and their coastal neighbors that the savanna peoples remained free from the worst ravages of maleficent witchcraft. "When anyone wishes to set up a new shrine," Field wrote of the forest state of Akyem Kotoku, "he usually travels to the distant home of one of the gods of the Northern Territory [sic] strangers whose reports of their own country first awakened interest . . . in their gods. . . . These strangers reported, in particular, that witchcraft was unknown in their country, for their gods protected them against it."[29]

The alternative interpretation is that far from being a new phenomenon, the twentieth-century anti-witchcraft movements were more likely to be the continuation of an older, precolonial tradition. This was argued with regard to Asante by Jack Goody, who in 1957 challenged the tendency to assume a causal connection between capitalism and colonialism on the one hand and the fear of witchcraft on the other.[30] Goody's critique of the orthodox view rested on two fundamental points: first, that the proliferation of witch-finding cults was not necessarily an indication of an escalation in the fear of witchcraft, as it may have been accompanied by a corresponding decrease in established ways of identifying witchcraft; and second, that there was little firm evidence that an increase in the resort to what he called "medicine shrines" from the northern savannas had in fact taken place. With regard to the first of these points, Goody simply noted in passing that the Akan funerary custom of "carrying the corpse" (i.e., *afunsua*), by which the movement of a corpse when borne aloft through the town was held to indicate the culprit in cases of suspected death by witchcraft, had fallen into disuse, "largely owing to the disapproval of the [British] Administration."[31] On the second point, Goody outlined a more detailed case. While acknowledging that the medicine shrines of the 1930s and 1940s were recent imports, he argued that the circulation of ritual powers between the savanna and forest was already well established in the precolonial period, drawing particular attention to the flourishing market in Asante for Muslim talismans, or *safi*. More generally, Goody raised a question mark over the whole notion that colonial conquest gave rise to a heightened sense of anomie, concluding that "the 'new witch-finding cults' provide an unsatisfactory index of an increase in individual anxieties in Ashanti."[32] Without knowing levels of witchcraft accusations before the watershed of colonial conquest and without any way to measure a society's "moral health," the alternative approach, with its emphasis on the modernity of inter-war eradication cults, remained an intriguing but essentially untested hypothesis.

The Akan Vocabulary of Witchcraft Belief

Before considering the historical record on witchcraft and anti-witchcraft in Asante and the Gold Coast, let us turn first to the vocabulary of Akan witchcraft belief.[33] The Twi word for "witchcraft" is *bayi;* a practitioner of *bayi* or a "witch" is an *obayifo* (pl. *abayifoo*).[34] An *obayifo* can be either a woman or a man, although the term is often used in the sources exclusively for the former as distinct from a male "wizard" or *obonsam*. The etymology of *bayi* is unclear, but a possible derivation is *oba* (child) + *yi* (to remove), the literal notion "to take away a child" underscoring the close association of witchcraft with issues of fertility, reproduction, and infant mortality.[35] As in many African societies, it was generally believed that *bayi* was effective only within the family or lineage (*abusua*)—in Geschiere's evocative phrase, it can be seen to represent the "dark side of kinship."[36] In matrilineal Akan culture, this was associated with the belief that a propensity toward *bayi* was inherited along with blood (*mogya*) through the female line. "'The right of killing, both visible and invisible killing [i.e., *bayi*], is on the mother's side,'" Field was told by one of her Akyem Kotoku informants. "'In the old days too the right of selling children into slavery was on the mother's side. So also in witchcraft the right of selling the children's *kra* is on the mother's. [T]he mother's *kra*, if angry, can take revenge and kill the children.'"[37] By the 1940s, however, this established belief appears to have been undergoing some revision. "It is not now generally believed," Field observed, "that witches can kill only members of their own *abusua*"— perhaps one manifestation of the broader renegotiation of kinship and gender relations under way in the colonial Gold Coast.[38]

Bayi could take two forms: *bayi boro*, "hot" or maleficent witchcraft, and, more rarely, *bayi papaa*, "cool" or beneficent witchcraft. *Bayi boro* was conceptualized as an evil power that lodged itself—sometimes by blood inheritance and sometimes not—inside its victim, who was transformed into an *obayifo*. Early European commentators (and, as we will see, later Christian converts) tended to equate this evil power with the devil, although at least one warned against the dangers of too loose a translation from indigenous concepts. Writing in the early 1850s, Brodie Cruickshank, a Cape Coast–based trader and one-time governor of the British settlements on the Gold Coast, noted of the Fante that

> we do not find that the opinion of a devil, or one great evil spirit, prevails among them. There are modes of expression in use which might lead us to entertain this idea; but it is found, on more minute investigation, that these are only translated forms of an expression suited to meet our European notions, such as "the devil tempted me," "to drive the devil out of town," and so forth, for which the literal Fantee terms express, "an evil spirit tempted me," "to drive all abomination and evil spirits away."[39]

The language of witchcraft practice also suggests that Evans-Pritchard's classic distinction between psychic "witchcraft" and physical "sorcery" can be sustained in the Akan case only with some qualification. In the early twentieth century, *bayi boro* often had nothing to do with sorcery, that is, the manipulation of physical objects, the casting of magical spells, or the use of evil medicine or "poison" (*aduto* or *aduru bone*).[40] Rather, it was seen as the projection from the mind of the *obayifo*—either consciously or unconsciously—of a maleficent psychic power that consumes, "eats" (*di*), or, in Ghanaian English, "chops" the victim. However, colonial documentation indicates that the concept often encompassed the use of both psychic power and physical objects.[41] The latter were particularly associated with Nzema in the extreme southwest of the Gold Coast, a region renowned for its potent charms and medicines.[42] In the 1940s, Field was struck by the "amazing collections" of physical objects handed over by penitents at anti-witchcraft shrines, from so-called *ogbaniba suman* employed to kill enemies to talismans (*asuman*) specially designed "to cause accidents with cutlasses, hoes, and motor-lorries, to 'suck away' others' money and enrich the *suman*-owner, to cause others' wives to leave them, and to make others unsuccessful in obtaining wives."[43]

Perhaps the best way to convey something of the popular perception of *bayi* is through the testimonies of *abayifoo* themselves. Colonial dossiers on Nana Tongo and other anti-witchcraft movements in the early twentieth century contain numerous detailed admissions of *bayi*, mostly by women who had been "caught" by the new shrines.[44] But let us turn to one discrete episode not specifically associated with an organized eradication movement and from a region relatively isolated from the main currents of economic and social change. Our evidence is from the village of Jenase, near Wiawso, the capital of the Akan state of Sefwi in the densely forested Western Province of the Gold Coast Colony. It dates from sometime between 1919 and the early 1920s, when District Commissioner W. Kilby conducted an inquiry into an apparent "outbreak" of witchcraft.[45] Twelve local women were accused of practicing *bayi*, four of whom admitted that they did in fact form a "company" (*fekuo*) of *abayifoo*, who gathered at night to kill and to eat their victims. "My mother bequeathed her witch to me when I was a girl," one of the women, Efua Gyenfua, explained. "Witches can distinguish one another; some carry their witch in their forehead and some in the back of their neck. My witch is a bird, perhaps a hawk. Ya Ejoe's witch is in her eye."[46] The matter-of-fact way in which the women spoke of the consumption of their victims was such that at first Kilby suspected that he had discovered a secret society practicing cannibalism similar to those rumored to exist in Sierra Leone and elsewhere. "There are plenty of witch companies all over the bush," said Effua Gyenfua. "In my company we always kill children." Children were easier victims, she explained, because unlike adults they did not use protective medicines.[47] They were hunted down, dismembered ("just like a butcher killing meat in the market"), cooked in a pot ("we add pepper and salt"), then eaten.[48] "It tastes like cow meat," said Yaa Ejoe. But after making further inquiries, Kilby realized that the language of consumption was purely metaphorical and that what was being eaten was the children's "souls" (either *kra* or *sunsum*). "My witch kills the children, I don't know how," testified Bua Kuwah, who was described as the *bayihene* or head of the company. "I catch their souls. When I go to sleep at night the witch goes away and kills the child." Crucially, all the women explained the death of their own children or of children within their *abusua* as being the result of existing "debts of flesh" between themselves and other companies. "I have conceived three times, [but] each time Bua Kuwah took the child to pay the debt," said Yaa Ejoe. "I killed my sister Ya Duah's child . . . four years ago. I seized her soul. We took some flesh to pay a debt and ate the rest." As Field pointed out, just as in the diurnal world senior family members had the authority to pledge (or "pawn") their juniors to secure a debt, so in the nocturnal realm of supernatural transactions those yet to be born could be earmarked to redeem a debt between *abayifoo*. According to Efua Gyenfua, "my grandmother pledged my aunt's womb to Kobina Fosuah for £4 of flesh. They sell the flesh to witches."

The assertion by these and many other women in the early colonial period that they belonged to highly organized *abayifoo fekuo*, "witch companies," is a striking feature of Akan perceptions of the supernatural that finds an echo in the witches' Sabbath of early modern Europe. Despite important differences, notably the role in much of Europe of a state apparatus willing to use torture to extract confessions, the widespread belief in the nocturnal activities of Akan witch companies—including those revealed by the admissions of *abayifoo* themselves—raises analytical problems similar to those faced by generations of historians of witchcraft in Europe.[49] A number of early, so-called "romantic" interpretations of European witchcraft argued that the belief in the witches' Sabbath was rooted in the reality of secret nocturnal assemblies, dedicated variously to pagan or diabolic worship, to protest against the established social order, or to the parody of the ecclesiastical hierarchy. Later scholars rejected this theory, arguing that confessions of collective pacts with the Devil and gruesome, cannibalistic rites were invariably extracted under torture and were more a reflection of the conspiratorial—and often highly sexualized—fantasies of male inquisitors. This debate has been advanced by Carlo Ginzburg, who has reconsidered "romantic" interpretations in order to develop a more textured reading of witchcraft narratives. In *The Night Battles*, Ginzburg argued that in the Italian province of Friuli in the late sixteenth and early seventeenth centuries, groups of people identified as witches were in fact members of an organized agrarian cult. Calling themselves *benandanti,* they claimed that their "spirits" traveled abroad at night combating witches in the defense of fertility.[50] Ginzburg's central argument is that belief in the witches' Sabbath in Europe was fashioned by a dialogue between two cultural currents: the anxieties of the agents of the early modern state on the one hand, and the accretions of folk culture on the other.[51] In short, even if the inversion of social reality was purely imaginary, many confessed witches appear to have believed that they did in fact fly about at night, copulate with demons, eat their victims, and all the rest.

While Ginzburg's analysis of the witches' Sabbath has in turn been subjected to vigorous critique, many of his insights can contribute to an understanding of African narratives of witchcraft and anti-witchcraft practices. If witchcraft in Africa operated as the "dark side of kinship," then there are some indications that the *abayifoo fekuo* of the Akan and their neighbors also consciously mirrored—or turned upside down—the political order. As Field wrote of *fekuo* amongst the Ga of the Accra region, "The company is organized like a chief's court and has a chief, an *otsame* [Twi: *okyeame:* spokesperson or "linguist"], an executioner [*obrafo*], a messenger, and so on."[52] As we will see, the history of the *benandanti* also has striking parallels to that of Akan anti-witchcraft cults, whose adepts sought to do battle with the perceived enemies of wealth and fertility but themselves suffered persecution at the hands of ruling orders deeply suspicious of their engagement with the supernatural. There are, of course, fundamental differences between the European witch craze of the fifteenth to seventeenth centuries and the apparent upsurge in witchcraft eradication measures in twentieth-century Africa. Most prominently, in contrast to the coercive role of the early modern European state, African "witch-hunts" were popular (if sometimes brutal) movements conducted in response to a state that refused to act against a perceived social evil. It must be stressed that there is no firm evidence either for early modern Europe or for colonial Africa that people actually did gather together to practice nocturnal rituals that could be interpreted in either context as "witchcraft."[53] Yet as Luise White stresses in her subtle analysis of the history of vampire rumors in colonial East and Central Africa, the widespread popular perception that this was the case must be taken seriously by historians.[54] Like the belief in blood-sucking lackeys of the colonial state—which White tentatively suggests developed from existing notions of witches—the idioms of witchcraft must be seen as metaphorical interrogations of social and political realities.

Bayi as Historical Process

The difficulty for the historian is to extrapolate the characteristics of *bayi* based largely on twentieth-century sources back into the precolonial past. As in early modern Europe, it is only when the fear of maleficent forces builds to such a point that it gives rise to organized eradication movements that details of witchcraft practice tend to emerge from the substrata of folklore and popular belief onto the retrievable historical record. There is no evidence for any such witch-finding movement on the Gold Coast or in the Akan forest before the second half of the nineteenth century. The first vague hints come in about 1855, when an association of towns on the eastern Gold Coast were reported to have hired a specialist "anti-witchcraft exorcist," an episode Debrunner regards as an innovation caused by the increasing interference of the inchoate British administration into "native customs."[55] In 1879–80, Domankama, the first recorded movement, enjoyed a brief efflorescence in Asante before being suppressed by the state. A second popular movement, Aberewa, erupted in metropolitan Asante in the opening years of British rule, although it can be shown to have been spreading into the northern reaches of the empire by the 1880s. Then from the 1920s onward we see wave after wave of eradication movements sweeping through colonial Asante and the Gold Coast. Was this apparent proliferation a response to a popular perception that *bayi* was on the increase or taking more menacing forms? Or was it, as posited by Goody, simply during the colonial period that an established pattern of anti-witchcraft practice began to appear in written sources? Having proscribed witch-finding (*yi abayi*, lit. the "taking out of witchcraft") by *afunsua* ("coffin carrying") in 1901 and by poison ordeal in 1906 and then outlawed Aberewa in 1908, colonial officials certainly paid a great deal of attention in the inter-war period to what many saw as a re-emergence under a new guise of these illegal customs and fetishes. The fragmentary, evasive nature of the sources for the precolonial period therefore stands in sharp contrast with the extensive dossiers on the various witch-finding cults compiled by alarmed British officials. Nonetheless, accounts from the early colonial period, such as those of the *abayifoo* of the village of Jenase, suggest that the idioms of witchcraft were strongly rooted in Akan thought. *Bayi* seems to have provided the standard, mundane explanation for "unnatural" disease and death, especially that of children. As McCaskie has argued, there can be little doubt that the precolonial Akan peoples inhabited a cognitive world "saturated with apprehensions respecting witchcraft" that ran "like a fever throughout the Asante historical experience."[56]

These apprehensions emerge most clearly from the precolonial sources with regard to the array of supernatural forces aimed at countering *bayi* and other acts of willful maleficence. The Akan acknowledged the existence of a supreme being (in Twi, *Onyame*), a hazy figure who, like the Talensi's Naawun, created the universe but subsequently withdrew from any direct discourse with mankind. Beneath the "withdrawn God" *Onyame* existed a world teeming with an extraordinary variety of spiritual beings, entities, and powers. These were perceived as belonging to two main cosmological categories, *abosom* and *asuman*.[57] *Abosom* (sing. *obosom*) may broadly be translated as "gods"—tutelary deities associated with bodies of water, the sky, and the forest that were seen to have originated before and to remain beyond human society. Like the *vodun* of the Aja-speaking peoples and the *orisa* of the Yoruba to the east, the *abosom* were capricious beings whose interventions into human affairs were unpredictable and potentially dangerous. Their most direct interventions were mediated by *akomfoo* (sing. *okomfo*, often rendered as "fetish priest"), individuals of either sex who were involuntarily "possessed" by particular *abosom* and through whom they spoke. In contrast, *asuman* (sing. *suman*) comprised a diverse range of powers that possessed less of an anthropomorphic "personality" and typically were manifested in the form of physical charms or amulets. As one Asante *okomfo*, Kwasi Broni, explained in 1946, *asuman* were more manageable and so could be utilized for specific purposes: "'Abosom' can give instructions for the making of a 'suman' which is [a] lower order of spirit beings operating through little 'jujus'. . . . 'Nsuman' are good or bad. 'Abosom' can be good and bad."[58] A third category of ritual power, *aduro* or "medicines," overlapped to some extent with *asuman* and ranged from herbal remedies to magical potions and charms.

Two key distinctions between these categories of spiritual forces have particular relevance for the Akan battle against witchcraft and the transformation of Tongnaab into Nana Tongo. First, unlike *abosom*, which tended to be associated with particular localities in the natural world, *asuman* were highly mobile and could be bought and sold. One famous example associated with the founding of the Asante state at the end of the seventeenth century was the *suman* Apafram, said to have been acquired by the first *asantehene* Osei Tutu in Akyem Abuakwa and carried to Kumasi inside the horn of a bongo antelope.[59] Second, *abosom*, although the "higher" of the two powers, were regarded as largely ineffectual against *bayi*. In the grim task of fighting fire with fire, the great tutelary gods were simply too lofty to enter the fray. Kwasi Broni's words on this point are revealing: "'Nsuman' . . . are very revengeful indeed. They borrow their power from

Figure 3.3. Healing and ritual practice in the Akan forest. A photograph taken during Governor Maxwell's tour of Asante and its savanna hinterland in 1897, captioned "Medicine Man [i.e., *odunsini* or *aduruyofo*] appealing to Fetish spirit on behalf of a woman with sick children at village on Pra River." Courtesy of the Foreign and Commonwealth Office Library, London.

lower, lower things which can act without reasoning properly."[60] The result was a pluralist ritual economy characterized by innovation, the commodification and mobility of *asuman* and *aduro*, and an attraction to exotic supernatural powers derived from nether regions beyond the carefully mediated realm of human culture.

The dramatic expansion of the Asante imperial system in the eighteenth century extended the scope of ritual commerce along with other forms of inter-regional trade. Given the utter dominance of Asante military power in the century before the catastrophic defeat at Katamanso on the eastern Gold Coast in 1826, it is notable that in this era of empire-building the one type of supernatural power most eagerly sought from subjugated peoples appears to have been "war medicines." These ranged from personalized *asuman* worn on the battle dress of warriors in order to divert the weapons of their enemies to royal access to the oracular insights of great *abosom*. These were all important elements in the special relationship between the Asante and the Ga, a non-Akan coastal people incorporated into the empire in the 1740s whom the former regarded as having exclusive access to a potent array of supernatural forces.[61] The Asante also drew on sacred sites within their orbit of power to the north. Two oracle shrines, both located on the forest-savanna borderlands of the Akan world, were especially famous: Dente, on the Volta River at Krakye, and Kukuro (in Bron-Twi, lit. "Lift it up"), at Nkyeraa in the Bron state of Wenkyi. Dente, whose wide renown was reported by Bowdich as early as 1817, was one of the many "sons" of the ancient Guan god Bruku—whose own ritual network, focused on the shrine at nearby Siare, would expand dramatically in the early twentieth century.[62] Oral traditions also stated that the *asantehene* would send his *nsumankwahene*, the head of the "court physicians," to consult Kukuro before any campaign.[63] It is significant that during the reign of Osei Kwame (1777–98), the growing numbers of Muslims in Kumasi were placed under the control of the office of *nsumankwahene*, the holder of which would remain a key link between the *asantehene* and the savanna countries.[64] The pioneering Ga historian Reverend Carl Reindorf recorded that in preparation for his fateful campaign against Accra in 1826, Asantehene Osei Yaw Akoto consulted, in turn, the greatest of all Asante *obosom*, Tano; Kumasi's leading Muslim diviner, Kramo Koko; and finally the oracle at Dente.[65] Half a century later, before the Anglo-Asante war of 1873–74, Asantehene Kofi Kakari reportedly sent *nsumankwafoo* emissaries first to Dagbon and then to the distant "Bariba" kingdom (i.e., Borgu) in the far north of present-day Benin in a desperate attempt to secure supplies of a potent war medicine.[66]

As Goody correctly observed, the thriving trade in Muslim talismans was a well-documented part of the Asante relationship with the northern savannas.[67] "If Muslim charms came down from Dagomba . . . at the beginning of the nineteenth century," Goody postulates, "then there seems little doubt that [anti-witchcraft] medicine shrines came as well."[68] No firm evidence exists to support this contention. It is of course possible that the Asante had already begun to show an interest in the exotic ritual resources of their *nnonkofoo* slaves in the eighteenth and nineteenth centuries. But if this were the case, then any resulting "medicine shrines" before the rise of Domankama in the late 1870s were likely to have remained as private *asuman* protecting against *bayi* rather than organized public cults seeking to eradicate it. Two points can be made in support of this argument. First, there is every indication that the judicial response to *abayifoo* on the part of Akan rulers was harsh and uncompromising. "Those accused of witchcraft, or having a devil, are tortured to death," Bowdich observed of Asante in 1817, stressing that those unfortunate enough to be inhabited by the "wandering evil spirit" were "immediately to be destroyed for the safety of mankind."[69] In the coastal states, too, capital punishment was the norm, Cruickshank citing one case near the Fante town of Anomabu where a man identified by *afunsua* was "unanimously pronounced a wizard" and drowned.[70] The emphasis, in other words, was on retribution and physical elimination rather than healing. Second, precolonial Akan rulers were reluctant to allow the influence of established "state" *obosom* to be challenged by popular cult movements mobilizing new and exotic ritual power. As we will see with Domankama, this was most evident in Asante. Just as the authorities in Kumasi monitored carefully the religious influence of Islam and from the 1840s refused the advances of Christian missions from the Gold Coast, so too were indigenous ritual accretions carefully incorporated into existing structures of power. This was stated emphatically in 1923 by the *omanhene* of Agona, Kwadwo Apaw, who evoked the genesis of the Asante state in order to explain his official approval for the new Hwemeso witch-finding cult: "After the conquering of Ntim the King of Denkira, Osei Tutu the king of Ashanti . . . elected Komfo Anokye, who prepared the war miracles against Ntim, and placed him at the head of all the Fetishes in Ashanti; consequent of which no other Fetish was introduced into Ashanti without the consent and approval of Komfo Anokye."[71] As McCaskie argues, "The uncontrolled, unmediated or teeming emanations of heterodoxy only came to play any significant part in Asante life *after* the collapse of the state."[72]

Anti-witchcraft Movements in Asante and the Gold Coast, 1870s–1920s

The ritual passage of Tongnaab to the Akan forest and its transformation into Nana Tongo was not an isolated phenomenon. It was part of a trajectory of heterodox religious cults devoted to the eradication of *bayi* that can be traced back to the emergence of Domankama in Asante in the late 1870s. Anti-witchcraft movements proliferated in Asante and the Gold Coast in the first decades of twentieth century, as the coming of colonial rule brought new problems and anxieties while serving to open up the ritual resources of the savannas of the Northern Territories. Drawing on an increasingly wider range of powers from outside the accepted realm of human culture, these movements were protean, polymorphous, and unstable. They also sought to create "instant utopias," cleansing communities of evil thoughts and deeds before uniting them under the watchful eye of exotic *asuman*.

Domankama, 1879–1880

The earliest recorded anti-witchcraft movement in the Akan region is Domankama ("The Creator"), which arose in 1879 in Asante during the troubled reign of Asantehene Mensa Bonsu (1874–83).[73] There is no trace of any similar movement before this and there are indications that Domankama was something quite new in Asante approaches to the problem of *bayi*. Little is known about either its origins or its ritual dynamics, but it is clear from the fugitive sources carefully assembled and analyzed by McCaskie that Domankama shared much in common with subsequent witch-finding cults in the colonial period.[74] It was founded in the village of Adwumakaase Wadie by one Okomfo Kwaku and appears to have spread rapidly, attracting hundreds and perhaps thousands of adherents. Like twentieth-century movements, Domankama developed a three-pronged approach to the eradication of witchcraft, first identifying those who were practicing *bayi boro*, then curing them of the affliction, and finally incorporating the cleansed ex-witches into its ranks.

In 1922, Rattray met a surviving adept of Domankama named Yaw Adawua, who four decades after the destruction of the movement by the Asante state was still renowned as a "famous witch-finder."[75] According to Yaw Adawua, in the "olden times"—and by this he may have meant either before the British conquest of 1896 or before the rise of Domankama—suspected witches were subjected to trial by the *odom* poison ordeal and if found guilty were immediately executed by strangulation.[76] Self-confessed witches were driven from village to village—a punishment which, if not resulting in physical death, represented the social death of permanent expulsion from human civilization. But Yaw's skill, and that of his fellow Domankama adepts, lay not in punishing but in assuaging *bayi*. "He said he could cure people of being witches without having to kill them, provided that once he had treated them they did not resort again to their evil practices; if they did so, they would die."[77] How was this achieved? "Yao Adawua also stated that the *abosom* (gods) were never consulted for the discovery of *bayi* (witchcraft), because it was recognized that they would not tell, 'being afraid of *bayi* which was more powerful than they.'"[78] Domankama instead drew its ritual power from the *sasabonsam*, the ferocious, part-human monster of the deep forest itself seen to be in league with witches. "'Sasabonsam* is my master,'" Yaw revealed; "'he helps the nation, he is very tall, has long thin legs, long hair, very large red eyes, sits on an *odum* tree and his legs reach the ground.'"[79] Yaw Adawua's testimony is crucial in understanding the nature of Akan anti-witchcraft movements. The ritual resources deemed necessary to identify and heal the terrible power of witches were derived not from within the realm of human culture or from the established hierarchy of tutelary deities that defended it. Rather, they came from outside that realm—in Kwasi Broni's evocative words quoted above, from the "lower, lower things" of nature. Domankama, apparently the first such movement, looked to the forest that surrounded and constantly threatened the fragile social order. Its successors would draw on an increasingly exotic and other-worldly range of ritual powers that led ultimately to the cultural and ecological "other" of the northern savannas.

In its ambivalent embrace of the powers of the *sasabonsam*, Domankama therefore resembles the classic "cult of affliction" model of Bantu-speaking Africa: an attempt to remove misfortune (in this case, to heal witches) by venerating and attempting to manipulate the actual agent of that misfortune. This would have profound implications not only for the structural characteristics of the movement but for its unfolding history. Asante in the late 1870s provided fertile ground for Okomfo Kwaku and his ranks of *abonsamkomfoo*.[80] Military defeat at the hands of the British and the destoolment of Asantehene Kofi Kakari in 1874, the loss of the northern provinces, building political unrest, and the increasingly predatory actions of Mensa Bonsu himself all contributed to a climate of uncertainty and anxiety. It is impossible to know for sure whether this accumulation of troubles gave rise to a popular perception that *bayi* was on the increase. What sources do indicate, however, is that Domankama's campaign against witchcraft was shaped by its identification of Mensa Bonsu's regime itself as the source of Asante's woes. Domankama therefore sought to restore the damaged social fabric of Asante by returning to the certainties of the past. Okomfo Kwaku himself assumed the name of Komfo Onokye, the demiurgic figure who ritually mediated the founding of the kingdom, and created a mirror of the state with laws, courts, officials, and the rest. It was this dangerous parody of the state—and here the similarity with Field's description of the nocturnal "office holders" of the witches' company is suggestive—that led to its inevitable demise. As with the *benandanti* of Friuli, the perception that the movement was openly consorting with evil forces may also have facilitated its persecution. In the wake of an alleged assault on Asantehene Mensa Bonsu by cult members in 1880, official policy turned quickly from wary toleration to violent suppression. Large numbers of *abonsamkomfoo* were rounded up and executed and the cult ceased to exist.

Sakrabundi and Aberewa, 1889–1908

The second documented anti-witchcraft movement in the Akan region was
Sakrabundi. Sakrabundi first appears in the historical record in 1889 and
in the first decade of the twentieth century emerged in a new form called
Aberewa: in Twi, "The Old Woman."[81] Under that name it swept through
Asante in 1906, ten years after the great forest kingdom had been occupied
and incorporated into the Gold Coast and five years after the final act of
military resistance to British rule, the Yaa Asantewaa War. The political
context in which it flourished, therefore, was dramatically different from
that which framed the brief efflorescence of Domankama a quarter of a century before. Moreover, whereas Domankama appears to have been a home-
grown affair, drawing its ritual power from the deep forest and its ideological inspiration from the founding charter of the Asante state, Aberewa
was an exotic import. The first of a wave of savanna gods that by the 1920s
would include Tongnaab, it entered Asante from the north via the Abron
kingdom of Gyaman. This ritual trajectory is revealing. Strategically located
on the edge of the forest, Gyaman was the northernmost outpost of Akan
culture and statecraft. It was also a cultural crossroads, with an important
Mande-speaking Muslim population and a variety of Gur-speaking savanna
migrants such as the Kulango, Degha, and Nafana.

The role of the frontier Bron kingdoms as arenas of ritual experimen-
tation and conduits for northern gods emerges from R. A. Freeman's account of the 1889 British diplomatic mission to Gyaman. Some fifty miles
south of its capital, Bonduku, in the neighboring state of Takyiman, the
British envoys were invited to a spectacular nocturnal "fetish dance."[82] Unusually for the Akan region, the dance involved the use of large wooden,
Gur-style masks. The object of worship was a "great inland fetish," Sakrabundi, whose sphere of influence was said to include Gyaman, "Gurunsi,"
and "several of the countries lying to the north."[83] Freeman was informed
that Sakrabundi was a new addition to the religious repertoire of the region, having been introduced from the savanna in comparatively recent
times. The "great inland fetish" was again encountered by the French ad-
ministrator-ethnographer Maurice Delafosse in 1902.[84] Unlike Freeman,
Delafosse understood that what Sakrabundi ("Sakara-Bounou") did was to
offer protection against evil and misfortune. As in later movements, individual protection together with the social harmony of the god's entire congregation was secured by the ingestion of a specially prepared sacramen-
tal liquid. Not only would this initiation rite identify witches and cure them
of their affliction, it thereafter bound all adherents—on pain of death at

the hands of the deity—to abide by a corpus of moral laws, most prominently a strict prohibition on the practice of witchcraft or sorcery. Herein lay a central tension that ultimately would bring Sakrabundi, Aberewa, and subsequent cults into conflict with both local African rulers and the colonial state. That is, deaths were often attributed to the watchful god, with the deceased identified either as an *obayifo* or someone who otherwise had contravened the laws of the cult. To suspicious outside observers, however, the "sacred water" was believed to be a poison targeted at preordained victims. Thus Delafosse regarded Sakrabundi as nothing more than a murderous extortion racket, responsible for the poisoning of large numbers of people who refused to join its ranks.

There is every indication that Sakrabundi drew strong inspiration from the anti-witchcraft "power associations" of Mande- and Gur-speaking peoples, traveling into Gyaman via the trade routes connecting Bonduku with Buna to the north and Kong to the northwest.[85] Yet a fundamental ideological adaptability meant that witch-cleansing gods tended to mutate over time and space, acquiring new accretions to their ritual personality as they traversed cultural and political boundaries. As would also be the case with Tongnaab, the spread of new shrines from region to region was characterized by deliberate disguise, rumor, and conflicting narratives of origin. The further they traveled, the more elaborated rumors of provenance often became. Indeed, such gods were often deliberately marketed from an intermediary shrine center as being from some ill-defined, exotic nether region. This was certainly the case with Sakrabundi and Aberewa, whose initial "take-off" beyond Gyaman was championed by one man, Osei Kwaku, a resident of Wirekye near Bonduku in what by the turn of the century was French Côte d'Ivoire. After a sustained attack on his family by *bayi* that resulted in a series of calamitous deaths, he was said to have traveled to Dagarti country in search of ritual protection, returning with the two exotic gods. Osei Kwaku therefore emerges as the first in a long line of enterprising individuals responsible for the dissemination of new anti-witchcraft movements in the colonial Gold Coast. Like the ill-fated Okomfo Kwaku in 1879–80, he appears to have possessed a certain degree of charismatic leadership in his ability to attract supplicants to new healing shrines. Yet the protean nature of the resulting cults tended to limit such figures to being vectors rather than the conscious "founders" of new religious movements. They are perhaps best described not as "prophetic" figures but as "ritual entrepreneurs."

Aberewa itself first appeared in the Asante heartland at Edweso, one of the centers of the anti-colonial uprising of 1900. It was acquired by the

British-appointed *omanhene* Yaw Awua in an apparent attempt to bolster his ritual armory in the face of widespread popular hostility. From there it spread with great rapidity throughout much of Asante and the Gold Coast. Its origin as an exotic Sarem power was indicated by the prominent use in its rituals of the kola nut (a commodity actually harvested from the Akan forest but popularly associated with savanna culture), the wearing of northern smocks by its officiating priests, and—in what may be a faint echo of Islamic influence—the designation of Friday as its sacred day. In terms of both geographical reach and numbers of adherents, then, Aberewa operated on a far larger scale than its precolonial predecessor, in some areas attracting what can only be described as a mass following. In the Gold Coast Colony state of Akuapem—also, it should be noted, an early stronghold of Christianity—the *omanhene* estimated in 1913 that "almost half of the heathen population . . . have partaken of the notorious drug or medicine."[86]

British officials were at first not inclined to regard Aberewa as a threat to colonial control. On the contrary, the chief commissioner of Ashanti, F. C. Fuller, was suitably impressed with the movement's injunctions against criminality and bad behavior—in particular the rule that adherents should obey the government. Following an inquiry in 1907 prompted by alarmist reports from the Basel Mission of subversive new "heathenish" customs, Fuller concluded that "Aberewa worship will work for law and order," citing the "metamorphosis it has caused in the Ejisu [Edweso] Country— formerly a hotbed of intrigue between people and chiefs and now a peaceful and united community."[87] Missionary warnings were dismissed as a cynical attempt to "counteract the proselytizing success of the 'Abirewa' propaganda" in the face of their own striking lack of success.

The following year, however, British opinion shifted, as leading chiefs in Asante and the Colony began to express unease at the increasing autonomy of the movement. Much was made of the practice of mutilating the corpses of those individuals believed to have been killed by Aberewa for practicing *bayi* or breaking one of the god's other injunctions. Officials were also concerned about the large amount of money that was draining across the colonial frontier to Osei Kwaku's shrine headquarters in French Gyaman. On 6 August 1908, Fuller announced the prohibition of the movement to a large gathering in Kumasi. In an extraordinary address he openly taunted the Asantes for being duped by northern peoples who were once their subjects and slaves, repeating rumors that the Gyamans "clap their hands and say 'By these tricks of Fetishes we are getting back from Ashanti all the moneys and tributes they took from us in the old days.' "[88] Fuller highlighted the role of one Yaw Nokwobo, an "ex-Grunshi slave in Ashanti and Chief Emissary from the High Priest," who was himself present: "I have here now, behind me, one of the leading men in this Religion. He happens to be, or used to be, an Ashanti slave. Now he is becoming a very big man. He has got a lot of money out of it, and hopes to get more. What does a slave like better than to turn on his former master?"[89]

Speaking only a few months after the abolition of the legal status of slavery in Asante, Fuller clearly sought to touch a raw nerve with his audience. He may have done even more than that, as his taunts inadvertently went to the very heart of the ambivalent relationship in Akan thought between savanna culture and ritual power. The most pronounced official fear, however—and it was one that would recur throughout the ensuing history of anti-witchcraft movements in the colonial Gold Coast—was that Aberewa represented an alien and therefore illegitimate religious form that was fundamentally subversive of "traditional" tribal authority. "The Ashantis have always had gods of their own; they have always worshipped their ancestors," Fuller insisted. "What have your ancestors done that you should stop worshipping them?"[90] Or, as a report on a suspected resurgence of Aberewa stated four years later, "The real danger that I see in them—I speak of the extra-tribal as distinct from the tribal or ancestral fetish—is their tendency to set aside tribal authority. Their service exacts a freemasonry that is . . . subversive of good order."[91] Like Domankama three decades before, Aberewa had incurred the hostility of an authoritarian state that was suspicious of its engagement with the supernatural and fearful of its ability to mobilize followers outside of established structures of belief. Throughout the second half of 1908, the paired shrines that had been popping up like mushrooms on the eastern and western outskirts of villages were systematically demolished by the colonial police. Although the cult continued in secret for a short time, by 1910 it had virtually disappeared as a large-scale, public phenomenon.

Hwemeso, 1919–1923

Following an almost ten-year lull, a fresh wave of witch-finding broke over much of the Gold Coast and Asante between 1919 and 1923. The new healing movement was called Hwemeso, "Watch Over Me."[92] In the light of the illegality of Aberewa, there was much debate within the colonial administration, as well as within African society, as to whether Hwemeso was a new phenomenon or a resurgence of the former under a different name. Certainly, the techniques for identifying and healing abayifoo were broadly similar to those employed by Aberewa. In terms of the trajectory of ritual movement, however, there was one key difference: Hwemeso entered the Akan heartland not from the north but from Appolonia in Nzema coun-

Figure 3.4. Witch-finding and healing ceremony at a Hwemeso shrine in
a village on the shores of Lake Bosomtwe in Asante, photographed c. 1922
by R. S. Rattray. Pitt Rivers Museum, University of Oxford 1998.312.566.1;
published as figure 26 of *Religion and Art in Ashanti*, facing 34.

try, at its own southeastern extremity. Hwemeso's distinctive origin means
that it does not fit the historical pattern that saw the ritual frontier moving steadily northward from forest to savanna, although it should be repeated that within the Akan world the Nzema were especially renowned
for their intimacy with the supernatural realm. It was this reputation that
was traded on by the one man, Kwabena Nzema from Appolonia, who
was almost single-handedly responsible for the initial dissemination of
Hwemeso. Over the course of three years of vigorous traveling salesman-
ship, Kwabena Nzema ranged widely through the Akan forest states, charging wealthy individuals, syndicates of operators, and entire farming communities anything between £50 and £400 for user rights to Hwemeso.
This most extraordinary of ritual entrepreneurs amassed a sizeable fortune
before he was apprehended by colonial officials and Hwemeso was proscribed at the end of 1922.[93]

Figure 3.5. Police pose with the confiscated contents of a Hwemeso shrine at Kwanyako in the Winneba District of the Gold Coast Colony, 1922. Photograph enclosed in file NAG ADM 11/1/1243, Hwemisu Fetish.

Yet it would be a mistake to view the spectacular if short-lived popularity of Aberewa, Hwemeso, and subsequent movements as due primarily to successful marketing. The increasingly detailed documentary evidence for the inter-war period suggests that the recurring waves of anti-witchcraft cults were created by a complex dialogue between supply and demand. "The Blackman knows his medicine," stated the powerful *omanhene* of Akyem Kotoku, Ata Fua. "I heard that someone ["Kobina Nsimaah"] was making a medicine, and that it was preventing witchcraft. Infant mortality has been very high: a woman might have one child, or two, and no more. Before I left to help the Government against Prempeh [i.e., the British expedition of 1896], I had more than 100 children—then I had another 100—but all are dead except 50."[94]

Whether this demand for exotic ritual resources was actually rising or simply becoming better documented is the key question. Two points emerge from the archival record on Hwemeso. The first concerns the timing of the movement. If *bayi* can be interpreted as an idiom with which wider concerns about the well-being of society are expressed, then social anxiety was obviously greatly heightened by the sudden breakdown of that well-being. Such a breakdown occurred during the influenza pandemic of 1918–19, an event that for many could be explained only by maleficent forces. Chief Kojo Amuakwa of the village of Agona Duakwa in the Swedru district of the Colony wrote in 1922 how he had applied to purchase Hwemeso three years earlier in a desperate attempt to counter the alarming death rates amongst his people. "The deceaseds [*sic*] had to suffer an illness of about two to three days the longest, both young and old. The nature of their sufferings and death signifies that it was bad and poisonous medicine that some people have brought to the town to injure people." "Truly speaking," he continued, "ever since we got this fetish into the town here, all these evil actions and practices of witchcrafts have ceased and we were enjoying a happy time."[95] Soaring death rates intersected with existing tensions within families, leading to the sort of confessions that would become so familiar in the 1930s. "I killed my sister, during the Influenza Epidemic," admitted a woman named Ampofuah from Akyem Oda who had been "cured" by Hwemeso. "I killed her by witchcraft. I liked her but she wronged me."[96] The years 1918–19 also witnessed the sudden expansion of two savanna healing cults, Kunde and Senyakupo, that would reach their florescence as contemporaries of Nana Tongo in the 1930s. As was the case with the emergence of the Aladura churches amongst the Yoruba, the influenza outbreak seems to have been a key catalyst in the search for new ritual solutions amongst the Akan.

The second point concerns the interaction between Christianity and indigenous systems of belief. Christianity had had only a very limited impact in Asante and in much of the rural Gold Coast Colony at the time of Aberewa and there is little evidence that it had any significant influence on the movement. Ten years later, however, the three leading missions—the Wesleyan Methodists, the Presbyterians (who had taken over the Basel Mission church during the First World War), and the Roman Catholics-were well established.[97] Congregations were growing and the Akan region stood on the cusp of large-scale conversions. Indeed, the well-informed Basel Mission pastor N. V. Asare had identified the public "fall" of Aberewa in Kumasi as a key breakthrough in the evangelical project.[98] Church authorities were alarmed by the sudden appearance of Hwemeso, which they regarded as a "dangerous new fetish" that in some congregations began to tempt the newly converted back into the arms of heathenism.[99] There are hints in some of the testimonies of Hwemeso followers—whether or not these individuals were "backsliders" is unclear—that Christianity had begun to have some impact on perceptions of witchcraft and the notion of evil. The most obvious indication is the increasing reference to the concept of the Devil in explanations of maleficent forces. "I am a witch," admitted one Yaw Krah, a cocoa farmer from Anyiman. "I took this medicine [Hwemeso] to get rid of this devil in me. I killed . . . my own sister."[100] Kojo Annan, described as "one of the medicine men at the rites," recited a song sung at his Hwemeso shrine: "I have brought my god with me; the medicine which I use, Edua Yaa; The Devil has dealt very bitterly with me."[101] In line with Cruickshank's warning from Cape Coast as early as the 1850s, too much can perhaps be read into these fragments. Such testimonies exist only in English translation, and it is quite possible that by "the Devil" the speakers were referring in the vernacular to a purely indigenous conception of witchcraft. Yet they are suggestive of the beginnings of a process of "diabolization," by which the missionary identification of African belief as essentially satanic was appropriated by both local Christians and "traditionalists" in a variety of ways that served to underscore the threat of evil forces.[102] Indeed, the impact of Christian idioms on indigenous thought was addressed explicitly in an intervention by the well-known Cape Coast lawyer and proto-nationalist politician Kwabena Sekyi. In 1922, Sekyi was hired by Omanhene Ata Fua as part of a campaign to prevent the colonial proscription of Hwemeso in Akyem Kotoku. The spread of Hwemeso, Sekyi argued, was fueled by two main factors: the discrediting of "old forms of worship" by the "irresponsible diffusion of badly-digested Christian tenets," and "the impossibility of obtaining in the British Courts decisions against, and punishment for, the more serious offences [of witchcraft]."[103]

Kwabena Sekyi was not the only public figure in the Gold Coast concerned about "badly-digested Christian tenets." British officials expressed similar worries regarding the wave of mass conversions associated with the crusade of the prophet Sampson Opong through the Eastern Province of Ashanti in 1920. At the same time that Kwabena Nzema was championing the efficacy of Hwemeso, Opong's success in attracting thousands of converts to the Wesleyan church provides evidence that the flow of religious ideas concerning the nature of *bayi* was far from one-directional. Indeed, the latter's crusade had much in common with the ecstatic embrace of indigenous cults. It is notable that Opong—like Yaw Nokwobo, Aberewa's man in Kumasi—was a "Gurunsi" ex-slave trained as an *asumanni* (a "master of the *asuman*" or "magician").[104] Following a revelatory experience while working in the cocoa belt during the First World War, he abandoned his *asuman* and, like other peripatetic preachers of the period, "asked a carpenter to make me a cross and a tailor to make me a long, white prophet's robe of the kind the people of the Bible times wore. . . . Everywhere I went, I told people to burn their fetishes and give up magic, witchcraft and everything evil."[105] Like other heterodox witch-finders, Opong soon found himself in conflict with established hierarchies of power. "The headmen became restless," he recalled. "My preaching undermined their power, which was based on heathen religion."[106] After serving a short prison sentence and being blocked from preaching by hostile chiefs in the Western Province of Ashanti, in 1920 Opong approached Wesleyan missionaries and began his crusade on their behalf to the east of Kumasi. The emergence of "something in the nature of a 'mass movement' towards Christianity" was greeted with mixed feelings by officials.[107] "Such a movement had attendant dangers," the annual report on Ashanti warned. "Possibly set native habits of morality and the valuable and . . . inspired elements in native religion will be cast aside in an excess of momentary enthusiasm."[108] Like Aberewa and Hwemeso, Opong's prophetic crusade was indeed a "momentary enthusiasm." But it is important to stress that from the 1920s, the spectrum of innovative ritual responses to the threat of *bayi* ranged from exotic savanna deities through to growing numbers of itinerant Christian preachers and indigenous prophetic churches.[109]

The Spread of Savanna Cults, 1900s–1920s

As was the case with Aberewa, the colonial campaign to stamp out Hwemeso met with considerable success. Shrines remained active in some rural areas into 1923, particularly in Akyem Kotoku, where the movement was especially widespread and had the support of Omanhene Ata Fua. But by the end of the year it was in rapid decline and British concern with new witch-finding "fetishes" would not be reawakened until Nana Tongo burst onto the scene in 1930. Yet the efflorescence of Hwemeso in the years following the First World War coincided with the accelerating spread of a whole wave of anti-witchcraft movements in Asante and the Gold Coast Colony drawing their ritual power from the north. Some of these gods enjoyed only brief or geographically circumscribed popularity, attracting adherents for a few years and then falling into decline. Many *asuman* collected on intrepid journeys to the Northern Territories and installed at local shrines probably never emerged onto the documentary record at all, quietly serving single communities or even individual households before being absorbed into local cosmologies. The ritual trajectory of others remains difficult to reconstruct, often fragmented by the bewildering variety of names and manifestations adopted in order to appeal to local constituencies or to avoid persecution by the authorities. Yet four gods originating at shrines in the northern savanna—Kunde, Senyakupo, Tigare, and Nana Tongo—developed from the 1920s along the lines of Aberewa and Hwemeso into major anti-witchcraft movements. Others, such as Kankamea and Asasi, developed important ritual networks of a lesser order of magnitude, while the established fame of the Bruku shrine at Siare also expanded dramatically. Of these deities, it is notable that only one, Asasi—from Kontrobo in the Ivory Coast—originated from beyond the Northern Territories of the Gold Coast. The rest were all identified with sites of sacred power located on the very extremities of the Protectorate, often just a few miles inside the border. McLeod observed that by the early 1960s, new anti-witchcraft powers were being sought from as far afield as Ouagadougou in Upper Volta and Gao in Mali.[110] But in the inter-war period, the coincidence of the ritual frontier and the colonial frontier is quite unmistakable. Indeed, it lends the entire phenomenon of pilgrimage and anti-witchcraft in the Gold Coast a striking "proto-national" character. It is almost as if the ritual potency associated in indigenous cosmological thought with liminal frontier zones had been mapped onto the arbitrary boundaries created just a few decades before by colonial conquest.

Let us briefly consider the origins and early diffusion of the movements that in the 1930s would emerge as Nana Tongo's principal competitors in the thriving ritual marketplace. Perhaps the first to embark on its passage south was Kunde. Kunde (also known as Kune or Brakune) originated from a Wala shrine devoted to the local High God, Kyaale, at Kandiau, southwest of Wa on the border with present-day Burkina Faso. The current Kandiau *tengdaana* told us that the shrine was already famous and attracted supplicants from Asante and elsewhere before the coming of British rule.[111] One of these pilgrims was Jabah Kojo, who sometime in the middle or late nineteenth century established a branch on the edge of the forest near the Bron trading center of Nkoranza.[112] This new "Kunde" shrine (a name derived from "Kandiau") was soon patronized by the ruling house of Nkoranza and its reputation began to travel down the old imperial road to metropolitan Asante and on to the Gold Coast Colony. As early as 1905, a delegation from one (unnamed) Gold Coast town deemed to be "full of witches" was dispatched to Nkoranza to obtain an "offspring" of the great "'Barakune' or 'Witchkiller' (Okum abayifoo)."[113] "I hate every evil man who hates his neighbour," the deity was reported to have informed the delegation through its *okomfo*. "When therefore I come to town, everybody must love his neighbour. If anybody hates his neighbour and seeks to injure him [i.e., by *bayi*], I will not let him live, but I will kill him. And

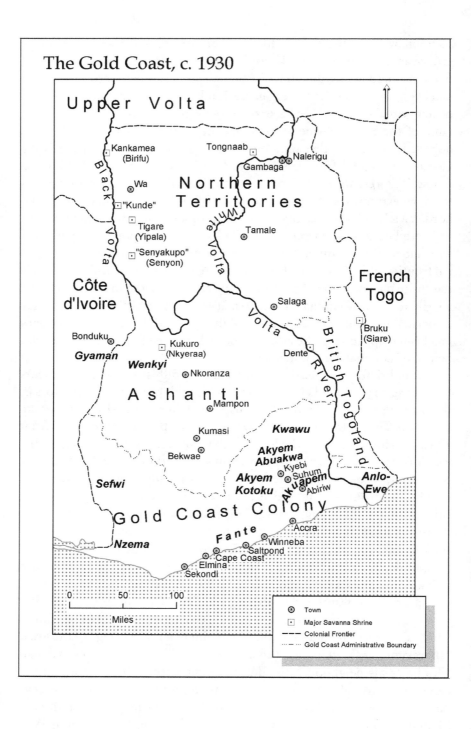

The Gold Coast, c. 1930

Upper Volta

Kankamea
(Birifu)

Tongnaab

Gambaga
Nalerigu

Wa

Northern
Territories

"Kunde"

Tigare
(Yipala)

Tamale

"Senyakupo"
(Senyon)

Côte
d'Ivoire

Salaga

French
Togo

Bonduku

Gyaman

Kukuro
(Nkyeraa)

Dente

Bruku
(Siare)

Wenkyi

Nkoranza

Ashanti

Mampon

Kumasi

Kwawu

Akyem
Abuakwa

Bekwae

Kyebi
Suhum
Abiriw

Akyem
Kotoku

Anlo-
Ewe

Sefwi

Gold Coast Colony

Fante

Accra

Nzema

Winneba
Saltpond
Cape Coast
Elmina
Sekondi

| 0 | 50 | 100 |

Miles

⊚	Town
▫	Major Savanna Shrine
———	Colonial Frontier
⋯⋯⋯	Gold Coast Administrative Boundary

I am very serious and unrelenting about this."[114] By the First World War, Kunde was sweeping through the heart of the cocoa-growing region in the southeastern Gold Coast state of Akyem Abuakwa, where the years following the suppression of Aberewa had seen a number of short-lived experiments with substitute anti-witchcraft powers. Sharing colonial officials' suspicion of exotic "foreign" deities, the influential *omanhene* Ofori Atta ruled in 1916 that his subjects were prohibited from conducting pilgrimages to the north "for the purposes of partaking of any fetish of that objectionable character."[115]

Ofori Atta's attempt to stamp out Kunde in Akyem Abuakwa was defeated by the god's protean nature. Whether authorized by local African authority or not, pilgrims continued to travel north and to establish their own shrines. Others purchased the *asuman* from itinerant ritual entrepreneurs, described with some accuracy as "a class of person not unlike the relic-mongering friar of the XV and early XVI centuries" who "imitate the rites of the local deity or carry with them either amulets or 'hosts' believed to possess some of its potency."[116] By 1925, Kunde in a variety of localized manifestations—such as Alafia (Hausa: "health"), Goro (Hausa: "kola"), or Breketey—had begun to cross the Volta river into the Ewe region.[117] As they were in Kunde's contemporaries, these prodigious forms were in some cases purchased from neighboring regions. In other cases they were acquired from Nkoranza or directly from the original Wala shrine at Kandiau, to which officiating *akomfoo* were required to return once a year to renew the efficacy of their "offspring."[118]

The movement of Kunde's principal contemporaries to about 1930 followed a similar pattern. Senyakupo took its name from the powerful Kupo shrine at Senyon near Bole, the westernmost site of a network of earth and medicine shrines stretching across the expanses of Gonja to Dente and Bruku in the east.[119] Lying near the "great road" north from Kumasi to Gonja, Senyon was well within the orbit of precolonial Asante power. Like Kandiau, it too attracted Asante supplicants in the nineteenth century and was said to have been brought south by the Banda "during one of their Gonja slave raids."[120] In about 1916, a "Senyakupo" shrine was established at Twenedurase in Kwawu, which by the late 1920s had become a major witch-healing center with subsidiary shrines in other Kwawu towns. From Twenedurase, Senyakupo spread widely through the forest zone before following Kunde east along the coast and across the Volta.[121]

Kwawu was also a crucial conduit in the southward dispersal of Tigare, which originated at a shrine at Yipala on the main route between Bole and Wa. Few references to Tigare crop up in the documentary record before

1930, although Field reckons that it had appeared in northwestern Asante by the First World War.[122] In 1931, an Asante chief, the *omanhene* of Ahafo, wrote that one of his subjects had returned from the Northern Territories with Tigare, "the advantage of which is just the same as that of Fitish 'Kukuro' at Nchira [Nkyeraa]"; that is, the "superiority of healing diseases of all kind . . . couple[d] with excellent powers of catching witchcrafts [*sic*] and persons who try to endanger human life with obnoxious medicines."[123] Six years later, one Kwasi Fofie established a Tigare shrine at Nkwantanang, which by the 1940s had surpassed that at Twendurase as Kwawu's leading witch-healing center.[124] Tigare's dispersal continued into the 1950s, by which time it had subsumed its rivals and extended its influence as far as southwestern Nigeria, where it emerged in a manifestation known to the Yoruba as Atinga.[125]

A fourth major *asuman* to follow the path of the old Asante road from the northwest of the Northern Territories was Kankamea. It was associated in the south with the Dagara (or "Lobi") settlement of Birifu, just inside the Ivorian frontier, and like Tigare reached its efflorescence in the late colonial period. Importantly, the Birifu *naaba* informed Debrunner in the 1950s that his father had obtained Kankamea (from *kpankpanbia:* lit. "I cannot live with evil men") from a Nabdam man who had in turn had acquired it in French Upper Volta. It was, Debrunner observed, merely the most prominent of the two-hundred-odd shrines in his compound. Kankamea's movements remind us that the search for exotic ritual powers was not just a southern phenomenon. The god's relocation to Birifu resulted in an extraordinary accumulation of wealth by the enterprising *naaba*, who owned an automobile and in 1953 attended the coronation of Queen Elizabeth II in London.[126]

Unlike the four relative newcomers, Nana Tongo, Senyakupo, Kunde, and Tigare, Bruku (variously Buruku, Burukung, or Brukum) did not attract the opprobrium of the colonial regime by suddenly exploding into a new and potentially subversive movement in the Akan forests during the inter-war period. Yet colonial mobility did enable the great oracle located atop the Siare mountains on the frontier of the British and French sectors of mandated Togoland to enlarge dramatically its long-established ritual network. A key source for Bruku is the redoubtable E. F. Tamakloe, the Ewe clerk, interpreter, and author of *A Brief History of the Dagbamba People* (1931), who first visited the shrine in 1899 when escorting a German expedition through the region. Tamakloe's 1926 account of the history of Bruku indicates that in its role as a focus of long-distance pilgrimage, the god functioned in a strikingly similar way to Tongnaab: "This 'god' has become [more] famous than all other 'gods' and is known all over the world for indescribable and wonderful powers of healing, making barren women to become mothers of children, determine the dispute of witchcraft, and saving people from all other troubles."[127] By the mid-1920s, Siare was reported to be visited by pilgrims from the Colony, Ashanti, the Northern Territories, Dahomey, and as far away as Senegambia, and to be equipped with translators "for all the principal tongues of West Africa."[128] As in the Tong Hills, the myriad transformations wrought by colonialism were both fueling the need and providing the means for a dramatic redrawing of regional ritual networks and identities.

Conclusions

The central point of this narrative outline of anti-witchcraft movements in the Akan world from Domankama in the late 1870s to the wave of cults animated by savanna gods in the 1920s is the ambivalent nature of ritual power. This ambivalence is apparent at a variety of levels. It can be seen to characterize Akan perceptions of their own tutelary deities, the great *abosom*, whose capricious, unpredictable interventions into human affairs could either offer protection or inflict punishment. It also lay at the heart of the historical relationship between the Akan forest kingdoms and the peoples of the savanna grasslands to the north. On the one hand, the "Gurunsi," "Frafra," and other *nnonkofoo* were generally regarded as primitive barbarians, who as slaves or subsequently as migrant wage laborers were fit only to perform the most menial of tasks. On the other hand, these uncivilized aliens possessed the esoteric knowledge to access a range of deities that could combat *bayi*, the greatest single threat to the civilized order. The ambiguity of ethnic "otherness" therefore intersected with a further ambivalence, that of the historical battle against witchcraft. As we have seen with Domankama, Aberewa, and Hwemeso, with Kunde and the other savanna gods, and as we will see in more detail with Nana Tongo, the eradication of *bayi* necessitated the embrace of ritual forces from outside the carefully constructed realm of human culture. This resulted not only in the obvious spiritual hazards, but also in the threat of persecution from ruling elites suspicious of heterodox cultic movements and their engagement with exotic powers. The ambivalence of ritual power therefore goes some way to explaining the uneasy relationship between the "new cults" on the one hand and the colonial state and its indigenous allies on the other. It also provides the context for the extraordinary scene Rattray and Aboya witnessed on the morning of 6 May 1928, when prosperous Asante pilgrims stripped down to their underclothes and entered the inner sanctum of Tongnaab's Yanii shrine.

As for the impact of colonial conquest on perceptions of *bayi*, the paucity of evidence for the nineteenth century means that any attempt to gauge the relative "modernity" of witchcraft and anti-witchcraft must be tentative and impressionistic. But there is every indication that anxieties created by rising tensions within kinship and gender relations, by the opportunities and inequalities opened up by the cash-based cocoa economy, by the individualism engendered by capitalism and Christianity, and by the outlawing of established methods of dealing with witches were increasingly being expressed in the idiom of *bayi*. At the same time, the imposition of colonial order on the recently "pacified" frontiers of the Northern Territories together with the increase in mobility facilitated a dramatic expansion in ritual dialogue between the forest and sites of sacred power in the savanna grasslands. Tongnaab's journey across that ecological and cultural divide is the focus of the next chapter.

4

From Savanna to Forest:
Nana Tongo and Ritual Commerce
in the World of Cash and Cocoa

Persons who have consulted the Fetish are satisfied that they
received value for their money.[1]

*A*s we have seen, a significant expansion in Tongnaab's rit-
ual field was well under way by the time of R. S. Rattray's visit in 1928. Building upon the established mobility of the great *bo'a* in its savanna heartland,
ritual intermediaries like Tengol began to grant to favored southern pilgrims the right to transport Tongnaab's *yihiyii* or "shadow" to the distant
south. The first to carry Tongnaab into the forest was a man named Kobina
Assifu.[2] Rather than having to make the arduous and expensive journey
north each time they needed to consult Tongnaab, southern acolytes like
Assifu instead founded "satellite" shrines in their home areas. "Not everyone was able to visit Northern Ghana," Debrunner wrote in 1959, "and
therefore the tendency arose to set up shrines of these tutelary spirits in
the south as well, in order to have 'a child' of Tongo . . . in one's own town
for constant consultation."[3] As the fame of Nana Tongo spread, Assifu and
others emerged as renowned ritual mediators (*akomfoo*, or "priests") in their
own right, paying yearly fees to their Talensi interlocutors in order to renew
the license for their shrines. In a pattern which was typical of the expansion of African religious systems across regional frontiers, the new shrines
took on a life of their own in the dramatically different cultural landscape
of the Akan forests.

Although continuing to offer the full range of services available in the
Tong Hills, Nana Tongo in the south became, like so many other savanna
gods, a specialized healing or "medicine" cult used to combat the threat of

maleficent witchcraft (*bayi*). By 1930, it had emerged as one of the most prominent of a whole constellation of anti-witchcraft movements that were consciously marketed—very like the rising numbers of Christian denominations—as potent new "exotic" ritual imports. In this chapter, we explore the rise of Nana Tongo as part and parcel of this dramatic efflorescence of organized witchcraft eradication. Expanding physical mobility in the inter-war period not only brought Talensi workers to the cocoa farms, the mines, and the trading towns of the south, but also enabled Akan, Ga, and Ewe peoples of southern Ghana who might never have traveled north of Kintampo to draw upon the powers of the distant savanna shrine. They did so in order to reinforce their spiritual armory in the face of a growing range of problems expressed in the established idioms of *bayi*. The resulting movement had a profound impact on the lived experience of many people throughout Asante and the Gold Coast. Hitherto obscured by the ultimate triumph of Christianity in narratives of religious change, Tongnaab's dramatic cross-cultural expansion is absolutely central, we argue, to the social history of twentieth-century Ghana.

Kobina Assifu's First Journey to Tongnaab, 1925

Some three years before Rattray and Aboya visited Tongnaab in 1928, Kobina Assifu made the first of what would be many pilgrimages to the Tong Hills. In July 1930, Assifu described his pioneering journey in a letter written to the ruler of Akyem Abuakwa, Okyenhene Nana Sir Ofori Atta, in whose kingdom Assifu had established his famous Nana Tongo shrine.[4] Aside from a few brief quotations included by Field in her discussion of the anti-witchcraft movements, Assifu's letter is the only detailed first-person account of a ritual journey from the Gold Coast or Asante north to a distant savanna shrine yet to emerge from the documentary record. Unlike Rattray's narrative, it contains no details of ritual practice or what Assifu encountered in the caves at the summit of the Tong Hills. What it does describe, however, is something of the motivation that lay behind his decision to embark on an arduous journey in search of spiritual help and of the process by which he came to establish his own anti-witchcraft business. It serves to highlight the key role played by individual agency in brokering the expanding cultural flows between savanna and forest.

"I have the honour to inform you or state to you the reason of getting this Fitish [*sic*] by name Nana," Assifu began.

> My reason was, before I . . . got this medicine, anything that I do it will never ends well. I have been to ditch four times by lorry. It was only about five years and six

months since I heard that there is some fitish at Frafra and whenever you approach it, it will tell you everything that is following you. Through this, I have my journey to the abovementioned station of which when I approached the fitish it reported to me that there is nothing that troubles but it is only Devil or Witchcraft. Before I will be leaving to Frafra for this Fitish, I was having little medicine that anybody who is sick I can cure him or her, but when there is witchcraft on the sick person, then the man or the woman will never be alive, through this I have to go to Frafra just to get medicine to clear away witchcraft on the sick person when I am on sick person curing. From Suhum to the place where the Fitish is, is mile 482 that is Tongo in the Northern Territories.[5]

Assifu, then, had both personal and professional reasons for undertaking his journey. He feared that the string of four truck accidents was the result of more than simply bad luck—a fact subsequently confirmed by Tongnaab's diagnosis of "Devil or Witchcraft." Assifu clearly knew something of the workings of witches. As he indicates, he was already a practicing herbalist (*odunsini*), although he believed he was ill-equipped to deal with serious cases of *bayi boro*. This is confirmed by information on Assifu's life and career provided by his descendants.

By all accounts, Assifu took an active interest in *abosonsem* ("religious" matters) from an early age. His grandfather, a Ga man who hailed from the Accra township of Osu, had settled in Abiriw in the Akan kingdom of Akuapem, where he married a Guan woman and raised his children. Assifu's father was one of the early pioneers, immortalized in Polly Hill's 1963 study, *The Migrant Cocoa Farmers of Southern Ghana*, who, from the 1890s, left Abiriw and other towns on the Akuapem ridge and moved into the forests of Akyem Abuakwa to establish cocoa farms.[6] Assifu himself was born around 1881 and began studying *aduro* (medicine) and *bayi* around the age of eighteen, possibly in the Fante kingdom of Oguaa (Cape Coast).[7] In 1925, the *omanhene* of Akuapem, Okuapenhene Kwasi Akuffo, officially certified and approved Assifu as a "native doctor" in the district. In his certification letter, Kwasi Akuffo noted that Assifu had been practicing "native medicine" in Abiriw since 1920.[8] Eventually, Assifu settled outside the trading town of Suhum on land his father had first acquired for cocoa farming sometime around the turn of the century. There, in the forest state of Akyem Abuakwa, in a small village known as Obretema a few miles from Suhum and just off the main road north from Accra, Assifu built extensively upon his father's cocoa interests in the area.[9] At the very same time he was acquiring his reputation as a successful cocoa farmer at Obretema, he was becoming known as a powerful *obosomfo* or "fetishman."[10]

Assifu, in fact, became a consummate collector of ritual power, a tireless religious entrepreneur who traversed ethnic, regional, and colonial

Figure 4.1. Kobina Assifu, c. 1930s. Photograph courtesy of his family.

frontiers in order to acquire a wide repertory of *asuman* and *abosom*. According to his son Paul Assifu, the current guardian of the Nana Tongo shrine at Obretema, his first acquisition was Kentenkren, which he obtained at nearby Agona Saban.[11] He then traveled north to the forest-savanna fringe at Kpandu and collected Adane. Next, as a result of the journey Assifu himself dates to around 1925, he acquired Nana Tongo. This is corroborated by testimony given in 1930 by Kobina Owusu, who operated a branch of Assifu's shrine at the coastal town of Winneba and stated that Nana Tongo was installed at Obretema by 1926.[12] Assifu subsequently added two more gods from the Northern Territories to his expanding armory: Yawtwere and Brukum, the latter from the great shrine at Siare on the eastern frontiers of Gonja. Finally, Paul Assifu said, he journeyed east into French territory and brought back Bobroto from Dahomey (present-day Benin). Each of these *abosom* had its ritual specializations. Brukum, for example, was especially associated with the fertility of the land and of women, while Bobroto, "the executioner," would rid you of your enemies.

In his letter of 1930, Assifu went on to describe how at Tengzug he was entrusted with the "shadow" of Tongnaab: "Before you will be given this medicine . . . you kill a fowl, and [if] . . . the fowl turn towards up . . . you will be given [the "medicine," but . . .] if you are witchcraft [i.e., an *obayifo*], whenever you kill this fowl it will never turn up but rather down"—the ritual technique used in the south by Nana Tongo and most of the other movements to detect *abayifoo*. "After this, I was given the medicine [and] . . . I was instructed by the man in charge to report to my Omanhene whenever I come. I did this by reporting to late Omanhene Nana Kwasi Akuffo at Akropong."[13] In these details of how he obtained the shadow of Tongnaab, Assifu's descriptions very much echo Talensi accounts of the process. In his letter to Ofori Atta, Assifu described why people from the south would turn to Nana Tongo for protection—the god's extraordinary ability to detect and to heal *abayifoo* on the one hand and to protect against their fearsome powers on the other. His emphasis was very much on *bayi boro* as a threat to health and to fertility, both of women and of the land. Barrenness, infant mortality, sickness, sudden death, the failure of cocoa farms, loss of money: "all these due to witchcraft." As at the shrines of Aberewa, Hwemeso, Kunde, Senyakupo, and the rest, the eradication of the social evil of *bayi* was dependent on a set of rules to which the acolytes were bound:

> These are the things the Fitish do not like. 1. You are not to steal. 2. You are not to follow somebody's wife. 3. You are not to talk lies. 4. You are not to poison some-

body. 5. You do not extort. . . . Its rules [are] this. Fitish is not kept at home but rather in the bush, and before you go where this fitish is, you are not to go with cloth, whether man or woman, but only underwear because where this fetish come from they do not use cloth. These are the rules and instructions of the fitish. It is called Nana Tongo. These were consented to by the whole of Akuapim.[14]

Margaret Field encountered Kobina Assifu at the height of his powers in the early 1930s. He was, she wrote, "perhaps the greatest witch-doctor-medicine-man in the Gold Coast . . . a man of fine intelligence, deeply versed in the theory of witchcraft, widely experienced in all its manifestations, willing with a veritable scientific detachment to discuss his 'cases' frankly and expound them clearly."[15] Paul Assifu recently made a similar claim, hyperbolic perhaps, but reflective of the challenge the new cults presented to long-established hierarchies of ritual power: "there was only one other *okomfo* in the whole of Ghana who was more powerful than my father and that *okomfo* was Okomfo Anokye."[16]

Tongnaab in the South

Kobina Assifu may have been the first southerner to bring Nana Tongo into the forests, but he was quickly joined by others, and became *primus inter pares* in an expansive anti-witchcraft movement mediated by southern pilgrims to the Tong Hills. Talensi accounts of how those pilgrims acquired Nana Tongo are very similar both to the story Assifu told Ofori Atta in 1930 and to the recollections of more recent pilgrims whom we have interviewed. "The way Tongnaab works," explained Tengdaan Dok,

> is that if the person is a regular customer here and has been coming here all the time and believes in it and his problems have always been solved, then we can make him a *tengdaana* in charge of Tongnaab and give him part of the god to make his own shrine. So people nearby can go to him and he can help people solve their problems.[17]

On some occasions, individuals who accompanied Assifu to the Tong Hills on one of his many pilgrimages brought Tongnaab down with them to their respective villages. Such was the case of Atta Kojo of the Akyem town of Kukurantumi who, in turn, trained several *akomfoo* in the ways of Nana Tongo, including his niece, Okomfo Aframea. Today, Aframea's portrait adorns the outside wall of her daughter's *abosonnan* (*abosom* room) in Kukurantumi.[18] Her granddaughter, Okomfo Sika, succeeded her as *okomfo*. Indeed, by 1930, the *Gold Coast Times* began to speak of the proliferation of Nana Tongo shrines as an "industry":

Following on the flourishing establishing at Suhum, Winneba has also opened a factory at Esuekyir, the local high priest being one Acken. We shall not be surprised to hear that other States have followed suit, each with its own factory, especially as the charges are said to be competitive.[19]

And so the web of ritual commerce expanded, through and across families of pilgrims, beginning with Kobina Assifu.

Other pilgrims, particularly Gas, Dangmes, and Ewes from outside the Akan axis on the eastern reaches of the Gold Coast, appear to have learned of Nana Tongo subsequent to, and independently of, Assifu.[20] Korkor Nartey from Prampram, who was born around 1912, received Nana Tongo from her father, Abraham Akron Nartey, who, she says, brought it down on his own.[21] Many of these pilgrims were already tending other *abosom* and describe being instructed by one of them to go and collect Nana Tongo. Although these recollections are from more recent times, they probably capture a process not unlike the one Assifu himself experienced. Okomfo Yaa Sekyibiaa of Hemang recalled, "I was frying fish and Mami Wata came and collected me and told me to come to Nana to get even more help. I was a fish fryer who got taken by Mami Wata." Yaa had traveled to the Tong Hills with Adwoa Ankoma and her brother in 1999. The latter said they had learned of Nana Tongo from Tano. "We got the power from River Tano and River Tano in turn directed us to come here to collect the shadow of Tongnaab. We were then sent back to be working there. So, now I want to help people, especially women."[22] In these stories, the acquisition of Nana Tongo is neatly woven into narratives of local *abosom* who turn to the savanna in order to augment their arsenal of ritual powers. As we saw in chapter 3, even the greatest of all Asante *abosom*, including Tano, felt the need to call on Nana Tongo for assistance because they were too far removed from the mundane world to work effectively against *bayi*. As Atta Kojo's grandson recently explained, the local *obosom* in Kukurantumi was called "Nana Buo." Nana Buo or Naabuo was "the chief here and actually paved the way for [Nana Tongo] to come down and then the two worked hand in hand."[23]

Because the activities of Assifu and other *akomfoo* and *abosomfoo* devoted to Nana Tongo gained the rapt attention of colonial authorities, we are fortunate to have several contemporary accounts which document how, in practice, Nana Tongo operated in the ritual landscape of the south. The "Statement of Amah Botchway" is particularly rich in detail and warrants quotation at some length:

> [F]ive months ago . . . Tetteh Quaye felt sick. The father Quaye Akpanga and mother Fofo said they have been to a fetish man and they were told that there is a

Figure 4.2. Okomfo Sika (on right) of Kukurantumi standing before a portrait of her grandmother Okomfo Aframea in 2000. Sika had a local painter reproduce a photograph of Aframea on the side of her compound.

witchcraft in the house we live and so all the families in the house will be taken to Asifu. . . . Kofi Elotey . . . called all the families and sworn oath that the following day . . . we shall go to Asifu to make "Aka" that is to know the party who is causing the death of Tetteh Quaye. All the families replied the oath that they will go with him. I didn't reply the oath. On Saturday . . . we were 21 in all. 11 women and 10 men left for Asifu. . . . Asifu asked us the matter on which we came to him and Kofi Elotey replied that we are all families and some of them are suspected to be witchcraft and so we have come to him to know the real witchcraft. Kofi Klotey and Annan gave Asifu one bottle gin, he opened it and drank it. Tuesday in the morning we all were taken to the Fetish place by Asifu. When we were about to reach the place where the fetish is preserved, Asifu ordered every one to loose cover cloth, beads and headkerchiefs. I loosed mine and became naked and we all bought native drawers from the village, 1/- each. I wore the native drawer and every one wore the same. When we started going to the fetish, Asifu said every one should walk backward and so we all walked backwards. When we reached the fetish place, he asked us to kneel down and we all knelt down before the fetish. He showed us some place to sit near the fetish and we sat down. He called us one by one and every one that he calls you should kneel before the fetish and tell all you know to the fetish. He said if you are before the Fetish and he cuts fowl and the fowl lies with face upwards then you are not a witchcraft, but if the fowl lies face downwards then you are a witchcraft. He called me and I knelt before the fetish. He cut 6 fowls all face downwards he told me I am a witchcraft. I agreed although I am not a witchcraft but all my fowls finished thus why I agreed. Asifu ordered that the people must hoot at me and all hooted at me. One of Asifu's subjects name unknown chewed kola and poured at my face and head. My head was shaved and barbered at the same time with knife. He charged me £3 10/- and 14/- for the 6 fowls. The whole money including one native drawers comes to £4 5/- and I paid. We were 21 persons went to the Fetish and 6 women including myself were found witchcraft. The said Tetteh Quaye is still lying sick and the families said I must cure him but if he die I shall be held responsible.[24]

In Amah Botchway's account we see described numerous practices which were fairly consistent among Nana Tongo shrines in the south. Generally, people were brought before or came to the shrine because of *bayi*— either to gain protection from it, to prove they were not possessed of it, or to accuse someone else of possession. They usually presented gin, kola, and a fowl to the priest or his or her aides and were charged an entrance or basic consulting fee of a few shillings to as much as £5. People were not allowed to approach Nana Tongo in clothes and, in Amah's case, were made to purchase special "native shorts" to appear before the god. In all cases, a fowl or fowls were sacrificed to Nana Tongo in order to ascertain whether *bayi* was present or not. If the fowl landed with its back upward, then Nana Tongo had refused to eat the fowl. For those accused of witchcraft, as in Amah's case, the individual was considered guilty and could be fined up to

£25.[25] For those merely seeking Nana Tongo's protection, "the rejected suppliant," as Field wrote, "publicly confesses a few sins and tries again. He repeats this till his gift is accepted. He then drinks the 'medicine.'" If, however, the fowl landed with its chest up, this indicated that Nana Tongo had "eaten" the fowl. The person was deemed not to be a witch and could immediately drink the special medicine to protect him- or herself from *bayi*. As Field wrote of her similar experiences with Senyakupo, the medicine "may consist of either real water, ceremonially treated by the priest, a herbal bath, the eating of a kola-nut, or being marked on the face with spots of white clay. He is then secure against witchcraft, bad medicine, theft, and adulterous intrigue for the rest of his life."[26] The special medicine connected to Nana Tongo was probably produced by Assifu at Obretema, the center of the movement in the south, and then distributed from there. As the district commissioner at Winneba reported in 1930, Nana Tongo had been in the area for some time, but had been "quite innocuous" until "it acquired witch-finding proclivities, this evidently encouraged by the purchase of 3 bottles of Tongo Fetish medicine bought from Suhum at the rate of £5 a bottle."[27]

Extensive detail on the practices associated with Nana Tongo was gathered in 1930 by a police constable who went undercover to Assifu's shrine at Obretema and reported that the "rules of the 'fetish'" were as follows:

1. If you have been accused of Witchcraft and brought before the 'Fetish' and found guilty of being a Witchcraft, then you have . . . violated the 'Fetish' rules. You are liable to a fine of £15 to £25, one life sheep, one dog, three fowls, seven eggs, and six bottles gin.
2. If you are brought to drink the 'Fetish' for protection £5, one bottle gin, and one fowl.
3. If you are brought before the 'Fetish' to ask your fortune, £1.7, one bottle gin and three fowls.
4. If you have already . . . drank the "Fetish" and were consequently brought before the 'Fetish' for violation of any of its rules, a fine not exceeding £20, one life sheep and two bottles gin.[28]

Rules such as these were fairly consistent among the different shrines, though prices varied and, as the *Gold Coast Times* reported, could be extremely competitive. For example, in the late 1920s there appear to have been several Nana Tongo shrines in the immediate vicinity of Suhum which vied with Assifu's vigorous trade at Obretema. Ohene Kwaku, the *odikro* (village head) of Suhum, claimed in a 1928 letter to Okyenhene Ofori Atta that he "went to Sahara Desert, in a town call Tongo," and "there bought the medicine."[29] In 1929, Kwame Amponsah set up a competing Nana Tongo shrine at Suhum Tetekasum and his all-inclusive price, which covered removing *bayi* from an individual and protecting that person from witchcraft in the future, was only twelve shillings, one fowl, and one kola— far less than Assifu charged a few miles down the road.[30]

Although fees might differ, there were important discursive constants among the shrines in the south, just as there were overriding continuities in practice. *Bayi* or witchcraft—depending upon the language being utilized— was absolutely central to every mention of Nana Tongo, whether oral or documentary. But encompassed by and expressed through *bayi* were numerous contemporary social concerns that were specific to the historical place and moment. First and foremost among these was cocoa. As we have seen, Assifu himself was a renowned cocoa farmer whose father was one of the pioneers who in the 1890s began to migrate from the Akuapem ridge down into the forests of Akyem Abuakwa.[31] Cocoa, therefore, was frequently mentioned in descriptions of Nana Tongo's powers. In his 1930 letter to Ofori Atta, Assifu explained, "Somebody may trouble himself of farming this cocoa farm when this cocoa farm is full grown it will never be alright, all these due to witchcraft; and whenever he drink this medicine and he takes some to the said cocoa farm it will never happen again, it will proof success until the end." Money was another discursive constant. Again, as Assifu explained, "If somebody who is having money and he do not know whatever he does with his money and loses them, whenever he drinks this medicine it will never happen again."[32] The third constant, protection against theft, was integrally connected to cocoa and money. These hallmarks of the new capitalist economy had brought a range of new commodities to successful farmers and traders, and with them, agonizing fears of theft. "Nobody can steal your things and be free unless [they] return them back," Kwame Amponsah explained of Nana Tongo's powers, as "the medicine will catch the party until he brings same."[33] These concerns animated the procurement of Nana Tongo by the people of the Fante town of Agona, whose chief notified the administration that they had "imported . . . a medicine by the name of 'Tongor Medicine' from Fra Fra in the Northern Territories, for the purpose of protecting the Town . . . from being destroyed by Witch Crafts, Robbers and other Evil Spirits, that generally interfere with the prosperity of a Town or village."[34] At £150, "Tongor" did not come cheap, but the entire community had chipped in and everyone seems to have been very happy with the results.

From North to South:
Continuity, Transformation, and Mimicry

With the dramatic expansion of the export economy and its attendant anxieties in Asante and the Gold Coast, Nana Tongo's reputation was directly linked throughout the forest country to cocoa, the securing of cash, and the ability to identify and cure witches. Such concerns differed dramatically from those connected to Tongnaab's reputation in the Tong Hills. For the Talensi, Tongnaab lay at the heart of a complex ritual system that included overlapping rites for ancestors and for the earth. Its connection to the fertility of land and of women was of paramount importance. In some ways, that specialization was retained in the ritual passage south. Nana Tongo, like Tongnaab, was considered to be extremely effective at helping women bring forth: "Barren women," wrote Chief Yaw Koi of Krabo, "are released by this medicine."[35] Yet what is particularly striking when looking at north and south are the ritual discontinuities, or, better, the ritual transformations by which the Talensi *bo'ar* Tongnaab became Nana Tongo. Over fifty years ago, Field wrote of this process:

> in their old homes, newly exported deities are tribal gods with a long-established priesthood [whose] festivals are a tribal affair. . . . They know nothing of witchcraft. . . . But as soon as they are established in Akim they are supposed to be specially competent to deal with witchcraft, and they furthermore occupy a curious position between gods and medicines (*Abosum* and *adru*). In their old homes they act as gods, that is, as intelligent, reflecting beings who exercise both caprice and judgement and listen to prayer and reason. In the new shrines they act as gods only when they are accepting or rejecting new adherents, exercising in this both knowledge and judgement. On all other occasions they act as medicine and their responses to their adherents' actions are as automatic and inexorable as the action of a fire in burning the hand put into it.[36]

As we have already shown, the notion that Tongnaab was a discretely bounded "tribal god" which in its original savanna setting knew "nothing of witchcraft" is somewhat misplaced. But Field's description does capture the process by which a northern deity could traverse the porous categories of the cosmological spectrum at the same time as it moved physically from savanna to forest. Her location of savanna witch-finders in the "curious position" between *abosom* and *aduru* further suggests that they tended to be regarded by the Akan as *asuman*, ambivalent spiritual forces that combined the caprice and judgment of "gods" with the healing and protective powers of "medicine."

But ritual transformations from north to south could invert this process, as well. Shown the statement of the accused *obayifo* Ama Botchway by colonial officials and asked to provide some insight into the workings of Nana Tongo, E. R. Addow of Abetifi emphasized just that. "There are private and public protective medicines," Addow pointed out. "When a medicineman's charm becomes celebrated to be powerful against devils, people who are unhappy and think that devils are after them flock to him for protection and his charm becomes a thing of public worship."[37] One of the most dramatic manifestations of such a transformation is evidenced in the emergence of Nana Boachi, known as Nana Tongo's "son" in parts of the south. Many who acquired Nana Tongo, including Assifu, also acquired "Nana Boachi" or "Tongo Boakye" at some point.[38] Bosomfo Nii Yaw, from the Ga seaside town of Oshieyie, inherited his gods, including Nana Tongo and Nana Boachi, from his father, who brought them down in the 1930s. Nii Yaw is now over eighty years old. He has built a shrine to Nana Tongo in the forest several hundred feet away and across the road from his house, and one to Nana Boachi, which he says also came from Tongo, right next to the road. Okomfo Atta Fordwo, in the Akyem town of Kukurantumi, also inherited Nana Boachi from his grandfather, Atta Kojo, who, he says, was the first to bring Boachi south. "Nana Tongo . . . wanted to give him something powerful, so it could get rid of all the evil things in this town," he recently explained. "Boachi is the eldest son of Nana Tongo. . . . He is the supreme one. His interests are the same as Nana Tongo's. He does Nana's work for him. From him you can get children, find witches."[39]

Yet in the Tong Hills, no one recognizes "Boachi" as the name of a *bo'ar*. If you ask about Nana Tongo, people inevitably point to Tongnaab, but that is not the case with Nana Boachi. What is the explanation? As noted in chapter 1, the "shadow" of Nana Tongo was and is given to individuals either to carry with them for protection or to establish a satellite shrine. Often soil or another substance from around the sacred space is placed in a container—a leather pouch or an animal horn—and given to the supplicant. This is a process that is widely recognized. "The thing that was given to that person to take away," explains the *tengdaana* of Gundaat, "is called *bo'artyii*" (literally the "bo'ar in a bag").[40] But in the south, the term *bo'artyii* was "Akanized," transmuted into the familiar Akan name "Boachi" or "Boakye." Similarly, Sakrabundi, a name of probable Mande origin, became translated into Twi as *sakra bone*, "change the sin." And eventually, Nana Boachi developed a separate status as an independent *obosom* in the south. Such a transmutation makes little sense to those in the Tong Hills. As the Gundaat *tengdaana* recently protested, "They are one thing. You cannot call the thing that was given to the person to go away with—you can't call

Figure 4.3. Bosomfo Nii Yaw's Nana Tongo shrine at Oshieyie, 1999. The painted letters read "Nana Tongo Buatsi *kee* [Ga: commands] keep off your light if you are devil."

it a separate god. They are one."[41] In the ritual landscape of the south, a northern "talisman" (for the Akan, a *suman*, or for the Talensi, a *bo'artyii*) could become a full-fledged *obosom*. Alternatively, as in the case Field describes, a northern "god" or *bo'ar* could be transformed into a simple protective medicine, or *oduru*. Such was the fluid nature of ritual commerce between savanna and forest. As Field noted in 1940, "the nature and attributes of any deity are not inherent in it but change with changing worshippers—sometimes out of all recognition."[42]

Another dramatic change that marked Tongnaab's passage from north to south involved gender. In the Tong Hills, Talensi women were never allowed near Tongnaab. It was, as we were often told, for men only. If a Talensi woman encountered problems with fertility, for example, her husband could visit Tongnaab, but his wife was forbidden. The justification for this gender exclusivity is consistently explained in terms of "secrets." Talensi society is patrilocal, so the wives of a house or lineage (Talen: *yir*) come from outside. To bring them into the *bo'a* congregations would be to reveal to them the innermost secret knowledge of the lineage, to which they should never be privy. In the south, however, Tongnaab was extricated from its Tale moorings—from webs of kinship, from specific *bo'a* congregations, and from the earth shrine, Ngoo. It retained many secrets, but none were gender-specific. Thus, from early on, southern women not only directly sought protection from Nana Tongo but served as important *akomfoo*. One of the earliest examples was probably Adwoa Aframea of Kukurantumi, who was taught by her uncle Atta Kojo, one of the first to travel north with Assifu. Moreover, the majority of those accused of witchcraft or who confessed to witchcraft before these savanna gods were women. Tongnaab's journey from north to south, in other words, incorporated a fundamental shift in the gender dynamics of ritual practice.

It also witnessed the integration of the great *bo'ar* into ritual calendars or cycles very different from those which obtained in the Tong Hills. There, Tongnaab was a central part of the *Bo'araam* festival—the celebration in late October or early November accompanying the harvest of the year's crops. *Bo'a* congregations also assumed very specific roles in *Gologo*—the March/April celebration focused on the earth shrine, Ngoo, aimed at guaranteeing good rains and good crops in the forthcoming farming season. In the south, Nana Tongo was woven into very different local calendars. In the Akan states, notably in Akyem and Asante, Nana Tongo was directly incorporated into the *adae* festival calendar. The *adae* calendar has a forty-two-day cycle. *Adae Kesee*, the "big" *adae*, is celebrated on Sunday; *Wukudae*, the smaller, occurs twenty-four days later, on a Wednesday. During the ceremony, mashed yams, plantains, and rum are offered to the king's ancestors. For supplicants of Nana Tongo in the south, *Wukudae* became the god's special festival day. It was on *Wukudae* that mashed yams and drink were and are offered; it is the day that Nana Tongo is "fed."

But to highlight the ritual discontinuities between north and south, to foreground the transformations in ritual calendars and gender dynamics, or to probe the translatability of a concept like "*bo'artyii*" is not to suggest that Tongnaab and the various Talensi rituals associated with it lost all original content and meaning as they migrated into the southern ritual landscape. The process was far more complicated. There were, for example, significant performative continuities in how one approached Nana Tongo in the south and how Tongnaab was approached amidst the rocks of the Tong Hills. Often a few Talen words were incorporated into southern rituals. When the *okomfo* beckoned to Nana Tongo, it was common for southerners to clap their hands and to repeat the Talen word *taari* ("okay" or "I am listening") during the summons. The role of sacrifice (Talen: *kaab*)—so fundamental to Talensi belief—was also consistent, as was the ban on clothing for those entering the ritual space. Yet the process of transmigration was not simply about con-

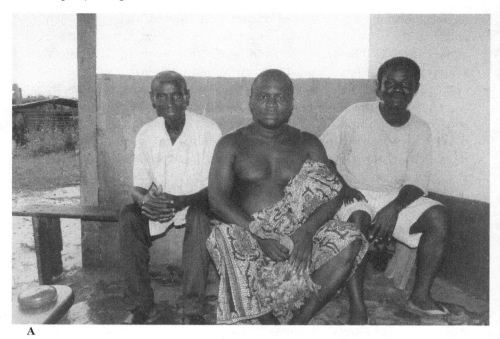

A

Figures 4.4A–4.4C. Atta Kojo of Kukurantumi (A) outside his shrine room,
wearing Akan-style cloth; (B) inside the shrine, wearing a Mossi smock and
summoning Nana Tongo; (C) possessed by Nana Tongo, with "northern" hat,
spear, and hoe.

tinuity or discontinuity, about what stayed the same and what changed.
What is most striking about movement, translation, and relocation are the
ways in which Tongnaab's exoticness or otherness remained integral to the
performance of its power in the forests of the south.

Nana Tongo was consistently surrounded by a mimetic collection of
"northern" objects which aimed to create an aura of savanna authenticity.
Margaret Field, one of the most astute observers of witch-finding activities in the Gold Coast, noted that "Practitioners who set up shrines in
Akim—whether shrines of [Senya] Kupo, Tongo, or any of the other Northern Territory gods—usually lay out a good deal of money on Northern Territory robes, spears, gong-gongs, talismans, and other trappings to impress
their customers."[43] Even though one was not supposed to approach Nana
Tongo in clothing, the attire of *akomfoo* could still be important as a signifier
of distant savanna origins. There is no discussion in our sources of Assifu's
attire in the 1930s, although present-day *akomfoo* like Kojo Fordwo of Kukurantumi signal their "possession" or "being caught" by Nana Tongo with

B

C

Figure 4.5. Bosomfo Nii Yaw wearing *batakari*, 2000.

the donning of a northern smock and hat.[44] Nii Yaa of Oshieyie recently told us that supplicants could not wear shirts before Nana Tongo, but "the *batakari* [the Mossi- and Gonja-style smock] can go there."[45] And, of course, the very absence of clothing when in the presence of Nana Tongo—a key signifier of the historical cultural divide within the savanna world—was central to most mimetic performances in the south.

That southern adherents of these savanna gods violated what many considered to be the boundary between the civilized and the uncivilized in their mimetic performances by removing their clothing or donning "northern" garb was a source of grave concern to many, especially southern Christians. Isaac Newman Boadu complained to Okyenhene Ofori Atta in 1935 about the activities of those involved with the Tigare cult: "We are sorry that true sons and daughters of Akim Abuakwa," he wrote, "have changed their custom, living and manner and language into Moshi."[46] The chief of Osina also complained to Ofori Atta about so-called "fetish practices" which had been imported from the north and established in his town. Not only were the southern adherents "bared nudely," but "during the course of the dance they will be employed as *kayakaya* [carriers] in different directions, some carrying water at the request of applicants for monetary reward and some too serving as menials after the fashion of the Northerners."[47] Here the Osina chief's remarks echoed both contemporary colonial discourses of the "civilized" vs. the "savage" and older Akan imaginings of the north and of northerners.

What are we to make of this ritual mimesis—of "south" performing "north?" Kramer, taking his argument a step further than Field, argued that savanna shrines lost all of their original meaning in the south. They became, in essence, southern shrines, "retaining nothing of their origins but their characteristic stamp and the ambience of the north."[48] Richard Werbner comes to a similar conclusion in his analysis of the cross-cultural diffusion of Tongnaab, positing that southern acolytes sought to blur the ideological boundaries between themselves and savanna strangers not only to "domesticate the exotic" but to "do away with their own resemblances." This semblance of equality, however, "was on the southerners' terms," and therefore constituted an "assertion of cultural dominance through the one-directional borrowing of exotic codes and ritual."[49]

But was it only "ambience" that was retained? Was the entire process of ritual movement so thoroughly manipulated by Akan acolytes of Nana Tongo? If it were simply the case that savanna "gods" moved south and there became part and parcel of the southern pantheon of titular deities, it would be easy to accept this characterization. But movement and migration were not unidirectional and were certainly not finite. Savanna and forest engaged in long-term commerce and dialogue through the language of the gods—of *abosom, asuman, bo'a,* and *bo'artyii*—and both were transformed, though in different ways, by the process. For us, the remarkable part of this story is not that savanna gods became forest gods, but that ordinary women and men, across the forest-savanna divide, used their own languages, as it were, to engage in a ritual conversation about the modern world.

This conversation did not end with the transplantation of a Talensi *bo'ar* to the heart of the forest and its concomitant transformation into an Akan *suman* or *obosom*. As in Tongnaab's established savanna heartland, pilgrims from the south were and are required to make yearly visits to the Tong Hills to "renew" the god.[50] Most do so during the annual *Bo'araam* festival, which these days can draw supplicants from throughout the sub-region of West Africa.[51] Of these "pilgrimages of thanksgiving," as Field described them, "after making money out of their shrines, they usually bring handsome gifts to the original priests."[52] Atta Fordwo returns to the Tong Hills every six months, after having "studied there for three good years." As an apprentice to the *tengdaana*s in the hills, Fordwo learned how to perform the rituals:

> So many go there to learn how to perform. It's like someone going to learn a trade. You have to go humbly, serve them, wash, work for your masters, and I did that and they were also open to me and taught me how to do everything. So the *batakari* and everything . . . inside [the shrine]—all of it came from up there. They gave it to me there.[53]

As important to ongoing ritual commerce as southern pilgrims returning north, however, were the annual visits by Talensi owners of Tongnaab to their clients in the south. Systemized visits to client areas had a long history in regions nearer the shrine, such as Builsa. As Anyaam from the Builsa town of Kadema recently explained, the "Tengzug people" come to him once a year, after the *Bo'araam* festival. "If we don't go there with the flour of the late millet," he explained, "they won't come here."[54] This process of reciprocation was extended to the far southern reaches of the country with the movement of Nana Tongo into the forests in the 1920s. At least once a year, often for *Wukudae,* men from the Tong Hills traveled to Asante, to Akyem Abuakwa, and on to the coastal towns of Accra, Sekondi-Takoradi, Winneba, Cape Coast, and elsewhere to visit the client villages that owed ritual allegiance to their *bo'ar.* "These ritual visits," Fortes wrote,

> are made in order to consecrate local shrines . . . , to release children born to them from special taboos, and to perform the ritual shaving of the children by which they

are formally placed under the spiritual guardianship of the *Bɔɣar*. But these services are paid for in cowries and other gifts, and portions of the animals sacrificed are taken home and added to the meat supply of the sponsors. Young men go along on these ritual tours carrying fowls for sale in the client villages, and sometimes buy grain or yams in return.[55]

One can only wonder if the "great export of fowls Southwards . . . chiefly by motor vehicles" noted in the 1928 Annual Report for Zuarungu had anything to do with these "ritual visits."[56] What is clear is that the movement of people, gods, and goods created a web of ritual commerce between forest and savanna that was consistently being renewed, rehearsed, and performed. In the context of this ongoing commerce, Nana Tongo could never become, *in toto*, an Akan or an Ewe deity, for its power was thoroughly grounded in its exotic—and deliberately exoticized—savanna identity. Nor could it remain simply a Talensi *bo'ar*—the "tribal god" of ethnographic discourse—once extricated from localized "dynamics of clanship." Transformation, mimicry, relocation, translation, performance—each of these words captures something of the dialogical processes that wove Tongnaab into the ritual landscape of the south. Together they were part and parcel of a multi-lingual, trans-regional, and cross-cultural conversation.

Spotlight on Obretema:
Nana Tongo and the Politics of Indirect Rule

Although Nana Tongo spread very quickly via a web of connections that extended from Tengzug through the Akan forest and on to the seaside towns of the Gold Coast, there is little disagreement regarding the primary, foundational role of Kobina Assifu. It was Assifu who brought Nana Tongo to the forests of Akyem Abuakwa and allowed the god to speak loudly and eloquently to the particular problems and concerns of people in the heart of cocoa country. And it was at Obretema that Assifu established one of the largest centers for ritual healing in the south, certainly the largest devoted to Nana Tongo. Although he assembled a whole pantheon of gods at Obretema, Nana Tongo was responsible for Assifu's growing Colony-wide reputation as one who could expertly detect, capture, and cure witches.[57] As Assifu's grandson recalled, it was

the activities of "Tongo" that made Assifu famous. During those days . . . there was the strong belief in witchcraft and, for that matter, if a member of any family got sick or [was] affected by any predicament, he/she would attribute [it] to the activities of witches. Members of the family were accused and a pronouncement of an oath was made which binds all the members of the family and compels all the family members to go to Assifu's Tongo shrine to prove their innocence. From among the family members, "Nana Tongo" will detect and arrest the witch or wizard who is responsible.[58]

Indeed, it was as a potent witch-finder that Nana Tongo burst into the colonial field of vision. Its activities first came to the notice of government officials in the Eastern and Central Provinces of the Gold Coast Colony at the end of the 1920s, when native tribunals began to refer cases involving *bayi* to Nana Tongo for judgment. The reemergence of witch-finding as an issue of concern for the colonial state appears to have been triggered in part by the 1927 Native Administration Ordinance, which rendered witchcraft a crime in the Colony. Under the new ordinance—which had been drafted and introduced into the Legislative Council by the influential Nana Ofori Atta of Akyem Abuakwa—witchcraft cases were to be tried before native tribunals.[59] Thus, from very early on, Nana Tongo was inextricably tied to the formalization and consolidation of indirect rule in the Colony. One of the first cases involving Nana Tongo to catch the attention of colonial officials did not directly involve Kobina Assifu, though many of the subsequent cases did. This early case occurred in the Akuapem town of Larteh in 1929 and involved a man named Atta Kwadjo who accused four of his relatives of witchcraft. The chief who initially heard the case, the local *benkumhene*, ordered the accused to go to the nearby Nana Tongo shrine at Aframsu, run by the Okomfo Yao Boadi—a ritual entrepreneur in his own right.[60] Boadi heard the case, consulted his oracle, and determined that the four accused women were guilty.[61] The results were reported to the *benkumhene* of Larteh and, in the end, the fees and fines amounted to over £100. The Birim district commissioner, Captain Warrington, was informed of the case, did some initial investigations, and placed Yao Boadi in custody. He then referred the matter to Ofori Atta, instructing him to hear the women's complaint. If the *okyenhene* wished to have Boadi arrested, Warrington agreed to retain the latter in custody.[62] In the end, the Akyem court did order Yaw Boadi to return the fees he had collected, but he was not imprisoned, nor was his shrine closed.[63]

By early 1930, it was clear to colonial authorities that the case at Larteh was not an isolated one. Tribunals throughout the Colony were increasingly sending litigants to several Nana Tongo shrines, but particularly to Assifu's healing center at Obretema. As the secretary for native affairs lamented, native tribunals had begun "almost to make a habit of sending [witchcraft] cases to Suhum for trial and decision."[64] Colony newspapers were soon running stories on Assifu's witch-finding activities. The *Gold Coast Times* reported in January that so wide has his fame spread that crowds of people, including those accused of witch-craft and desiring to establish their innocence as well as those seeking for their rel-atives relief from the spell of witches, have been resorting to the village of Suhum for his professional services; and some of the Native Tribunals have now been known to refer witchcraft cases to the oracle who is doing a lucrative business.[65]

A few months later, the same paper reported that the "smelling out of witches" was an "industry" that was expanding throughout the major towns of the Colony. "With the extension of this business all over the country," an editorialist wrote, "the question will arise as to the raw products to feed the factories; and we do not know how the supply will be kept up unless the people begin to indulge in a mutual accusation of witchcraft which may end in provoking riots and causing suicides to the extent that will impel the Government to put an effective check to this wretched business."[66] In a subsequent letter to the editor, one C. Kingsley William put the entire blame on the 1927 Native Administration Ordinance. The "truth" is, he argued, "that witchcraft is something that no man living can define, that witchcraft is, therefore, not the proper subject of a criminal investigation, that the retention of this clause in the Native Administration Ordinance will inevitably lead to a revival of terrorism; and that the words in the Na-tive Administration Ordinance 'the practice of witchcraft' should there-fore be deleted."[67]

As debate over the "Suhum Fetish" filled the pages of the Gold Coast press, concerns about Assifu's work were raised primarily by two groups: by missionaries and Christian converts who feared being victimized by the shrine, and by colonial officials worried about the impact of a new witch-finding movement on the consolidation of indirect rule and the jurisdic-tion of native courts. In March 1930, Harry Webster, the general super-intendent for the Wesleyan Methodist Missionary Society, wrote to the secretary for native affairs to express his concern about the "Suhum Fetish." Branches of the fetish, he wrote, "have been established in some of the vil-lages [of the Apam District, on the coast near Winneba] and to these are being daily charged poor people who cannot help themselves, among whom are some of our own church members."[68] On the very same day, Joseph Strebler, the acting head of the Catholic Mission, wrote to the Colonial Secretary to report

the unjust and revolting dealings of a certain fetish priest, who is enjoying great popularity since several months as "witch doctor" at Suhum, near Nsawam in the Akim District. . . . The witch doctor of Suhum has become famous all along the Coast for his professional successes and it is now quite common practice of the Na-tive Tribunals here to refer witchcraft cases . . . to this impostor. . . . In many places

Catholics have been accused to be "witches" and were ordered to go to Suhum for the doctor's verdict. This is against Christian and natural law.[69]

Such complaints came not only from mission authorities. Rank-and-file Christians also registered their concern, including one Brakato Ateko, an employee of the Bank of British West Africa in Accra. In a March 1930 letter to the secretary for native affairs, he told of visiting his home town of Boso near the Volta river some two years before and observing Christian women accused of witchcraft being forced either to appear before a local Nana Tongo shrine or to make the journey to Suhum. Ateko argued that his aim in raising the matter was to get the government "to take steps to protect Christians and other innocent persons who, as a result of the NAO [Native Administration Ordinance] which recognizes witchcraft, are being oppressed in a way less admirable than our present stage of civilization, while fetish practices which have been prohibited by Government are revived under the guise of native customs as sanctioned by the NAO."[70]

Given the connections drawn publicly between indirect rule, the Native Administration Ordinance, and witchcraft accusations, British officials' concerns about Nana Tongo were not surprising. Following the suppression of Aberewa in 1908 and Hwemeso in 1923, there was considerable speculation about whether the latest exotic import was simply a new, disguised form of these illegal cults. Many colonial officials were opposed to the introduction of any "fetishes from foreign countries"—that is, to *asuman* and *abosom* that did not originate in the area concerned.[71] On receiving *odikro* Ohene Kwaku's petition for a license to practice native medicine after his return from the "Sahara Desert" with Nana Tongo, Okyenhene Ofori Atta forwarded the request to the district commissioner. "I deprecate the importation into this state of new-fangled foreign Fetishes from the 'Sahara Desert,'" the latter responded, "as these have no claim to sympathetic recognition because of time-honoured usage and the reverence which the people attach to them." The commissioner suggested that Ohene Kwaku be advised "to leave 'Tongo' in the 'Sahara Desert' whence it comes, and . . . that the State Council tell him so."[72] But in the context of a fully elaborated system of indirect rule in the 1930s, it was not so easy to simply outlaw a movement, especially given the fact that chiefs were utilizing the powers of witch-finders in their native courts.[73] Thus, rather than immediately banning Nana Tongo, the government attempted to gather information on Assifu's activities. In March 1930, officials sent plainclothes detective James Obeng undercover to Obretema, where he posed as a supplicant troubled by suspected witchcraft. Beginning in March, weekly reports were then sent to the provincial commissioner by the police. Obeng told his superiors that when he looked around Assifu's village, he saw

> three big "JUJUS" made in pots, one was placed at the outskirt of the village, and two were in the house. I also saw one man and two women admitted for treatment. . . . On the 25th instant I went to the village and hid myself among the cocoyam leaves watching as if there will be any celebration of Fetish . . . but none . . . was done. . . . On the 26th instant, while I was standing at Asifu Nkwanta [i.e., "Assifu Junction"], a Stewart Lorry . . . brought in an old Lady named Abba Dakoma, two men and one girl . . . alleged the woman is a witchcraft and sending her to Assifu's village just to Worship the Fetish.[74]

In his April report, Obeng noted that despite Assifu's absence there were still some one hundred visitors to the shrine, about twenty of whom he described as "in patients."[75]

Meanwhile, in the coastal town of Winneba, inquests were held into two separate suicides which could be linked to witchcraft accusations and to individuals being compelled to appear before Nana Tongo. Although neither of these suicides implicated Kobina Assifu directly, one involved a Nana Tongo shrine at Mankessim, and the other a shrine at Winneba run by one Kobina Owusu, who claimed to be an "assistant to the Suhum Fetish Priest."[76] Throughout April and May there was thus a flurry of correspondence among colonial officials as they tried to gather information across districts and then sort out how to handle the predicament created by a Native Administration Ordinance that seemed to empower native tribunals to do precisely what they were doing—sending women and men accused of witchcraft to experts in *bayi* detection. The commissioner for the Eastern Province wrote to all of his district commissioners in April informing them that native tribunals had no right to compel individuals to consult the "fetish at Suhum." Some chiefs may have construed the ordinance as "conferring upon their Tribunals the power of compelling persons suspected of witchcraft . . . to proceed to Suhum," he argued, "[but] no such power is conferred."[77] Yet this announcement was much easier circularized than enforced. In the same month, the superintendent of police in Kyebi informed his superior that he had tried to arrest Assifu several times under section 105 (3), which forbade "charlatanic practices." But as the superintendent lamented, "The confidence the people have in Asifu makes it difficult to get independent evidence to support this charge. . . . The last time we raided his village, I saw a good number of patients and from what I heard from them Asifu is obviously a genuine therapeutist who is using this fetish for diagnostic purposes."[78] Meanwhile, District Commissioner

Warrington argued in April that until he received a "definite complaint" or "evidence of [an] eyewitness is obtained . . . it is impossible for me to take any direct action in the matter."[79]

Colonial government opinion on how to respond was far from unanimous and even individual officials could be equivocal. The provincial commissioner himself admitted that he "had some doubts as to the illegality of this Fetish and even so, if there were real extortion I think the Police or the District Commissioner would have heard complaints, remembering that Suhum is a big commercial town and not a secluded bush village."[80] The complicating factors for colonial officials deciding how to react were many, not least the fact that Assifu had fashioned a close connection with the influential Nana Sir Ofori Atta, whose native administration was one of the major success stories of indirect rule in the Gold Coast Colony. At least part of that connection was financial. As Assifu's grandson recently explained, because witchcraft cases were initiated with the swearing of the great oath, which "was identified with the throne of *okyenhene* and as such belonged to him," Assifu gave one-third of his fees from any case to Ofori Atta.[81] Moreover, Assifu was also reported by 1930 to have "a host of lawyers behind him," led by Ofori Atta's brother, Dr. J. B. Danquah, the leading light of the Colony intelligentsia who would later emerge as the doyen of Gold Coast nationalism.[82] When Assifu became the subject of so much public scrutiny and then was placed under constant police surveillance, he appealed to Ofori Atta for concrete assistance and he received it. In March 1930, the *okyenhene* offered protection, as well as a certificate "recognizing his practice and granting him permission to practice as a Native Physician at Bretema."[83] Although we have no documentary evidence of how "protection" was given, Assifu's grandson has written that Ofori Atta "deployed a group of traditional policemen to Assiful's village to provide security."[84]

In late June 1930, District Commissioner Warrington discussed with Ofori Atta at length the problems surrounding the "Suhum Fetish." The *okyenhene* promised to make a full inquiry into the matter. He interviewed Assifu on 1 July, at which time Assifu handed him the letter describing his first journey to the Tong Hills and "the reason of getting this Fitish by name Nana." On 3 July, Ofori Atta informed Warrington that he had interviewed "the medicine man called Assifu," and saw no reason to interfere with his work. "I am convinced that it is harmless," he insisted, emphasizing that both he and the late *omanhene* of Akuapem, Kwasi Akuffo, had already given their consent "to the practice of this medicine." "Supported by my Council," he concluded, "I am ready to acknowledge the existence of such medicines and unless there is practice of extortion or of inhuman treatment, I should be the last man to attempt to intimidate the medicine men with the view to the abandonment of the skill used in counteracting the ill-effects of witchcraft."[85] In a follow-up letter to Assifu, Ofori Atta enclosed copies of his correspondence with Warrington. "I truly hope," he concluded, "you will carry on the practice of your medicine in such a way as will cause no anxiety on the part of the Authorities and myself."[86]

Yet, by all indications, the anxiety continued. At the same time that Ofori Atta was trying to convince the Birim district commissioner of the benign nature of Assifu's Nana Tongo shrine center, the commissioner for the Central Province reported that at least 250 cases involving the "Suhum Fetish" had come to his attention. Moreover, those cases represented only a proportion, "since the Native Tribunal records are silent in many cases and numerous Chiefs without tribunals have mulcted witches." The commissioner's recommendation in July was that the "Fetish be suppressed."[87] Yet there still remained substantial disagreement among colonial officers on how to proceed. In November, the commissioner for the Eastern Province made a personal visit to Obretema in the company of Assifu. In contrast to his counterpart for the Central Province, he was suitably impressed by all that he saw and heard. Assifu informed him

> that it is the Tong Fetish, which has its habitat at Tongzugu (Tong) near Zuaragu in the Northern Territories. This Fetish is of a benevolent nature, being devoted mainly to producing fertility in child bearing, though it also professes to cure evil practices such as witchcraft. It was recognised by the Chief Commissioner of the Northern Territories as being a harmless Fetish in 1921, and Mr. Cardinall, who lived for many years in Zuaragu, assures me that the White Fathers under Monsiegneur Morin have no objection to offer to the practice of this Fetish beyond the normal religious objections of a Christian sect to a Heathen Fetish.[88]

Although the letter's syntax makes it difficult to discern whether it was the commissioner or Assifu himself who revealed the origins of the shrine and connected it to events in the Tong Hills in the 1920s, it is clear that the former was largely convinced of the benevolent nature of Nana Tongo. "Assifu was completely frank with me as to the functions of his Fetish," he reported, "and created a decidedly favourable impression." He concluded that there was "no reason to recommend that the Suhum Fetish be proclaimed."[89]

The commissioner's impressions notwithstanding, officials were still being inundated with complaints about activities at Suhum. By the end of 1930, the government felt it was under increasing pressure to react.[90] Despite the divisions within its ranks and the direct intervention of key players in the indirect rule system like Ofori Atta, the government finally responded. On 19 December it passed the Order in Council (No. 28) of 1930—the Native Customs (Witch and Wizard Finding) Order, which replaced the apparently ineffective 1906 law proscribing the "Yi Abeyi Custom" in the Gold Coast Colony. Similar legislation would be framed for Ashanti four years later. It "took witchcraft off the books," as Gray has recently summarized, "and made witch-finding illegal."[91] No longer could native tribunals legally be implicated in the trying of *bayi* cases.

From "Fetish Priest" to "Psychoanalyst": Nana Tongo and the Legitimation of "Traditional Medicine"

Taking witchcraft off the books was one thing. Exorcising it from the lived world of cash and cocoa was quite another. While the colonial archive overwhelmingly focuses on the "problems" generated by the Suhum fetish, there are other bits and pieces of documentary evidence which provide some access to the broader, and in many cases more positive, public perceptions of events taking place at Suhum. Often that evidence is buried within troubled colonial accounts. For example, as he was considering the possibility of charging Assifu with "witchfinding," the solicitor general admitted that "any witness from Kwahu called to give evidence against Asifu would do so most reluctantly and would probably be only too glad to take advantage of differences in detail in order to avoid having to say that witchfinding as practiced at Suhum is the custom known [and banned] as Yi Abeyi."[92] Meanwhile, the commissioner for the Eastern Province was convinced that those who consulted with Nana Tongo "are satisfied that they received value for their money."[93] Yet perhaps the most telling statement in support of the benefits wrought by Nana Tongo was sent to the secretary for native affairs in April 1930 by anonymous "Well Wishers of the Country" from the Bekwae region of Asante. The letter warrants quotation in full:

> Before the late Governor Guggisberg took over [in 1919] . . . there was a serious infantile mortality and also a deplorable loss in mothers after child-birth.
>
> The incidence was so alarming that large sums of money were spent by the Government on Infant Clinics and Maternity Hospitals in order to arrest the loss of life. These losses in infants and mothers are the work of witches all over the country. It is regrettable to remark that the majority of the witches are refuged in the Christian churches of the Colony, notably in the Wesleyan Churches of the Colony and Ashanti.
>
> Recently the depredations of the witches are becoming so alarming that a certain big Fetish has been set up at Suhum and branches at other places to catch and punish these human devils. It is interesting to note that it is only through Fetish

methods that these witches can be successfully caught and dealt with. It is rumoured that the Christian Churches are trying to persuade Government in order to inter-fere or put a stop to the actions of the Fetish.

We beg to ask Government not to do such a thing. The duty of Christian Missions is to try to induce or to teach their members to give up such evil practices, but if they are unable to do so the Suhum Fetish must stay to rid the country of such destructive beings.

An exhaustive enquiry by Government into the mystery of how and why women become witches will enable Government to understand the destructive powers of such people.

An attempt by the Christian Missions of the Colony to induce the natives to give up such evil practices would have been far more beneficial to the Country than their serious attempt to prohibit the liquor traffic. Liquor is not taking toll of in-fant life as witchcraft is doing at present.

Any representation by the Christian Missions must not be entertained. Gov-ernment must use his own judgment in the matter.[94]

In this fascinating missive, the "well wishers of the country" inserted witches directly into a modern discourse of money, Christianity, infant mor-tality, temperance, and western biomedicine. Theirs was not a language of tradition versus modernity. The petitioners argued that Christianity had already shown itself incapable of combating the evils of the current day. Indeed, it had served as a last refuge for many of those infected by *bayi*. The evils of infant and maternal mortality, they insisted, could not be addressed by welfare clinics or churches. Nana Tongo was the strongest weapon avail-able in a very modern struggle and it could not be abandoned.[95]

Two weeks after the ban was in place, on 2 January 1931, Commissioner for the Eastern Province Applegate, in the company of Birim District Com-missioner Warrington, went to inspect Assifu's shrine at Obretema to de-termine if it was operating in violation of the "Witch and Wizard Finding Order." We have three very different accounts of that visit, two contem-porary and one recent. All three point to the fact that Nana Tongo con-tinued to operate as it had been, basically in defiance of the new ordinance. The first account comes from Warrington's diary, in which he describes "the ceremony of finding the witch." "This ceremony, if well-staged," he wrote, "would make a popular 'talkie' in London, but locally I'm afraid it comes under the ban. I am sending Asifu a copy of Order No. 28/30 for information."[96] Warrington's brief account, then, suggests that he saw what he expected to see and rather regretted the fact that the performance was not legal under the new ordinance—an ordinance that Warrington him-self did not fully support. Assifu's own recollection of this day is preserved in the petition he would submit to the government in 1932. For Assifu, what was memorable about the day was not the ritual performance itself. In fact, the officials "appeared satisfied with what they saw." Rather, the extraordinary event of the day was "a certain sudden invasion of black ants at the shrine . . . [which] did not permit the Political officers to prolong their enquiries."[97] In 1999, Assifu's son shared with us a more elaborate rendition of this story, but one that may very well capture local memories of a rather extraordinary day. Initially, Paul Assifu explained, the British

> had made up their mind to arrest my father and just kill him. Formerly, there was no road here. There was only one way to get here. The white people who plotted to kill my father . . . came by that one way. . . . And when they were getting closer to this village, ants starting cropping up and so they made up their minds to just run over the ants, but the ants just kept coming; they were growing and growing in number . . . some of them scattered. . . . They went back the way they came. After realizing the powers that my father had, they later went back and told their own story. So, later they granted him a permit to be the fetish over all fetishes from here to Enchi.[98]

That the story of the ants appears in two accounts—one oral and one archival—offered some seventy years apart is remarkable, even if the story only passed from father to son. Whether one understands the story literally or figuratively, the meaning is the same in both cases. Implicit in the first and explicit in the second account is one central point: Assifu, through Nana Tongo, wielded extraordinary powers that were capable of interfering directly with the colonial project. In Paul Assifu's interpretation, the appearance of the ants represented a crucial turning point in the relationship between his father and the colonial state. Once colonial authorities came to appreciate, if not fear, the magnitude of Assifu's extraordinary powers, they gave up on their battle and awarded him the recognition he had so long sought.

The year 1931 was a turning point not only for Nana Tongo, but for the broader history of witchcraft and anti-witchcraft movements in the Gold Coast. As colonial pressure against Assifu mounted in the new year, so too did a broad-based defense of the Suhum "fetish." In February, the Council of Chiefs in the Central Province passed a resolution denouncing the government's decision to take witchcraft off of the books,

> with the unhappy result of the Native Authorities of this Country being forever deprived of the Statutory powers of duly apprehending and trying persons . . . who may be found by some skillful detection or by their confessions to possess the means of practicing Witchcraft with intent to use the dangerous spiritual powers it involved to endanger or destroy human life. . . . from time immemorial it has been

the firm belief of all Native African peoples—Christian and non-Christian—that Witchcraft positively exists.[99]

But the defense of Assifu soon entailed much more than affirming the existence of witchcraft. It took on a nationalist tenor in asserting the value of local culture and the legitimacy of indigenous healing practices. Like other early nationalist efforts, it was a defense launched from among the western-educated urban elite, in coalition with sympathetic chiefs. In a letter to Ofori Atta, Sydney Spencer-Hayford of the *Gold Coast Leader* decried the passage of the Order in Council: "The whitemen may take a different view on the matter, or may pretend . . . not to believe in witchcraft but you and I do know that it does exist . . . and I shall be gratified, if you will use your influence to cast away the ban that the Government and the so-called 'Christian Council' have sought to put on it."[100] In his reply, Ofori Atta assured Spencer-Hayford that he was completely sympathetic and noted that both the provincial and district commissioners also "took special interest in [Assifu] and the latter did everything he could on my advice to exonerate him from the accusations which were erroneously leveled against him."[101]

By February, J. B. Danquah was on the case, preparing Assifu's petition to the government in defense of Nana Tongo. This was not an entirely new endeavor for Danquah. He had represented one Kofi Agyeman in his efforts to be allowed to operate a Bruku shrine in Akyem in 1927 and had sought to defend the Nkona "fetish" against government proscription earlier in the same year.[102] Neither was Danquah the first Gold Coast lawyer to mount an intervention into ritual affairs. Indeed, the legal defense of indigenous gods against government suppression and Christian condemnation can be traced back to at least the mid-1890s, when the Accra advocate Edmund Bannerman and his barrister son C. J. Bannerman represented *obosomfo* Kwamin Asare, detained as a "political prisoner" following the outlawing of the Katawere cult in the Akyem region in 1894.[103] The archives offer no evidence that elite voices challenged the official suppression of Aberewa in 1908. Yet fourteen years later, the outspoken Cape Coast barrister Kwabena Sekyi mounted an eloquent defense of Aberewa's successor, Hwemeso. As we have seen, Sekyi was hired by the powerful *omanhene* of Akyem Kotoku, Ata Fua. Ata Fua, it should be noted, had also been a leading guardian of the *obosom* Katawere in the 1890s. It is therefore striking that Sekyi sought to explain the widespread diffusion of new, exotic anti-witchcraft cults in part on the grounds that the colonial state had banned established "state" gods such as Katawere.

In his 1930 petition on behalf of Kobina Assifu, Danquah took Sekyi's arguments a stage further by utilizing a discursive strategy that boldly equated indigenous knowledge with western biomedicine.[104] After carefully setting out the long history of how Assifu obtained Nana Tongo, was licensed to practice in Akuapem and later Akyem Abuakwa, and had the implicit support of officials like Warrington, Danquah got down to business. He began by establishing that Assifu and the government shared a common ground: they both agreed that the majority of inhabitants of the country believed in witches. Whether *bayi* was "real" was open to question, but the fact that people believed in it was not. Danquah's central contention was that Assifu could help individuals "unbelieve" that they had become *abayifoo*. The fundamental distinction between legal and illegal witch-finding, he argued, should be between "those who voluntarily and of their own free will, seek to be relieved from their pains, and those [who,] being unwilling, are compelled by some superior authority such as a family, a Tribunal or some other community." Danquah then argued that the new ordinance left individuals with no right "to consult a legitimate native doctor versed in the practices of witchcraft to analyze the cause of that person's troubles by a process of psycho-analysis, and to find remedies for the BELIEF, whether groundless, hallucinatory or not, which that person entertains in regard to his own health and well-being." This constituted the key passage in the petition—one that marked a fundamental discursive shift in how "native medicine" could be discussed. The existence or not of *bayi* was taken off the table and the only issue left on was appropriate treatment. And it was not treatment by just anyone. Assifu signed the petition as "one of the said medicine men . . . speaking for himself and his profession."[105] In the early nationalist language of indigenous healing, "fetish" became "medicine," a "fetish priest" became a doctor, and the ritual process became an indigenous form of psychoanalysis. In 1928, the Birim district commissioner had queried Ofori Atta about what was meant by "medicine" in all of these discussions. "Is it strictly speaking merely a medicine, as the word is understood in English, or is it a 'Fetish'?"[106] Assifu's 1932 petition, rendered in early nationalist language, demonstrated that there were no easy answers to this question. The petition foregrounded professionalization and sought the legitimation of indigenous knowledge, but via the language of western biomedicine. In the end, it was a discursive strategy the colonial regime found compelling, if only because it offered a way out of a most difficult situation by allowing officials to support the rule of the chiefs without having to acknowledge in colonial law the existence of *bayi*.

In March 1932, the commissioner for the Eastern Province wrote at length to the secretary for native affairs about the efficacy of Assifu's "medi-cine" after visiting him at Obretema:

> if a man or woman feels that she is under the influence of an evil spirit I do not think these persons, though they are obviously mentally affected, should be denied the right to approach a native physician who may have powers to exercise [*sic*] the spirit. Kobina Assifu in charming away (for a consideration!) malign influence is nothing more than the modern psychiatrist whose treatment is a form of psycho-analysis.[107]

Assistant Secretary for Native Affairs J. C. De Graft-Johnson, a Fante from Cape Coast, shared these sentiments in his file minutes: "Order No. 28 was certainly not intended to prevent neurotics from obtaining relief from the expert treatment of psycho-analysts or psychiatrists (if there be any such among the Gold Coast 'witchdoctors'). . . . If the so-called witch-doctor or psychiatrist . . . can effect a 'cure' without bringing accusation against other persons as being the cause of such illness, I do not think Govern-ment should interfere."[108] Sentiments such as these soon won the day, and Assifu's appeal succeeded in April 1932.[109] The secretary for native affairs and the governor agreed that as long as individuals came to Assifu or other native doctors of their own free will and were not forced by families or na-tive tribunals, they could legally be treated by Nana Tongo.

The discursive strategy that was so important to the success of Assifu's petition was not employed in a vacuum. It was in the 1920s that *abosomfoo* and *adunsinfoo*—both women and men—calling themselves by the English terms "native physicians" or "herbalists," began to organize themselves as healers and to seek legitimation through the state apparatus of indirect rule. Many began to approach native councils throughout Asante and the Gold Coast Colony in the aftermath of the 1923 suppression of Hwemeso, often asking for a license to certify that they were utilizing medicinal or ritual powers other than those of the outlawed god.[110] Assifu was licensed in Akuapem in 1925. This licensing more or less went on outside the purview of the colonial state. Indeed, as late as 1938 the chief commissioner of As-ante was surprised to discover that the police had come across an individ-ual who was carrying a "Native Physician's License." It was clear that he had never seen or heard of such a license and wanted to know by what au-thority such certification was issued and by whom.[111] In part, the issuing of licenses was a money-making proposition for native councils. But more importantly, physicians were seeking the protection of their chiefs from what must have appeared as capricious maneuvers against local medicines by colonial authorities. As many applicants wrote, they wanted "to pursue [their] work as . . . native Medicine men, without infringing the Law of the

Colony."[112] Local healers thus sought to defend indigenous knowledge, as well as their own expertise.

New organizational forms also began to take shape in the expanding ritual marketplace. Four years before the chief commissioner of Ashanti chanced upon the licensing system, Colony officials were startled to discover the existence of a registered firm called the Senyakupo Trading Company. Following hurried inquiries, it emerged that the firm had been formed in 1928 by a consortium led by the then *omanhene* of Akyem Bosome, Mafo Ahenkora, and his "medicine-man," Kwadwo Obeng. According to Obeng, "this company has entered into contracts with well qualified Native Fetish Priests and Native Doctors for the supply of all West African herbs and medicines for a period of years."[113] Given that the Senyakupo movement in Akyem Bosome was said to incorporate not only the deity of that name but also Tigare, Bruku, and Nana Tongo, there can be little doubt that one of those doctors was Kobina Assifu.[114]

In 1931, the formal professionalization of indigenous healing was marked by the founding of the Society of African Herbalists at Sekondi. Its objectives were

a. to preserve the knowledge of the healing virtues and uses of our native plants that have been bequeathed to us by our forefathers.
b. to improve upon the local practice of medical herbalism, freeing it from superstition and raising it to a high standard.
c. to examine old remedies and make herborisations [investigations of plants] to discover new medicines.
d. to encourage the study of scientific books on herbal medication.
e. to write treatises on herbal medication for the guidance of the rising generation.
f. to see that members of the society should be left free and unhampered in the practice of their profession or art.[115]

As Gray argues, Ofori Atta was one "of the early supporters of the Society which appealed to him as part of his larger project of modernizing Akan traditions, both political and social."[116] Part of that project was achieved in June 1940, when the Akyem Abuakwa State Council focused at length on native medicines and "fetishes" and finally regularized licensing procedures so that all herbalists or native physicians in the state had to be licensed and abide by a series of specific rules. Individuals who sought to establish "any cult" had to introduce themselves to the divisional chief and pay the sum of £1.4 and then the Native Authority Treasury a further sum of £2.8. Every herbalist or cult had to obtain a license, renewable each year, at a

Figure 4.6. Native physician's license, from file RAG ARG 6/1/27.

cost of £1.2. Meanwhile, the State Council listed those activities that it would not countenance:

1. The exposal of the victim by stripping him or her naked in public.
2. Any attempt to accuse any person who is not before a cult as having caused illness or a complaint of the victim.
3. Any act or attempt to claim from the family or relatives of any person supposed or believed to have died as a result of an offence committed against a cult any money, gunpowder or any other property for the purpose of releasing to the family or relatives, the dead body for internment, or for the purpose of redeeming the deceased's obligations to the cult. . . . etc.
4. Any act or attempt to compel, induce, coerce or threaten any person, whether adherent of such cult or not, with a view to exact confession or to implicate any other person as to the cause of the illness or disability or death of any person whatsoever.[117]

In a similar move three years later, the Asante Confederacy Council regularized a policy of licensing for the Ashanti region. However, it divided "native physicians" into three classes and established a scale of fees for each class. Thus, "suman" paid £4.3, while "ordinary physicians" and "physician hawkers" paid £1.3.6 for their licenses.[118] In short, by the opening years of the 1940s, many of the primary structures of indirect rule in Asante and the Colony were busy certifying the legitimacy of native medicine through the rather lucrative business of issuing official licenses to indigenous physicians.[119] In 1944, with the legitimation and professionalization of local medicine continuing apace, the Society of African Medical Herbalists—now under the patronage of the Joint Provincial Council of Chiefs in the Colony—began to solicit support for the establishment of a West African Institute of Natural Medicines and Bio-Psychology.[120]

Elsewhere, the ongoing spread of anti-witchcraft movements was marked not by accommodation and legitimation but by division and conflict within the ranks of African society. This was generally the case amongst the Ewe-speaking peoples of the southeastern Gold Coast and in particular in the coastal state of Anlo. By the early 1930s, Nana Tongo, Senyakupo, Kunde, and other savanna gods had crossed the Volta River into the Anlo-Ewe region. There they encountered not only the established deities of local *vodun* cults but also other recent arrivals from Dahomey to the east as well as growing numbers of Christian converts.[121] The result was an explosive political conflict over the control of ritual resources, as coalitions of discontented and aspirant commoner men challenged the power of established chiefs by associating themselves with the new gods. On the one hand, these exotic deities took on a bewildering variety of new local identities, but on the other, they were identified by many observers as being fragments of one all-encompassing religious cult, known as "Kunde" and led by one Mensah Hiator Lawson of Adina. While Kunde's opponents charged the new movement with crimes ranging from the destruction of local culture to mass murder by poison, its members countered that the god merely offered protection against witchcraft and other forms of anti-social behavior. "The 'Friendly Society' under which this sect has been . . . consolidated," ran one petition from Kunde followers, "is the surest . . . protection against the secret evil of the chiefs in former times towards . . . well-to-do subjects."[122] By the end of the decade, Kunde shrines appear to have sprung up on the outskirts of nearly every town and village in Anlo, with more than six thousand followers reported to attend an annual festival in Adina.[123] In 1939, the besieged chiefs of the Anlo State Council passed a resolution appealing to the colonial government to act. Disturbed by reports of extortion, intimidation, and murder, the latter acquiesced, banning Kunde in the Gold Coast Colony by Order in Council No. 43 of 1939. In contrast to Nana Tongo, which was strongly supported by influential chiefs like Ofori Atta and eloquently defended by Kobina Assifu and J. B. Danquah, Kunde in the Ewe region—into which there is every indication that Nana Tongo was subsumed—became associated with those opposed to the indirect rule chiefs. Like Aberewa and Hwemeso, it therefore ultimately fell afoul of the colonial state.

If the "translation" of indigenous healing from "fetish" to "medicine" can be located in terms of developing nationalist thought, so too must be the anti-witchcraft movements and the threats they posed to colonial law and order. It is easy to overlook this point in light of subsequent events, but it should be remembered that before the rise of anti-colonial nationalist parties after the Second World War, the European rulers of tropical Africa often regarded syncretic religious movements as the most dangerous vehicles of "nationalist" sentiment.[124] This emerges clearly in the debate surrounding Kunde, which was seen by many observers—both European and African—as a heady and potentially subversive mix of indigenous belief, Islam, and Christianity. "Nationalistic movements in Africa have shown themselves openly since the Great War of 1914," railed Father Dufontey of the Catholic mission in Eweland, and "should they come to understand one another and to fusion, it would be all Africa against Europe. Whatever the name of these movements, whether it be Ki[m]banguism, Amieda, Amatsi or Kunde and the rest, they . . . all have the same goal: leave Africa for the Africans."[125] A somewhat hysterical Christian reaction perhaps—although by the late 1930s Kunde was reported to have been carried around the coast of West-Central Africa as far as French Congo and Gabon.[126] Indeed, it was the trans-regionalism and incipient pan-Africanism of the new religious movements that was seen as their most subversive aspect, challenging hallowed "state" deities and established hierarchies of rule. As colonial authorities in both the southeastern Gold Coast and neighboring French Togo struggled to suppress Kunde and its offspring into the 1940s, it is telling that one new manifestation of the cult adopted that most pan-African of names, "Abyssinia."[127]

Conclusion: Ritual Conversations

By opening up a public space wherein *bayi* could be treated by native physicians licensed by indirect rule chiefs, Assifu's case represents something of a watershed in the history of "traditional medicine" in twentieth-century Ghana. It also marks a significant shift in colonial discourse regarding indigenous belief systems, as chiefs and the educated elite, as well as ordinary *akomfoo* and *abosomfoo*, challenged and ultimately transformed early-twentieth-century vocabularies of "fetishes" and "native gods" into a more "rational," translatable discourse of (comparative) "medicines." Through such state-sanctioned processes, initiated by early nationalists like Danquah and formalized by powerful *amanhene* like Nana Ofori Atta, Tongnaab was entrenched in the ritual landscape of the southern colonial Gold Coast. There, as Nana Tongo, it became a vibrant part of the spiritual armory of Akan, Ewe, and Ga women and men who sought personal protection in a world being reshaped by colonialism, cash, and cocoa. But Nana Tongo's protection required constant renewal and thus, via ongoing ritual commerce, Tongnaab remained integral to the production of spiritual power in the south. The savanna world, through repeated mimetic performance and the careful assemblage of "northern objects," remained ever-present. Southern supplicants and savanna *tengdaana*s did not speak the same language, but important ritual conversations still took place.

For most colonial officials and Christians (especially missionaries and clergymen), the conversation looked far more like a one-way importation of uncivilized "foreign fetishes" into the civilizing south than a debate about the present. Their view was powerful and salient, and embraced a range of predictable binaries: "tradition" versus "modernity," "civilized states" versus "primitive tribes," "north" versus "south," and "legitimate local gods" versus "illegitimate exotic fetishes." These stark dualities made for great newspaper copy in the 1930s, but they are of little use to the historian trying to see past the colonized and colonizing discourse of the colonial archive.

They certainly do not help us understand the historical processes which saw the leading Gold Coast nationalist of the 1930s and 1940s, J. B. Danquah, at the forefront of legal efforts to defend a savanna *bo'ar* which, dutifully tended by a wealthy cocoa farmer, developed extraordinary *bayi*-detecting abilities after being transplanted into the forest. Tongnaab/Nana Tongo, far from being a "traditional" response to a rapidly modernizing world, embodied a very modern response to that world—one that could be spoken in multiple vernaculars as it crossed the ritual and political boundaries between north and south, savanna and forest. It should, in fact, come as little surprise that the Talensi *bo'ar* Tongnaab ended up being implicated in some of the earliest articulations of Ghana-as-nation. Such was the modernity of ritual commerce.

5

Tongnaab, Meyer Fortes, and the Making of Colonial Taleland, 1928–1945

*T*he inter-war period witnessed the greatest efflorescence of organized witchcraft eradication in Ghanaian history. Expanding physical mobility and ritual commerce enabled the peoples of southern Ghana to draw on the powers of distant savanna shrines and to deploy those powers in new and innovative ways. They did so in order to reinforce their spiritual armory in the face of a growing range of problems expressed in the established idioms of witchcraft. The resulting movements, Nana Tongo, Kunde, Senyakupo, Tigare, and the rest, had a profound impact on the lived experiences of many people throughout Asante and the Gold Coast. They are, as we have argued, absolutely central to the social history of twentieth-century Ghana.

In this chapter, we leave the forests and coastlines of the south and return to the epicenter of Tongnaab's ritual network in the Tong Hills. Our aim is to demonstrate that the sites of sacred power dotted across Ghana's northern savannas remained integral to that same unfolding social history. While historians and anthropologists have long recognized that most southern anti-witchcraft movements derived from savanna shrines, those originative sites have been excluded from core narratives of religious and social change. They have stood in synchronic silence. Just as British rulers saw the Northern Territories first and foremost as a marginal reservoir of labor power, scholarly accounts of anti-witchcraft movements have tended to treat the region as an unchanging reservoir of sacred power. Yet if the inter-war period witnessed an expansion in Tongnaab's cross-cultural ritual network, there were also dramatic changes at the sacred center of the Tong Hills. Tongnaab, in other words, did not just make history once it was swept into the flows of social change coursing through the cocoa farms and trading towns of the south. It remained pivotal in local, Talensi histories.

The focus of this chapter is the role of Tongnaab and its lucrative pilgrim trade in struggles over the implementation of indirect rule in and around the Tong Hills. We examine three principal episodes in Talensi history from the late 1920s to the close of the Second World War: the return of the hill folk to the Tong Hills after a generation of exile from their ancestral homes; the reformulation of the terms of colonial control with the construction of "indirect rule"; and Golibdaana Tengol's consolidation of power as the leading ritual entrepreneur in Tongnaab's expanding pilgrimage network. Woven into all three of these interrelated stories is the pivotal figure of Meyer Fortes, who spent a total of two years conducting anthropological research at Tongo between 1934 and 1937. If Tongnaab has been excluded from historical accounts of twentieth-century Ghana, so too has been this renowned scholar who, in many ways, authored the terms of colonial control for the Tong Hills in the 1930s.

As we observed in the introduction, Fortes's name has become virtually synonymous with that of the Talensi. This is not just the case in the ivory tower of Africanist anthropology. When we began talking with Talensi people about the history of Tongnaab in 1999, we were struck by how often Fortes came up in conversation, sixty-five years after he first appeared and almost thirty years after his final, brief visit. Even in the hilltop settlement of Tengzug, where he spent relatively little time, many older people remember him conducting his research.[1] Down on the flat in Tongo, where he lived under the patronage of Tongrana Nambiong and other elders, his name (always "Doctor Fortes") is revered. When we interviewed Nayina, the eighty-five-year-old acting *tengdaana* of the Gbezug section of Tongo, he disappeared into his compound at the end of our conversation and emerged with a framed photograph of himself as a young man standing beside Fortes.[2] Meyer Fortes put the Talensi on the emerging ethnographic map of colonial Africa. But he also inserted himself, whether intentionally or not, into the historical narratives flowing in and around the Tong Hills. In this chapter, we seek to restore both Tongnaab and Meyer Fortes to the colonial history of the Tong Hills. We demonstrate the ways in which the great Talensi *bo'a* and the social anthropologist were implicated in the consolidation of indirect rule in Taleland and, ultimately, in the formulation of political structures and hierarchies that have held sway since the Second World War.

The Resettlement of the Tong Hills, 1931–1935

Despite the lifting of the official ban on the use of the Yanii site of Tong-naab in 1925 and the subsequent expansion of pilgrim traffic from Asante and the Gold Coast, the Tong Hills remained off-limits to permanent habitation until the mid-1930s. The settlement of 1925 meant that the Talensi were no longer forced to visit the earth and ancestor shrines of Tengzug secretly at night or to make do with furtive, circumscribed forms of the great annual festivals. But the colonial authorities continued to enforce the exclusion zone within the stone boundary that ringed the hills and those communities expelled from their homes in 1911 remained confined to the surrounding plains. "If the British saw us accompanying a stranger to the shrine, they would guide us there to make sure we had no bows and arrows," explained Diegire Baa of the years after 1925. "So they didn't prevent us from going, but we had to return straight back after we had sacrificed."[3] Our informants from Tengzug and the other hill communities—many of whom were born during the generation of exile between 1911 and 1935—often regard these decades with a certain ambivalence. Memories of dislocation and frustration abound. But these are often tempered by recollections of the real economic and social advances made at Santeng and further afield in the lands south of the White Volta, always referred to simply as "Dagbon." "The area where we went was virgin forest, so it was very fertile," said Tii from Yinduri. "We were growing plenty of food there."[4] "We were happy," remembered Yiran Boare, who witnessed the destruction of 1911, "because those who survived had many children to replace those who were killed. Many women had children at the time we were at Santeng."[5] Yet the desire to return was powerful. "Just as you are here and will return to your home, so we wanted to return," responded the old blacksmith Wayanaya Songbazaa to our questioning. "We were not settled. Even if we were happy, we would have been happier in our homes."[6] These sentiments were echoed by Zimemeh, an elder of Yinduri, as he looked out from the southern slopes of the hills toward "Dagbon": "This is our ancestral land. Our ancestors originated here and we could never be happy away from here. We lost some of our fathers down there, but before they died they told us that when the British gave us permission to return, then we must come back."[7]

It is likely that the imperative to return to ancestral homes in the Tong Hills was heightened by a succession of poor harvests and famines that gripped Taleland and neighboring areas of the Zuarungu District in the late 1920s and early 1930s. Great care is needed when considering changing levels of food production and nutrition in the region and when making connections between these and broader dynamics of social history. Data are extremely scanty and where they do exist are often too vague to allow anything more than the most impressionistic glimpse of historical change. Highly localized incidence of rainfall alone meant that in any given season one part of the countryside may have had an abundant harvest while another part less than ten miles away may have experienced crop failure and food shortages. Within communities, moreover, households and even individuals could be affected by subsistence crises in very different ways. As the specter of hunger loomed in 1928, Victor Aboya explained to Rattray how socio-economic differentiation became more pronounced at times of food shortages:

> When a man has many sons, corn [i.e., millet] cannot fail in his house. Why? Because they are many. When going to the bush farm, soon they have finished, passing on to the next; when this farm fails, that one does not. . . . Such people are better off than their neighbours. Starving people's best goats, sheep, the biggest of the heifers, find their way to their place in exchange for corn; their belly is washed (i.e., they are happy because not in want) and you have to agree to what they give you (in exchange for your stock).[8]

After a starving household's livestock had all gone, one further option was the pledging or even the outright sale of kin. It will be remembered that such was the fate of Aboya himself in the 1890s—exchanged for a few baskets of grain and sold down to Asante.

Still, despite the growth of local markets in the 1920s and the availability of wage labor in the south, the Talensi as a whole were yet to escape either the cyclical "hungry season" in the months before the harvest of the early millet or periodic severe subsistence crises.[9] Such a crisis occurred in the Zuarungu District in the first half of 1928, when what was described in colonial records as a "serious famine" resulted in "a large exodus of the population to other districts."[10] The harvest later that year appears to have been fair, but records for November 1929 note a serious threat to the late millet from plagues of locusts. Locusts struck again in 1930, 1931, and 1932, combining with poor rains to cause acute food shortages in Taleland and elsewhere in the Northern Territories.[11] Hard times were made worse by the downturn in the colonial economy caused by the world depression. By 1931, unemployment was rising in Asante and the Gold Coast, pushing down wages for migrant laborers and forcing many to return north into the teeth of the food crisis.[12]

The succession of poor rains and locust plagues between 1927 and 1932 resulted in the most serious subsistence crisis faced by the Talensi since the great famine of the mid-1890s. As was the case three decades before—when, according to Yiran Boare, "Tongnaab decided to punish the people"— ritual mismanagement was believed to have been the reason for such devastating agricultural failure.[13] In September 1930, a diviner (*bakoldaana*) apparently succeeded in identifying the source of the problem as the unseemly delay in the funeral rites of a renowned *tengdaana* who had died some years before. "The spirit of the dead Tindana is angry," it was reported from Tongo, "and has brought the locusts as a sign of his anger."[14] Two failed farming seasons later and with the rains again delayed, recriminations continued to fly about the countryside:

> Rain! Rain! Behold the shouts escaping from the chests of the famished people. No more food, no more grass to make soup; it is really a misery. Some people say that the Chief of Nangori [i.e., the Nabdam *nangodinaaba*] is the cause for it not raining, wanting to punish the Chief of Zuarangu, who it seems has reduced his kingdom.[15]

"If the poor blacks, instead of spending the little that they have on sacrifice upon sacrifice, wanted to beg the Master of rain, God would listen," despaired the diarist at the White Father's station at Bolgatanga. "But these poor pagans even go to the extent of saying that it is us who are the cause of the drought, that it is the medals, the rosaries and the crosses that our Christians and catechumens are wearing that drive away the rain."[16] Recalling the crisis some seventy years later, Ba'an also emphasized the importance of *kaab* ("sacrifice") in restoring ritual and ecological harmony:

> Before we returned [to the hills], all the elders each had to deliver a cow to the chief [i.e., the *sipaatnaab*] so he could sacrifice to the land. After we did that we had a good harvest . . . but two or three years later there was a drought . . . [and] locusts came and chopped all the produce—that year there was much hunger. We reported this to the British, who came to our aid. The chief and *tengdaana*s also made various sacrifices, and since that time hunger has decreased.[17]

Perhaps the most intriguing readings of the crisis come not from Talensi sources but from far beyond the Tong Hills in Dagomba and Gonja. Here, in a huge swathe of savanna country that fell within the established ritual field of Tongnaab, it was widely recognized that the swarms of locusts plaguing the land issued forth from a hole in the Tong Hills. In February 1930, the "Chief of Kombi" (i.e., the *kumbung-na* of Dagomba) told the chief commissioner in Tamale that he had received messengers from the "Chief of the Tong Hills" (presumably Tengol) requesting "one dog, six hoes and six chickens or their equivalent in money in order that his Fetish might recall

all the locusts."[18] Similar messengers were despatched as far as Bole and Salaga in Gonja. "Usually this hole is stopped up by the iron heads of native hoes," it was reported from Gonja, "but the . . . Tindana decided that money was a more efficacious barrier than mere hoes."[19] Whether or not the Talensi themselves subscribed to the notion that the locusts issued forth from within the Tong Hills is uncertain.[20] Yet far away in Dagomba and Gonja, the "fetish" believed to exercise power over the destructive insects was none other than Tongnaab.[21]

Now, there is no direct evidence to link all of this with the agitation on the part of the exiled Talensi to return to their homes. But it is highly suggestive that the onset of drought, insect plague, and hunger in 1928 coincided with the beginning of regular appeals from Tengol and the *tengdaanas* of Tengzug to be "allowed to live up near the fetish."[22] Certainly, the wealth-generating potential of the expanding pilgrimage trade to Tongnaab meant that Tengol had every reason to want to consolidate his control over access to the main Yanii shrine. Yet given the role of the great *tongbana* and *bo'a* in guaranteeing the well-being and continuity of all Talensi society, it is inconceivable that the deepening subsistence crisis did not shape an increasingly urgent desire to return to the hills that had offered both spiritual and physical protection to their inhabitants for so long. In the words of Naoh, son of Dakuar, who was the second man allowed to return, "Tengol . . . told the British that all Tengzug's people's gods are here. They sacrifice here, they get their water here. Now we are driven from here, how are we to get our ancestors' help?"[23] Moreover, it is significant that popular pressure to return to the hills arose at a time when the British were mounting a campaign of "systematic and continuous propaganda" to encourage people to move away from the region and to resettle permanently in the thinly populated plains of Mamprugu to the south.[24]

The chief commissioner finally granted permission for Tengol alone to rebuild and reoccupy his compound in Tengzug in mid-1931.[25] Tongnaab certainly appeared to smile on his return, as the run of poor harvests was broken the following year with the belated arrival of the rains and a bumper crop.[26] It would take another four years of negotiations before all those expelled in 1911 and their descendants were allowed to return. Unfortunately, the official file containing the records of these negotiations was lost some years later. It is therefore to the oral testimonies of some of those who reclaimed their ancestral homes in the 1930s that we must turn in order to reconstruct this key moment. One of the first to return was Boarnii, who was born about 1905 in Gbeog, on the plain to the immediate west of Tongo. Sometime in the 1920s, her father Nangena arranged for her to be married to Dakuar of the Bukiok clan of Tengzug, whom she joined around the other side of the hills at Santeng. Having re-established himself below the rocks housing the Yanii site of Tongnaab, Boarnii remembers, Tengol set about pleading with the British to allow his immediate family and associates to join him in Tengzug. The British acquiesced, and Tengol was joined first by Dakuar, accompanied by Boarnii and their children, by the then *yiran*, Naoh, and his family, and then by the *tengdaana* Tiezein.[27] "When we first came, the whole area had returned to bush. There were tall trees everywhere, and the bush was full of wild animals: lions, leopards, hyenas. We would be at home and hyenas would be outside howling. We were always afraid, and it was hard work to clear the area to build our homes. . . . Life really was difficult at that time."[28] Boarnii's picture of the civilized heart of the Talensi world having reverted to dangerous wilderness was repeated by other informants, most of whom at the time of re-settlement had never set foot in Tengzug. "The bush was full of wild animals," Azabu confirms. "Only our fathers knew the way back. If they had died, we would not have known the way back here."[29]

In 1932—the very year that Kobina Assifu won the right to operate his Nana Tongo shrine far to the south in Akyem Abuakwa—the hill folk secured a further concession from British officials. The "chief" and the leading *tengdaana* from each of the four communities on the outer slopes of the Tong Hills that had taken up arms in 1911, Gorogo, Shia, Sipaat, and Yinduri, were permitted to reoccupy their homes within the exclusion zone.[30] Two of our most insightful elderly informants, Diegire Baa of Shia and the late Yiran Boare, offered interesting interpretations of the negotiations leading to the eventual return of all the exiles. Both placed great emphasis on changing British perceptions of Tongnaab. Diegire Baa told us, "After we were reconciled with the British, they questioned us about the shrine. We told them that it doesn't harm people; rather it helps them. They took some sample of the god, and three years later said yes, they can see that the shrine really is not harmful. Then we were allowed to stay and sacrifice properly."[31] Yiran too stressed the spatial dislocation of *kaab* during the years of exile. Like Diegire Baa, he saw the settlement with colonial power as the belated British acknowledgment of Tongnaab's ritual power. Intriguingly, he recalled one intervention as being particularly crucial: "We had to sacrifice where we were staying [at Santeng]. Later, however, a British man came with his wife to Tongnaab, as they wanted a child. When they came to the shrine it helped them, and they succeeded in having children. When the British saw that Tongnaab is helpful rather than harmful . . . [they] asked us to return and make the shrine nice so it could solve all people's problems."[32]

Figure 5.1. Boarnii (c. 1905–2001).

Figure 5.2. Diegire Baa (born c. 1910).

Seventy years on, Yiran was uncertain as to the identity of this British couple. It is possible that he is referring to the governor of the Gold Coast, Sir Ransford Slater (1927–32), and Lady Slater, who during a tour of the Northern Territories visited Taleland with much pomp and circumstance on 17 April 1929. Motoring "to Tong amid rows of Bow and Arrow men lining the route straight to the foot of the Hill," the governor and his party then proceeded to trek to the summit housing the Tongnaab shrine.[33] Coming shortly before the easing of the ban on settlement in the hills, the visit was certainly a memorable one. But Sir Ransford and Lady Slater appear to have been accompanied by their daughters, so do not fit Yiran's description of a childless couple in search of Tongnaab's legendary gift of fertility. More likely candidates for the couple whose pilgrimage would precipitate the final resettlement of the Tong Hills are the social anthropologist Meyer Fortes and his wife Sonia, who arrived for a rather longer sojourn in Taleland some five years later, in January 1934.

Fortes would become intimately involved with the reformulation of colonial rule in Taleland. However, there is no evidence that he intervened directly into the question of the resettlement of the Tong Hills during his first period of fieldwork, between January 1934 and February 1935. In the absence of the relevant documentation, all that can be said is that sometime early in the dry season of 1934, the chief commissioner ruled that "as a reward for their obedience" all the exiled hill people could return to their homes.[34] In addition, the ban on the use of the Bonaab shrine, which had remained in place after the inquiry of 1925, was lifted. "How attached the people are to their ancestral homes," the chief commissioner reported,

> is shown by the fact that within two months of the removal of the ban over one hundred and twenty compounds had been rebuilt. These concessions have earned the gratitude of the chiefs and people. They are happy now that their ancient constitution and form of worship have been restored with the sole proviso, to which they unhesitatingly agreed, that the Administrative Officers shall at all times have free access to the shrines and be permitted . . . to attend the ceremonies connected with their worship.[35]

Fortes estimated that the total number of homesteads built over the course of two dry seasons was at least three hundred and that in all over two thousand people returned to the hills.[36] It is noteworthy that the full reoccupation of ancestral lands and the rebuilding of household shrines was followed in 1936 by another outstanding harvest.[37]

Although this period of dramatic social reconstruction in the Tong Hills—the making of new farms, the removal of bush, the construction of

Figure 5.3. The return to the Tong Hills. Unpublished photograph by Meyer Fortes captioned "Housebuilding at Yinduri Dec. 1934."

new houses—coincided with Fortes's fieldwork, he had remarkably little to say about it in his published work. What he did have to say, however, is important, as it has featured prominently in subsequent debate over his particular vision of Talensi social structure. Like the chief commissioner, Fortes stressed that the desire on the part of the hill folk to return to their "ancient constitution" of clan and lineage relationships was the key motivation, "in spite of the economic sacrifice this meant for a great many of them."[38] "Down on the plains most of them had all the land they needed [and] . . . were better off for food than they had been on the hills," he argued. "For all their rationalizations about the better climate and pleasanter surroundings of the hills, the truth was that it was a matter of faith. On the hills they were back among their fathers and forefathers, and this gave them a sense of religious security they had lacked on the plains."[39] This determination to privilege "moral" at the expense of "rational" materialist factors in shaping both Talensi behavior and the entire kinship struc-

Figure 5.4. Tengol's extensive, newly built compound nestled in the rocks below the Yanii Tongnaab shrine. Unpublished photograph by Meyer Fortes captioned "A flat roofed compound on Tenzugu (Beukyeok) [i.e., Bukiok]," 1934–37. All houses within a certain radius of the great earth shrine (*tongban*) Ngoo must have flat mud roofs rather than thatch. The house still stands and is now occupied by Tengol's sons John Bawa Zuure and Golibdaana Malbazaa and their families.

ture was challenged by a number of early critics, who in turn have been criticized by Hart for espousing a "vulgar materialism."[40] Whether or not the rocky valley of the Tong Hills provided a better agrarian livelihood than the surrounding flatlands must remain a moot point—although Hart does support Worsley's contention that this was indeed the case.[41] We would agree with Hart that these two theoretical positions are far from mutually exclusive. No doubt like Fortes's informants in the 1930s, those to whom we have recently spoken put great emphasis on religious factors in explaining the desire to return to their homes. But as the ancestors accessed through the Tongnaab *bo'a* of the hills were seen to preside over and to determine the fate of human society, then there was certainly nothing "irrational" in that desire, particularly in the wake of four years of recurring crop failures and serious subsistence crises.

The resettlement of the Tong Hills years after the violent expulsion of March 1911 represents a key moment in the encounter between the Talensi and British colonialism. If the 1935 restoration of the Ashanti Confederacy has long been recognized as a watershed in the twentieth-century history of the great forest kingdom, then far to the north in Taleland the same year can be seen as marking the end of the prolonged process of conquest and pacification. Yet it also marks the point at which the Talensi began to achieve another kind of fame above and beyond their reputation as the stubbornly independent mediators of a powerful cult complex. They became subjects not only of colonial rule, but of intense anthropological inquiry—processes which were not unconnected. Through the work of Meyer Fortes, the Talensi would finally be brought more fully into the purview of the colonial state. At the same time, they would become inextricably linked to British social anthropology in tropical Africa, enshrined as the very model of a traditional, stateless society. It is to the nature of this anthropological project that we now turn.

Meyer Fortes and the Talensi, 1934–1937

As we have seen, Meyer Fortes was not the first figure engaged in the production of ethnographic knowledge about the Talensi. His immediate precursor was Gold Coast Government Anthropologist R. S. Rattray. With regard to the succession of theoretical paradigms that form the basis of the intellectual history of anthropology, the short gap separating Rattray's research in the Northern Territories in 1928–30 and Fortes's fieldwork in 1934–37 can be seen as marking a fundamental dividing line in the practice of the discipline in West Africa. Rattray, it should be remembered, was a colonial official turned amateur ethnographer, a rare British example of the tradition of "scholar-administrator" that in neighboring French territories had produced such major figures as Delafosse, Tauxier, and Labouret. To the extent that he was at all interested in grand theories, Rattray tended to look back to the nineteenth century—to the evolutionism of Morgan and the primeval ancient law of Maine.[42] In contrast, Fortes belonged to the vanguard of a new generation of professional academic anthropologists. Not only did they arrive in Africa armed with a distinctive and more sophisticated set of theoretical tools, they were also independent academics affiliated with British universities and not directly answerable to colonial regimes. That said, it is important not to take the contrast between Rattray and Fortes too far in terms of their respective locations within the structure of colonial power. As already argued, Rattray was far from being the well-connected colonial "insider." Despite his official position, he was regarded with suspicion and sometimes outright hostility by district commissioners in the north and by his superiors in Accra. Fortes—for different reasons—was also regarded warily at first. But by the time of his second period of fieldwork, in 1936–37, he had won the trust of officials and was working closely on the project of colonial reform.

Meyer Fortes was born in 1906 in Britstown, a small railway town in the northern Cape Colony of South Africa, the son of two Russian Jewish immigrants.[43] "I came into anthropology by a roundabout route, in common with a number of my contemporaries," he wrote four years before his death in 1983.[44] After graduating from the University of Cape Town in 1926, Fortes moved to London, where he enrolled for a Ph.D. in psychology at University College. He was awarded his doctorate in 1930, and in the following year, while he was working on a study of juvenile delinquency in the East End of London, a chance meeting with Bronislaw Malinowski set him on the path to a career in anthropology. Fortes began attending Malinowski's seminar at the London School of Economics, where since 1923 the latter had been advocating a new type of social anthropology along the lines of his own research on the Trobriand Islanders of Melanesia. Moving away from the sweeping hypothetical reconstructions of the history of "primitive" peoples that had characterized the discipline from the mid-Victorian age, Malinowski favored a strictly synchronic approach based on extensive fieldwork amongst one people or tribe. Although Fortes claimed he was at first unimpressed with the explanatory value of Malinowski's "functionalist" theory, he recognized that it "represented a revolution in fieldwork method."[45] Crucially, Malinowski was also successful in selling his new approach to the International Institute of African Languages and Cultures (later renamed the International African Institute [IAI]). Founded in London in 1926 by a group of missionaries, educationalists, linguists, and colonial administrators, the IAI was committed to furthering the acquisition of knowledge about Africa's peoples with a view to social amelioration. In 1931, it attracted financial backing from the Rockefeller Foundation, enabling the launch of an active research program that looked for its first recruits to Malinowski's emerging cadre of acolytes. The first intake of IAI research fellows included Fortes, S. F. Nadel, S. Hofstra, Godfrey and Monica Wilson, Margery Perham, Hilda Kuper, Lucy Mair, the black South African Z. K. Matthews, and, subsequently, Audrey Richards. Together with E. E. Evans-Pritchard and Isaac Schapera, two of

Malinowski's earlier students who had already secured funding for field-work, they would go on to form the core personnel of postwar Africanist anthropology.

Jack Goody has argued at length that the extraordinary diversity of the pioneering generation of Malinowskian ethnographers in terms of nation-ality, gender, race, religion, and political persuasion belies any simplistic notion that they were somehow in league with the colonial establishment and therefore part and parcel of the project of colonial rule in Africa.[46] To a very great extent, this is convincing. These is no doubt that Fortes's iden-tity as a South African Jew of left-wing persuasion was an issue in the pro-longed negotiations involved in securing permission for him and his wife Sonia to enter the Gold Coast. Indeed, Sonia, a Russian emigrée with a Soviet upbringing whom Fortes had met in South Africa and married in London, was very much part of the problem. It is also clear that any agenda that might have been imposed by funding bodies such as the Rockefeller Foundation was easily side-stepped in the field. When Fortes was awarded an IAI fellowship to conduct fieldwork in 1932, his proposal was entitled "A Psychological Approach to the Study of African Society: The Social Development of the African Child." His plan was to investigate child psy-chology in order that "the task of inculcating new habits, motives, and at-titudes in the African child" through Western education avoid unneces-sary "disruption of African society in the course of this new teaching."[47] Aside from Malinowski's concern with what he called "practical anthro-pology," this proposal was shaped by two proximate factors: first, Fortes's own previous work in child psychology, and second, the interest of the Rockefeller Foundation in "culture contact"—in other words, the perceived threat to the fabric of "traditional" African societies from the combined forces of colonialism, capitalism, and modernity. However, once in Tongo, Fortes was soon diverted from his envisaged research focus on child psy-chology and demonstrated little interest in the whole IAI–Rockefeller Foun-dation notion of "culture contact."

Fortes had decided to conduct fieldwork in the Northern Territories of the Gold Coast on the advice of Rattray, with whom he had been in con-tact in London and whose *Tribes of the Ashanti Hinterland* appeared as he was preparing his research proposal in 1932.[48] "I wished to work in a society that was minimally acculturated, economically and politically traditional, and above all with a 'family system' . . . that was distinctively 'African,'" he wrote in the 1970s. "The Tallensi proved to be ideal in all these respects."[49] Yet it is clear from his first fieldwork report to Malinowski that Fortes did not actually intend to work amongst the Talensi.[50] On arriving at Accra in

January 1934, he was uncertain exactly where in the Northern Territories he and Sonia should base themselves. The couple spent their first fortnight in the Gold Coast acclimatizing at the Prince of Wales College at Achimota on the outskirts of the colonial capital. Fortes was impressed with the "new social values" being inculcated at the school and spent a lot of time chatting with the older students, who were "interested in discussing the advantages and disadvantages of the kinship system with me."[51] "We . . . consulted a number of people at Accra and Kumasi," he wrote to Malinowski, "and were advised to make for Zuarungu . . . which is in the middle of a populous Nankanni district."[52] Fortes hoped to start work among the Nankani immediately, but on arrival at Zuarungu was disappointed to find the recently abandoned colonial station unsuitable for fieldwork. The rest house was occupied too often by traveling commissioners and was in any case "segregated from the native compounds in such a way as to make free and easy contact with the people difficult." More problematically, "the natives have a fixed idea that all white men are government officials, and were convinced that we were emissaries of the DC in disguise. They were very friendly but not forthcoming." Perhaps because of the great weight of ethnographic data on the Nankani already available in *Tribes of the Ashanti Hinterland,* he was loath to deviate from his original plan, and only very reluctantly accepted the suggestion of District Commissioner Gibbs at Gambaga that he should instead base himself amongst the neighboring Talensi at Tongo. Gibbs instructed Tongrana Nambiong to organize the repair of the rest house, during which time the Forteses started work at Zuarungu on the understanding that "the Tallense and the Nankanni . . . belong to a single culture, and . . . we should be able to apply experience gained at Zuarungu to Tongo." This they found only partially true and were frustrated to have to begin their language training all over again when they relocated to Tongo a month later.

Despite these early hiccups, Fortes soon came to regard his last-minute change of plans as fortuitous. The main advantage of Talensi country, he reported to Malinowski, was its relative isolation: "While only six miles from Zuarungu and the main motor road, we are not on a motorable road. Tongo is rarely visited by European officials, who stop at Zuarungu if any business with the Tallense chiefs calls them here. . . . The nearest focus of effective culture contact is Navrongo, about twenty-six miles away, where there is a hospital, a DC and a store." This last observation was not quite accurate. Fortes had overlooked the presence at Bolgatanga, some eight miles away, of the Catholic White Fathers, who in 1925 had been granted permission to open a mission station and a school serving the Frafra countryside.[53] Moreover, because his definition of "culture contact" was limited to that between "traditional" African society and the forces of European modernity, he chose not to recognize the shrines of the Tong Hills as sites of cross-cultural encounter.[54] Yet, although Fortes's functionalist approach pushed him toward treating Talensi society as if it were hermetically sealed, he was well aware of the changes wrought by colonial conquest: "Twenty-five years of European occupation have left an appreciable mark. As recently as 1911 a military expedition came to Tongo to suppress a revolt of the people in the neighbouring hills. The expedition is well remembered—we have been reproached for the misdeeds of our predecessors! The political organization and legal system have been profoundly affected by the control exercised by the European administration." It was in the economic sphere that Fortes believed that the impact of outside contact was most pronounced: "Money is well established as a medium of exchange, and a large percentage of the younger men have been away to work in Ashanti and the Colony. . . . The open communication and the *Pax Britannica* have contrived to make the population very mobile. People travel a good deal in search of work, or buying and selling grain and livestock." Although he believed that these changes had had a negative influence on the morale of Talensi society, he concluded that "the indigenous institutions seem to be firmly established" and contact had "not led to a breakdown of the culture."

By the time Fortes reported all of this to Malinowski in July 1934, he had already departed from his original research agenda. Indeed, almost as soon as he and Sonia were established under the wing of Nambiong at Tongo, "unexpected contingencies" began to divert him away from his planned focus on child development and toward what he referred to as the "wider contexts" of Talensi society.[55] "Thus," he wrote, "we arrived at the season of communal fishing expeditions, in some of which we were able to participate. Forearmed with a functional plan of enquiry we soon discovered that this ostensibly purely economic activity has great political significance."[56] Arriving in the depths of the dry season and feeling their way into life at Tongo during the lean, hungry months before the next harvest, the Forteses unsurprisingly directed their attention to the local food economy—a topic that must have been the one overriding concern of their Talensi hosts.[57] After the years of recurring hardship between 1928 and 1932, delayed rains and locusts again threatened devastation, enabling the couple "to observe the social processes of dealing with this threat to the very life of the people. Once again we were led into the fields of political organisation, and especially—again guided by a functional plan—to investigate the magical sanctions of chieftainship and its traditional back-

Figure 5.5. Meyer Fortes and Tongrana Nambiong. Unpublished photograph, probably by Sonia Fortes, 1934–37.

ground."[58] But investigation in this direction was constrained by Fortes's limited command of Talen. By the middle of the year, he and Sonia had "progressed so far with the language as to be able to do a certain amount of work without an interpreter."[59] It was in "the sphere of magic and religion," however, that they remained most dependent on their local assistant—an unnamed individual whom Fortes describes only in passing as "the only literate member of the tribe at home."[60]

The Forteses appear to have had very little if any contact with British officialdom for the first six months of their sojourn at Tongo. By the time Fortes submitted his second fieldwork report in October 1934, however, that had changed. On several occasions he had met with District Commissioner Gibbs, who he described to Malinowski as "one of the men organising a group of 'Native States' under indirect rule in the Northern Territories."[61] These meetings appear to have resulted in a further shift in his research agenda toward the political realm:

> Colonel Gibbs very frankly discussed with us the administrative problems with which he is grappling in this area. We were led, in consequence, to give more attention than before to political organisation in relation to the plans of the Government. To deal adequately with this would require several months. What we have learnt so far, however, is enough to show both that the government is tackling a more formidable task than its officers seem to realise and that it has been seriously misinformed, perhaps even deliberately misled about the existing state of affairs.[62]

Where the government had been led astray was with regard to the nature of Talensi chieftaincy—although Fortes's explanation of this to Malinowski suggests that what he actually meant was that the British had been misinformed or misled about the role of chiefs in the precolonial past, rather than the "existing state of affairs." Namoo chiefs such as the *tongrana*, he argued, had long exercised a degree of authority, especially that associated with "magical sanctions like rain making." Where the administration had gone wrong was, first, in regarding such chiefs as "autocratic potentates" and, second, in creating *kambonaaba*s amongst the autochthonous Tale clans. The latter, Fortes stressed, "are regarded as upstarts by the 'Mamprussi' [i.e., Namoo] community and indeed often behave as such. On the other hand, it is amongst these new chiefs . . . that progressive and vigorous personalities are often to be found, men eager to benefit by whatever the white man has to offer." Fortes mentions no names, but it is clear that the vigorous personality he had most in mind here was the British-appointed "Chief of Tengzug," Tengol.

Rattray had sounded a similar warning regarding the direction of administrative policy in the Northern Territories four years earlier. Yet senior British officials initially were as unimpressed with Fortes's concerns as they had been with those of his ethnographic precursor. After thirteen months' fieldwork at Tongo, Fortes and Sonia returned to England early in 1935. That June, Chief Commissioner W. J. A. Jones expressed deep reservations about the value of such prolonged anthropological research. "From a brief conversation with Dr. Fortes," he wrote to Accra, "I formed the opinion, possibly erroneous, that he was reactionary in his outlook. He did not appear to favour the efforts that are being made to establish local government on a proper basis, and he certainly deplored the fact that the Telansi [*sic*] were becoming money-conscious, preferring that the system of barter should continue to be practised."[63] What Jones expected was information "of practical value from an administrative point of view," and until he had got it he was inclined to suggest that Fortes "should not be encouraged to resume his studies in the Northern Territories."[64] The chief commissioner was particularly interested in the growing pilgrimage trade to the Tongnaab and Bonaab shrines, asking Fortes to provide him with information "on the ceremonies connected with two fetishes which I recently allowed to be resuscitated after a period of prohibition of over twenty years." While still at Tongo, Fortes had fobbed off Jones's initial request for a research report on the grounds that he first needed the permission of the IAI in London. Whether or not he later became aware of the chief commissioner's antipathy toward his return is unclear. But in August 1935, shortly after he had secured the funding that would enable him to proceed with a second period of fieldwork, Fortes agreed to co-operate, writing to Secretary for Native Affairs Hugh Thomas that he was now "anxious to write down my conclusions in a form which will be of use to the administrative officers" and requesting a set of specific problems concerning the Talensi "which require anthropological information."[65]

After consulting with the local field administration, Jones compiled a list of six questions that was forwarded to Fortes in London.[66] The first three questions addressed a topic that lay at the heart of the envisaged next phase of indirect rule in the north, the imposition of direct taxation: "What instances of commutable tribute" existed amongst the Talensi? "What is the capacity of those people to pay taxation?" and "What in view of local customs would be the most convenient and best understood sanction for non-payment?" The fourth question asked about Talensi laws of succession to the positions of "family head" and *kambonaaba*. The fifth addressed a problem that British officers had wrestled with for decades: "How was seduction dealt with previous to the advent of the European? What has been the trend of the native law or custom dealing with seduction since the advent of the European?" The final question returned to the one issue that had already been raised with Fortes, that of the working of the Tongnaab shrines at Tengzug. Once again, Jones's inquiries in this direction were to prove fruitless. Fortes replied that he would do his best to answer the first five questions, but refused to address the sixth, which he insisted "will have to await a later date."[67] Without access to Fortes's papers, it is difficult to know exactly why he was so reluctant to discuss Tongnaab with the colonial administration. The answer may simply be that he did not yet know enough about the great ancestor shrines of the Tong Hills to commit himself on the subject. His two 1934 fieldwork reports indicate that most of that year was spent exclusively down on the plain in Tongo. In a paper published in 1974, he referred in passing to a 1963 visit to "the old friend who had first enabled me, in 1935, to break the resistance of the Hill Tallis and be initiated into their Boghar [i.e., *bo'ar*] cult."[68] He must have observed a variety of pilgrims passing by on their way up to Tongnaab, but the fact that Tengzug remained almost entirely depopulated until early 1935 offered little incentive to spend valuable research time on the dispersed and "resistant" hill folk. Accompanied again by Sonia, Fortes returned for a second year-long stay amongst the Talensi in May 1936, and there can be little doubt that the bulk of research on what he called the "External *Bɔyar* cult" of the hills was conducted in this period.[69]

It is clear from Fortes's treatment of the External *Bo'ar* cult in the first of his two monographs, *The Dynamics of Clanship*, that the role of Tongnaab did represent something of a problem for his functionalist vision of Talensi society. *The Dynamics of Clanship* ends with an eight-page section entitled "Modern Factors of Disequilibrium," a brief and somewhat startling departure from the notion maintained throughout the previous 250 pages of the book that the Talensi political system observed in the ethnographic present of 1934–37 is to be equated with that which existed in a normative precolonial past. Fortes identifies two modern factors that had disturbed this primordial equilibrium: "British rule" and what he terms "pecuniary competition among the Hill Talis." British rule is dealt with in a cursory four paragraphs. On the one hand, Fortes applauds the "enforcement of peace and the substitution of an embryonic judicial system for the arbitrament of the bow and arrow." On the other, he points out the failings of the "artificial hierarchy" of chiefs and headmen created by colonial power before the indirect rule reforms of the 1930s.[70] The military conquest of 1911, British attempts to destroy and to prohibit the great earth and ancestor shrines, the quarter-century of exile imposed on the hill folk, forced labor, migration to the south, and the recent resettlement of the Tong Hills—events noted only in passing earlier in the book—go unremarked. The imposition of direct taxation, described by colonial officials as "the most important accomplishment" of 1936,[71] receives no mention at all.

The second factor of disequilibrium, "pecuniary competition among the Hill Talis," is discussed in slightly more detail. Fortes begins his concluding section by reiterating the central thesis of *The Dynamics of Clanship*:

> The integration of the Hill Talis in the native social structure depends, as we have seen, on a meticulous balance of local, clanship, and ritual ties and cleavages focused on the politico-ritual offices vested in the heads of maximal lineages. So nicely calculated is the distribution of these politico-ritual functions amongst the various

maximal lineages that none can claim precedence over the others. All are equally essential for the maintenance of the social equilibrium and competition between them is absolutely excluded.[72]

All this had been upset, however, by the advent of Akan pilgrimage to the Tong Hills, a "traffic in ritual benefits comparable to that of the notorious Southern Nigerian oracles" that "has brought violent competition into the sphere of the common ritual interests and values which form the bulwark of their cohesion."[73]

It is important to reiterate that Fortes was quite aware of the existence in the precolonial period of the ritual networks focused on Tongnaab that spread beyond the Talensi region to neighboring peoples of the middle Volta basin. As shown in chapter 1, he provides much valuable information on the organization of these networks, which he regarded as "an intrinsic and obviously old-fashioned feature" of the External *Bo'ar* cult. "The pilgrim traffic was . . . in former times an economic asset of the first importance as the Hill Talis and their neighbours themselves point out. It gave them also a wider range of social and cultural relationships than their own restricted community."[74] Although Fortes did not explore the full implications of this last statement, he felt able to accommodate the established trans-ethnic extension of the External *Bo'ar* cult into his overall picture of Talensi social equilibrium. What he patently was unable to accommodate, however, was the dynamics of the pilgrim trade as it had evolved by the time of his fieldwork in the mid-1930s. The very bonds of social cohesion, he argued, were being threatened by the sudden extension of ritual traffic to Asante and the Gold Coast, from where pilgrims "bring gifts in money and kind beside which the traditional gifts of Mamprusi or Bulisi client villages pale into insignificance."[75] The problem was not so much that the Talensi were becoming "money-conscious"—the concern for which Fortes had been branded a "reactionary" by Chief Commissioner Jones in 1935. It was more that the bulk of this sudden influx of cash was falling into the hands of one man, Golibdaana Tengol, "a shrewd and resolute man of unbounded ambition" whose "response to the opportunity offered by the pilgrim trade has been a mixture of cupidity, calculation, and unbridled self-interest."[76] Along with the impact of colonial rule, all of these tumultuous changes are relegated by Fortes to a perfunctory afterword. As Barnes observed, "These discrepancies do not necessarily invalidate his analysis, but it is apparent that Fortes's interest in any given situation is likely to lie in the analysis of those features that are characterized by homogeneity and persistence, rather than in a description of the possibly heterogeneous whole."[77]

Meyer Fortes's relationship with the colonial government during his second period of fieldwork, from May 1936 to April 1937, was profoundly different from what it had been during his first sojourn in the Northern Territories. In his annual report for 1934–35, Jones had taken a sideways swipe at the anthropologist, describing his views more or less as inimical to progress. A year later, the tone could not have been more different, with Jones applauding the Forteses' research and quoting extensively from their paper on the Talensi food economy.[78] Whether or not this transformation was due to Fortes's willingness while in London to respond to the administration's request for information is unclear and need not concern us here. What is important is the result of the rapprochement: the fact that during his second year at Tongo, Fortes would play a crucial role in determining the shape of indirect rule in Taleland. The extent to which Fortes's research findings began to shift colonial perceptions and policies is apparent from the official response to his memorandum on Talensi marriage. "The sections describing the formalities of the marriage contract demonstrate how logical and clear the thinking of the primitive African may be and how little we can teach him in that respect," enthused the district commissioner at Gambaga, with Jones concurring that the memorandum "provides proof that even the comparatively primitive Furfura [*sic*] possess a logical, and not unjust, code of laws."[79]

The 1935–36 annual report signaled the intention of the administration to push forward to the next phase of reform. "The end of the year finds us ready, with nominal rolls prepared, to start what we have been aiming at for the last six years," stated the chief commissioner, "namely direct taxation, the cornerstone of indirect rule."[80] The transition from a forced labor regime to one based on taxation would also allow the British to do away with the *kambonaaba*s and to begin the task of restoring the authority of *tengdaana*s and other customary family heads. That the *kambonaaba*s "ever came into existence was the result of the failure to study the organisation and delegation of responsibility among the tribes comprising the Mamprusi Division and particularly those in the Zuarungu area where the Kombenaba [*sic*] have in the past reaped a rich harvest and consequently created a spirit of antagonism against native authority."[81] The decision to formally recognize the role of decentralized "family" authority throughout the Protectorate, Jones reported, was also influenced by recent events in the Tong Hills, where the absence of disputes over farm boundaries among the returning Talensi exiles was seen as a "remarkable testimony to the soundness of the family system of administration."[82] Both these pieces of evidence cited to support the shift in government policy bear all the marks of having been furnished by Fortes.

If, by 1936, officials had acknowledged that the *kambonaaba*s were a purely colonial creation often regarded with hostility within their own communities, then fresh doubts also began to emerge about the legitimacy of the Mamprusi *kunaaba* as the head chief of the Talensi. The British, of course, were neither willing nor able to dispense with the idea of chiefs altogether. Despite pronouncements on the virtues of the "family system of administration," some sort of indigenous hierarchy was still seen as indispensable for the functioning of indirect rule amongst the Frafra and the other stateless peoples of the northern frontier. A plan therefore emerged to replace the *kunaaba* with the *tongrana* and to further enhance the latter's authority by reconstituting his tribunal as the solitary Talensi native court. In August 1936, the chief commissioner invited comments from Fortes, who had signaled his readiness to assist the government. "We anthropologists come out to study primitive tribes such as the Talansi primarily out of professional interest in the Science of Man and generally under the auspices of academic bodies," Fortes explained to the new assistant district commissioner with responsibility for the Frafra region, A. F. Kerr. "But we realise that the test of accurate observation and inference must always lie in its applicability in practice. That is why I asked you, the practical man, to indicate to me those fields of 'practical politics' in which observations such as mine can be tested."[83] Fortes duly drafted a memorandum on the office of *tongrana*, which was broadly in favor of official proposals.[84] While pointing out that neither the Tongo chief nor any of the other Namoo clan leaders historically had any direct authority over each other or over any of the autochthonous Tale clans, he was convinced that in precolonial times the *tongrana* was "recognized as the man of highest rank in the district inhabited by the Talensi." This Fortes contrasted with the *kunaaba*, who, he confirmed, was entirely without legitimacy and seen by many Talensi as a "stranger." From his vantage point at Tongo, it was clear that Fortes was highly impressed with the personal qualities of Nambiong, who had been *tongrana* since 1918 and was widely regarded by British officials and the Talensi alike as a forceful, imposing character.

For the remainder of the year, Fortes collaborated closely with Kerr in further elaborating these recommendations for an enhanced judicial role for Tongrana Nambiong. It can be said without qualification that it was Fortes himself who drew up the final plans for indirect rule in Taleland. These are contained in a memorandum entitled "Tallensi Divisional Court" that he delivered to the government in January 1937 and that Kerr adopted lock, stock, and barrel for the constitution of what five months later would emerge as the "Talensi Confederacy."[85] Fortes's memorandum is in effect a very preliminary, distilled version of *The Dynamics of Clanship among the Tallensi*. What he did was identify "the age old traditional networks of loyalties and bonds based on kinship, clan organization, religious ideas and so forth" that lay "vigorously alive" beneath the system of chiefs and *kambonaaba*s that had been foisted on the Talensi during the first decades of colonial rule.[86] It was these networks—the famous "fields of clanship" and the "scheme of ritual collaboration" of the first monograph—that Fortes proposed should be rehabilitated as the basis for a new Native Authority. In short, he identified nine distinct groups of clan settlements, six predominantly Namoo and the remaining three Tale, which in turn were bound together by further sets of overlapping ties. He then suggested that from each of these nine groups, the senior clan head should go forward to sit on a joint council. The key to the system was the "ingenious device" that made it "impossible for any one clan head—even the one recognized as the *primus inter pares*—to act without the cooperation of the others."[87]

There was only one outstanding concern, and that concern brings us back to Tongnaab and the cross-cultural pilgrimage trade. "The Tong Hills offer, in my opinion, a serious problem," Fortes concluded. "It is the most distracted corner of the country and a settlement of the Gologdana's position is essential before the representation of this area is settled."[88] The language here is striking: "The most distracted corner of the country" could easily have come straight from colonial reports dating from the era of colonial conquest before 1911. Despite the progress made in bringing the recalcitrant hill folk "in," the historical dynamics of Tongnaab's ritual network still jarred with the colonial—and the ethnographic—vision of a "settled" Talensi society.

The Distracted Corner:
Ritual Collaboration and the Problem of Tengol

Rattray's striking portrait of Tengol, taken on the morning of 6 May 1928, captures something of the presence and authority of this pivotal figure in the history of Tongnaab. "A really magnificent-looking man, standing well over six feet and very finely proportioned," Tengol—probably in his fifties at the time—gazes from the photograph with all the poise and self-confidence of a man well on the way to carving a name for himself in the world.[89] A British-appointed *kambonaaba*, he appears to have been acutely conscious of the fragility of that position in Talensi society. Like many others, he also chafed under the ongoing exclusion from his ancestral home. "I was made chief by the Europeans," he told Rattray, "but have not yet been enskinned by the Nalelego [Nalerigu, i.e., the *nayiri*] because I am really an exile from my land and live at Tileg."[90] Nonetheless, Tengol's role as a colonial power-broker had allowed him to emerge by 1928 as the key intermediary in the expansion of Tongnaab's pilgrimage networks to Asante and the Gold Coast. It was Tengol whom Kobina Assifu approached on his pioneering journey in 1925 and it was Tengol whom subsequent pilgrims from the south sought out to guide them to the ritual sanctuary at the rocky summit of the Tong Hills. In 1931, he and his immediate family were the first Talensi to be permitted to return to Tengzug. Four years later, Tengol was finally presented with the red fez of office by the *nayiri*, although British officials were uncertain whether this was "only in respect of his position as priest of a fetish [worshiped?] in Nalerigu [i.e., Tongnaab?]" or "as chief of Tonzugu."[91] It was probably shortly after he received the red fez that Tengol succeeded Diema as *golibdaana*, thereby combining a degree of acquired power with ascribed ritual authority.

As we have seen, the principal sites of the Tongnaab cult in the Tong Hills all had long-established ritual constituencies among surrounding savanna peoples. The sphere of influence of the Degal *bo'ar*, for example, was especially strong in the southeast of Mamprugu, and that of Bonaab in the south-west of Mamprugu and amongst the *Dagbon-sabelig* or "Black Dagombas," while Yanii had long attracted supplicants from other Dagomba communities and from the Builsa. By the early 1930s, Yanii was also attracting the vast bulk of the new southern pilgrim trade. This was in part due to the fact that its main rival, Bonaab, continued to languish under a British ban throughout the crucial "take-off" period in southern pilgrimages from the mid-1920s. By the time the ban on Bonaab was lifted in 1935, Yanii was already regarded by southerners as *the* "Nana Tongo" shrine and Tengol as *the* intermediary on the hill. Yet there can be little doubt that Tengol exploited this situation to the full. Just as, in the south, exotic ritual commodities were marketed by entrepreneurs like Hwemeso salesman *extraordinaire* Kwabena Nzema, so the more business-minded guardians of savanna shrines actively developed their own strategies to attract the increasingly lucrative pilgrim traffic. Fortes, it should be reiterated, thought that such conscious marketing strategies had been a feature of the new transregional ritual commerce from the outset: "Men from the Hills, with a mixture of inborn business acumen and sincere faith in the magical powers of their oracle cult, advertised the cult quietly. A trickle of pilgrims from these

Figure 5.6. Tengol (d. 1949), photographed by R. S. Rattray on 6 May 1928. Pitt Rivers Museum, University of Oxford 1998.312.1057.1; published as figure 73 of *Tribes of the Ashanti Hinterland*, captioned "The Chief of Teng'zugu," facing 362.

wealthy and comparatively sophisticated areas began to flow northwards. And the trickle soon became a broad stream."[92] It was Tengol's return to Tengzug a full four years before the remainder of the exiled hill population that enabled him to press home his early advantage. Ensconced in a newly rebuilt and imposing compound nestled under the granite heights containing the Yanii shrine, he tightened his hold over this growing stream of pilgrims who made their way to his doorstep from the towns and villages of Asante, the Gold Coast, and beyond.

Although we can question the validity of Fortes's model of a static, perfectly balanced Talensi political structure suddenly threatened by "disequilibrium," there is no doubt that the extension of pilgrimage networks to the Akan forests did result in fierce "pecuniary competition" in the Tong Hills. Nor should this be especially surprising in the years after the period of recurring hunger, given that access to cash could mean physical survival in times of acute subsistence crisis. Present-day informants assert that supplicants have never actually "paid" for access to Tongnaab. Rather, pilgrims were (and are today) expected only to bring "gifts" for the god's ritual intermediaries—a point borne out by Fortes's own account of the pilgrimage trade.[93] This distinction notwithstanding, the result of such gifts in cash and in kind, plus the income generated by the purchase of sacrificial livestock, of food and accommodation, and, finally, of the "shadow" of Tongnaab itself, was an influx of money "on a scale unprecedented in Tale history."[94] The chief beneficiary was, of course, Tengol. "What made Tengol powerful was that people were giving him gifts, especially the Asante," remembered Yiran Boare. "The Asantes would dash him with money, cloth, big *kentes* and other gifts. These things made him great and rich, not money paid for sacrifices at Tongnaab."[95]

By the mid-1930s, Golibdaana Tengol stood at the center of a complex business operation that made him one of the wealthiest men in the Northern Territories. In 1938, he was reported to have "touts" permanently stationed in the Asante capital, Kumasi.[96] "All the members of his maximal lineage, except one segment, co-operate in running it and benefit from it," Fortes wrote.

> His closest partners are some of his own half brothers and cousins, and their share of the profits is enough to make them considerably more wealthy than the average native. Two or three henchmen belonging to other Tenzugu clans and the other ritual functionaries of the *Byar* whose presence is essential for the performance of the rites of accepting the pilgrims get about the same "rake-off" as his near agnates. On a rough estimate I would say that the Golibdaana keeps about half the profits and divides the other half among the other men interested in the business.

This enables the others . . . to have from five to nine wives each, where the ordinary native of similar age and status would have at most two or three wives; and the number of wives a man has is a good indication of his income in terms of food-supply and cash.[97]

Tengol himself was reported to have accumulated an extraordinary eighty wives by the mid-1930s, a number rising to over one hundred by the time of his death in 1949.[98] In a conversation with the current *golibdaana*, Tengol's son Malbazaa, we asked how many children his father's wives had borne. "Thirty-six," he answered emphatically, "—apart from women. The children who died we also don't count. Thirty-six grown men!"[99] Born at the height of his father's powers in 1938, Malbazaa recalled the streams of southern pilgrims passing through to Tongnaab: "I learnt to speak Twi from these people staying here in this house. I did not go to Kumasi or Accra to work, but learnt the Twi language here in this house, because of the Akan people coming."[100]

The impact of the pilgrim traffic and the wealth it generated was not limited to Tengol's house. In many ways, the traffic was at the root of transformations in relationships between generations and genders across the hills. Tengol commanded the allegiance of the majority of "youngmen" belonging to all the hill clans, as well as "by necessity, the many Tongzugu people who are his debtors."[101] Men who had access to wealth generated by pilgrims often used it to purchase cattle and, subsequently, to acquire wives. For a young man, such access could mean an earlier marriage than would have been possible if he had relied upon his father or uncles for cattle or traveled south to work as a migrant laborer. A son's dependence upon his elders, in other words, could be eroded. For older men, new-found wealth meant the ability to marry multiple times. The results of these shifting power differentials included a notable rise in polygyny from the 1930s and a marked decrease in the age of marriage of young women. For men who did not have access to wealth generated by the pilgrim trade, the marriage horizon could be rather bleak. There is evidence that as the average marriage age of women declined in these years, that of men rose.[102] Fortes noted that at the *Gologo* festival one year in the 1930s, the young dancers improvised a song lamenting "the sorry plight of the young men who could get no wives because the chiefs were greedily snapping up all the young women to add to their already huge harems."[103]

Some of those in Tengzug who lost out in the contest for the lucrative new pilgrim trade reacted angrily to Tengol's rise to prominence. Leading the opposition was the Kpatar clan, whose elders collaborated with those of the Samire, Gundaat, Nachire, and Sakpee clans in managing the

Bonaab shrine.[104] Claiming a superior position in the finely wrought structure of "ritual collaboration" so painstakingly reconstructed by Fortes, Kpatarnaaba Tiezien challenged the right of his Bukiok neighbors to maintain their monopoly over southern pilgrims. By 1935, he was in open conflict with Tengol. But the Kpatar position was weak and was further undermined when early in 1936 the Sakpee and Samire clans effectively broke their established ritual ties with the *kpatarnaaba* and "went over" to Tengol.[105]

Beyond the Tong Hills, Tengol also mobilized his new-found wealth in cultivating some impressive political connections. Kerr noted rumors that he had loaned large amounts of money both to the *ya na*, the paramount chief of Dagbon, and the *yagbumwura*, the paramount of Gonja.[106] If this was indeed the case, then, given his confirmed financial relationship with the *nayiri* of Mamprugu, Tengol was bankrolling the three most important African kings in the Protectorate.[107] Down on the surrounding plains, however, the Namoo-dominated Talensi communities appear to have remained aloof from the political infighting in the Tong Hills. Fortes's comments in this regard are fascinating. Tongrana Nambiong, he noted, certainly resented the fact that Tengol had received a red fez from the *nayiri*. Yet Fortes was adamant that the people of Tongo "do not in the least envy the Golibdaana his pecuniary monopoly. Frankly despising the fertility and oracle aspects of the *Bɔyar* cult as a piece of fraudulent magic, they look on the money gained through the pilgrim traffic as tainted."[108] If Fortes's description of Tongo perceptions was accurate, then there was much in his own accounts of Tongnaab that closely echoed those of his patrons and interlocutors in Tongo.

The ensuing stand-off between the *golibdaana* and the *kpatarnaaba* created real problems for Fortes in his research and for Kerr as he moved to implement the envisaged "Talensi Confederacy." "Thirty years earlier, everyone agreed, before the white man's peace was established, arrows would have flown on the hill," Fortes later wrote. "I was bombarded from both sides with acrimonious accusations against the other and had to step warily to assert my neutrality."[109] Despite this assertion, by the beginning of 1937 he appears to have convinced the administration that the underlying cause of conflict in the Tong Hills was the wealth being accumulated by Tengol. Chief Commissioner Jones—who only two years before had criticized the anthropologist on account of his hostility to the advancing cash nexus— toyed with a variety of solutions. "If peace and progress among the Talensi is to be assured," he wrote, "we must obviously curtail the activities and pretensions of the Gologdaana. This I think can best be done by insisting on all payments made in cash by the Ashanti pilgrims forming part of the native revenue."[110] Other suggestions were more drastic, ranging from forbidding access to the Tong Hills to Asantes and other southerners, through blowing up the Tongnaab cave, and on to the extraordinary idea of "encouraging the competition of rival fetishes."[111] All of these ideas were rejected as impracticable by Kerr, who had been advised by Fortes that it would be impossible even to establish the extent of Tengol's shrine income, let alone to enforce measures to control that income.[112] In the end, the administration pulled back from intervening directly in the pilgrim trade and imposed a temporary solution to the political stand-off in the Tong Hills. It was agreed that the *tongrana* should represent Tengzug on the new federal council until such time as the *golibdaana* and the *kpatarnaaba* could work out the order in which each would act in turn as the Tengzug representative.

In May 1937, Kerr spent ten days trekking around the Talensi communities "explaining and discussing the scheme at each place."[113] "A further visit to the Tongrana convinced me that so long as Kunaba remained north of the scarp little progress was likely to be made"[114]—a clear victory for Nambiong over his old Mamprusi rival. On 16 June, the old Kurugu Native Authority ceased to exist and the Talensi Native Authority came into being. The new ten-man federal council was composed of the *naaba*s of the predominantly Namoo communities of Tongo, Shiega, Yamelega, Duusi, Pwalugu, Datoko, and Winkogo, the Baari *tengdaana*, and the Shia *bo'arana* (representing the Tale hillside communities of Shia, Gorogo, Sipaat, and Yinduri), plus, in time, the *golibdaana* and the *kpatarnaaba* acting in turn as the representative of Tengzug. Tongrana Nambiong was selected as the first president of the council on the firm understanding that he was *primus inter pares* and not a "head chief." While he and the other Namoo chiefs would still receive the red fez from the *nayiri* at Nalerigu, the *kunaaba* was ordered to return to Mamprugu proper and "to no longer have anything to do with the Zuarangu area."[115] Twenty-six years after the British had stormed the Tong Hills, a system of colonial control was finally put into place that bore, in profound ways, the authorship of Meyer Fortes. Tengol, as *golibdaana*, was to "collaborate" with his rival *kpatarnaaba*, as the dynamics of clanship dictated. Meanwhile, Tongrana Nambiong, Fortes's old friend and patron, was recognized as the president of a modernized political structure—the Talensi Federation.

Aftermaths: "The Gold Coast Religion Racket" in History

Meyer and Sonia Fortes left Tongo and returned to England in May 1937. By the beginning of the following year, Fortes was busy writing up his fieldwork. Although his analysis of the "pecuniary competition" created by what he regarded as the cynical manipulation of the "External *Bɔyar* cult" was not published until after the war, Fortes aired his views on the subject in 1938 in a paper given to the anthropology section of the British Association's annual conference at Cambridge. He must have been in good form. Unusually for a paper on colonial ethnography, his address was reported in the London press, appearing in the *Daily Telegraph* and the *Courier and Advertiser* before being picked up by *West Africa* magazine.[116] Under the headline "Scientists Told of Gold Coast Religion Racket: Natives' 'Ancestors' Who Charge Fee for Giving Advice," the *Telegraph* reported that scientists at the meeting "rocked with laughter yesterday when they were told about the religion racket on the Gold Coast of Africa."[117] "Dr. M. Fortes . . . described the racket, which, he said, was based on the belief of some of the most 'civilised' and even Christian tribes that their ancestors could bring them children or wealth or anything else. The advice of the 'ancestor' was, in fact, the voice of the racketeer concealed behind a rock." Tongnaab— or at least one vision of the ancestor-deity—had made the London papers.

Despite some obvious confusion on the part of the *Telegraph*'s reporter regarding the status of the "ancestor" shrine, it is worth quoting the report at some length:

> People travel by the lorry load as much as 500 miles to consult their "ancestor"— who, of course, charged a fee for his favours. The first fee was a levy of 16s for board and lodging which the devotee has to pay to the racketeer. Worshippers had to make a gift of at least £1 before they could consult their dead grandfather and also promise a "commission" of at least £5 on favours received. One man had promised as much as £100—"almost a millionaire's sum." But before the mysterious voice would condescend to proffer advice, the pilgrim had to promise to tout for backsliders from the cult who, he was warned, would be visited by terrible distress if they slighted their ancestors. . . . Dr Fortes said that there was more than one clan working the racket, in each case members of a primitive tribe living on the credulity of partly Westernised natives. They divided the territory among themselves and "organised" the scheme by appointing local "agents" and even "commercial travellers" who made periodic tours to remind pilgrims of the terrible consequences of leaving their ancestors in the lurch. It was a common thing for pilgrims to be waylaid by touts who tried to persuade them to go to a rival shrine where they could consult the oracle at "half-price." "Two of the most enlightened, politically conscious and highly-educated chiefs in the country, whose names," said Dr. Fortes, "are so well known that I cannot mention them, happened to pass through a district where one of these fetishes is practised. They had come hundreds of miles ostensibly on a political visit, but really because they were obviously impressed with the cult." He told of one racketeer who had 80 wives and was making an income of from 300 to 400 cows a year—"obviously a man of very considerable wealth in a country where a cow is worth £2 and a wife is valued at £4 10s."

Figure 5.7. Tongrana Nambiong (r. 1918–41). A version of this photograph (minus the figure on the right) appeared as the frontispiece to *The Dynamics of Clanship among the Tallensi* with the caption "Na Naam Bioŋ of Tongo (d. 1941), wearing his red fez (*muŋ*) the chief emblem of his office, and clad in his finest ceremonial robes." 1934–37.

Fortes's account throws considerable light on his attitude toward the Tongnaab cult and its leading entrepreneur, Tengol. It also contains valuable details of the organization of the pilgrim trade subsequently left out of his published work—details that further undercut the normative, static picture of Talensi society drawn in the pages of *The Dynamics of Clanship*. Evidence from Fortes's photograph collection also reveals the identity of one of the two "enlightened, politically conscious and highly-educated chiefs" whom he was too polite to mention by name in 1938. The high-ranking pilgrim was none other than the *okyenhene* of Akyem Abuakwa, Nana Sir Ofori Atta, under whose patronage Kobina Assifu operated his renowned shrine at Obretema.[118]

In 1945, after having been held up by the war, *The Dynamics of Clanship* finally appeared. The book boasted a frontispiece of the late Tongrana Nambiong, resplendent in flowing ceremonial robes and bearing the insignia of office: a leather-clad staff, the "four inch" chiefs' medallion embossed with the profile of King George V, and the red fez. Fortes's old friend, "a proud, intelligent, and forthright man whose support stood us in good stead and whose great store of knowledge was freely open to us," had died in 1941.[119] The fine photograph of Nambiong, which in time would become familiar to generations of anthropology undergraduates, can be compared to that taken by Rattray of Tengol. The image of Tongrana Nambiong, looking every inch the Namoo chief, stands in contrast to that of Golibdaana Tengol, the Tale ritual entrepreneur, stripped down to loincloth and protective amulets before descending into the inner sanctum of Tongnaab. They were clearly two powerful men who mobilized quite different resources in order to negotiate to their best advantage the opening decades of the colonial encounter. But for Fortes, the former was an industrious leader of men, the latter a cynical racketeer. Fortes was quite able to accommodate the fact that twenty-five years of colonial rule had fundamentally altered the role of the *tongrana* and thus rendered Nambiong the obvious choice for *primus inter pares* in the new Talensi Federation. Yet he refused to recognize that Golibdaana Tengol had also by force of character and by the manipulation of "modern" resources—notably the great *bo'ar* Tongnaab—accrued authority, power, and wealth in a rapidly changing world. The irony was that Tongrana Nambiong spent the last four years of his life intriguing tirelessly to subvert the new constitution drafted so carefully by Fortes. As early as 1938, he had persuaded Nayiri Badimsuguru to delegate to him the power to install all Talensi chiefs, and by the end of his life effectively had transformed himself from *primus inter pares* to "head chief."[120] As Anafu points out, "This was the beginning of the Tongo paramountcy over Taleland"—a paramountcy that has survived to this day.[121]

What does this say about Meyer Fortes as a historical actor—as a maker of history in Taleland? We have not intended to suggest that Fortes was simply a "handmaiden of colonialism," although he played a far more central role than hitherto has been recognized in the reformulation of colonial rule.[122] Did the constitution he crafted in 1937 set the stage for the political ascendancy of the office of *tongrana* in the second half of the twentieth century? One could argue that this was, in effect, the case. But in so doing, Fortes's role would be greatly exaggerated. We want to restore Fortes to Talensi history, but not to move him to the center of that very complicated story. The process of constructing a new Talensi paramountcy was not a one-man show and was determined, more than anything, by Talensi realities—by the shifting bases of power and authority in and around the Tong Hills, much of which was centered on Tongnaab. These were realities that Fortes witnessed and at times commented upon, but for which he could find no place in his timeless scheme of ritual collaboration. Tengol was not a strange aberration in a perfectly balanced kinship system. He was a symptom of—living evidence for—profound, ongoing historical change. Fortes's draft constitution may have "demoted" the ritual authority of Tongnaab and its guardians relative to the secular power of Namoo chieftaincy. But it could not undercut Tengol's real power; nor, in the final analysis, could it extricate Tongnaab from modernity—from the world of ritual commerce, colonialism, and cross-cultural encounter. It could not, in other words, stop history. After Tongrana Nambiong died, his successor, Salima, was reportedly "backed" by Golibdaana Tengol.[123] New forms of wealth and authority not only created "pecuniary competition," they necessitated new forms of collaboration—collaboration based no longer on *teng* (earth) or *bo'a* (ancestors) alone, but on wealth and political office.

The historical forces whirling about Meyer Fortes in the 1930s had little impact on *The Dynamics of Clanship, The Web of Kinship*, or his subsequent theoretical extrapolations. Although Fortes certainly did not conspire to do so, the result of his strictly synchronic analysis was effectively to maroon the Talensi and other stateless peoples of the West African savannas outside history. And herein, we would argue, lay Fortes's complicity with imperial culture. His "colonizing theoretical gaze," as the anthropologist Charles Piot has termed it, quite literally made people—and gods—without history.

6

Tongnaab and the Dynamics
of History among the Talensi

R. S. Rattray sketched them onto the edges of an amorphous Asante hinterland. Meyer Fortes painted them into intricate webs of kinship that, in their overlapping complexity, embodied wider dynamics of clanship. For decades the western ethnographic pen, sometimes retracing the very lines drawn by early colonial officials, interned the Talensi and their gods in a timeless, unchanging present. There they have constituted for the western imagination the archetype of the stateless, a manifestation *par excellence* of a "people without history." Yet we have seen that neither the Talensi nor their great *bo'ar* Tongnaab were immobilized—in space or in time—by synchronic functionalist structures, by the "traditions" that colonial officials and western scholars landed upon them. If there is a dynamic story to be told here, it is one not just of kinship and clanship, but of history. Active and ongoing change enveloped the Tong Hills and their immediate environs just as surely as it did the forests of Asante or the littoral of the Gold Coast—areas of the West African sub-region that have most often been the subject of rigorous historical inquiry.

That dynamic of change was not simply contingent upon the powerful personalities of men like Golibdaana Tengol or Tongrana Nambiong—influential though they may have been. Long after they had traveled to join their ancestors (Nambiong in 1941 and Tengol in 1949), the historical processes of ritual commerce and entrepreneurship, of sacred authority and secular power, continued unabated. As in the opening phase of the colonial encounter in the first decades of the twentieth century, all forms of rule in and around the Tong Hills had to be brokered through Tongnaab, despite the fact that formal political power was increasingly vested in the office of *tongrana*. Tongrana Nambiong eventually became first among equals in the governing structure of Taleland, and his successor, Salima, was solemnly declared to be the "elder" over his Talensi compatriots in 1947. By 1962, Kwame Nkrumah's Convention People's Party (CPP) government had upgraded the position of *tongrana* to that of paramount chief over all Talensi.[1] Still, formal political recognition from the colonial state and, subsequently, from the postcolonial state did not bring with it either ritual or economic paramountcy. Ritual authority still resided with Tongnaab in the hills, and along with it came an expanding range of economic resources that flowed to those who tended the god's sacred sites—especially the men from the house (*yir*) of Tengol. The cash and the cross-cultural connections generated by the pilgrim trade to Tongnaab, in other words, would continue to shape in profound ways the political terrain of Taleland long after Tengol's passing. As British colonial authorities had slowly come to learn, Tongnaab's ritual influence could not easily be challenged.

Tongnaab's resilience was rooted not, as Fortes argued, in timeless, localized "dynamics of clanship," but in the historically constructed and carefully nourished network of ritual commerce that reached far beyond the boundaries of Taleland. This trans-regional network survived the demise of Tengol, Kobina Assifu, and the rest of the pioneering generation of entrepreneurs that between the 1920s and 1940s engineered its diffusion from savanna heartland to Akan periphery. Tongnaab's keepers in the hills continued to reinforce and cultivate connections with client shrines throughout the region, while non-Talensi practitioners—often the daughters and granddaughters, sons and grandsons of that first generation—continued to make annual pilgrimages to Tengzug, usually during the harvest celebration of *Bo'araam*. Unlike the god's initial expansionist phase in the interwar period, these ongoing stories of ritual commerce and collaboration have left few traces in the documentary archive. Once the Talensi were brought more fully within the parameters of the colonial state, once Assifu and others had renegotiated their identities from "fetish priests" to "native physicians," and once Nana Tongo had shifted from being a subversive witch-finder to a benign "medicine," the colonial state and its successor perceived few threats to their stability from these quarters. Tongnaab, along with its practitioners and pilgrims, slipped off the pages of official surveillance and inquiry. But the silence of the colonial archive after 1940 should not be read as a decline in either cross-cultural ritual dialogue or local concerns about witchcraft. Stories very much continue, they ebb and they flow—but they can only be traced in the memories of those who have lived them, rarely in the archives of the state.

Tongnaab's Ritual Network, 1950s–1990s

Every year during the *Bo'araam* or harvest festival, pilgrims still journey from far and wide to give thanks for the previous year's bounty and to nourish and renew their connections to Tongnaab. During the festivities of November 1999, we were able to witness just how extensive the ritual network remains and to hear personal narratives that weave Tongnaab or "Nana Tongo" into the local histories of communities from across Ghana. Prominent among festival-goers are devotees from the Builsa region to the southwest of Taleland, long an integral part of Tongnaab's core savanna hinterland. Atop the Tong Hills we also met Okomfo Sika, who had traveled north with her son and *okyeame* (spokeswoman) Tawia from Kukurantumi in Akyem Abuakwa. Sika, an imposing woman of middle age, has made the four-hundred-mile pilgrimage to Tengzug every year for over two decades. She first came with her grandmother, Okomfo Aframea, who was a famous *okomfo* in Kukurantumi. As noted in chapter 4, Aframea learned of Nana Tongo from her father's brother, Atta Kojo, who originally traveled to Tengzug with Kobina Assifu in the 1930s.[2] Kofi Obeng of the Akyem town of Asiakwa was also in Tengzug in 1999. He had come to renew the shrine for his wife, Ama Boatema, who is the *okomfo*, but who was unable to travel that year. Boatema learned of Nana Tongo from Okomfo Aframea and she and her husband began making yearly pilgrimages in 1969.[3]

Taken together, the interlaced stories of supplicants form intricate patterns of ritual collaboration that have only continued to expand since the 1940s. They are patterns that defy notions of "tradition," of "stasis," or, indeed, of "the local." Since 1999, we have been able to trace large sections of this far-flung network by doing informally, as researchers, precisely what Tongnaab's Talensi mediators have long done—that is, by visiting supplicants in their hometowns. Representatives from the Tong Hills continue to make these reciprocal journeys in order to reinforce the ties that bind distant client shrines to the sacred center. Likewise, we set out to witness firsthand how Nana Tongo operates today in different local contexts and how it has managed to survive across generations in Ghana's busy and fiercely competitive ritual marketplace.

The ongoing vitality of the network was especially evident when we visited Bosomfo Nii Yaw in the Ga coastal settlement of Oshieyie to the west

Figure 6.1. Southern pilgrims from Kukurantumi at Tengzug, waiting to be escorted to the Tongnaab *bo'ar*. Okomfo Sika is second from right.

of Accra. Nestled between Botianor, whose beach is a popular weekend destination for day-trippers from the capital, and Kokrobite, with its internationally renowned drumming academy, Oshieyie represents one of the furthermost extensions of Tongnaab's ritual field inside Ghana. In a compound within sight of the Atlantic Ocean, Nii Yaw presides over a thriving shrine center studded with ritual effigies and other power objects. Over eighty years old now, he inherited Nana Tongo from his father Yaw Kwashi, who had acquired the god from Tengzug after hearing about it from Kobina Assifu "four years before the Accra earthquake," that is, in 1935.[4] Like Assifu, Yaw is an *obosomfo* who has collected several gods and has a reputation that extends well beyond the limits of his own community. In addition to Nana Tongo, he tends Bruku as well as two Ewe deities, Adjakpa(ne) and Futuagbas. Nii Yaw's grandson, Pra, who is fifteen years old, currently serves as his apprentice and has already spent four months at Tengzug learning how to properly tend Nana Tongo. Pra will inherit the gods from his grandfather—thus securing the future of Nana Tongo in this Ga coastal area into the twenty-first century.

Many of these Akyem and Ga pilgrims found their way to Tengzug by way of the long lineage of supplicants originating with Kobina Assifu in the mid-1920s. Others whom we met encountered Tongnaab quite independently of Assifu's shrine center at Obretema. Kwao Ahoto, an Ewe from Aklayawaya, learned of Nana Tongo from his grandfather, who had come directly to Tengzug in the early 1950s.[5] That decade marked a significant expansion of the Tongnaab network amongst the Ewe peoples to the east of the Volta River. As we have seen, a range of savanna witch-finding gods had begun to cross the Volta by the early 1930s, a process marked by intense ritual competition in Anlo that culminated in the outlawing of the Kunde cult in 1939. But John Bawa Zuure of Tengol's Bukiok house is adamant that Ewe (or "Ayibge") supplicants only began to travel to Tengzug after the latter's death in 1949. Zuure identifies one Bosomfo Adjebu as the "Ayigbe Assifu"—a pioneering pilgrim who in the 1950s was the first Ewe to be actually granted the *yihiyii* or shadow of Tongnaab.[6] The late Adjebu installed the *yihiyii* in a satellite shrine near Kedzi, an Anlo town on the main road leading to the frontier with Togo, from where his "sons" and others continue to make regular pilgrimages to the Tong Hills.

It was from such new Nana Tongo shrines, from the remnants of the outlawed Kunde, and from the rising influence of Tigare that northern ritual powers entered into a new expansionist phase in the late 1940s and 1950s, sweeping down the coast through Togo and Dahomey (modern-day Benin), and on to southwestern Nigeria. As reported by Geoffrey Parrinder in the quotation from *West Africa* magazine that featured in the introduction, the resulting anti-witchcraft movement in the latter took the Yoruba name Atinga (or Alatinga), a formulation with echoes of both "Nana Tongo" and "Tigare."[7] It is unlikely that Tongnaab's sudden diffusion beyond the eastern frontier of the Gold Coast resulted in the development of routinized links with the Tong Hills such as those developed by Kobina Assifu and Bosomfo Adjebu. But that diffusion left powerful cultural traces nonetheless. In the 1980s, the anthropologist Judy Rosenthal identified "Papa Kunde," "Nana Ablewa," "Sacra Bode," "Sunia Compo," and "Nana Wango" as five of the savanna spirits of the Gorovudu possession orders of the Ewe and Guin-Mina peoples of coastal Togo.[8] Evidently Kunde, Aberewa, Sakrabundi, Senyakupo, and Nana Tongo, these spirits are said by many Gorovudu practitioners to embody the souls of departed captives who passed from the savanna hinterland through the ports of the old Slave Coast and into the vortex of the Atlantic slave system. In Rosenthal's subtle analysis, Nana Tongo and the rest—summoned into the bodies of adepts by "northern" *breteke* drum patterns—represent a present-day historical interrogation and memorialization of the slave trade and its attendant cross-cultural ritual dialogue.

But in this new century, it will be increasingly difficult to track the full extent of Tongnaab's ritual hinterland. In an age of rapidly accelerating information flow and trans-national movement, that hinterland continues to expand in new directions. The extent of this change was described for us by ninety-two-year-old Yikpemdaan Wakbazaa of Gorogo, a thoughtful observer of ritual affairs in the Tong Hills:

> Before, not so many people knew of the importance of Tongnaab. It was limited to the Asantes ["*Kambonse*"], the Builsas, the Dagombas, the Mossi, but now it has spread widely. In the old days you could never walk freely about from one town to the next, so just a few people got to hear about Tongnaab. But now that everybody has the freedom to move anywhere at all, Tongnaab has spread its fame, and a lot more people come. . . . Some are from Burkina Faso, some are from Togo, others from Ivory Coast. Many people who come are Muslims, both from within Ghana and from outside, [including] Hausas ["*Zangbe*"] from Nigeria. . . . The strangers are still coming, especially white people ["*solamiya*"].[9]

Wakbazaa's emphasis on the growing numbers of *solamiya* now making their way to Tongnaab is crucial in this respect. For many years, the Tong Hills have been a minor tourist attraction, especially for those travelers making their way overland between Accra and Ouagadougou in Burkina Faso. As early as 1959, Kwame Nkrumah's government began to explore possible sites for tourist development in the north and listed "the Tong Hills including the fetish cave, which is of great sociological interest," as a strong possibility.[10] By 1962, the government reported that "Tourists to the Northern Area are showing a great interest to [*sic*] places of scenic and historical interest, such as . . . the Tongo Hills and Caves."[11] While some of these visitors continue to visit Tongnaab exclusively as tourists—drawn by exotic descriptions of the area and its inhabitants in a range of travel guides—it is sometimes difficult to draw a clear distinction between tourists on the one hand and supplicants or potential supplicants on the other.[12] As motorized transportation to the area has improved over the last decade, the number of international visitors to Tengzug has increased dramatically. African American tour groups, drawn to the historic slave castles along Ghana's coast and to the heart of Asante culture in Kumasi, are now beginning to venture to the northern regions of the country and to visit the Tongnaab shrine. There is also a consistent trickle of young European and American backpackers, two of whom left a record of their journey in a 1998 issue of the Web travel magazine *Wanderlust*. Their article, "Losing Their Shirts," describes in highly exoticized prose how "two women find that to see a fetish priest in Ghana, they have to bring a lot of money—and take off their tops."[13] While the cultural baggage these new visitors carry with them obviously differs in important ways from that borne by the first southern pilgrims who arrived in the 1920s, these differences are more a matter of degree than of kind. Like their Akan predecessors, recent international visitors appear to share a sense of the hills as remote, timeless, exotic, and beyond the reach of history and of recognized civilization.

Witchcraft and Anti-witchcraft in the Postcolony

The ongoing ritual conversations that engage pilgrims, clients, tourists, and the keepers of Tongnaab, like those from earlier generations, have not been monologues through which a savanna god is simply transplanted into or translated for another ritual landscape. In chapter 4, we explored the complex dialogical processes that wove Tongnaab into the ritual landscape of the south. By the 1950s, we begin to have evidence of inverted processes whereby southern belief systems and practices begin to be woven into the ritual landscapes of the north, as part of the same trans-regional conversation. Witches and witch-finding, which early on appear to have played a relatively minor role in savanna cosmologies, begin to emerge as more central components. Indeed, some of the very same gods who left the savanna in the first decades of the twentieth century began to move back during the terminal phase of colonial rule, carrying their enhanced witch-finding powers with them.

This inversion of the established direction of ritual flows is most dramatically illustrated by a sudden wave of witch-finding that swept through parts of Dagbon and Mamprusi in the mid-1950s. The belated emergence of organized anti-witchcraft in the Northern Territories—the only documented instance throughout the entire colonial period—was associated with a powerful new deity known simply as "Nana." The use of the Akan title is telling. Colonial authorities were first alerted to the existence of Nana in July 1955 by reports of truckloads of elderly women traveling to a healing center in the Gushiegu district of northern Dagbon.[14] Nana had apparently spread to Gushiegu from a shrine in nearby Cherepong, a region straddling the frontier with French Togoland. But it emerged that the deity had only recently been installed there by a migrant worker turned ritual entrepreneur named Ndaka Chakosi, who had acquired it in Asante. There is every indication that Nana was in fact a protean offshoot of Tigare, which in the postwar period had succeeded Nana Tongo as the most prominent witch-finder in the Gold Coast after an extended passage from its orig-

inal home in Yipala on the northwestern frontier of the Northern Territories.[15] It appears too that interaction between savanna and forest in the
form of expanding flows of northern migrant workers may to some extent
explain the startling appearance of "Akan-style" anti-witchcraft practice in
Dagbon. According to Tait, a recurring theme running through the Nana
witch-hunt was concern "with the departure of young men for the South."[16]
He noted that in the past, few Dagomba had joined the procession of migrant workers to the cocoa farms and trading towns of the south. "But now
the genealogies record a high percentage . . . as 'Gone to the Coast'; that
is, their locations are not precisely known, in sharp contrast with the contact kept as a rule by Dagomba."[17] The result was not only anxiety about
the lack of manpower in the subsistence economy, but growing alarm over
rumors that the those missing had been either killed or driven away by local witches. In accordance with established Dagomba thought, the latter
were seen exclusively to be elderly women, thousands of whom began to
make the journey to Nana in order to prove their innocence or to cleanse
themselves of the curse of witchcraft.

Like many of the exotic anti-witchcraft deities that emerged in southern Ghana during the first half of the twentieth century, Nana enjoyed a
spectacular moment of efflorescence before fading away into relative obscurity. Highly attenuated from its Tigare origins and lacking a hallowed
sacred center such as the Tong Hills, it is unlikely to have left more than a
residual trace in the present-day sacred landscape of Dagbon.[18] But just as
Domankama in 1879–80 and Aberewa in 1906–10 represented an innovative approach to dealing with *bayi* in the Akan world, so the rise of Nana
in 1955–56 suggests a shift in attitudes toward the problem of witchcraft
in the savanna societies of the middle Volta basin. We are not equipped to
make any broad generalization on this point regarding the diverse peoples
of northern Ghana. In contemporary discourse about Tongnaab in and
around the Tong Hills, however, witchcraft and witches (*soi*) appear to figure
more prominently than in our sources for the period before the Second
World War. In a 1999 conversation with a southern pilgrim and John Bawa
Zuure, the district assemblyman for Tengzug and one of the successors of
Tengol, Zuure explained,

> when you go up the hill, you will see so many clothes lying there. Those are the
> property of witches—people who Nana Tongo has revealed are witches. He doesn't
> harm people; he protects people by harming people who want to harm others. So,
> when someone dies and we consult with a soothsayer and the soothsayer says that
> the person died because he or she is a witch, because he or she is bewitching people,
> and that is why Nana Tongo decided to kill you. Sometimes the witches even admit

it when they are dying. So, when they are dying, they can confirm that it is true. If the person then dies, after confessing, they will bring his or her belongings . . . to Nana Tongo.[19]

Just how much Zuure's explanation was shaped by the presence of a southern pilgrim at this conversation is hard to determine, but certainly in the stronghold of Tongnaab there is now a central space for talk of witches and witch-finding in a language that is not foreign.

And increasingly, we would argue, that language is a national language— one that is thoroughly embedded in Ghana's nationalist project. The process begun by J. B. Danquah with his defense of Assifu in 1935, whereby colonial notions of "fetish" and "witches" were destabilized by discourses of biomedicine, local healing practices, and psychoanalysis, continued into the postcolonial era and very much continues today.[20] As such, it has been central to the ongoing construction of Ghana-as-nation. We have seen how in the 1940s and 1950s traditional councils were empowered to issue licenses to practitioners of "native medicine" as part of the process of professionalizing and thereby legitimizing the practice of local healing. In 1962, the CPP Cabinet decided that Nkrumah should accept the invitation of the newly formed Ghana Psychic and Traditional Healing Association to serve as its patron. The aims of the Association were to

> uphold, protect and promote the best in psychic and traditional healing in Ghana and to collectively cooperate with the Ghana Medical Association and the Ghana Academy of Sciences in the promotion of the Science of herbalism, as well as psychiatric and psychosomatic treatment. . . . membership is open to any person actively engaged or interested in psychic and traditional healing.[21]

The modern translation of the idioms and the practices of anti-witchcraft and other forms of healing have also remained highly contested. In 1962, the Cabinet decided that it was in "the national interest" that "all herbalists and fetish priests" should register with the government-sponsored Psychic and Traditional Healing Association.[22] Chiefs and their traditional councils were thus disempowered in the field of traditional medicine, as they were in many other sectors of government, by the centripetal force of the new nation-state under Nkrumah's CPP government. In fact, the entire issue of licensing and organizing local healers was thoroughly entangled in struggles between the CPP and "traditional authorities," especially Asante chiefs who had actively campaigned for Asante autonomy vis-à-vis the central government in the 1950s. When Nkrumah was overthrown by a military coup in 1966, chiefs sought to reassert their authority over local licensing.[23] By the end of the decade, a breakaway national body calling itself the Psychic and Traditional Healers Association was formed. Meanwhile, in Asante, where Nkrumah's policies had been most actively opposed, a regional association called the Ashanti Herbalists Union also emerged. At its head was the *nsumankwahene*, the *asantehene*'s chief physician and the office-holder who since the eighteenth century had been responsible for overseeing the ritual relationship between the Asante state and the northern savannas. In short, "traditional" medicine and the place and power of chiefs in relation to the state remained issues as vexed for the new nation as they had been for the colonial regime in the 1930s and for the precolonial imperial state in the eighteenth and nineteenth centuries.

Richard Werbner, the only other scholar who has attempted to trace the twentieth-century trajectory of Tongnaab, has presented a very different perspective on the continuities and discontinuities in ritual commerce from the early twentieth century to the decade of nationalist mobilization. By the 1950s, he argues, there was a revival of indigenous Akan anti-witchcraft powers in the form of so-called *obosom-brafo* or "executioner's" shrines, many of which originated in the Bron region on the northwestern frontier of Asante. He explains this shift from the use of savanna gods to more locally based deities by the advance of nationalist politics, which, he suggests, altered how Akan and other southern inhabitants of the Gold Coast/Ghana perceived strangers. In the first half of the twentieth century, the key outsiders in the Akan region were northern laborers, "external strangers" whose presence created the attraction for savanna powers. But by the 1950s, Werbner argues, "the rise of provincialism or quasi-nationalism made internal strangers and indigenous identity to be matters of concern far overriding the earlier concern about alien strangers and the exotic."[24] The main vehicle for this "quasi-nationalism" in his view was the Asante-based National Liberation Movement, which between 1954 and Ghanaian independence in 1957 mounted a regionalist challenge to Kwame Nkrumah's CPP government.[25] Suddenly, the imperative on the part of southern Ghanaians to domesticate the exotic northerners in their midst faded from view, replaced, he argues, by the more pressing question of what exactly constituted citizenship amongst the Akan peoples themselves. As the NLM threatened secession and Nkrumah responded by supporting the efforts of the northern Bron kingdoms to break away from Asante, it was "the power and danger in Ashantiness that had to be managed through cults."[26]

While Werbner's insights are thought-provoking, there is little or no empirical evidence to support the contention that a fundamental shift in Akan notions of "stranger-hood" occurred in the 1950s and that this in turn led to a profound shift in ritual affiliations. Indeed, Field—who was only too aware of the importance of Akan perceptions of savanna migrants— explicitly rejected any direct link between the trajectories of religious change on the one hand and political change on the other.[27] Moreover, the notion that Tongnaab and other northern gods had been "displaced" from the south is misleading. Far from being swept aside by a wholesale return to Akan deities, pilgrimage networks focused on the principal savanna shrines actually entered a new phase of expansion after the Second World War. Tigare certainly reached its greatest efflorescence in the 1950s, while Tongnaab had already achieved a degree of routinization that continues today. In independent Ghana, Tongnaab certainly faded from the purview of the state, but its disappearance had far more to do with its ongoing successes than its failure.

Tongnaab: Local Politics and Global Connections

That histories of healing, of medicines and gods, priests and pilgrims, were and are integrally bound up with contested histories of the nation would come as no surprise to people in the Tong Hills, who have never considered themselves to be on the hinterland of anything and who see themselves as centrally located in Ghana's national body politic. Many stories have been shared with us in recent years of the rich and famous, the powerful and titled, making their way to the Tong Hills for advice and counsel. Nkrumah and his opposition feature prominently in many of these stories. "When Nkrumah was in power," we were told one day,

> whenever he would come north, he would stop at Pwalugu and leave a cow there. Then he would send a cow here for Nana Tongo. Then one year he was coming and he left Nana Tongo's cow at Pwalugu and asked someone else to bring it here. Nana Tongo then said, "If he now thinks he is bigger than me, they shouldn't even come and bring the cows." That was very near the time he got bombed at Kulungugu. Then a few years later, he sent his mother and father, but he himself didn't come. And Nana Tongo said, "You say you believe in Nana Tongo, but Nana Tongo sees that you didn't come." That was the year they seized power and the coup came. All his power was taken away. Everything was taken away.[28]

We have not located archival sources confirming Nkrumah's visits to Tengzug, but whether stories such as these can be substantiated or not is beside the point. Accounts of commanding statesmen making their obligatory pilgrimage to Tongnaab evidences in powerful ways that people in the hills view their own history and the history of their great *bo'ar* Tongnaab as integral to Ghana's unfolding national history. Unfortunately, we do not know the other side of the story—how those in the limelight of that national history have viewed Tongnaab and the sacred power of the Tong Hills. The politicians of the post-independence period have rarely reflected publicly on the nature of deities like Tongnaab in the same way that J. B. Danquah and men of his generation did. Because of this, we can only imagine the role Nana Tongo and many other savanna gods have played in the politics of the postcolonial state.

Still, there is enough evidence available to discern a marked political continuity—writ locally or nationally—for the Tong Hills. Tongnaab continues to broker political power, largely behind the scenes, just as it did at the moment of colonial encounter in the early twentieth century, while the Namoo town of Tongo remains formally paramount in the political landscape of Taleland. But there have also been important shifts—shifts that underscore the fact that historical change in the Tong Hills is constant. One of the most profound of these is the emergence of a new, alternate site of power that complicates, if not transcends, the longstanding tension between chiefly power and the ritual power of *tengdaana*s. That site is the District Assembly. As we have seen, new forms of wealth made possible by the expanding pilgrim trade generated new forms of authority that were based not just on the earth and the ancestors, but on political office. Tengol's effort to be recognized as the chief of Tengzug was one of the earliest examples of this process—a process that Fortes termed "pecuniary competition." He considered it an unhealthy competition that pitted the Yanii congregation of Tongnaab (dominated by Tengol's Bukiok clan) against those of Bonaab (the Kpatar clan and its allies). Down to the present, that ongoing tension has not disappeared, though it has ebbed and flowed since the 1920s. The *golibdaana*'s house has generally retained the upper hand in terms of access to resources and the paramountcy of Yanii, but it has never successfully captured political paramountcy vis-à-vis Kpatar and the other clans.

That stalemate has now been complicated by recent developments in the structure of local government. In 1989, the government of Flight Lieutenant J. J. Rawlings put new district assemblies in place throughout the country. One of Tengol's many "sons," John Bawa Zuure, won the seat in the assembly for Tengzug.[29] Over the course of the past decade, Zuure has transformed the position of district assemblyman into one of significant authority. As an alternate constellation of political power and resources, the new office has trumped chieftaincy in more ways than one. Unlike his predecessor, Tengol, Zuure has no designs on "traditional office." He is, however, intimately connected to it through his brother, Joseph Bugli Tengol, a former teacher who in 2000 was "enskinned" as the new *golibdaana*, taking the name Malbazaa. As "the Assemblyman," the name by which he is now most commonly called, Zuure has been a zealous advocate for his community and has overseen significant growth and development in the area— a good deal of it centered on Tengzug. He initiated the building and staffing of a primary school, as well as a grinding mill. Many of the compounds atop the hills now have solar panels to provide light in the evenings—a realistic concession to the fact that it will probably be many years before Tengzug is put on the national electricity grid. A medical clinic is also in the planning stages. Zuure, with his brother, Golibdaana Malbazaa, has also put tremendous effort into promoting Tengzug as a global tourist site. In 1998–99, he worked closely with the Upper East Regional Museum in developing a proposal to have the Tong Hills recognized by UNESCO as a World Heritage site.

The new power of the Assemblyman is perhaps nowhere more evident than in Zuure's successful efforts to stop the quarrying of granite from the northern face of the Tong Hills. In 1978, a European firm, the Granite and Marble Company, received a ninety-nine-year concession to cut granite from that section of the hills next to Wakii. Without seeking the permission of anyone from Tengzug and after exerting tremendous pressure on the Wakii *tengdaana*s, the *tongrana*, along with local government administrators, granted the concession. According to Volker Riehl, the company promised in exchange to put up a guest house at Tongo, provide employment to young men in the area, and give "a certain amount of money for every cubic yard of granite exported" to the *tongrana*.[30] The quarry was a source of very serious friction among Wakii, Tengzug, and Tongo from the moment it began its operations. Open conflict might have erupted sooner were it not for the fact that during the late 1980s and early 1990s the site was largely inactive. Then suddenly, in the dry season of 2000–2001, quarrying started up again in full force. Before long, the company was blasting granite atop the Tong Hills, far from the original site at Wakii and encroaching well into Tengzug—a dramatic and enormously destructive expansion that coincided with efforts to have the hills designated a World Heritage site! As tensions rose, there were mutterings from some quarters that, as in the old days, the situation might have to be solved with "bows and arrows." However, through pressure he was able to generate locally and nationally, the Assemblyman succeeded in getting the Regional Coordinating Council to convene a fact-finding committee on the quarry in June 2001. Only two months later, the regional minister ordered the company to cease operations immediately.[31] In these ways new forms of political power and authority in the Hills have manifested themselves. Tengol may have lost the battle for formal political power and legitimacy in the

Figure 6.2. Assemblyman John Bawa Zuure at the opening of the photographic exhibition "The Cultural Landscape of the Tong Hills" at the Regional Museum, Bolgatanga, 28 June 2000.

Figure 6.3. Golibdaana Malbazaa, 2002.

Figure 6.4. "Visitors Welcome": new signpost pointing tourists and pilgrims to Tongnaab, 2000.

1930s, but his descendants appear to have won the war—in no small part because of the tenacious and ongoing ritual power of Tongnaab.[32]

Since the termination of quarrying, developments have continued apace. There are now very visible indicators of the paramountcy of Tongnaab and the new forms of political power that have developed around it. In December 2001, the Tengzug community formed its own "Ecotourism Committee" (TEC), joining broader efforts in the region sponsored by USAID and implemented by the Ghana Tourist Board and the Nature Conservation Research Centre.[33] There are now striking billboards along the main road north and south of Tengzug pointing visitors to the "Tongo Hills and Tengzug Shrines." The TEC has also established fees for visitors to the area. Non-Ghanaians are charged 10,000 cedis (a little over one U.S. dollar), Ghanaians are charged 2,000 cedis, and Ghanaian students 1,000. This entrance fee includes a tour of the "chief's home," "other village attractions, unlimited picture taking, guide services and hiking in the hills and surrounding areas."[34] Beginning in 2003, it also includes a visit to a "model Talensi home" that has been constructed specifically for visitors. Two rooms of the compound contain an array of cultural items—one room for items used by women, the other for those used by men. There is also a guest room where visitors can stay overnight for an additional fee. It is furnished with a double bed, a desk, and mosquito netting on the window. The TEC has also built special bathing quarters and flushing latrines for its guests. Several Tengzug women have received training in catering for international visitors; others have attended workshops on batik and other crafts in order to build up a local craft industry. Young men have also received training in various forms of craft production and in tour guiding.

The Yanii pilgrimage site, far atop the hills, sits in a rather ambiguous position vis-à-vis these tourist developments. The entrance fees do not include a visit to this Tongnaab shrine. Those who come are told that "due to the sacred nature of the shrine . . . certain customs must be performed . . . thus the reason for a separate fee"—15,000 cedis for groups of one to four people.[35] Visits to Tongnaab clearly complicate the eco-tourism agenda, which is modeled around the idea of tourism rather than that of ritual consultation. The tension between the two has given rise to a series of pressing issues that are currently being worked out within the community. Will annual pilgrims at *Bo'araam* time be expected to pay an "entrance fee?" Will it be possible to differentiate between tourists on the one hand and pilgrims and supplicants on the other? What of Ghanaian visitors from the south who come as part of the growing local tourist market? What of international visitors who wish to undertake a full consultation with the oracle? These are not easy questions. But surely neither were those generated by the arrival of the first Akan pilgrims from the south some eighty years ago.

The TEC intends to use the various fees collected to pay the salaries of the guides (25 percent) and fund the tourist committee (25 percent). The other half of the money collected is to be put in a "Community Development Fund . . . [that] will be used to support development projects within the community."[36] Another challenge, of course, will be determining just who constitutes "the community." Will the funds so collected and utilized help heal the longstanding rift between those who tend Yanii and the congregations who tend Bonaab and the other sacred sites in the hills? Will these other sites be opened to visitors, and if so, at what cost? As importantly, will any of these expanding resources have a positive effect on Talensi communities besides Tengzug—settlements around the outer slopes of the hills such as Shia, Gorogo, and Yinduri, which tend to be bypassed by the growing numbers of tourists? Or will the emergence of eco-tourism serve to reinforce the dominant position of Bukiok within Tengzug, as well as that of Tengzug within broader Talensi society?

It is too early to answer these sorts of questions. But they were probably present in the minds of many Talensi as they watched the first graded and tarred road wind its way up the northern slope of the Tong Hills in 2002. When we first visited the area in 1992, all of the roads were in an equally sorry state of disrepair, including the main route from Tamale north to Bolgatanga and the frontier with Burkina Faso. Although the highway itself is now tarred, all of the feeder roads remain unpaved. However, these days, if you drive toward the hills from Bolgatanga, turn left at Winkogo onto the feeder road to Tongo, and then proceed through Gbeog, Tongo, and finally Wakii, you no longer come to an abrupt stop, as we did in September 1992 when the road turned into a footpath through the millet. Suddenly you come upon the first meters of a beautifully graded and tarred road that begins at the rusty remains of the quarry and then scales the northern face of the hills. After winding its way through the central valley of Tengzug, the road ends at the sprawling compound of the *golibdaana* and his brother, the Assemblyman—a powerful marker, etched into the landscape, of the legacy of Tengol and the power of Tongnaab.

As we recount these events and bring this story to an end, it is important that we acknowledge our own complicity in recent Talensi history. Although Meyer Fortes wrote himself out of the web of history-making in the hills, Talensi today are still debating the long-term impact of his presence and work in the area.[37] We do not want to make the same omission. We would be remiss were we not to acknowledge that, for better or for worse, we too have been entangled in the unfolding history of the hills. We wonder, in fact, if it is possible, much less desirable, to be detached scholars who somehow stand outside of history. If that is the mission of our discipline, then we suspect we have failed miserably. We have delighted in working with the staff of the Upper East Regional Museum in Bolgatanga in developing the UNESCO proposal to have the Tong Hills designated a World Heritage site. In 2000, again working with the museum and community leaders, we mounted a photographic exhibit on the cultural landscape of the hills. Central to the exhibit were portraits of many of the elderly men and women we have interviewed over the years. Next to their portraits were mounted excerpts, in English, from the interviews we had done. With assistance from the United States Cultural Affairs Officer in Accra, we were able to hire a bus to bring many of these elders from Tengzug and surrounding Talensi settlements to the exhibit opening.[38] Some had not been into Bolgatanga for years, and after lengthy speeches from assorted

Figure 6.5. Azabu studying his portrait at the Regional Museum, Bolgatanga, 28 June 2000.

dignitaries, they were the first to enter the exhibit and view their portraits. Many came with grandchildren who then translated their excerpted stories back into Talen for their grandparents. It was an extraordinary day that neither of us would wish to trade for the badge of scholarly objectivity and detachment. We were also entangled in the struggles over the quarry and received immediate word of the victory, though we were then thousands of miles away from the hills. And in 2002, we arranged for some fifteen secondary school teachers from the United States, touring Ghana as part of a Fulbright-sponsored study program, to spend the day as "tourists" in the hills. They were in the first tour bus to make it up the newly graded road and to pay the TEC entrance fees. We could go on, but the point is made. We could not be detached scholars, even if we had wanted to be. We were drawn into the history of the Tong Hills—a history that is local, regional, national, and now global—and there has been no turning back.

Although we have been a part of the last pages of this history, let us be clear: it remains a Talensi story—one into which we have been written by Talensi themselves. And as we were written into this story, we came to understand the necessity of historicizing "tradition" and plotting chronologies of belief. We witnessed the complexity and vibrancy of African modernity—a modernity that long predates European conquest—and we watched as the boundaries between the local, the national, and the global melted before our eyes. And as we read and reread Fortes and then sat in the very same places he once sat, often being queried as to whether or not we were "his children," it was clear we had to interrogate the pioneering ethnographer, not just for the cultural baggage that came with him, but as a historical actor who acted in real places, in real chronological time. We also had to interrogate our own subject positions.

Some may be concerned as they ponder these final pages that what we in fact have witnessed in the past decade, and have been complicit in, is the logical and final result of the "pecuniary competition" Fortes so bemoaned. Commercialization, international tourism, and the onward march of globalization have finally and inevitably destroyed the traditional culture and belief systems of the Talensi. Their fragile web of kinship has torn in the raging storm of modernity and Tongnaab has reached its final destination— another desecrated stop on an expanding tourist map. We disagree. If we have learned anything over this past decade, it is that commerce and ritual dialogue between the savanna and forests of West Africa have long been intertwined—as far back as the historical record can take us. And, the weight of colonial ethnography aside, Tongnaab's Talensi guardians have long defied any notion of "traditional." Theirs has been a vibrant, changing, and very modern tradition that has grown and transfigured from the days of the slave trade to the era of the tourist trade. As two among many who have been written into the history of the Tong Hills, we think the evidence before us is incontrovertible. Tongnaab and the people of the hills will continue to make history and they will continue to make it largely on their own terms.

Glossary

Talen (or Talni) Terms

ba'er (pl. *ba'a*): ancestor shrine
bakoldaana: diviner, soothsayer
bo'ar (pl. *bo'a*): ancestor shrine devoted to the founder of a lineage or clan
Bo'araam: the annual harvest festival focused on the *bo'ar* cult
Bo'arana: a ritual office, esp. in Shia, lit. "the custodian of the *bo'ar*"
bo'artyii: a portable shrine, lit. "*bo'ar* in a bag"
Golibdaana: a ritual office in Tengzug, lit. "the custodian of the *golib* drum"
Gologo (or *Golib*): the annual festival marking the start of the farming season
kaab: ritual sacrifice, "prayer"
kambona (pl. *kambonse*): Asante "gunman," used in northern Ghana for an Asante
kambonaaba: local "chiefs" created in the early colonial period
Kpatarnaaba: head of the Kpatar clan of Tengzug and senior custodian of the *tongban* Ngoo
kpeem: the dead, ancestors (see also *yikpem*)
moog (or *mo'o*): uncultivated land, wilderness, "bush" (cf. *teng*)
mung: red fez, the symbol of chiefly office
na or *naaba:* a secular office-holder or "chief"
Naawun (or *Naayin*): the creator god, "heaven"
Namoo: Talensi descended from migrants from Mamprugu and elsewhere
soob (pl. *soi*): witch
Talis menga: autochthonous Talensi, lit. "real Tale" (cf. *Namoo*)
teng or *tong:* the earth, soil, settled or cultivated land, the cult of the earth (cf. *moog*)
tengdaana: earth priest, lit. "custodian of the earth"
tongban (pl. *tongbana*): earth shrine
Tongnaab: the ancestor-deity of the *bo'ar* cult, lit. "lord of the earth"
Tongrana: the chief of Tongo, the leading Namoo office-holder
yihiyii (or *yilenyilug*): the "shade" or "shadow" of a god or ritual power
yikpem: lineage ancestors (see also *kpeem*)
Yikpemdaan: a ritual office, lit. "the custodian of the lineage ancestors"
yin: destiny, fate
yir: family, lineage
Yiran: a ritual office in Tengzug, the caretaker of the Yanii Tongnaab shrine

Twi (or Akan) Terms

abusua: matrilineage

aduruyofo (or *odunsini*): herbalist, "medicine man" (see also *oduru*)

afunsua: "carrying the coffin," funerary custom used to determine cause of death

batakari: "northern"-style woven smock, often studded with protective talismans

bayi: witchcraft

bayi boro: maleficent witchcraft, lit. "hot *bayi*"

kwaem: the forest (cf. *sarem*)

obayifo: (pl. *abayifoo*): witch

obosom (pl. *abosom*): tutelary deity, "god"

obosomfo (pl. *abosomfoo*): ritual specialist, collector and guardian of *abosom*

odikro: village head

odom: poison bark used in ordeals

odonko (pl. *nnonkofoo*): slave of northern origin

oduru (pl. *aduru*): medicine (see also *aduruyofo*)

oduru bone (or *oduto*): bad medicine, poison

okomfo (pl. *akomfoo*): ritual specialist, "fetish priest," one who is "possessed" by a god

okyeame: spokesperson or "linguist"

omanhene (pl. *amanhene*): the paramount chief or king of an Akan state

sarem: the savanna grasslands, "the north" (cf. *kwaem*)

suman (pl. *asuman*): lesser "god" or talisman (see also *obosom*)

Notes

Abbreviations

Terms that appear frequently have been abbreviated as follows:

AASA	Akyem Abuakwa State Archives
CCNT	Chief Commissioner of the Northern Territories
CCA	Chief Commissioner of Ashanti
CCP	Commissioner for the Central Province
CEP	Commissioner for the Eastern Province
CNEP	Commissioner for the North-Eastern Province
CNP	Commissioner for the Northern Province
CS	Colonial Secretary
DC	District Commissioner
JAH	*Journal of African History*
JRA	*Journal of Religion in Africa*
MRO	Manhyia Record Office, Kumasi
NAG	National Archives of Ghana, Accra
NEP	North-Eastern Province
NTs	Northern Territories
PRO	Public Record Office, Kew
RAGCC	Regional Archives of Ghana, Cape Coast
RAGK	Regional Archives of Ghana, Kumasi
RAGKD	Regional Archives of Ghana, Koforidua
RAGSK	Regional Archives of Ghana, Sekondi
RAGSN	Regional Archives of Ghana, Sunyani
RAGT	Regional Archives of Ghana, Tamale
RAI	Royal Anthropological Institute, London
SNA	Secretary for Native Affairs
THSG	*Transactions of the Historical Society of Ghana*

Introduction

1. E. G. Parrinder, "The Prevalence of Witches II," *West Africa*, 26 May 1956, 320.

2. Ibid. Parrinder's publications included *West African Religion, Illustrated from the Beliefs and Practices of the Yoruba, Ewe, Akan, and Kindred Peoples* (London, 1949); *West African Psychology* (London, 1951); and *African Traditional Religion* (London,

1954). He would go on to produce the first comparative study of European and African witchcraft belief, *Witchcraft* (Harmondsworth, 1958).

3. We draw here on the well-established literature on similar "regional," "trans-regional," and "territorial" cults in central, eastern, and southern Africa, esp. Willy de Craemer, Jan Vansina, and Renée C. Fox, "Religious Movements in Central Africa: A Theoretical Study," *Comparative Studies in Society and History* 18 (1976): 458–75; Richard P. Werbner, ed., *Regional Cults* (London, 1977); J. M. Schoffeleers, ed., *Guardians of the Land: Essays on Central African Territorial Cults* (Gwelo, 1978); and idem, *River of Blood: The Genesis of a Martyr Cult in Southern Malawi, c. A.D. 1600* (Madison, 1992).

4. R. S. Rattray, *The Tribes of the Ashanti Hinterland* (Oxford, 1932).

5. See Jean Comaroff and John Comaroff, *Of Revelation and Revolution*, vol. 1, *Christianity, Colonialism, and Consciousness in South Africa* (Chicago, 1991), esp. 11–13.

6. For critiques, see Louis Brenner, "'Religious' Discourses in and about Africa," in *Discourse and Its Disguises: The Interpretation of African Oral Texts*, ed. Karin Barber and P. F. de Moraes Farias (Birmingham, 1989), 87–103; and Rosalind Shaw, "The Invention of 'African Traditional Religion,'" *Religion* 20 (1990): 339–53.

7. Brenner, "'Religious' Discourses," 87; and Jonathan Z. Smith, *Imagining Religion: From Babylon to Jonestown* (Chicago, 1982), 89.

8. Brenner, "'Religious' Discourses," 91. Mircea Eliade's influential notion of the importance of a fixed site in sacred landscapes has been challenged by a more historically sensitive "metamorphic vision" of ritual and place. See Jonathan Z. Smith, *Map Is Not Territory: Studies in the History of Religions* (Leiden, 1978). For a recent case study from Ghana, see Sandra E. Greene, *Sacred Sites and the Colonial Encounter: A History of Meaning and Memory in Ghana* (Bloomington, 2002). The foundational text is Mircea Eliade, *The Sacred and the Profane* (New York, 1959).

9. Sandra T. Barnes, ed., *Africa's Ogun: Old World and New*, 2nd ed. (Bloomington, 1997).

10. Max Gluckman, "Analysis of a Social Situation in Modern Zululand," *Rhodes-Livingston Papers* 28, Manchester, 1958; and J. C. Mitchell, "The Kalela Dance," *Rhodes-Livingstone Papers* 27, Manchester, 1956.

11. See Victor W. Turner, *Schism and Continuity in an African Society: A Study of Ndembu Village Life* (Manchester, 1957); idem, *The Forest of Symbols: Aspects of Ndembu Ritual* (Ithaca, 1967); idem, *The Drums of Affliction* (Oxford, 1968); and Turner's widely cited comparative elaboration, *Dramas, Fields, and Metaphors: Symbolic Action in Human Society* (Ithaca, 1974).

12. See John M. Janzen, "Drums of Affliction: Real Phenomenon or Scholarly Chimaera?" in *Religion in Africa*, ed. Thomas D. Blakely, Walter van Beek, and Dennis C. Thompson (London, 1994), 161–81; also idem, *Ngoma: Discourses of Healing in Central and Southern Africa* (Berkeley, 1992); and Rijk van Dijk, Ria Reis, and Marja Spierenburg, eds., *The Quest for Fruition through Ngoma: Political Aspects of Healing in Southern Africa* (Oxford, 2000).

13. Three pioneering historical collections are Terence O. Ranger and Isaria Kimambo, eds., *The Historical Study of African Religion* (London, 1972); Terence O. Ranger and John Weller, eds., *Themes in the Christian History of Central Africa* (London, 1975); and Schoffeleers, *Guardians*. On indigenous shrines, see the essays in Werbner, *Regional Cults*, many of which develop Turner's typologies. Key mono-

graphs growing out of this body of work include John M. Janzen, *Lemba, 1650–1930: A Drum of Affliction in Africa and the New World* (New York, 1982); Karen E. Fields, *Revival and Rebellion in Colonial Central Africa* (Princeton, 1985); Wim van Binsbergen, *Religious Change in Zambia: Exploratory Studies* (London, 1981); idem, *Tears of Rain: Ethnicity and History in Central Western Zambia* (London, 1992); Schoffeleers, *River of Blood*; and Terence O. Ranger, *Voices from the Rocks: Nature, Culture, and History in the Matapos Hills of Zimbabwe* (Oxford, 1999).

14. van Binsbergen, *Religious Change*; Fields, *Revival and Rebellion*; and Janzen, *Lemba*.

15. de Craemer, Vansina, and Fox, "Religious Movements," 458.

16. Robert M. Baum, *Shrines of the Slave Trade: Diola Religion and Society in Precolonial Senegambia* (New York, 1999); and Rosalind Shaw, *Memories of the Slave Trade: Ritual and the Historical Imagination in Sierra Leone* (Chicago, 2002).

17. Richard P. Werbner, *Ritual Passage, Sacred Journey: The Process and Organization of Religious Movement* (Washington, 1989), esp. 1–15.

18. The same year, Louis Brenner regretted that "there are virtually no published first-hand accounts of possession in Africa" ("'Religious' Discourses," 97), a situation that has been transformed over the past decade. See Janice Boddy, "Spirit Possession Revisited: Beyond Instrumentality," *Annual Review of Anthropology* 23 (1994): 407–34; and Heike Behrend and Ute Luig, eds., *Spirit Possession, Modernity, and Power in Africa* (Oxford, 1999).

19. Werbner, "'Totemism' in History: The Sacred Crossing of West African Strangers," in *Ritual Passage*, 223–44.

20. See Fritz W. Kramer, *The Red Fez: Art and Spirit Possession in Africa*, trans. Malcolm Green (London, 1993), esp. chapter 1, "The Asante and the People from the Grasslands"; Paul Stoller, *Colonial Memories: Spirit Possession, Power, and the Hauka in West Africa* (New York, 1995); Judy Rosenthal, *Possession, Ecstasy, and Law in Ewe Voodoo* (Charlottesville, 1998); and Charles Piot, *Remotely Global: Village Modernity in West Africa* (Chicago, 1999).

21. On Rouch, the Hauka, and *Les maîtres fous* (1956), see Paul Stoller, *The Cinematic Griot: The Ethnography of Jean Rouch* (Chicago, 1992).

22. For example, Piot, *Remotely Global*, chapter 2, "History." For a similar criticism of the new "historical anthropology," see T. C. McCaskie, *Asante Identities: History and Modernity in an African Village, 1850–1950* (Edinburgh, 2000), 21–22 and passim.

23. Werbner, *Ritual Passage*, 9.

24. See the comments in Ivor Wilks, Nehemia Levtzion, and Bruce M. Haight, *Chronicles from Gonja: A Tradition of West African Muslim Historiography* (Cambridge, 1986), 30; also Nehemia Levtzion, *Muslims and Chiefs in West Africa: A Study of Islam in the Middle Volta Basin in the Pre-colonial Period* (Oxford, 1968).

25. Ivor Wilks, *The Northern Factor in Ashanti History* (Legon, 1961); idem, "The Position of Muslims in Metropolitan Ashanti in the Early Nineteenth Century," in *Islam in Tropical Africa*, ed. I. M. Lewis (London, 1966); idem, *Asante in the Nineteenth Century: The Structure and Evolution of a Political Order* (Cambridge, 1975), esp. chapter 7; and for a recent overview, idem, "The Juula and the Expansion of Islam into the Forest," in *The History of Islam in Africa*, ed. Nehemia Levtzion and Randall L. Pouwels (Athens, Ohio, 2000), 93–115.

26. Wilks, *Asante*, 243.

27. See esp. David Owusu-Ansah, *Islamic Talismanic Tradition in Nineteenth-Century Asante* (Lewiston, Mass., 1991); and also many of the essays in Enid Schildkrout, ed., *The Golden Stool: Studies of the Asante Center and Periphery* (New York, 1987). For an important exception to the focus on Islam in savanna-forest ritual dialogue, see Donna J. E. Maier, *Priests and Power: The Case of the Dente Shrine in Nineteenth-Century Ghana* (Bloomington, 1983).

28. Jack Goody, introduction to Meyer Fortes, *Religion, Morality, and the Person: Essays on Tallensi Religion*, ed. Jack Goody (Cambridge, 1987), vii; Meyer Fortes, *The Dynamics of Clanship among the Tallensi: Being the First Part of an Analysis of the Social Structure of a Trans-Volta Tribe* (London, 1945); and idem, *The Web of Kinship among the Tallensi: The Second Part of an Analysis of the Social Structure of a Trans-Volta Tribe* (London, 1949).

29. See, too, Fortes's earlier adumbration of the concept of "statelessness" in "The Political System of the Tallensi of the Northern Territories of the Gold Coast," in *African Political Systems*, ed. Meyer Fortes and E. E. Evans-Pritchard (London, 1940), 239–71.

30. On the "writing" of African peoples into the structures of colonial and ethnographic knowledge, see Sean Hawkins, *Writing and Colonialism in Northern Ghana: The Encounter between the LoDagaa and "The World on Paper"* (Toronto, 2002).

31. Thanks to the research of Douglas Johnson, we know that Evans-Pritchard's work amongst the Nuer took place in the immediate aftermath of—and was significantly shaped by—a British military campaign aimed at terminating the influence of Nuer prophets. Douglas H. Johnson, "Evans-Pritchard, the Nuer, and the Sudan Political Service," *African Affairs* 81 (1982): 231–46; and idem, *Nuer Prophets: A History of Prophecy from the Upper Nile in the Nineteenth and Twentieth Centuries* (Oxford, 1994). For an equally insightful reinterpretation of Audrey Richards's work, see Henrietta L. Moore and Megan Vaughan, *Cutting Down Trees: Gender, Nutrition, and Agricultural Change in the Northern Province of Zambia, 1890–1990* (Portsmouth, N.H. 1994).

32. On the intellectual history, see esp. Adam Kuper, *Anthropologists and Anthropology: The Modern British School*, 3rd ed. (London, 1996); useful Africanist surveys include Keith Hart, "The Social Anthropology of West Africa," *Annual Review of Anthropology* 14 (1985): 243–73; and Sally Falk Moore, *Anthropology and Africa: Changing Perspectives on a Changing Scene* (Charlottesville, 1994).

33. See Talal Asad, ed., *Anthropology and the Colonial Encounter* (Ithaca, 1973); and Henrika Kuklick, *The Savage Within: The Social History of British Anthropology, 1885–1945* (Cambridge, 1991).

34. Jack Goody, *The Expansive Moment: The Rise of Social Anthropology in Britain and Africa, 1918–1970* (Cambridge, 1995).

35. Fortes's other major writings on Talensi ritual and religion are "Ritual Festivals and Social Cohesion in the Hinterland of the Gold Coast," *American Anthropologist* 38 (1936): 590–604; *Oedipus and Job in West African Religion* (Cambridge, 1959; reprinted 1983 with an introductory essay by Robin Horton); and the essays collected in *Religion*.

36. Both de Craemer, Vansina, and Fox, "Religious Movements," and Werbner, *Ritual Passage*, 6, argue that terms such as "witch-finding movement" or "anti-

witchcraft cult" are too narrow to describe the broad covenants that bound the members of such movements. The former opt simply for "religious movement" and Werbner for "personal security cult." There is merit in this, but we choose to retain the emphasis on anti-witchcraft because historically in southern Ghana it was the idiom of witchcraft that was mobilized to explain and to interrogate a broad range of personal and collective security issues.

37. The phrase "occult economies" is borrowed from Jean Comaroff and John Comaroff, "Occult Economies and the Violence of Abstraction: Notes from the South African Postcolony," *American Ethnologist* 26 (1999): 297–303.

38. T. C. McCaskie, "Anti-witchcraft Cults in Asante: An Essay in the Social History of an African People," *History in Africa* 8 (1981): 125–54. See also the recent article by Natasha Gray, "Witches, Oracles, and Colonial Law: Evolving Anti-witchcraft Practices in Ghana, 1927–1932," *International Journal of African Historical Studies* 34 (2001): 339–64.

39. See esp. the collections of essays in Jean Comaroff and John Comaroff, eds., *Modernity and Its Malcontents: Ritual and Power in Postcolonial Africa* (Chicago, 1993); "Containing Witchcraft: Conflicting Scenarios in Postcolonial Africa," special issue, *African Studies Review* 41 (1998); and George Clement Bond and Diane M. Ciekawy, eds., *Witchcraft Dialogues: Anthropological and Philosophical Exchanges* (Athens, Ohio, 2001). See also Peter Geschiere, *The Modernity of Witchcraft: Politics and the Occult in Postcolonial Africa* (Charlottesville, 1997).

40. For the use of idioms of witchcraft in the postcolony, see Jean-François Bayart, *The State in Africa: The Politics of the Belly*, trans. Mary Harper, Christopher Harrison, and Elizabeth Harrison (Harlow, 1993).

41. For notable exceptions, see Baum, *Shrines of the Slave Trade;* Fields, *Revival and Rebellion;* and Luise White, *Speaking with Vampires: Rumor and History in Colonial Africa* (Berkeley, 2000).

42. As with other Christian missions in Africa and elsewhere, the White Fathers' desire to conduct ethnographic research declined dramatically after the first generation—so those insights into local religious belief and practice that do exist are dominated by observations made of the Kasen people in the distant Navrongo area. In terms of direct religious encounter, there was very little mission outreach from Bolgatanga into the Talensi area until the 1960s.

43. Because formal conversations in Taleland between strangers, even those carried out in Talen, are usually mediated by an individual known to both parties, this arrangement was not unfamiliar to those with whom we spoke.

1. Tongnaab and the Talensi in the History of the Middle Volta Savanna

1. See McCaskie, *Asante Identities*, 238–40.

2. The best general account remains Ivor Wilks, "The Mossi and the Akan States, 1400 to 1800," in *History of West Africa*, vol. 1, ed. J. F. A. Ajayi and Michael Crowder, 3rd ed. (Harlow, 1985), 465–502.

3. See Robin Law, *The Horse in West African History* (Oxford, 1980), 13–16, 181–84; and Jack Goody, *Technology, Tradition, and the State in Africa* (London, 1971).

4. See Wilks, "Mossi," 470–71; and the pioneering work by Emmanuel Forster Tamakloe, *A Brief History of the Dagbamba People* (Accra, 1931). The names Dagbon and Mamprugu refer to the kingdoms; Dagomba (or Dagbamba) and Mamprusi, to their respective ruling classes.

5. For pioneering analyses, see Louis Tauxier, *Le noir du Soudan: Pays Mossi et Gourounsi* (Paris, 1912); and Rattray, *Hinterland*.

6. Wilks, "Mossi," 470–71; see also Robin Horton, "Stateless Societies in the History of West Africa," in Ajayi and Crowder, *History of West Africa*, 98.

7. See esp. Jan Vansina, *Paths in the Rainforest: Towards a History of Political Tradition in Equatorial Africa* (Madison, 1990).

8. See Tony Naden, "The Gur Languages," in *The Languages of Ghana*, ed. M. E. Kropp Dakubu (London, 1988), 12–49. The Oti-Volta group was formerly called Mole-(i.e., Mooré-) Dagbani.

9. See Fortes's influential opening statement, "Political System of the Tallensi"; and Jack Goody, "The Political Systems of the Tallensi and Their Neighbours, 1888–1915," *Cambridge Anthropology* 14 (1990): 1–25.

10. For theoretical and comparative perspectives, see Igor Kopytoff, ed., *The African Frontier: The Reproduction of Traditional African Societies* (Bloomington, 1987); and cf. Barrie Sharpe, "Ethnography and a Regional System: Mental Maps and the Myth of States and Tribes in North-Central Nigeria," *Critique of Anthropology* 6 (1986): 33–65; and Benedict G. Der, "The Traditional Political Systems of Northern Ghana Reconsidered," in *Regionalism and Public Policy in Northern Ghana*, ed. Yakubu Saaka (New York, 2001), 36–65.

11. The earliest recension of Talensi traditions of origin is Rattray, *Hinterland*, 339–44, which should be supplemented with RAI, Rattray Papers, MS 109, Field Notes 1928–1930, No. 34: Northern Territories Notebook 5, "Notes on Talanse [*sic*]." See too NAG ADM 68/5/4, Zuarangu [i.e., Zuarungu] District Record Book [begun 1927, but compiled using material dating back to the 1900s]; NAG ADM 68/5/5, Zuarangu District Record Book [begun 1935].

12. A note on the form of these various ethnonyms: Fortes followed Rattray in using "Tallensi" (which the latter spelled "Talense"), observing that it was the term in the neighboring Guruni tongue for all the inhabitants of Taleland, who called themselves Talis (sing. Taleng): Fortes, "Political System," 240. He used the term "Hill Tali" to distinguish the autochthonous clans of the Tong Hills from the Namoo of the surrounding plains.

13. Horton, "Stateless Societies," 102–104.

14. See, for example, Boubacar Barry, *Senegambia and the Atlantic Slave Trade*, trans. Ayi Kwei Armah (Cambridge, 1998); and Richard Roberts, *Warriors, Merchants, and Slaves: The State and the Economy in the Middle Niger Valley, 1700–1914* (Stanford, 1987).

15. For two case studies from the Voltaic region, see Charles Piot, "Of Slaves and the Gift: Kabre Sale of Kin during the Era of the Atlantic Slave Trade," *JAH* 37 (1996): 31–49; Andrew Hubbell, "A View of the Slave Trade from the Margin: Souroudougou in the Late Nineteenth-Century Slave Trade of the Niger Bend," *JAH* 42 (2001): 25–47; and more generally, Martin Klein, "The Slave Trade and Decentralized Societies," *JAH* 42 (2001): 49–65.

16. John O. Hunwick, ed. and trans., *Timbuktu and the Songhay Empire: Al-Sa'di's Ta'rikh al-sudan down to 1613, and Other Contemporary Documents* (Leiden, 1999), lii.

17. Wilks, "Mossi," 473.

18. For an overview, see Levtzion, *Muslims*.

19. The last Ghanaian census, conducted in 2000, revealed the following figures for religious affiliation for the Northern, Upper West, and Upper East Regions: Muslim, 18 percent; Christian, 10 percent; "African Traditional Religion," 70 percent.

20. Wilks, *Asante*, 20–22, 66–68, 305.

21. Despite the extensive literature on slavery within Asante and the Gold Coast, the northern slave trade has been neglected by historians. For an overview of the relationship between Asante and its northern provinces, see Wilks, *Asante*, 243–309; Kwame Arhin, "Savanna Contributions to the Asante Political Economy," in Schildkrout, *Golden Stool*, 51–59; and for a brief corrective, Benedict Der, *The Slave Trade in Northern Ghana* (Accra, 1998).

22. Christian Oldendorp, *Geschichte der Mission der Evangelischen Bruder auf . . . St Thomas, St Croix und St Jan* (Leipzig, 1777), cited in Michael Schottner, "'We Stay, Others Come and Go': Identity among the Mamprusi in Northern Ghana," in *Ethnicity in Ghana: The Limits of Invention*, ed. Carola Lentz and Paul Nugent (Edinburgh, 2000), 50.

23. Thomas E. Bowdich, *Mission from Cape Coast Castle to Ashantee* (London, 1819; repr. 1966), 208; S. W. Koelle, *Polyglotta Africana* (London, 1854).

24. See esp. Tauxier, *Le noir du Soudan*; idem, *Nouvelles notes sur le Mossi et le Gourounsi* (Paris, 1924).

25. See Arhin, "Savanna Contributions"; and Enid Schildkrout, "The Ideology of Regionalism in Ghana," in *Strangers in African Societies*, ed. W. A. Shack and E. P. Skinner (Berkeley, 1979), 183–207.

26. On the importance of Islamic ritual services, see Owusu-Ansah, *Talismanic Tradition*.

27. Thomas Birch Freeman, *Journal of Various Visits to the Kingdoms of Ashanti, Aku, and Dahomi in Western Africa* (London, 1844), 132.

28. See Brodie Cruickshank, *Eighteen Years on the Gold Coast of Africa* (London, 1853; repr. 1966), vol. 2, 244–47, which reports that the majority of slaves imported into the Akan states of the Gold Coast in the mid-nineteenth century were *nnonkofoo*. On the situation of *nnonkofoo* in Asante, see T. C. McCaskie, *State and Society in Pre-colonial Asante* (Cambridge, 1995), 95–101.

29. J. J. Holden, "The Zabarima Conquest of North-West Ghana," *THSG* 8 (1965): 60–86; Tamakloe, *History of the Dagbamba*, 45–55.

30. For the slave trade to Salaga in the 1880s–90s, see Marion Johnson, ed., *Salaga Papers* (Institute of African Studies, Legon, n.d.).

31. NAG ADM 56/1/61, Report on the Navarro District, Jan.–June 1911, by S. D. Nash.

32. Jack Goody, "Population and Polity in the Voltaic Region," in *The Evolution of Social Systems*, ed. J. Friedman and M. J. Rowlands (London, 1977), 535–45.

33. Fortes, *Clanship*, 3. The 1931 census recorded the Talensi population as 35,000, a figure not including the many migrant workers in the south.

34. Ibid.

35. For some discussion, see Keith Hart, "The Economic Basis of Tallensi Social History in the Early Twentieth Century," *Research in Economic Anthropology* 1 (1978): 185–216; and for a general formulation that draws on Goody's hypothesis, Akin L. Mabogunje and Paul Richards, "Land and People: Models of Spatial and Ecological Process in West African History," in Ajayi and Crowder, *History of West Africa*, vol. 1, 45–46.

36. Richard Fardon, *Raiders and Refugees: Trends in Chamba Political Development, 1750–1950* (Washington, 1988).

37. Fortes, *Clanship*, 23. The literature is vast, but for the different theoretical positions, see Joseph Miller, ed., *The African Past Speaks: Essays on Oral Tradition and History* (Folkestone, 1980); and Jan Vansina, *Oral Tradition as History* (Madison, 1985).

38. RAI Rattray Papers, MS 109, "Notes on Talanse," evidence of Poyel. For evidence that Asante *kambonse* may have penetrated directly into the Navrongo region—some twenty-five miles northwest of the Tong Hills—around 1850, see Timothy Garrard, "An Asante *Kuduo* among the Frafra of Northern Ghana," in Schildkrout, *Golden Stool*, 73–80.

39. RAI Rattray Papers, MS 109, "Notes on Talanse."

40. NAG ADM 68/5/1, Zouaragu [i.e., Zuarungu] District Informal Diary, 5 Nov. 1913. A typescript version of this important source, with different marginalia, is located at NAG ADM 68/5/2.

41. An important early source compiled from interviews with local elders is NAG ADM 11/1/824, Essays by Assistant DCs on Tribal History, "Navarro District," by Captain J. O'Kinealy, dd. Navarro [i.e., Navrongo], 1 Nov. 1907.

42. Rattray, *Hinterland*, 259–60. Rattray's informant and the speaker of the sections in quotes was probably Victor Aboya: see below. On the enslavement of strangers by precolonial "chiefs," see Meyer Fortes, "Strangers," in *Studies in African Social Anthropology*, ed. Meyer Fortes and Sheila Patterson (London, 1975), 231–32.

43. Interview with Ba'an (c. 1910–2000), dd. Sipaat, 19 Aug. 1999; also interviews with Yiran Boare (c. 1905–2002), dd. Tengzug, 23 Aug. 1999; Yikpemdaan (or Gorogonaaba) Wakbazaa (born c. 1910), dd. Gorogo, 21 Aug. 1999; Tengdaana Pehibazaa (born c. 1916) and Siikabani (born c. 1920), dd. Zubiung, Tongo, 5 Aug. 1999.

44. On the famine of the 1890s, see NAG ADM 56/1/128, "Food Supply in Fra-Fra," by H. Wheeler, CNEP, 31 May 1911; and Fortes, *Clanship*, 173; on continuity from the precolonial era to the 1910s in the practice of pawning children, see NAG ADM 68/5/1, Zouaragu District Informal Diary, 15 Dec. 1913, by S. D. Nash.

45. Interview with Ba'an, dd. Sipaat, 19 Aug. 1999; on the sale of kin, see too interview with Tengdaana Pehibazaa and Siikabani, dd. Zubiung, 5 Aug. 1999; and Rattray, *Hinterland*, 340.

46. Rattray, *Hinterland*, 347–48.

47. Ibid., 130. For more on Victor Aboya, see chapter 3.

48. NAG ADM 56/1/207, "Report on the Fetish Shrine in the Tong Hills," by C. Ievers, DC Zuarungu, 28 Jan. 1915.

49. NAG ADM 68/5/1, Zouaragu District Informal Diary, 7 Nov. 1913.

50. Interview with Yiran Boare, dd. Tengzug, 10 Aug. 1999.

51. NAG ADM 56/1/207, CNP to CCNT, 19 Sep. 1925.

52. Goody, *Technology*, 57–72.

53. Fortes, *Clanship*, 129.

54. Ibid., 121–22, quoting an unnamed informant, and see 121–46 *passim*.

55. For comparative insights, see Elizabeth Colson, "Places of Power and Shrines of the Land," *Paideuma* 43 (1997): 47–57.

56. Fortes, *Clanship*, 252.

57. Ibid., 253.

58. Fortes, *Clanship*, 106. A note on orthography: following the standard orthography recommended by the International African Institute, Fortes used the form *Bɔγar, Bɔγaraam*, etc., in his writings of the 1930s–40s. In later decades he switched to *boghar, Bogharaam*, etc. Rattray, in *Hinterland*, used the form *bogere, bagere*, etc. In an attempt to approximate the sound of this key set of words as spoken in Talen, we have used the form *bo'ar, Bo'araam*, etc., as the "g," "γ," or "gh" of the earlier forms is in fact almost silent, a guttural aspiration making *ba'a*, for example, sound similar to the Spanish *baja*.

59. See Fortes, *Religion*, 260; and Robin Horton, "Social Psychologies: African and Western," introductory essay in Meyer Fortes, *Oedipus and Job in West African Religion* (Cambridge, 1983), 46–50.

60. See esp. Fortes, *Religion*, 22–23.

61. Fortes, *Clanship*, 80.

62. Ibid., 114.

63. See esp. ibid., 104–108, 164–66.

64. Fortes, *Religion*, 12 and *passim*; see too idem, *Time and Social Structure and Other Essays* (London, 1970), 166–91.

65. Horton, "Social Psychologies"; Goody, introduction to Fortes, *Religion*.

66. Fortes, *Kinship*, 21, 227; see too interview with Tengdaana Zienbazaa (born c. 1910), dd. Gbeog, 1 July 2002. An extensive debate has emerged among indigenous Christian clergy and historians concerning the extent to which the term "God" can be used to describe the withdrawn deity amongst the Dagara peoples of northwestern Ghana: see esp. Benedict Der, "God and Sacrifice in the Traditional Religions of the Kasena and Dagaba of Northern Ghana," *JRA* 11 (1980): 172–87; and Sean Hawkins, "The Interpretation of *Naangmin*: Missionary Ethnography, African Theology, and History among the LoDagaa," *JRA* 28 (1998): 32–61.

67. Fortes, *Kinship*, 229, and see 226–30.

68. See the useful description by Rattray, *Hinterland*, 352–55, of one compound, that of Sayebere, a Tongo *tengdaana*.

69. Fortes, *Clanship*, 106.

70. Fortes, *Time*, 157.

71. Fortes, *Clanship*, 100, and, generally, 98–108, 130–40.

72. Ibid., 253.

73. Interview with Yikpemdaan Wakbazaa (born c. 1910), dd. Gorogo, 21 Aug. 1999.

74. Rattray, *Hinterland*, 361; and interview with Yiran Boare, dd. Tengzug, 23 Aug. 1999.

75. Fortes, *Clanship*, 79; also interview with Tengdaana Pehibazaa and Siikabani, dd. Zubiung, 5 Aug. 1999.

76. Fortes, *Clanship*, 106.

77. In RAI Rattray Papers, MS 109, Rattray suggests "eight compounds" as a translation for "Ya ni," a reference to the number of *tengdaana*s who manage the

shrine—but his guess remained unpublished; while Fortes, *Clanship*, 106, expresses puzzlement at the form Wannii. Elsewhere, Rattray notes in passing the terms *Yini*, "The Sky God" *(Hinterland*, 257), and *Yini zug*, "God Above" (ibid., 353), clear rearrangements of the compound term Naayin or Naawun that come very close to Yanii. Another possible derivation is from *yaab* (grandfather or ancestor), a word often ritually used to invoke Tongnaab: Fortes, *Clanship*, 137.

78. See esp. file NAG ADM 56/1/207, Tong Hills Affairs; NAG ADM 68/5/5, Zuarangu District Record Book, "Tonzugu"; Fortes, *Clanship*, 252; and interview with John Bawa Zuure, dd. Tengzug, 23 Aug. 1999.

79. John M. Chernoff, "Spiritual Foundations of Dagbamba Religion and Culture," in *African Spirituality: Forms, Meanings, and Expressions*, ed. Jacob K. Olupona (New York, 2000), 262.

80. NAG ADM 56/1/207, Enquiry into the Alleged Opening of the Tong Hill Fetish, evidence of Billa Moshi, Interpreter of Zuarungu Station, 26 Dec. 1920.

81. RAI Rattray Papers, MS 109, "Notes on Talanse," "History of Si."

82. On Builsa, see NAG ADM 56/1/123, Report of a Tour of Kanjarga Country, by E. Warden, 2 Oct. 1911; on Yagaba and the slave trade, see Der, *Slave Trade*, 22; on Tongnaab in Yagaba, see evidence from Fortes photograph collection, Museum of Anthropology and Archaeology, University of Cambridge, notebook titled "Labelled Negatives, 1st Field Trip," roll 21.

83. Fortes, *Religion*, 156. Fortes uses the rather Akanized spelling *bogharkyee*.

84. Rattray, *Hinterland*, 355.

85. NAG ADM 56/1/207, Inquiry Regarding the Use of the Tong Fetish, 14 Sep. 1925.

86. Interview with Anyaam (born c. 1920), dd. Kpikpaluk, Kadema, 11 June 2001.

87. Interviews with Ben Atongnaab Akanisoam, dd. Akannyokyiri, Gbedema, 4 July 2002, and Asiidem Akanguli, dd. Wiaga, 11 June 2001. See further R. Schott, "Sources for a History of the Bulsa in Northern Ghana," *Paideuma* 23 (1977): 141–68.

88. Rattray, *Hinterland*, 340–41.

89. Interview with Atulum Angiaknab and Gariba Angiaknab, dd. Abangyire, Fumbisi-Kasiesa, 4 July 2002.

90. Fortes, *Clanship*, 131.

91. Ibid., 132.

92. Ibid., 19. For description and analysis of the two great festivals, Fortes, "Ritual Festivals," and idem, *Religion*, chapter 3, "Ritual Festivals and the Ancestors"; also see Rev. Joseph Awiah, "Tongo Festivals, Dances, and Marriage Customs," mimeograph, n.d.

93. Fortes, "Ritual Festivals," 158.

94. Ibid., 154.

95. See his passing comments at ibid., 159; *Religion*, 63; and *Clanship*, 138.

96. Fortes, *Clanship*, 138.

97. Interview with Yiran Boare, dd. Tengzug, 23 Aug. 1999; see too Fortes, "Strangers."

98. On this point, cf. de Craemer, Vansina, and Fox, "Religious Movements."

99. NAG ADM 68/5/1, Zouaragu District Informal Diary, 5 Nov. 1913.

100. Ibid., 2 Oct. 1913.

101. The conquest of the "Gurunsi" region from the French perspective is re-constructed in Anne-Marie Duperray, *Les Gourounsi de Haute-Volta: Conquête et colonisation, 1896–1933* (Stuttgart, 1984); and Jeanne-Marie Kambou-Ferrand, *Peuples voltaïques et conquête coloniale, 1885–1914: Burkina Faso* (Paris, 1993).

102. Captain L. G. Binger, *Du Niger au Golfe de Guinée: Par le pays de Kong et le Mossi* (Paris, 1892), vol. 2, 25. For some discussion, see Goody, "Political Systems," 2–3; and Kambou-Ferrand, *Peuples voltaïques*, 30–34.

103. Binger, *Du Niger*, 56, and 409 for the comparative scarification diagrams. Note too Binger's famous map, which incorrectly locates the Talensi to the west of his route but does suggest that he was informed of their importance. See also the compendium by former chief commissioner C. H. Armitage, *The Tribal Markings and Marks of Adornment of the Natives of the Northern Territories of the Gold Coast Colony* (London, 1924).

104. Many of Ferguson's writings are conveniently collected in Kwame Arhin, ed., *The Papers of George Ekem Ferguson: A Fanti Official of the Government of the Gold Coast, 1890–1897* (Leiden, 1974).

105. Ferguson to Governor, dd. Yendi, 18 Aug. 1894, in Arhin, *George Ekem Ferguson*, 99. He would later amend his descriptions to "1. semibarbarous tribes with a form of organized government; 2. wild tribes, naked [and] living in independent family communities" and add a third category, "Mahomedan converts and traders": ibid., 109.

106. PRO CO 879/41, *Further Correspondence Respecting the Missions of Mr. G. E. Ferguson*, Ferguson to Governor, dd. Gambaga, 7 June 1894, 2.

107. Ferguson to Governor, dd. Yendi, 18 Aug. 1894, in Arhin, *George Ekem Ferguson*, 100; further commentary by Ferguson on nudity can be found at ibid., 68, 76, 142.

108. PRO CO 96/289, Maxwell to Chamberlain, 5 Feb. 1897, enclosed: Stewart to Colonial Secretary, Accra [CS], dd. Gambaga, 29 Dec. 1896.

109. Ferguson to Governor, enclosed in PRO CO 96/277, despatch dd. 5 Oct. 1896, in Arhin, *George Ekem Ferguson*, 140.

110. See, for example, PRO CO 879/54, *Correspondence Relating to the Northern Territories, June–Dec. 1898*, Hodgson to Chamberlain, 23 June 1898, and enclosures, 54–57; see also A. A. Illiasu, "The Establishment of British Administration in Mamprugu, 1898–1937," *THSG* 16 (1975): 1–28.

111. PRO CO 879/52, *Correspondence Relating to the Northern Territories, Jan.–June 1898*, Northcott to Governor, dd. Gambaga, 8 Apr. 1898, 391. For the term *"furra furra"* and early colonial perceptions of Frafra ethnicity, see NAG ADM 63/5/2, Navrongo District Record Book, entries by J. O'Kinealy, June 1907; for some discussion, see Moses Anafu, "The Impact of Colonial Rule on Tallensi Political Institutions, 1898–1967," *THSG* 14 (1973): 17–37.

112. PRO CO 879/52, No. 366, enclosed: "Report on Mamprussi," by Captain D. Macksworth, 30 May 1898.

113. A further note on ethnonyms: just as "Talensi" was a term used originally by their neighbors rather than the Talensi themselves, so the term "Nankani" (or sometimes Nankanse) was used by the Kasena to the west to describe a people who tended collectively to call themselves Gurunsi—a name, Rattray noted, "in most cases objected to by other tribes": *Hinterland*, 232. The Nankani in turn called the Kasena

"Yulse." To further complicate the issue, because the Nankani straddled the emerging ethnic frontier between Gurunsi and Frafra, individuals and communities often referred to themselves as "Frafra-Gurunsi."

114. PRO CO 879/58, *Correspondence Relating to the Northern Territories, 1899*, Northcott to Colonial Office, 9 July 1899, 180.

115. Note that the Dagomba kingdom had been bifurcated by the Anglo-German frontier, with its capital Yendi located in German Togoland: see Martin Staniland, *The Lions of Dagbon: Political Change in Northern Ghana* (Cambridge, 1975).

116. On the role of the *imam* of Gambaga in supplying the British with information on the Frafra and Gurunsi to the north, see PRO CO 879/52, Northcott to Governor, dd. Gambaga, 8 Apr. 1898, 391. According to Rattray, the term Gurunsi "is very much the equivalent of the word 'Kaffir'—unbeliever; eater of dogs—as bestowed by Mohammedans on those who do not follow the prophet": *Hinterland*, 232.

117. PRO CO 879/52, "Report on Mamprusi," 30 May 1898.

118. On the role of "fetish priests" amongst the Dagara (or "LoDagaa"), cf. Hawkins, *Writing*, 48–51, 64.

119. PRO CO 879/58, Low to Chamberlain, 2 May 1899, enclosed: "Report on Expedition to Fra-Fra Country, Jan.–Feb. 1899," by Captain W. Gifford.

120. PRO CO 879/58, *Correspondence Relating to the Northern Territories, 1899*, Stewart to CS, 12 Sep. 1899, 304.

121. Ibid., 306.

122. Rattray, *Hinterland*, 341. Like those of neighboring peoples, Talensi men on succeeding to the office of *tengdaana* or *naaba* would be addressed only by their title or nickname (*sam-wur*).

123. NAG ADM 56/1/46, Watherstone to CS, dd. Gambaga, 4 Mar. 1905; for accounts of the punitive forays out of Gambaga, see PRO CO 879/78, *Despatches Relating to Field Operations in the Northern Territories, 1899–1902*, 11–14, 21–29.

124. See esp. file NAG ADM 56/1/62, Asana Moshi's Case.

125. NAG ADM 56/1/46, Rodger to Lyttelton, 12 Apr. 1905; and enclosed: Watherston to CS, dd. Gambaga, 4 Mar. 1905.

126. See file NAG ADM 56/1/38, Fra Fra—Proposed Establishment of a Post In [1905].

127. NAG ADM 63/5/2, Navrongo District Record Book, "Zoko," by Lt. Partridge, 29 Dec. 1905.

128. PRO CO 96/460, Bryan to Elgin, 24 Dec. 1907, enclosed: O'Kinealy to CCNT, 8 Nov. 1907; CO 98/16, Annual Report on the NTs, 1907, 9.

129. NAG ADM 63/5/2, "Tongzugu," by J. O'Kinealy, 30 Sep. 1907.

130. On clothing, bodily adornment, and "nakedness" in the region, see Esther Goody and Jack Goody, "The Naked and the Clothed," in *The Cloth of Many Colored Silks: Papers on History and Society, Ghanaian and Islamic, in Honor of Ivor Wilks*, ed. John Hunwick and Nancy Lawler (Evanston, 1996), 67–90; Hawkins, *Writing*, 71–86; and generally, Jean Allman, ed., *Fashioning Africa: Power and the Politics of Dress* (Bloomington, 2004).

131. NAG ADM 56/1/456, Annual Report on the NTs, 1904.

132. NAG ADM 5/1/46, Watherstone to CS, 6 June 1906, enclosed: "Reorganization of the Administration of the Northern Territories," n.d. [but 1906].

133. Indeed, the same report goes on to point out the problems that cheap Eu-

ropean "fancy prints" had in breaking into an existing market dominated by the durable Mossi cloth; on the wearing of European and Mossi cotton cloth in the 1930s, see Fortes, *Clanship*, 11.

134. NAG ADM 63/5/2, Navrongo District Record Book, "Tong," 24 Nov. 1909. The school is the one opened in December 1907 by the Catholic White Fathers, who the year before had extended their operations from French territory with the opening of a station in Navrongo: see file NAG ADM 56/1/33, Catholic Mission.

135. Fortes, *Clanship*, 22; also field-note on a visit to Tengdaana Nimbazaa, Wakii, 6 Aug. 1999. Compare here the Mamprusi oral tradition of how the third *nayiri*, Banmalagu, was taught the art of weaving by a stranger, after which no Mamprusi would "ever be content to wear animal skins": NAG ADM 11/1/824, "A Short Essay on the History and Customs of the Mamprusi Tribe," by G. Mackay, n.d. [but 1920s]; and for an analysis of cultural exchange that takes as its starting point the symbol of the fez, see Kramer, *Red Fez*.

136. Interviews with Kpalbil Mebogire, dd. Wakii, 6 Aug. 1999, and Yikpemdaan Wakbazaa, dd. Gorogo, 21 Aug. 1999.

137. Interview with Yiran Boare, dd. Tengzug, 10 Aug. 1999.

138. NAG ADM 56/1/124, Report on a Tour of Inspection of the NEP, by C. H. Armitage, July 1911.

139. See PRO CO 96/495, Rodger to Crewe, 19 Apr. 1910.

140. NAG ADM 11/1/464, Annual Report on the Navarro District, 1910, by H. Berkely, n.d. [but Jan. 1911].

141. NAG ADM 56/1/441, Report on the NEP for the Quarter Ending 31 Dec. 1910.

142. PRO CO 96/506, Bryan to Harcourt, 19 Apr. 1911.

143. Interview with Tengdaan Kuruk, Kuribil Waadan, and Kpalbil Mebogire, dd. Wakii, 6 Aug. 1999. Kurugunaab was the Mamprusi office-holder who acted as intermediary between the *nayiri* and the Namoo chiefs; see chapter 2.

144. Interviews with Diegire Baa, dd. Shia, 17 Aug. 1999, and Bo'arnaab Dilimit, dd. Tengzug, 13 Aug. 1999.

145. Interview with Yiran Boare, dd. Tengzug, 10 Aug. 1999.

146. The operation is voluminously reported in PRO CO 96/506, Bryan to Harcourt, 19 Apr. 1911, esp. enclosure 2: Festing to CS, 12 Mar. 1911.

147. Ibid., 14. Note that the area on the southeast of the hills called Tiliga in British accounts is known to the Talensi as Santeng.

148. Interviews with *sipaatnaaba*, Ba'an, Putehinga, Doabil, and Sapak, dd. Sipaat, 19 Aug. 1999, and Pahinooni (born c. 1915), dd. Sipaat, 19 Aug. 1999.

149. Interview with Ba'an, dd. Sipaat, 19 Aug. 1999. Ba'an (c. 1910–2000), who of all our informants gave the most extensive and finely grained account of the British conquest, insisted that Yigare was from Tumu, in Sisala country some eighty miles to the west.

150. PRO CO 96/506, Festing to CS, 12 Mar. 1911, 22.

151. Interview with Yiran Boare, dd. Tengzug, 23 Aug. 1999.

152. Fortes, *Clanship*, 241, 243; see too idem, "Ritual Festivals."

153. Fortes, *Clanship*, 235.

154. Ibid. For further suggestive clues—albeit frustratingly vague—to a "mys-

tical calamity" arising from armed conflict during *Gologo* "in the very year that the British appeared on the scene in Tale life," see ibid., 241.

155. PRO CO 96/506, Festing to CS, 12 Mar. 1911. Festing refers to two episodes from the British conquest of southern Nigeria: the expedition against the Benin kingdom in 1897, spurred on by rumors of human sacrifice and other criminal activities, and that of 1901–1902, which destroyed the famous oracle shrine at Arochukwo in the southeast.

156. Ibid., Festing to Elkan, 12 Mar. 1911.

2. Gods and Guns, Rituals and Rule, 1911–1928

1. From an address given by Governor Shenton Thomas at Navrongo in 1933, in RAGT NRG 6/3/1, Asst. DC Navarro to CCNT, 23 Dec. 1933.

2. Rattray, *Hinterland*, 344, reporting a conversation with a Talensi *tengdaana* in 1928.

3. PRO CO 96/506, CCNT to CS, 12 Mar. 1911.

4. Colonial correspondence characterizes the postconquest process in the Northern Territories as one whereby peoples were either persuaded or forced to "come in" to the colonial state. See NAG ADM 56/1/441, Monthly Reports for the NEP, Feb. 1910, Mar. 1910, and Aug. 1910.

5. PRO CO 96/506, CCNT to Elkan, 12 Mar. 1911.

6. NAG ADM 63/5/2, District Record Book, Navarro, Mar. 1911.

7. PRO CO 96/506, CCNT to CS, dd. Nasia, 12 Mar. 1911.

8. NAG ADM 56/1/463, Annual Report on the Zouaragu District for 1911.

9. NAG ADM 56/1/61, Handing Over Reports, Navarro District, May 1912.

10. The prisoners originally numbered five—four "headmen" and one "fetish priest." At first they were jailed at Tamale, but in July 1911 they were allowed to be at liberty in Tamale as long as they did not return to the Frafra District or cross the Nasia river: NAG ADM 56/1/59, CNEP to CCNT, 29 July 1911; NAG ADM 56/1/127, CCNT to CNEP, 17 July 1912, and CNEP to CCNT, dd. Navarro, 12 Aug. 1912.

11. NAG ADM 56/1/124, Report on a Tour of Inspection of the NTs . . . between 19 November 1912 and 23 January 1913, by CCNT Armitage.

12. NAG ADM 68/5/2, Zouaragu Official Diary, 7 Nov. 1913.

13. NAG ADM 56/1/476, CCNT to CNEP, 27 Apr. 1914.

14. See, for example, NAG ADM 56/1/130, CNEP to CCNT, 3 Oct. 1911; NAG ADM 56/1/468 Quarterly Reports, NEP, 31 Dec. 1913; and NAG ADM 56/1/145, Handing Over Report, by A. Lundie, date unclear [but 1911].

15. PRO CO 96/557, Extract from Diary of CCNT, 2 Jan. 1915.

16. NAG ADM 56/1/207, Tong Hills Affairs, DC to CNEP, 28 Jan. 1915.

17. PRO CO 96/557, Extract from Diary of CCNT, 9 Feb. 1915.

18. NAG ADM 56/1/207, DC Zouaragu to CNEP, Notes of Evidence . . . taken on the 9th day of February 1915 . . . in connection with the renewal of the Fetish in the Tong Hills.

19. PRO CO 96/557, Extract from Diary of CCNT, 10 Feb. 1915.

20. Ibid., 11 Feb. 1915.

21. NAG ADM 56/1/207, CCNT to CNEP, dd. Zouaragu, 12 Feb. 1915.

22. PRO CO 96/557, Tong Hill Fetish, minute dd. 28 May 1915.

23. NAG ADM 56/1/207, CNEP to CCNT, dd. Paragu [i.e., Pwalugu], 10 June 1915.

24. Interview with Naoh (born c. 1927), dd. Tengzug, 9 Aug. 1999; also interviews with Yiran Boare, dd. Tengzug, 10 Aug. 1999, and Ba'an, dd. Sipaat, 19 Aug. 1999.

25. Fortes, *Clanship*, 114.

26. Ibid., 106.

27. Ibid., 111.

28. In physical space, Bonaab is very close to Ngoo, the great *tongban* on which the British were said to have set up their camp in 1911. It is logical, given this location, that the British would first discover the *bo'ar* Bonaab.

29. Goody, "Political Systems," 19.

30. NAG ADM 56/1/121, CCNT to CNEP, 3 July 1911.

31. PRO CO 96/506, CCNT to CS, dd. Nasia, 12 Mar. 1911.

32. NAG ADM 56/1/123, CNEP to CCNT, dd. Navarro, 2 Oct. 1911.

33. NAG ADM 56/1/476, CCNT to CNEP, 27 Apr. 1914.

34. NAG ADM 56/1/441, NEP Monthly Reports, June 1910. Sulsiba had been "enskinned" as *kunaaba* in 1909: NAG ADM 68/5/4, Zuarangu District Record Book, entry "Kurugu."

35. NAG ADM 56/1/441, NEP Monthly Reports, June 1910.

36. NAG ADM 56/1/121, Extract from letter to CS, 11 Sep. 1911.

37. NAG ADM 56/1/137, DC Zouaragu to DC Gambaga, 6 Dec. 1911.

38. NAG ADM 56/1/462, NEP, Report for the Quarter Ending 31 Mar. 1912.

39. NAG ADM 56/1/121, Declaration by CCNT, 14 Apr. 1912.

40. NAG ADM 56/1/137, CNEP to DC Zouaragu, dd. Navarro, 1 Feb. 1913.

41. Anafu, "Colonial Rule," 28–29.

42. See Roger Thomas, "The 1916 Bongo 'Riots' and Their Background: Aspects of Colonial Administration and African Response in Eastern Upper Ghana," *JAH* 24 (1983): 73; and Iliasu, "British Administration," 17.

43. NAG ADM 56/1/468, NEP Quarterly Reports, 30 Sep. 1913.

44. NAG ADM 68/5/2, Zouaragu Official Diary, 15 Oct. 1913.

45. Iliasu, "British Administration," 8.

46. An excellent example of this process comes from neighboring Zuarungu, where the chief in 1923 was the slave of the previous chief, "who made him his representative in the Commissioner's Court . . . and was misnamed by the Court Interpreter as the 'chief's son.'" See NAG ADM 56/1/118, CNEP to CCNT, dd. Navrongo, 15 Mar. 1923.

47. NAG ADM 56/1/165, CNEP to CCNT, dd. Navarro, 25 June 1913.

48. For example, NAG ADM 56/1/165, CNEP to CCNT, dd. Navarro, 25 June 1913; and NAG ADM 56/1/468, NEP Quarterly Reports, 30 Sep. 1913.

49. See, for example, NAG ADM 56/1/468, NEP Quarterly Reports, 30 June 1913; NAG ADM 68/5/2, Zouaragu Official Diary, 23 Mar. 1916; RAGT NRG 8/4/10, Zouaragu Informal Diary, 26 Aug. 1920; and NAG ADM 56/1/125, DC Navarro-Zuarugu to CNEP, 8 July 1919.

50. NAG ADM 68/5/2, Zouragu Official Diary, 27 Oct. 1913.

51. NAG ADM 56/1/137, CCNT to CNEP, dd. Tamale, 16 Jan. 1914.

52. James Lance, "Seeking the Political Kingdom: British Colonial Impositions and African Manipulations in the Northern Territories of the Gold Coast Colony" (Ph.D. dissertation, Stanford University, 1995). See also Iliasu, "British Administration," 8.

53. Anafu, "Colonial Rule," 26.

54. Interview with *sipaatnaaba* and elders Putehnya, Doabil, Ba'an, and Sapak, dd. Sipaat, 19 Aug. 1999.

55. NAG ADM 63/5/2, Navrongo District Record Book, 20 Feb. 1909.

56. Roger Thomas, "Forced Labour in British West Africa: The Case of the Northern Territories of the Gold Coast, 1906–1927," *JAH* 14 (1973): 80.

57. Interview with Bo'arana Volemeng (born c. 1912), dd. Shia, 17 Aug. 1999.

58. See NAG ADM 56/1/128, "Food supply in Fra-Fra," by H. Wheeler, 1 May 1911.

59. Interview with Lambazaa Naoh (born c. 1925), with Zampahi, dd. Tengzug, 14 Aug. 1999.

60. Interview with Pahinooni (born c. 1910) and her brother Tengdaana Dukbazaa (born c. 1915), dd. Sipaat, 19 Aug. 1999.

61. NAG ADM 56/1/473, Annual Report on the NTs, 1913.

62. RAGT NRG 8/3/41, Annual Report for the Zuarungu District, 1931–32. Nash's statement from 1913 is revisited in the 1931 report.

63. NAG ADM 45/1/476, NEP Quarterly Report, 30 Sep. 1914; see too NAG ADM 56/1/479, Annual Report on the NTs, 1914.

64. Thomas, "Bongo 'Riots,'" 61.

65. NAG ADM 68/5/2, Zouaragu Diary, 10 Aug. 1910.

66. Ibid., 18 Jan. 1915.

67. See the voluminous correspondence and reports assembled in PRO CO 96/570; NAG ADM 56/1/193, "Report on the Recent Disturbances at Bongo," 5 Aug. 1916; NAG ADM 68/5/1, Zouaragu District Informal Diary; and Thomas, "Bongo 'Riots.'"

68. Thomas, "Bongo 'Riots,'" 60. For accounts of similar stories unfolding north and west of the border, see Mahir Saul and Patrick Royer, *West African Challenge to Empire: Culture and History in the Volta-Bani Anticolonial War* (Athens, Ohio, 2001), 120–72.

69. NAG ADM 56/1/165, Notes of Enquiry into Unrest in Zouaragu District, 16 Nov. 1916.

70. Ibid.

71. Interview with Tengdaana Pehibazaa (born c. 1916) and Siikabani (born c. 1920), dd. Zubiung, Tongo, 5 Aug. 1999.

72. NAG ADM 68/5/2, Zouaragu Official Diary, 3 Aug. 1917.

73. Ibid., 4 Aug. 1917.

74. Ibid., 6 Aug. 1917.

75. Ibid., 5 Aug. 1917.

76. Ibid., 9 Aug. 1917.

77. Thomas, "Forced Labour."

78. NAG ADM 56/1/319, NP Diary, 19–22 Aug. 1922.

79. As Thomas has shown, many men were already going south to work in the

mines before heavy recruitment began, "but they objected to any form of contract, wishing to be free to come and go as they pleased": Thomas, "Forced Labour," 99.

80. NAG ADM 68/5/2, Zouaragu Official Diary, 14 Oct. 1913; also NAG ADM 56/1/463, Annual Report for Navarro-Zouaragu District, 1914.

81. For the migration statistics from the late 1920s and 1930s, see RAGT NRG 8/17/2, Return of Unorganised Labour . . . 1926–27 to 1930–31.

82. NAG ADM 56/1/118, CNP to CCNT, dd. Navrongo, 25 June 1923.

83. Taleland is noted for extreme variation in rainfall patterns: one area can receive ample rainfall in a given year, yet a few miles down the road another area can be suffering drought. Fortes, *Clanship*, 1–2, notes that differences in rainfall can vary from 25 to 45 inches per year. See too Hart, "Economic Basis," 190, and chapter 5 below on the late 1920s–early 1930s.

84. John Sebiyam Nabila, "The Migration of the Frafra of Northern Ghana: A Case Study of Cyclical Labor Migration in West Africa" (Ph.D. dissertation, Michigan State University, 1974), 71, argues that government recruitment efforts "formed the embryo of voluntary labor migration from the North to the South." The evidence that we have uncovered suggests that voluntary migration coincided with (and at times preceded) recruitment drives. Manchuelle's study of the Soninke argues against the pivotal role of taxation and coercion in the development of migrant labor systems: François Manchuelle, *Willing Migrants: Soninke Labor Diasporas* (Athens, Ohio, 1998), 8, 148–78.

85. Interview with Atuli Asamane (born c. 1900), dd. Yorogo, 21 Oct. 1999. "Prempeh House" refers to the building erected by the British in Kumasi to house the repatriated *asantehene* (or "Kumasihene") Nana Prempeh I.

86. NAG ADM 56/1/61, Handing Over Reports, Navarro District, July 1911.

87. Teresa Barnes does a wonderful job of unpacking the distinctions embedded in the differing notions of "travel" and "migration" in her "Virgin Territory? Travel and Migration by African Women in Twentieth-Century Southern Africa," in *Women in African Colonial Histories*, ed. Jean Allman, Susan Geiger, and Nakanyike Musisi (Bloomington, 2002), esp. 170–72.

88. Interview with Azabu (born c. 1914), dd. Samire, Tengzug, 20 Oct. 1999.

89. Interview with Atuli Asamane, dd. Yorogo, 21 Oct. 1999.

90. Again, cf. Manchuelle, *Willing Migrants*, 2, which stresses the internal dynamics of the labor migration process.

91. Meyer Fortes, "Some Aspects of Migration and Mobility in Ghana," *Journal of Asian and African Studies* 6 (1971): 1–20. Fortes estimated that this 10 per cent were away, mainly in the south, during the dry, non-farming season.

92. Interview with *Sipaatnaaba* (born c. 1925), dd. Sipaat, 19 Aug. 1999.

93. Interview with Bo'arnaab Dilimit, *tengdaana* of Gundaat (born c. 1924), dd. Tengzug, 13 Aug. 1999.

94. NAG ADM 56/1/463, Annual Report on the Navarro-Zouarugu District for 1916.

95. See, for example, NAG ADM 56/1/207, DC Zuarungu to CNEP, 29 Dec. 1915.

96. RAGT NRG 8/4/3, Navarro-Zuaragu Informal Diary, 12 Feb. 1919.

97. NAG ADM 68/5/2, Zouaragu Official Diary, 29 Dec. 1918.

98. NAG ADM 56/1/207, CCNT to CNEP, 23 Nov. 1920.

99. Ibid., DC Zuarungu to CNEP, 29 Oct. 1920.

100. Ibid., CNEP to DC Navarro-Zuaragu, dd. Gambaga, 9 Nov. 1920.

101. Ibid.

102. Ibid., "Enquiry into the Alleged Reopening of the Tong Hills Fetish," by Louis Castellain, 26–27 Dec. 1920.

103. Ibid., CNEP to CCNT, 5 Jan. 1921.

104. NAG ADM 56/1/207, "Enquiry into the . . . Tong Hills Fetish," 27 Dec. 1920.

105. NAG ADM 68/5/4, Zuarangu District Record Book, "Tongo." See also NAG ADM 56/1/207, CNP to CCNT, dd. Navrongo, 19 Sep. 1925.

106. Ibid., "Enquiry . . . Regarding the Use of the Tong Fetish," 14 Sep. 1925.

107. Ibid., citing evidence of Shia *bo'arana*.

108. RAGT NRG 8/3/48, Annual Report on the NTs, 1925–26.

109. NAG ADM 56/1/207, CNP to CCNT, dd. Navrongo, 19 Sep. 1925.

110. Ibid.

111. Ibid. See also NAG ADM 56/1/363, Handing Over Reports, NTs, 30 Nov. 1925.

112. NAG ADM 56/1/207, CCNT to CNP, 13 Nov. 1925.

113. NAG ADM 56/1/207, "Notes of Evidence . . . in connection with the removal of the fetish in the Tong Hills," 9 Feb. 1915.

114. NAG ADM 68/5/2, Zouaragu Diary, 27 Nov. 1916.

115. Ibid., 3 Jan. 1917.

116. Ibid., 25 June 1917.

117. See Fortes, *Clanship*, 105.

118. What evidence we do have is sketchy. The position of *golibdaana* was neither a *tengdaana*-ship nor a chiefship. It is possible that Tengol was the *golibdaana* in 1915 and used that position to put himself forward to the British as a leader of the Tengzug people. It is more likely, however, that Tengol parlayed his colonial chiefship, as "Chief of Tengzugu," into a more legitimate customary office in the late 1920s or early 1930s—an office whose powers he then greatly expanded. The current *golibdaana* insists that his father, Tengol, succeeded Diema as *golibdaana* only after they had all returned to the hills in 1935. Moreover, in Rattray's account of his conversation with Tengol, there is no explicit mention of the latter being the "keeper of the drums." Finally, it is customary for the position of *golibdaana* to go to the most senior man in the house. In 1915, it is unlikely that Tengol had achieved that seniority and stature. See interview with *Golibdaana* Malbazaa (born 1938), dd. Tengzug, 24 July 2000; and Rattray, *Hinterland*, 342–43.

119. The ban on Bonaab was not removed until 1935. See NAG ADM 68/5/5, Zuarangu District Record Book, "Tonzugu," n.d.

120. Barbara E. Ward, "Some Observations on Religious Cults in Ashanti," *Africa* 26 (1956): 53.

121. Fortes, *Clanship*, 253.

122. On the arrival of perhaps the first truck from Kumasi, see NAG ADM 11/1/495, Report on North Mamprussi for the Quarter Ending 30 June 1922.

123. Sacred Heart Parish Diaries, vol. 1, 1925–1931, translated by George Apolala, 14 Apr. 1926.

124. NAG ADM 56/1/512, Annual Report on Zuarungu District for year ending 31 Mar. 1928.

125. NAG ADM 11/1/886, Witchcraft, Cardinall, DC Kwahu, to CEP, 8 July 1930. On these other shrines, see chapter 3.

126. Fortes, *Clanship*, 254.

127. Rattray, *Hinterland*, 343.

128. Fortes, *Clanship*, 24.

129. Ibid.

130. Ibid., 25. Still, by 1932, Tengol would have his red fez: see NAG ADM 68/5/5, Zuarangu District Record Book, "Tonzugu," and chapter 5 below.

131. As Manchuelle argues, this perspective on labor migration is reproduced in much of the academic work on African labor migration: *Willing Migrants*, 6–8.

3. "Watch Over Me"

1. One of the features of the earliest written descriptions of Tongnaab is the emphasis on the mass of cloth crammed between rocks and hanging from trees around the vicinity of the shrine. This cloth can still be seen today at the Yanii *bo'ar* and is said to have been left by *soi*, "witches," who have been sent to the shrine to be healed of their affliction. Not surprisingly, Meyer Fortes downplayed the role of witchcraft amongst the Talensi, believing that it occupied a "minor place in Tale mystical thought and ritual action . . . [because it] is not easily reconcilable with the structure of Tale society": Fortes, *Kinship*, 32–35.

2. *Nana*, a term of deference and respect used when addressing Akan office-holders and elders, was also commonly used to refer to powerful deities. On the similar use of the Yoruba term *baba*, cf. J. D. Y. Peel, *Religious Encounter and the Making of the Yoruba* (Bloomington, 2000), 72–73.

3. NAG ADM 56/1/179, Rattray to CS, dd. Zuarungu, 21 May 1928. Compare Fortes's similar description of the journey in *Clanship*, 1.

4. NAG ADM 56/1/179, Rattray to CS, 21 May 1928.

5. Ibid.

6. See Sacred Heart Parish Diaries, 5 June 1925 and 14 Dec. 1925. On the negotiations between the Catholic Church and the colonial government over the extension of the mission from Navrongo to Bolgatanga, see NAG ADM 56/1/298, Catholic Mission.

7. Aboya's writing is found in Rattray, *Hinterland*, 130–228.

8. See T. C. McCaskie, "R. S. Rattray and the Construction of Asante History: An Appraisal," *History in Africa* 10 (1983): 189.

9. Rattray, *Hinterland*, 130.

10. Ibid., 339.

11. Ibid., 361.

12. The following account is based on ibid., 361–65, and RAI Rattray Papers, MS 109, "Notes on Talanse."

13. Rattray, *Hinterland*, 362.

14. Ibid.

15. Ibid., 362–63.

16. Rattray suggests in a note that Takuru-nab is "possibly *Ta-kora*," the most famous manifestation of the Asante tutelary deity (*obosom*) Tano.

17. Rattray, *Hinterland*, 363. Rattray notes that his request to "return like a hawk" was granted, as eight months later, on 12 January 1929, he was indeed to fly directly over the Tong Hills on the last stage of his pioneering solo flight from England to the Gold Coast.

18. Ibid. For the Twi texts, see RAI Rattray Papers, MS 109, and for Rattray's English translations, *Hinterland*, 364–65.

19. All quotations in this paragraph from ibid., 365.

20. See esp. NAG ADM 56/1/179, Rattray to CS, 15 Apr. 1930.

21. Ibid., 19.

22. Ibid., 10.

23. Ibid., 17.

24. On the symbolic drama of pilgrimage, see Turner, *Dramas*, 166–230, esp. 183, where Turner draws on Fortes's treatment of Tongnaab; and Werbner, introduction to *Ritual Cults*.

25. Margaret J. Field, "Some New Shrines of the Gold Coast and their Significance," *Africa* 13 (1940): 138–49; idem, *Akim-Kotoku: An Oman of the Gold Coast* (London, 1948), 171–97; idem, *Search for Security: An Ethno-psychiatric Study of Rural Ghana* (London, 1960); and Ward, "Religious Cults." For overviews of the literature, see Malcolm McLeod, "On the Spread of Anti-witchcraft Cults in Modern Asante," in *Changing Social Structure in Ghana: Essays in the Comparative Sociology of a New State and an Old Tradition*, ed. Jack Goody (London, 1975): 107–17; McCaskie, "Anti-witchcraft Cults"; and, more generally, R. G. Willis, "Instant Millennium: The Sociology of African Witch-Cleansing Cults," in *Witchcraft Confessions and Accusations*, ed. Mary Douglas (London, 1970), 129–39.

26. Field, "New Shrines," 141.

27. Ibid.

28. Hans Debrunner, *Witchcraft in Ghana: A Study of the Belief in Destructive Witches and Its Effect on the Akan Tribes* (Accra, 1959), esp. 61–62.

29. Field, *Akim-Kotoku*, 179.

30. Jack Goody, "Anomie in Ashanti?" *Africa* 27 (1957): 356–63.

31. Goody, "Anomie," 356, following a short account by Rattray in *Religion and Art in Ashanti* (London, 1927), 167–70. *Afunsua* was in fact proscribed by the British in the Gold Coast Colony in 1901, but not formally outlawed in Asante until 1918: NAG ADM 11/1/1437, "Suppression of Objectionable Customs," n.d. [c. 1930].

32. Goody, "Anomie," 362. The debate on the dynamics of witchcraft and anti-witchcraft in the Gold Coast emerged in parallel with that in other parts of the continent in the wake of the publication in 1937 of *Witchcraft, Oracles, and Magic among the Azande* by E. E. Evans-Pritchard (Oxford, 1937). See also Douglas, *Witchcraft Confessions;* and Audrey I. Richards, "A Modern Movement of Witchfinders," *Africa* 8 (1935): 448–61.

33. The focus here is on the dominant Twi-speaking Akan culture of present-day southern Ghana, although it should be noted that witchcraft belief was shared by neighboring peoples, notably the Ga-, Dangme-, and Ewe-speaking groups to the southeast of the Akan. This cluster of shared beliefs in turn shaded into those of

the Aja-speaking peoples of the "Slave Coast"—present-day Togo and Benin—further to the east. M. J. Field, *Religion and Medicine of the Gã People* (London, 1937), 137, noted that there was no term in the Ga language for a witch and that terminology had been borrowed from the Akan. For a brief account of Ewe witchcraft belief, see Birgit Meyer, *Translating the Devil: Religion and Modernity among the Ewe in Ghana* (Edinburgh, 1999), 88–92. The most assiduous chronicler of witchcraft in postcolonial Ghana is the U.S.-based Ghanaian professor of English Gabriel Bannerman-Richter; see his trilogy *The Practice of Witchcraft in Ghana* (Elk Grove, Calif., 1982), *Don't Cry! My Baby, Don't Cry! Autobiography of an African Witch* (Elk Grove, Calif., 1986), and *Mmoetia: The Mysterious Little People* (Elk Grove, Calif., 1987).

34. In Fante-Twi, spoken on the central Gold Coast and slightly different from Asante-Twi, the term for *bayi* is *ayene*, and for *obayifo*, *obayen* or *ayen*. For the various forms, see Rev. J. G. Christaller, *A Dictionary of the Asante and Fante Language Called Tshi (Chwee, Twi)* (Basel, 1881), 9. The term has also traveled via the trans-Atlantic slave trade to the Caribbean and North America, where it became "obeah."

35. McCaskie, *State and Society*, 274.

36. Geschiere, *Witchcraft*.

37. Field, *Akim-Kotoku*, 185. *Kra* was one of four elements, with *sunsum*, *mogya*, and *ntoro*, seen to constitute each human being, and can be broadly translated as "soul." Other sources identify the *sunsum* rather than the *kra* as the element most susceptible to attack by witchcraft. For a useful summary, see McCaskie, *State and Society*, 167–68.

38. Field, *Akim-Kotoku*, 185.

39. Cruickshank, *Eighteen Years*, vol. 2, 134.

40. *Aduto*: from *aduru* (medicine) + *to* (to throw, or to put on). On the various types of Akan "medicine," see Dennis M. Warren, "Bono Traditional Healers," in *African Therapeutic Systems*, ed. Z. A. Ademuwagun et al. (Waltham, 1979), 120–24.

41. See, for example, RAGK ARG 1/30/1/5, Fetish Priest Adawua, Statement of Edu Wura [i.e., Yaw Adawua], 10 Oct. 1906.

42. On so-called "Nzima-bayi," charms used "positively" to acquire wealth, see Debrunner, *Witchcraft*, 1. The use of *bayi* for commercial gain was noted by Christaller as early as 1881: *Dictionary*, 9.

43. Field, *Akim-Kotoku*, 184–85.

44. For published first-person accounts, see Field, *Religion and Medicine*, 135–60; idem, *Search for Security, passim*; Debrunner, *Witchcraft*, part 2 *passim*; and from a later period, Bannerman-Richter, *Don't Cry*.

45. All quotations in this paragraph are from Rhodes House Library MSS Afr. s.849, Notes of an Enquiry by W. W. Kilby, DC, into a Case of Alleged Witchcraft at Jenase, near Wiawso, n.d. [1919–23].

46. Cf. McLeod, "Anti-witchcraft Cults," 112: "*bayi* are most often kept in a woman's belly or vagina, the bodily areas associated with reproduction, or in her waist beads (*toma*) which support the red pubic cover cloth (*etam*) and are inextricably linked with female sexuality." Field, *Religion and Medicine*, 145, noted that the animal most commonly associated with *bayi* was the snake. "My *obeye* [*sic*] is a snake, *Onanka*," one woman told her, "and I keep it inside my vagina."

47. On protective medicine charms or *kunkuma*, see NAG ADM 11/1/886, J. C. De Graft Johnson to SNA, 21 Dec. 1937.

48. Field, *Religion and Medicine*, 142, notes that the Ga used the circumlocution *akpasa* ("scissors") to refer to *abayifoo*, "signifying that the witch cuts through the blood-vessels round her victim's heart."

49. The literature on the European "witch craze" is now enormous; useful recent overviews include Brian P. Levack, *The Witch-Hunt in Early Modern Europe* (Harlow, 1995); and Robert W. Thurston, *Witch, Wicce, Mother Goose: The Rise and Fall of the Witch Hunts in Europe and North America* (Harlow, 2001).

50. Carlo Ginzburg, *The Night Battles: Witchcraft and Agrarian Cults in the Sixteenth and Seventeenth Centuries*, trans. John Tedeschi and Anne Tedeschi (London, 1983).

51. Ginzburg further developed this idea in *Ecstacies: Deciphering the Witches' Sabbath*, trans. Raymond Rosenthal (London, 1992).

52. Field, *Religion and Medicine*, 139.

53. Field, ibid., 147–49, and Debrunner, *Witchcraft*, 32–33, assess their own evidence on this point. Both remain inconclusive.

54. White, *Vampires*.

55. Debrunner, *Witchcraft*, 106, citing the Basel missionary H. Bohner, *Im Lande des Fetishes* (Basel, 1890), 214–18.

56. McCaskie, "Anti-witchcraft Cults," 126, 129, and *passim*.

57. See McCaskie, *State and Society*, 102–43; for the corresponding cosmology of the Ga, see Field, *Religion and Medicine*.

58. Quoted in McCaskie, *State and Society*, 111.

59. Ivor Wilks, *Forests of Gold: Essays on the Akan and the Kingdom of Asante* (Athens, Ohio, 1993), 115.

60. McCaskie, *State and Society*, 111. For further insights, see Bannerman-Richter, *Witchcraft*, 54–59, 107–10.

61. John Parker, *Making the Town: Ga State and Society in Early Colonial Accra* (Portsmouth, N.H., 2000), 56–57.

62. Maier, *Priests and Power*. Bruku's influence had reached as far east as Yorubaland by the 1850s: Peel, *Religious Encounter*, 105, 108.

63. RAGK ARG 1/30/1/18, "Kukuro," by W. J. Pitt, n.d. [but 1928].

64. Arhin, "Savanna Contributions," 53; and Wilks, *Asante*, 250.

65. Parker, *Making the Town*, 56.

66. R. Lonsdale's Report from Salaga, 1882, cited in Johnson, *Salaga Papers*; and Wilks, *Asante*, 239.

67. Goody, "Anomie." See further Owusu-Ansah, *Talismanic Tradition*.

68. Goody, "Anomie," 358.

69. Bowdich, *Mission*, 260, 508.

70. Cruickshank, *Eighteen Years*, 177–79; see too John Beecham, *Ashanti and the Gold Coast* (London, 1841), 214–15. Drowning or strangulation were the preferred methods of execution, so as to avoid spilling the "contaminated" blood of the *obayifo*.

71. RH MSS Brit. Emp. s.344 Harper Papers, Kwadjo Apaw to DC Kumase, 28 Feb. 1923.

72. McCaskie, *State and Society*, 143, emphasis in original.

73. *Domankama* was one of the many appellations of the supreme being, *Onyame*. The cult was also known as Abonsamkom, i.e., *abonsam*, "wizard" + *akom*, the dance of the possessed *akomfoo*.

74. McCaskie, "Anti-witchcraft Cults," 129–33; see too idem, *State and Society*, 133–35; also Wilks, *Asante*, 519–21.

75. Rattray, *Religion*, 29. For Yaw Adawua's activities in 1906, see file RAGK ARG 1/30/1/5, Fetish Priest Adawua.

76. The ordeal involved the accused swallowing a copious amount of water into which the poisonous bark of the *odom* tree (or sasswood, *Erythrophleum guineese*) had been dissolved; if this caused vomiting and the accused survived, the verdict was innocent. The poison ordeal formed a standard part of judicial practice throughout much of the forest zone of precolonial West Africa.

77. Rattray, *Religion*, 30.

78. Ibid., 31.

79. Ibid., 29. *Odum (Chlorophora excelsa)* is not to be confused with *odom*. For Asante perceptions of the *kwae bibrem*, the "deep forest," and the *sasabonsam*, see T. E. Kyei, *Our Days Dwindle: Memories of My Childhood Days in Asante* (Portsmouth, N.H., 2001), 4, 182; and, from the very pinnacle of society, NAG CSO 21/9/25, Native Customs, Asantehene Osei A. Prempeh II to CCA, 7 Nov. 1944.

80. McCaskie, "Anti-witchcraft Cults," 130–32; and idem *State and Society*, 133–34.

81. For a full discussion, see John Parker, "Witchcraft, Anti-witchcraft, and Trans-regional Ritual Innovation in Early Colonial Ghana: Sakrabundi and Aberewa, 1889–1910," *JAH* 45 (2004): 393–420; also McCaskie, "Anti-witchcraft Cults," 138–41.

82. R. A. Freeman, *Travels and Life in Ashanti and Jaman* (London, 1898), 148–55.

83. Ibid.

84. Maurice Delafosse, *Les frontières de la Côte d'Ivoire, de le Côte d'Or et du Soudan* (Paris, 1908), 119–20.

85. For a review of the evidence, see Parker, "Witchcraft."

86. NAG ADM 11/1/1154. "Information regarding the Fetish Aberewa," by Owusu Ansa, *omanhene* of Akwapim, n.d. [1913].

87. PRO CO 96/471, Rodger to Crewe, 17 Aug. 1908, enclosed: Fuller to CS, 8 Aug. 1907.

88. Ibid., Fell to CCA, 5 July 1908.

89. Ibid., "Meeting Held on the 6th August 1908 Outside the Fort at Coomasie."

90. Ibid.

91. RAGK ARG 1/30/7, minute by SNA, 6 July 1912.

92. For Hwemeso, see Rattray, *Religion*, 31–34; McCaskie, "Anti-witchcraft Cults," 141–45; RH MSS Brit. Emp. s.344 Harper Papers, file on "Fwemiso or Kwaku Fetish"; NAG ADM 36/1/8, Fetish 1920–46; and NAG ADM 11/1/1243 Hwemisu Fetish (Fwe-me-sa).

93. McCaskie, "Anti-witchcraft Cults," 143.

94. NAG ADM 36/1/8, "Hwe Mi Su Fetish," 20 Oct. 1921.

95. NAG ADM 11/1/1243, Chief Kojo Amuakwa to CCP, 8 Aug. 1922; on mortality levels, see K. David Patterson, "The Influenza Epidemic of 1918–19 in the Gold Coast," *JAH* 24 (1983): 485–502.

96. NAG ADM 36/1/8, "Hwe Mi Su Fetish," 20 Oct. 1921.

97. For statistics on church membership in Asante, see NAG ADM 11/1/1907, Report on Ashanti for 1921, 33–37.

98. Basel Mission Archive D-1, 90/74, Annual Report of Kumase Congregation, 22 Feb. 1909.

99. See for example NAG ADM 11/1/1243, De Carteret to CEP, 6 Aug. 1922, on the situation at the cocoa trading town of Pakro.

100. NAG ADM 36/1/8, "Hwe Mi Su Fetish," 20 Oct. 1921.

101. Ibid; see too RAGKD ADM/KD 29/6/69, "Abayi-yie (Taking out Witch-craft)," by E. R. Addow, n.d. [but 1930].

102. For an ethnographic analysis of this process in the Peki region east of the Volta, see Meyer, *Translating the Devil.*

103. RAGCC ADM 23/1/452, Sekyi to CCP, 27 Aug. 1922.

104. See Hans Debrunner, *The Story of Sampson Opong* (Accra, 1965), 11–12. Debrunner's account is based on an interview with the elderly Opong himself in 1957.

105. Ibid., 23–24.

106. Ibid., 24.

107. NAG ADM 11/1/1907, Report on Ashanti for 1921, 33–37.

108. Ibid.

109. See esp. Debrunner, *Witchcraft*, part 5; and C. G. Baëta, *Prophetism in Ghana: A Study of Some "Spiritual" Churches* (London, 1962).

110. McLeod, "Anti-witchcraft Cults," 113; see too Bannerman-Richter, *Witchcraft*, 40, on the draw of the "Kankam" oracle shrine in the Republic of Guinea.

111. Interview with Kandiau *tengdaana*, dd. Kandiau, 19 July 2000; and NAG ADM 66/5/5, Wa District Informal Diary, Wuchiau, 22 Oct. 1916, by S. D. Nash.

112. Kunde's history can be reconstructed from NAG ADM 11/1/637, Kune Fetish; and RAGK ARG 1/30/1/18, DC Wenchi to CCA, 28 June 1932.

113. Debrunner, *Witchcraft*, 109–10, 112, citing an article by J. P. Atiemo in the Basel Mission newspaper *The Christian Messenger* in 1909.

114. Debrunner, *Witchcraft*, 112.

115. NAG ADM 11/1/637, Ofori Atta to DC Birrim, 22 Sep. 1916.

116. Ibid., F. Crowther to CS, minute dd. 7 Nov. 1916.

117. See Field, *Search for Security*, 90; and RAGKD ADM/KD 29/6/106, "Memorandum on 'The Fetish Kundi,'" by M. J. Field, 12 Jan.1940.

118. RAGKD ADM/KD 29/6/69, DC Kwahu to CEP, 2 Aug. 1933.

119. NAG ADM 11/1/886, Witchcraft, Cardinall to CEP, 8 July 1930; Field, *Akim-Kotoku*, 180–81; and Jack Goody, "The Over-Kingdom of Gonja," in *West African Kingdoms in the Nineteenth Century*, ed. Daryl Forde and P. M. Kaberry (London, 1967), 201.

120. RAGK ARG 1/30/1/18, DC Wenchi to CCA, 7 Mar. 1936; see too interview with *Senyonwura, Senyon Kupo*, and *Kuluwura*, dd. Senyon, 17 July 2000.

121. RAGKD ADM/KD 29/6/69, CEP to DC Kwahu, 23 Aug. 1930; and NAG ARG 1/30/1/18, CS to CCA, 6 Feb. 1935.

122. Field, *Search for Security*, 90.

123. RAGK ARG 1/30/1/18, Nana Kwaku Mensah to [DC?], 14 Aug. 1931.

124. RAGKD ADM/KD 29/6/69, A. Akainyah, Sub-inspector, Gold Coast Police, Nkawkaw, to Asst. Superintendent, Koforidua, 2 Aug. 1944; and NAG ARG 2/2/119, *omanhene* of Kwahu to DC Mpraeso, 17 Jan. 1945.

125. Peter Morton-Williams, "The Atinga Cult among the South-Western

Yoruba: A Sociological Analysis of a Witch-Finding Movement," *Bulletin de l'IFAN* 18 (1956): 315–34.

126. Debrunner, *Witchcraft*, 108. See too Goody, "Anomie," 357: "I spent a year in the village . . . containing the parent shrine of the Kpankpanbia exported to Ashanti." This year in Birifu (1950–51) resulted in *The Social Organisation of the Lo-Wiili* (London, 1956) and *Death, Property, and the Ancestors: A Study of the Mortuary Customs of the LoDagaa of West Africa* (Stanford, 1962), but it is striking that Goody fails to mention the thriving pilgrim trade, a phenomenon that Fortes had described for the Tong Hills fifteen years before.

127. RAGT NRG 8/19/2, "The 'God' Bruku of Siari," by E. F. Tamakloe, 16 Sep. 1926.

128. A. W. Cardinall, *Tales Told in Togoland* (London, 1931), 52; see too RAGT NRG 8/19/2, DC Eastern Dagomba to Commissioner for the Southern Province of the NTs, 7 Oct. 1926; and on Bruku's influence throughout the Gold Coast, Togo, Dahomey, and Nigeria by the 1940s, Parrinder, *West African Religion*, 28. The extension of ritual networks as far as Senegambia might seem doubtful were it not for reports of Senegalese traders passing through Bolgatanga en route to Kumasi and Accra by this period: Sacred Heart Parish Diaries, 14 Feb. 1928.

4. From Savanna to Forest

1. NAG ADM 11/1/886, CEP to CS, dd. Koforidua, 31 Oct. 1930.

2. Interviews with John Bawa Zuure, dd. Tengzug, 23 Aug. 1999, and Shia *Bo'arana* Volemeng (born c. 1913), dd. Shia, 17 Aug. 1999.

3. Debrunner, *Witchcraft*, 108.

4. AASA 3/283, Kwabena Assifu to Omanhene of Akyem Abuakwa, dd. Suhum, 1 July 1930.

5. Ibid.

6. For a full account, see Polly Hill, *The Migrant Cocoa-Farmers of Southern Ghana: A Study in Rural Capitalism* (Cambridge, 1963). See also Natasha Gray, "The Legal History of Witchcraft in Colonial Ghana: Akyem Abuakwa, 1913–1943" (Ph.D. dissertation, Columbia University, 2000), 118–29.

7. NAG ADM 11/1/886, Assifu to Governor, Gold Coast, dd. Bretema, near Suhum, 12 Feb. 1932.

8. The politics of Abiriw, a predominantly Guan town in the Akan state of Akuapem, were complex and highly contested in the late nineteenth and early twentieth centuries. For some fugitive indications that Assifu and/or his father were involved in political conflict and in the management of the Bosumpra *obosom* in the period, see file NAG ADM 11/1/23, Abirew Native Affairs, esp. Kwesie Mfodjo to CS, 4 Jan. 1909.

9. See Robert Addo-Fening, *Akyem Abuakwa, 1700–1943: From Ofori Panin to Sir Ofori Atta* (Trondheim, 1997); and Richard Rathbone, *Murder and Politics in Colonial Ghana* (New Haven, 1993).

10. Christaller considered *obosomfo* and *okomfo* to be synonymous: *Dictionary*, 2nd ed., 43. However, there is an important difference: an *obosomfo* collects or ac-

quires the *obosom* and tends it, but is never possessed by it. The *okomfo*, on the other hand, is possessed by the *obosom* and speaks as it. Technically, Assifu was not an *okomfo* because he was never possessed by Nana Tongo. See interview with Paul Assifu, dd. Obretema, 13 Nov. 1999.

11. Ibid. See also Bismark Enoch Larbi (Assifu's grandson), "Assiful's Relationship with Nana Tongo," typed ms., May 2002; and interview with Bismark Enoch Larbi, dd. Kokomlemle, Accra, and Abiriw, 17 June 2000.

12. NAG ADM 11/1/886, G. Smith, Cape Coast Divisional Court, to Governor, 14 May 1930, enclosed: testimony of Kobina Owusu.

13. AASA 3/283, Assifu to Omanhene of Akyem Abuakwa, 1 July 1930.

14. Ibid.

15. Field, *Religion and Medicine*, 135.

16. Interview with Paul Assifu, dd. Obretema, 13 Nov. 1999.

17. Interview with Tengdaan Dok (Tamboo *tengdaana*, born c. 1930), dd. Tengzug, 12 Aug. 1999. See also interviews with Zimemeh (born c. 1930) and Yin Kudoog (born c. 1927), dd. Yinduri, 16 Aug. 1999.

18. Interviews with Okomfo Sika, Okomfo Yaa, and Okyeame Tawia, dd. Tengzug, 8 Nov. 1999; Okomfo Sika and Okyeame Tawia, dd. Kukurantumi, 16 June 2000; and Okomfo Atta Fordwo, dd. Kukurantumi, 16 June 2000. Okomfo Sika learned her trade from her grandmother Okomfo Aframea, who was the niece of Atta Kojo. It should be noted that the introduction of Nana Tongo into Kukurantumi was marked by political conflict when in 1931 the deity identified the queen mother as an *obayifo* responsible for the death of members of the local *adontenhene*'s family: see the *West African Times*, "Queen-Mother Destooled for Alleged Witchcraft," 5 May 1931.

19. *Gold Coast Times*, 12 Apr. 1930.

20. Interview with Kwao Ahoto, from Aklayawaya, dd. Tengzug, 8 Nov. 1999.

21. Interview with Korkor Nartey (born c. 1912) and Lardje Nartey (born c. 1916), dd. Suhum, 13 Nov. 1999.

22. Interview with Adwoa Ankoma and Kofi Obeng (of Amaase, Asikwaa), Okomfo Yaa Sekyibiaa and her husband Kwaku Opoku (of Hemang), Efia Nyakoaa (of Saaman Osino), and Isaac Tetteh-Nartey (of Suhum), dd. Tengzug, 8 Nov. 1999.

23. Interview with Okomfo Atta Fordwo, dd. Kukurantumi, 16 June 2000.

24. NAG ADM 11/1/886, "Statement of Amah Botchway," n.d. [but c. 1930].

25. For Field's account of the very similar fowl sacrifice at a Senyakupo shrine, see Field, *Akim-Kotoku*, 179.

26. Ibid., 184.

27. NAG ADM 11/1/886, CEP to DC Mpraeso, dd. Koforidua, 28 July 1930.

28. NAG ADM 11/1/1051, Police Constable Obeng to Senior Superintendent of Police, dd. Suhum, 21 Apr. 1930.

29. AASA 3/72, Odikro Ohene Kwaku, Odikro Suhum, to Omanhene, Akyem Abuakwa, dd. Suhum, 7 May 1928.

30. AASA 8/85, Kwame Amponsah, Native Doctor Suhum Tetekasum, to Omanhene, Akyem Abuakwa, dd. 19 Dec. 1929.

31. Among the most easily accessible sources on the spread of cocoa farming are Hill, *Migrant Cocoa-Farmers;* Gareth Austin, "The Emergence of Capitalist Relations in South Asante Cocoa-Farming, c. 1916–33," *JAH* 28 (1987): 259–79; Beverly Grier,

"Pawns, Porters, and Petty Traders: Women in the Transition to Cash-Crop Agriculture in Colonial Ghana," *Signs* 17 (1992): 302–28; Gwendolyn Mikell, *Cocoa and Chaos in Ghana* (New York, 1989); and John Dunn and A. F. Robertson, *Dependence and Opportunity: Political Change in Ahafo* (Cambridge, 1973).

32. AASA 3/283, Kwabena Assifu of Abiriw to Omanhene, Akim-Abuakwa, dd. Suhum, 1 July 1930. The idea that Asantes visit Tongnaab especially for money is widely held by northern followers of Tongnaab today. As Atulum and Gariba Angiaknab of Fumbisi (in the Builsa region) recently explained, "Now the Ashantis . . . They only go there to ask for wealth. When they go, they say that 'OK, if I go back and I get rich, I'll come with a cow'": interview with Atulum Angiaknab and Gariba Angiaknab, dd. Abangyire, Fumbisi-Kasiesa, 4 July 2002.

33. AASA 8/85, Kwame Amponsah, Native Doctor Suhum Tetekasum, to Omanhene, Akyem Abuakwa, dd. 19 Dec. 1929.

34. RAGCC ADM 23/1/213, Nana Torpor II to DC Cape Coast, 6 May 1930.

35. AASA 3/283, Chief Yaw Koi to Omanhene, Akim-Abuakwa, dd. Krabo, 1 Aug. 1930.

36. Field, *Akim-Kotoku*, 182.

37. RAGKD ADM/KD 29/6/69, "Abayi-Yie (Taking out witch-craft)," by E. R. Addow of Abetifi [Kwawu], n.d. [1930].

38. Interview with Bismark Enoch Larbi, dd. Accra and Abiriw, 17 June 2000.

39. Interview with Okomfo Atta Fordwo, dd. Kukurantumi, 16 June 2000.

40. Interview with Tengdaana Boana'ab Dilimit, dd. Gundaat, Tengzug, 8 June 2001.

41. Ibid. See also interview with Yikpemdaan Wakbazaa, dd. Gorogo, 9 June 2001.

42. Field, "New Shrines," 145.

43. Field, *Akim-Kotoku*, 181.

44. On mimesis and north-south dialogue within present-day Ewe cults in neighboring Togo, see Rosenthal, *Possession;* also Kramer, *Red Fez;* and for theoretical insights, Michael Taussig, *Mimesis and Alterity: A Particular History of the Senses* (New York, 1993).

45. Interview with Bosomfo Nii Yaw, dd. Oshieyie, 4 June 2000. We have not encountered any evidence that would let us know whether the laxity in enforcing the prohibition of clothing is a recent phenomenon, or whether it existed in the early days of Nana Tongo's proliferation in the south. Atta Fordwo recently stated that people who were only coming to consult could keep their shirts on. "Up there, Nana speaks directly," he explained. "But down here he has to go through a fetish priest to give his messages out. We don't go so hard on people down here as they do up there. Here, the rules are a bit minimized": interview with Okomfo Atta Fordwo, dd. Kukurantumi, 16 June 2000.

46. AASA 3/282, Isaac Newman Boadu and others to Omanhene, Akyem Abuakwa, dd. Abomosu, 15 Aug. 1935.

47. Ibid., Ohene of Osina, Barima Otu Darko II, to Omanhene of Akyem Abuakwa, dd. Osino, 13 Aug. 1935. See too the comments on nudity at a Nana Tongo shrine in the Fante town of Komenda in RAGCC ADM 23/1/213, Komeh V, *omanhene* of Komenda, to DC Cape Coast, 26 Apr. 1934.

48. Kramer, *Red Fez*, 43.

49. Werbner, *Ritual Passage*, 232–33.

50. See interviews with Bosomfo Nii Yaw, dd. Oshieyie, 4 June 2000; Okomfo Atta Fordwo, dd. Kukurantumi, 16 June 2000; Isaac Tetteh-Nartey, dd. Tengzug, 7 Nov. 1999; and Okomfo Sika, Okomfo Yaa, and Okyeame Tawia, dd. Tengzug, 8 Nov. 1999.

51. It was, in fact, by attending the 1999 *Bo'araam* that we were able to access the vast network of *akomfoo* and *abosomfoo* in the south. We then conducted follow-up interviews in the south with many of those pilgrims we met in Tengzug.

52. Field, *Akim-Kotoku*, 182.

53. Interview with Okomfo Atta Fordwo, dd. Kukurantumi, 16 June 2000.

54. Interview with Anyaam, dd. Kpikpaluk, Kadema, 11 June 2001; see also interview with Asiidem Akanguli, dd. Wiaga, 11 June 2001. Asiidem stated that he visits Shia right before *Bo'araam* and then comes back to Wiaga. After *Bo'araam* is finished, then people from Shia "will send two or three people here to perform sacrifices."

55. Fortes, *Clanship*, 253.

56. NAG ADM 56/1/512, Annual Report for Zuarungu District, 31 Mar. 1928.

57. Even today, those gods are still residing at Assifu's old house in Obretema. Each has its own room and is carefully attended by an *okomfo* and by Assifu's son, Paul.

58. Larbi, "Assiful's Relationship."

59. For a thorough legal history of witchcraft in colonial Akyem Abuakwa, see Gray, "Legal History," esp. chapter 5; and idem., "Witches."

60. Like Assifu, Yao Boadi was quite the collector of *abosom*. We know from the archival record that he had obtained Kwasi Biriku (i.e., Bruku) by 1924 and both Senyakupo and Nana Tongo by 1930: see AASA 3/264, Elders of Akwabuoso to Omanhene, Akyem Abuakwa, dd. Akwabuoso, 7 Aug. 1924; and AASA 3/283, DC Birim to Omanhene, Akyem Abuakwa, 2 Jan. 1930, and Yao Boadi, Odikro of Pramkese, to Omanhene, Akyem Abuakwa, 7 June 1930.

61. AASA 1/2/19, Criminal Record Book, Afua Kuma, Adwoa Botwe, and Ama Aku v. Yao Boadi, 10 Jan. 1930. For a full account of the case, see Gray, "Legal History," 190–202. For the *Benkumhene's* account, see AASA 2/27, Okanta Ofori III, *benkumhene*, to Omanhene, Akyem Abuakwa, dd. Larteh, Ahenease, 15 Jan. 1930.

62. AASA 3/283, DC Birim to Omanhene, Akyem Abuakwa, 2 Jan. 1930.

63. See AASA 1/2/19, Afua Kuma et al. v. Yao Boadi, 10 Jan. 1930; Gray, "Legal History," 200–201.

64. NAG ADM 11/1/886, minute by Acting SNA, 4 Nov. 1930. "Assifu's fetish" or the "Suhum fetish" appears in the archival record before 1930, but not in the context of tribunal cases being referred to it. See, for example, AASA 1/1/91, Civil Record Book, Kwame Minta v. Kwasi Koranteng, 20 Nov. 1928.

65. "Smelling Out Witches at Suhum," *Gold Coast Times*, 18 Jan. 1930. Founded at Cape Coast in 1923, the weekly *Gold Coast Times* was edited by the radical lawyer Kwabena Sekyi.

66. *Gold Coast Times*, 12 Apr. 1930.

67. *Gold Coast Times*, 12 June 1930.

68. NAG ADM 11/1/886, Webster to SNA, dd. Accra, 24 Mar. 1930.

69. NAG ADM 11/1/1051, Joseph Strebler to CS, dd. Cape Coast, 24 Mar. 1930.

70. Ibid., Brakato Ateko to SNA, dd. Accra, 26 Mar. 1930.

71. See, for example, AASA 3/264, Kwame Atia, Nifahene Asiakwa to Oman-hene, Akyem Abuakwa, 13 Sep. 1924, and DC Birim to Omanhene, Akyem Abuakwa, 31 May 1924.

72. AASA 3/272, Odikro Ohene Kwaku, Odikro Suhum to *omanhene*, Akyem Abuakwa, 7 May 1928; and DC Birim to Omanhene, Akyem Abuakwa, dd. Kibi, 11 May 1928.

73. NAG ADM 36/1/8: F. W. Applegate to DCs, dd. Koforidua, 8 Apr. 1930.

74. NAG ADM 11/1/1051, "Report on Enquiries . . . re: Fetish called Tongo," by PC Obeng, 27 Mar. 1930.

75. Ibid., 21 Apr. 1930.

76. See NAG ADM 11/1/886, "Inquisition on a Death . . . taken at Winneba on 10 April 1930," and "Inquisition on a Death . . . taken at Winneba on 12 April 1930." Also discussed in Gray, "Legal History," 207–209. Both inquests received extensive coverage in the *Gold Coast Times*, 12 Apr. 1930.

77. NAG ADM 11/1/1051, CEP to all DCs, dd. Koforidua, 8 Apr. 1930. See also NAG CSO 21/1/1, minute by SNA, 29 Apr. 1930.

78. NAG ADM 11/1/1051, J. S. Manyo Plange, Senior Superintendent of Police, Kibi, to Commissioner of Police, Eastern Province, dd. Kibi, 23 Apr. 1930.

79. NAG ADM 11/1/886, DC Birim to CEP, dd. Kibi, 28 Apr. 1930; a copy of the letter is also in NAG ADM 11/1/1051.

80. NAG ADM 11/1/1051, CEP to SNA, dd. Koforidua, 1 May 1930.

81. See interview with Bismark Enoch Larbi, dd. Accra and Abiriw, 17 June 2000. The three-way division of shrine fees appears to have been very common, with one-third of the fees going to the paramount chief, one-third to the chief who referred the case to the shrine, and one-third to the *bosomfo* or *okomfo*. See also Debrunner, *Witchcraft*, 110–11.

82. NAG ADM 11/1/1051, Manyo Plange to Commissioner of Police, 23 Apr. 1930.

83. NAG ADM 11/1/886, Kofi Assifu to Governor, 12 Feb. 1932. The certificate, located in AASA 3/283, reads as follows:

TO ALL WHOM IT MAY CONCERN: KWABENA ASIFO
native of Abiriw in the State of Akuapem but now residing at Bretema
near Apedwa in Akyem Abuakwa has applied to me for permission
to practice as a NATIVE PHYSICIAN at Bretema and I have
no objection to this being done.

KWABENA ASIFO is responsible for his actions, especially where
the life or reputation of a person is involved, and this paper does
not assign to him any right or power other than reasonable fair
and ordinary.
Dated at Ofori Panin Fie, Kibi, this 22nd day of March, 1930
[signed] Ofori Atta
Omanahene, Akyem Abuakwa

84. Larbi, "Assiful's Relationship."

85. AASA 3/283, Omanhene, Akyem Abuakwa, to DC, 3 July 1930. Copies of Assifu's licenses are included in the file.

86. AASA 3/283, Omanhene, Akyem Abuakwa, to Kobin Sifu, 8 July 1930.

87. NAG ADM 11/1/886, CCP to SNA, 1 July 1930; see also ibid., CCP to SNA, dd. Cape Coast, 4 Nov. 1930, regarding cases involving the Suhum fetish.

88. Ibid., CEP to CS, dd. Koforidua, 18 Nov. 1930.

89. Ibid.

90. See AASA 3/283, DC Birim to Omanhene, Akyem Abuakwa, 17 Dec. 1930.

91. For a fuller discussion of the legal debates within government, see Gray, "Legal History," 210–12.

92. NAG ADM 11/1/886, Acting Solicitor General to SNA, dd. Accra, 20 Aug. 1930.

93. NAG CSO 21/1/1, CEP to CS, dd. Koforidua, 31 Oct. 1930.

94. NAG ADM 11/1/1051, "Well-Wishers of the Country" to SNA, dd. Bekwai, Ashanti, 30 Apr. 1930. It is worth noting that the debate over the Suhum shrine coincided with the Commission of Inquiry Regarding the Consumption of Spirits in the Gold Coast, which reported in February 1930. In many ways, both constituted a moral debate driven forward by the missions, by Christian converts, and by sections of the middle-class urban elite. For a discussion of the debate over alcohol consumption, see Emmanuel Kwaku Akyeampong, *Drink, Power, and Cultural Change: A Social History of Alcohol in Ghana, ca. 1800 to Recent Times* (Portsmouth, N.H., 1996), 70–94.

95. As Birgit Meyer has demonstrated, for pentecostal Christians, Christianity could also serve as a powerful weapon against witchcraft. See *Translating the Devil*, 175–216 *passim*.

96. RAGKD ADM/KD 29/6/58, Birim District Diary, 2 Jan. 1931.

97. NAG ADM 11/1/886, "The Petition of Kobina Assifu," 12 Feb. 1932.

98. Interview with Paul Assifu, dd. Obretema, 13 Nov. 1999.

99. NAG ADM 11/1/886, "The Provincial Council of Chiefs . . . in the course of the 18th Session," dd. Saltpond, 17 Feb. 1931.

100. AASA 3/280, Spencer-Hayford to Omanhene, Akyem Abuakwa, dd. Sekondi, 14 Mar. 1932.

101. Ibid., Omanhene, Akyem Abuakwa, to Spencer-Hayford, dd. Kibi, 19 Mar. 1932.

102. See AASA 3/270, J. B. Danquah to Omanhene, Akyem Abuakwa, 10 Dec. 1927; Omanhene, Akyem Abuakwa, to DC Birim, dd. Kibi, 10 Sep. 1927; Omanhene to CEP, dd. Kibi, 27 Oct. 1927. For a full discussion of the Nkona defense, see Gray, "Legal History," 170–88.

103. See the extensive documentation in file NAG ADM 11/1/1298, Katawere Fetish [1891–1906].

104. NAG ADM 11/1/886, "The petition of Kobina Assifu," dd. Accra, 12 Feb. 1932.

105. Ibid.

106. AASA 3/272, DC Birim to Omanhene, Akyem Abuakwa, dd. Kibi, 11 May 1928.

107. NAG ADM 11/1/886, CEP to SNA, 18 Mar. 1932.

108. Ibid., Minute by J. C. De Graft-Johnson, 29 Mar. 1932.

109. AASA 11/1/886, SNA to CEP, dd. Accra, 5 Apr. 1932.

110. See the dozens of applications from the Central Province of the Gold Coast in file RAGCC ADM 23/1/213, Fetishes.

111. RAGK ARG 6/1/27, CCA to DC Kumasi, 8 June 1938.

112. Ibid., Offinsuhene to DC Kumasi, dd. Offinsu, 14 July 1938.

113. NAG ADM 36/1/8, Fetish 1920–46 [Oda District Records], Kwadwo Obeng to DC Western Akim, 30 May 1935; and ibid., Nana Kuragye Ampaw II to DC Western Akim, 31 May 1935.

114. See ibid., DC Western Akim to CCP, 2 Aug. 1934. The firm also had agents in Ashanti: see RAGK ARG 1/30/1/18, CS to CCA, 6 Jan. 1935.

115. AASA 3/295, "Memorandum: African Herbalism and Cultism: Conditions relating to practice or operation of cults etc. in Akyem Abuakwa," by the State Council of Akyem Abuakwa and approved by the Joint Provincial Council, forwarded to DC on 21 June 1941. On the society and its relations with Ofori Atta, see Gray, "Legal History," 226–28.

116. Gray, "Legal History," 227.

117. See RAGKD ADM/KD 29/6/106, Extract from minutes of Akyem Abuakwa State Council, dd. Kibi, 12–21 June 1940. For a detailed legal analysis of this session, see Gray, "Legal History," 223–31.

118. See RAGK ARG 6/1/27, CCA to CS, dd. Kumasi, 1 Jan. 1943.

119. Files full of petitions for licenses can be found at both the AASA and the MRO.

120. AASA 3/298, Society of African Medical Herbalists and Training Centre to Omanhene, Akyem Abuakwa, dd. Sekondi, 18 Jan. 1944.

121. See files RAGKD ADM/KD 29/6/69, Fetishes and Charms; NAG ADM 39/1/67, The Asogli State; NAG CSO 21/10/4, Kunde Fetish; and for a brief discussion, Greene, *Sacred Sites*, 103.

122. NAG ADM 39/1/67, Kofi Kumi and others to CEP, dd. Ho, 6 Dec. 1933.

123. RAGKD ADM/KD 29/6/69, D. Venour, for Commissioner, Gold Coast Police, to SNA, 27 May 1939, "Kunde Fetish—Alleged Murders for."

124. On this point, see the pioneering analysis by Thomas Hodgkin, *Nationalism in Colonial Africa* (London, 1957), chapter 3, "Prophets and Priests," 93–114.

125. RAGKD ADM/KD 29/6/69, cited by A. C. Duncan-Johnstone, CEP, to SNA, 10 Aug. 1939. "Kimbanguism" refers to the syncretic Christian movement in the lower Congo led by the prophet Simon Kimbangu; Amieda and Amatsei (the equivalent in Ewe of the Twi *aduro*, "medicine") were two of the many alternative names for Kunde.

126. Ibid.

127. RAGKD ADM/KD 29/6/106, DC Kpandu to CEP, 12 Feb. 1940.

5. Tongnaab, Meyer Fortes, and the Making of Colonial Taleland, 1928–1945

1. Interview with Manyanme (born c. 1940), Sapak (born c. 1930), Zong (born c. 1925), and Azabu (born c. 1915), dd. Samire, Tengzug, 11 Aug. 1999.

2. Interview with Nayina (born c. 1914), dd. Gbezug, Tongo, 5 Aug. 1999.

3. Interview with Diegire Baa (born c. 1910), dd. Shia, 17 Aug. 1999.

4. Interview with Tii Kaha (born c. 1920) and Kumahe Puhibazaa (born 1954), dd. Yinduri, 19 Aug. 1999.

5. Interview with Yiran Boare (1905–2002), dd. Tengzug, 10 Aug. 1999.

6. Interview with Wayanaya Songbazaa (born c. 1920), dd. Sakpee, Tengzug, 11 Aug. 1999.

7. Interview with Zimemeh (born c. 1930) and Yin Kudoog (born c. 1927), dd. Yinduri, 16 Aug. 1999.

8. Rattray, *Hinterland*, 138.

9. See NAG ADM 56/1/128, "Food Supply in Fra-Fra," by H. Wheeler, 31 May 1911; PRO CO 96/751/14, *Agriculture in Northern Mamprusi*, by C. W. Lynne, Bulletin No. 34, Gold Coast Department of Agriculture (1937); and Meyer Fortes and S. L. Fortes, "Food in the Domestic Economy of the Tallensi," *Africa* 9 (1936): 237–76.

10. NAG ADM 56/1/294, Handing Over Report, Zuarangu District, 28 July 1928; see too Sacred Heart Parish Diaries, 28 May and 17 June 1928.

11. NAG ADM 56/1/294, Handing Over Report, Zuarangu District, 15 Nov. 1929; Sacred Heart Parish Diaries, 1 Nov. and 15 Nov. 1929, 1 Apr., 1 May, and 23–24 Sep. 1930, 2–6 May 1932; NAG ADM 56/5/2, Diary of CNP, 4 Mar. 1931; RAGT NRG 8/3/37, Annual Report for the Zuarangu District, 1930–1931; and Fortes and Fortes, "Food in the Domestic Economy," 252.

12. RAGT NRG 8/3/37, Annual Report for the Zuarangu District, 1930–1931.

13. Interview with Yiran Boare, dd. Tengzug, 23 Aug. 1999.

14. NAG ADM 63/5/6, Navrongo Informal Diary, 27 Sep. 1930.

15. Sacred Heart Parish Diaries, 7 May 1932.

16. Ibid., 10 May 1932.

17. Interview with Ba'an (c. 1910–2000), dd. Sipaat, 19 Aug. 1999. "To chop" is Ghanaian English for "to eat" or "to consume."

18. RAGT NRG 8/4/53, CCNT's Informal Diary, 26 Feb. 1930.

19. NAG ADM 63/5/6, Navrongo Informal Diary, 27 Sep. 1930.

20. Suggestive material is, however, found in Fortes, *Religion*, 35–36. In a discussion of Talensi prayer, Fortes includes verbatim extracts from the invocations of the Wakii *tengdaana* at the opening of the *Gologo* festival of either 1934 or 1935, including exhortations that locusts "not come into this land, let them go down in holes, go down in holes."

21. In the early 1960s, Nayiri Sheriga-Abdulai (1948–66) reported that he continued to send iron hoes to the Tong Hills in order to prevent the appearance of locusts: personal communication from Susan Drucker-Brown.

22. NAG ADM 68/5/4, Zuarangu District Record Book, "Tongzugu," 18 Aug. 1929; and RAGT NRG 8/4/5, Zuarangu District Informal Diary, 10 June 1931.

23. Interview with Naoh (born c. 1927), dd. Tengzug, 9 Aug. 1999.

24. NAG ADM 56/1/278, CCNT to CNP, 28 Aug. 1928.

25. Ibid.; and NAG ADM 68/5/5, Zuarangu District Record Book, "Tonzugu."

26. PRO CO 96/751/14, *Agriculture in Northern Mamprusi*, 34.

27. Interview with Boarnii (c. 1905–2001), dd. Tengzug, 12 Aug. 1999; confirmed by interviews with Naoh, dd. Tengzug, 9 Aug. 1999, and Yiran Boare, dd. Tengzug, 10 Aug. 1999.

28. Interview with Boarnii, dd. Tengzug, 12 Aug. 1999. On the presence of leopards in the area, see RAGT NRG 8/4/26, Zuarangu District Informal Diary, 9 July 1927; and on hyenas in the Tong Hills, NRG 8/4/31, Northern Mamprussi District Diary, 27 May 1926.

29. Interview with Azabu (born c. 1915), dd. Samire, Tengzug, 11 Aug. 1999.
30. NAG ADM 68/5/5, Zuarangu District Record Book.
31. Interview with Diegire Baa, dd. Shia, 17 Aug. 1999.
32. Interview with *Yiran* Boare, dd. Tengzug, 10 Aug. 1999.
33. NAG ADM 68/5/4, Zuarangu District Record Book, "Tongo," 17 Apr. 1929; and RAGT NRG 8/4/32, Extract from Zuarangu Office Diary, 17 Apr. 1929.
34. RAGT NRG 8/3/49, Annual Report on the NTs, 1934–1935. The timing of the decision can be inferred from Fortes's photograph collection: by late 1934, intensive rebuilding work was under way in the hills.
35. Ibid.; see too NAG ADM 68/5/5, Zuarangu District Record Book, "Tonzugu," 1935; and NAG CSO 21/9/6, Dr M. Fortes—Visit to the Gold Coast, CCNT to CS, 8 June 1935.
36. Fortes, *Kinship*, 185.
37. PRO CO 96/751/14, *Agriculture in North Mamprusi*, 28.
38. Fortes, *Kinship*, 185.
39. Ibid.
40. Hart, "Economic Basis," 206. The first and most substantial critique of Fortes's analysis of Talensi kinship is P. Worsley, "The Kinship System of the Tallensi: A Revaluation," *Journal of the Royal Anthropological Institute* 86 (1956): 9–10.
41. Hart, "Economic Basis," 207.
42. McCaskie, "R. S. Rattray"; Kuklick, *Savage Within*, 227–29; Carola Lentz, "Colonial Ethnography and Political Reform: The Works of A. C. Duncan-Johnson, R. S. Rattray, J. Eyre-Smith, and J. Guiness on Northern Ghana," *Ghana Studies* 2 (1999): 138.
43. For biographical details, see Susan Drucker-Brown, "Notes towards a Biography of Meyer Fortes," *American Ethnologist* 16 (1989): 375–85; Meyer Fortes, "An Anthropologist's Apprenticeship," *Annual Review of Anthropology* 7 (1978), reprinted in *Cambridge Anthropology* 8, special issue in memory of Meyer Fortes (1983): 14–51; Raymond Firth, "Meyer Fortes: An Appreciation," in *Cambridge Anthropology* 8 (1983): 52–68; and Goody, *Expansive Moment, passim*.
44. Fortes, "Apprenticeship," 15.
45. Ibid., 17.
46. Goody, *Expansive Moment, passim*, esp. chapter 3, "Making It to the Field as a Jew and a Red."
47. NAG CSO 21/9/6, J. H. Oldham, Director, IAI, to Gov. Slater, 3 June 1932, enclosed: memorandum by M. Fortes, 26 Mar. 1932.
48. Ibid., Oldham to Slater, 3 June 1932; and Fortes, "Apprenticeship," 21.
49. Fortes, "Apprenticeship," 21.
50. RAI MS 298.1, "First Report on Field Work," by Meyer Fortes, dd. July 1934.
51. This and all subsequent quotations in the following two paragraphs are from ibid.
52. See too NAG CSO 21/9/6, CS to CCNT, 16 Jan. 1934.
53. But cf. Meyer Fortes, "Culture Contact as a Dynamic Process: An Investigation in the Northern Territories of the Gold Coast," *Africa* 9 (1936): 24–55, which notes the existence of the mission and the fact that in 1934 some half-dozen Talensi boys were attending the school.
54. Again, cf. ibid., 52–53, where Fortes admits that he has not "mentioned the

Toŋnaab fertility cult of the Talensi living in the Tong Hills, which attracts thousands of pilgrims annually from all over the Gold Coast."

55. RAI MS 298.1, "First Report on Field Work."

56. Ibid. See M. Fortes, "Communal Fishing and Fishing Magic in the Northern Territories of the Gold Coast," *Journal of the Royal Anthropological Institute* 67 (1937): 131–42.

57. This formed the topic of another of Fortes's first published papers—and the only one he co-wrote with Sonia: Fortes and Fortes, "Food in the Domestic Economy."

58. RAI MS 298.1, "First Report on Field Work"; see too Fortes, "Apprenticeship," 23–24.

59. RAI MS 298.1, "First Report on Field Work."

60. Fortes, "Culture Contact," 43; see too *Clanship*, xii, where this unnamed assistant is demoted to the status of a "semi-literate interpreter."

61. RAI MS 298.2, "Second Report on Field Work," by Meyer Fortes, 14 Oct. 1934.

62. This and subsequent quotations in this paragraph from ibid.

63. NAG CSO 21/9/6, CCNT to CS, 8 June 1935.

64. Ibid. Jones repeated his dissatisfaction with Fortes—although without mentioning the latter's name—in his annual report, observing that "to the average person the desire to abandon the system of barter and to obtain money wherewith to purchase cloths and other articles . . . denotes progress. Yet an anthropologist of unquestionable ability and some repute remarked to the writer how regrettable it was that the Talansi [*sic*] were becoming money conscious and generally criticised the efforts that are being made to develop trade in the Protectorate": RAGT NRG 8/3/49, Report on the NTs, 1934–1935. See Kuper, *Anthropologists*, 108, on the cash economy as a common source of conflict between British officials and anthropologists.

65. NAG CSO 21/9/6, Fortes to Thomas, dd. London, 27 Aug. 1935.

66. Ibid., 21/9/6, CCNT to SNA, 21 Oct. 1935.

67. Ibid., Fortes to Thomas, n.d. [but late 1935]. Fortes's report could not be located, although he was to develop his response to the question of seduction into an extended memorandum on "Marriage Law among the Tallensi," published by the Gold Coast Government: copies are located in ibid. and in RAGT NRG 8/2/200, Marriage Law.

68. Fortes, *Religion*, 63; see too *Clanship*, vii.

69. *Clanship*, vii.

70. Ibid., 250–51.

71. RAGT NRG 8/3/59, Annual Report on the Mamprusi District, 1936–1937.

72. Fortes, *Clanship*, 251–52.

73. Ibid., 251.

74. Ibid., 253.

75. Ibid., 254.

76. Ibid., 254–55.

77. J. A. Barnes, *Three Styles in the Study of Kinship* (London, 1971), 209.

78. RAGT NRG 8/3/53, Annual Report on the NTs, 1935–1936 [compiled c. Apr. 1936].

79. RAGT NRG 3/2/6, DC Gambaga to CCNT, 18 Feb. 1937; and NAG CSO 21/9/6, CCNT to SNA, 1 Mar. 1937.

80. RAGT NRG 8/3/53, Annual Report on the NTs, 1935–1936.

81. Ibid.

82. Ibid.

83. RAGT NRG 3/2/11, Fortes to Kerr, dd. Tongo, 9 Sep. 1936; see too RAG NRG 3/2/9, Kerr to Fortes, dd. Gambaga, 26 Aug. 1936. Fortes would subsequently elaborate on this relationship in "An Anthropologist's Point of View," in Rita Hinden, ed., *Fabian Colonial Essays* (London, 1945).

84. RAGT NRG 3/2/9, Fortes to CCNT, 24 Aug. 1936.

85. Ibid., "Tallensi Divisional Court," by Meyer Fortes, n.d. [but c. Jan. 1937], CCNT to DC Mamprusi, 23 Jan 1937, and Asst. DC Zuarungu to DC Mamprussi, "Talensi Federation," 7 June 1937. For earlier interventions by Fortes, see RAGT NRG 3/2/11, Fortes to Kerr, 9 Sep. 1936, and "Co-operation between the Furafura Native Authorities," by A. F. Kerr, 17 Oct. 1936.

86. RAGT NRG 3/2/9, "Tallensi Divisional Court," by Meyer Fortes.

87. Ibid.

88. Ibid.

89. Rattray, *Hinterland*, 362. Tengol's great height and obvious physical prowess should not be overlooked as a factor in his early rise to prominence in a society that placed great stock in both physical and mental "toughness." The comments of Manyanme are interesting in this respect. "Our fathers and ancestors were very, very tough men. . . . Now, however, people try to be as big as their fathers and do not succeed. You now see much shorter people": interview dd. Samire, Tengzug, 11 Aug. 1999.

90. RAI Rattray Papers, MS 109, "Notes on Talanse."

91. NAG ADM 68/5/5, Zuarangu District Record Book, "Tonzugu," Nov. 1932.

92. Fortes, *Clanship*, 253.

93. For an anthropological analysis of the importance of gift exchange in the formulation of identity amongst the Kabre peoples of nearby northern Togo in the 1980s–90s, cf. Piot, *Remotely Global*, 52–75.

94. Fortes, *Clanship*, 251.

95. Interview with Yiran Boare, dd. Tengzug, 10 Aug. 1999. "Dash," from the Portuguese verb *dar*, to give, is a common term in West African English for a gift or for the act of giving a gift; *kente* is the famous and highly prestigious multi-colored woven cloth closely associated with Akan kingship.

96. RAGT NRG 8/4/88, Zuarangu District Informal Diary, 4 Sep. 1938.

97. Fortes, *Clanship*, 254.

98. Ibid. Aside from Tengol, Fortes identified two other Talensi chiefs with extraordinarily large numbers of wives: Tongrana Nambiong (over thirty) and the *datokonaaba* (between fifty and a hundred): *Kinship*, 72.

99. Interview with Golibdaana Malbazaa, dd. Tengzug, 24 July 2000.

100. Ibid.

101. NAG ADM 68/5/5, Zuarangu District Record Book, entry dd. 1937.

102. See Hart, "Economic Basis," 195–96; Fortes, *Kinship*, 84, no. 1.

103. Fortes, *Religion*, 51.

104. On the management of Bonaab, see interviews with Manyanme, Sapak,

Zong, and Azabu, dd. Samire, Tengzug, 11 Aug. 1999; and Bo'arnaab Dilimit, dd. Gundaat, Tengzug, 13 Aug. 1999.

105. NAG ADM 68/5/5, Zuarangu District Record Book, 18 Mar. 1936. The DC's entry states that "of their own choice, the families of Sapei, Tamboo, Samin and Digali will serve Tongrana through the Gologdana. The Gundari family will also of their own choice serve Tongrana through the Patanaba." In short, with the exceptions of Kpatar and Gundaat, most of the congregations broke from their *bo'a* constituencies by supporting the *golibdaana*. See also Fortes, *Clanship*, 257–58.

106. NAG ADM 68/5/5, Zuarangu District Record Book, entry dd. 1937.

107. Fortes, *Religion*, 46.

108. Fortes, *Clanship*, 257.

109. Fortes, *Religion*, 46.

110. RAGT NRG 3/2/9, CCNT to DC Mamprusi, 23 Jan. 1937.

111. Ibid., Asst. DC Zuarangu to DC Mamprusi, 2 May 1937.

112. Ibid.; cf. Fortes, *Clanship*, 254: "it would be hopeless for an outsider to attempt to estimate his wealth."

113. RAGT NRG 3/2/9, Asst DC Zuarangu to DC Mamprusi, 7 June 1937.

114. Ibid.

115. Ibid., Asst DC Zuarangu to Acting CCNT, 16 June 1937.

116. The clippings are found in PRO CO 96/752/8.

117. *Daily Telegraph*, 23 Aug. 1938.

118. Fortes Photograph Collection, Museum of Anthropology and Archaeology, University of Cambridge, Notebooks of contact sheets, Roll 27, image labeled "The departure of Sir Ofori Ata [*sic*] and his group to Tong Hills," n.d. [but c. Apr. 1937].

119. Fortes, *Clanship*, xii.

120. See Anafu, "Colonial Rule," 32–34.

121. Ibid., 34. For official commentary reflecting the growing power of the *tongrana*, see RAG NRG 8/4/101, Zuarungu Informal Diary, 1 Mar. 1943, 22 July 1944, 2 Dec. 1945, and 19 Dec. 1945. In 1943, the *tongrana* was appointed president of the Talensi Federation "for an unspecified term following continual disagreement over the Presidency": NAG ADM 68/5/5, Zuarangu District Record Book, "Tongo," 1943.

122. Cf. Piot's argument on anthropology and colonialism in *Remotely Global*, 24.

123. NAG ADM 68/5/5, Zuarangu District Record Book, marginalia dd. 1 June 1948.

6. Tongnaab and the Dynamics of History among the Talensi

1. NAG ADM 13/2/90, Cabinet Minutes, 13 Mar. 1962. For a synopsis of the transformations in official rule in Taleland, see Anafu, "Colonial Rule," 34–35. For the debates, see RAGT NRG 9/2/14, Traditional Council, Tongo, 1965, much of it authored by the late Donald Balagumyetime, the CPP Member of Parliament for the Talensi Area. Balagumyetime, a native of Baare, was concerned with the issue of which chiefs would become divisional chiefs under the *tongrana*'s paramountcy. The debate he initiated in June 1965 ended with the military overthrow of the CPP government in February 1966.

2. Interviews with Okomfo Sika, Okomfo Yaa, and Okyeame Tawia, dd. Tengzug, 8 Nov. 1999; and with Okomfo Sika and Okyeame Tawia, dd. Kukurantumi, 16 June 2000.

3. Interviews with Adwoa Ankoma and her brother, Kofi Obeng (from Amaase Asiakwaa); Komfo Yaa Sekyibiaa and her husband, Kwaku Opoku (from Hemang); Efia Nyakoaa (from Saaman Osino); and Isaac Tetteh-Nartey (from Suhum), dd. Tengzug, 8 Nov. 1999.

4. Interviews with Bosomfo Nii Yaw, dd. Oshieyie, 4 June 2000; and Nii Kofi Akrashie, dd. Oshieyie, 29 July 2000. On the annual pilgrimages of Ga "priests" to the Tong Hills after the Second World War, see Parrinder, *Witchcraft*, 168. We did not first encounter Nii Yaw in Tengzug, but rather heard of his shrine from our Legon colleague, Mary Esther Kropp Dakubu, who first noticed a sign for Nana Tongo while traveling along the road between Kokrobite and Botianor. We are grateful to Dr. Kropp Dakubu for her assistance.

5. Interview with Kwao Ahoto and John Bawa Zuure, dd. Tengzug, 8 Nov. 1999.

6. Interview with John Bawa Zuure, dd. Tengzug, 24 July 2000.

7. See Morton-Williams, "Atinga Cult." For evidence that points to a degree of conflation of the Nana Tongo and Tigare cults in southern Ghana from the 1940s, see RAGK ARG 2/2/119, Akuamoa Akyeampong, Omanhene of Kwahu, to DC Mpraeso, "Tegare Alias Gare Fetish," 17 Jan. 1945; and Parrinder, *Witchcraft*, 169.

8. Rosenthal, *Possession*, 22, 73–99. A sixth prominent Gorovudu spirit, Banguele, appears to be derived from the one large-scale Gold Coast witch-finding god missing from this list, Hwemeso: ibid., 89.

9. Interview with Yikpemdaan Wakbazaa, dd. Gorogo, 3 July 2002.

10. RAGT NRG 8/25/7, Tourism in Ghana: Northern Region, 1959–1962, undated minute [but likely 20 Dec. 1959].

11. RAGT NRG 8/25/13, Tourism in Ghana: Progress Report—Northern and Upper Regions [1962].

12. See, for example, Jim Hudgens and Richard Trillo, *West Africa: The Rough Guide* (London, 1999), 758.

13. Tanya Shaffer, "Losing their Shirts," *Wanderlust*, 1998, http://archive.salon.com/wlust/feature/1998/06/04feature.html.

14. Nana is documented in files RAGT NRG 8/19/18, Fetish in the Northern Region; RAGT NRG 3/21/4, Fetish Witchcraft 1955; and RAGT NRG 8/4/110, Dagomba District Diaries, 1951–57.

15. See RAGT NRG 8/19/18, Government Agent, Dagomba-Yendi, to Chief Regional Officer, 2 Aug. 1955; and the account by the anthropologist David Tait, who had been working for some years among the Konkomba: ibid., "A Sorcery Hunt in Dagomba," typescript, 1955, 26, a version of which was published posthumously in *Africa* 32 (1963): 136–47.

16. Tait, "Sorcery Hunt," 145.

17. Ibid.

18. Our efforts to research further the history of "Nana" as well as to trace Tongnaab's pilgrimage network in Dagomba were thwarted by the high levels of insecurity in the region following the assassination of the Dagomba paramount, the *ya na*, in 2002.

19. Interview with Isaac Tetteh-Nartey and John Bawa Zuure, Tengzug, 7 Nov.

1999; also interviews with Yikpemdaan Wakbazaa, dd. Gorogo, 3 July 2002, and Lambazaa Naoh, dd. Tengzug, 6 July 2002.

20. See Gustav Jahoda, "Traditional Healers and Other Institutions Concerned with Mental Illness in Ghana," *International Journal of Social Psychiatry* 7 (1961): 199–215. For a useful survey of the main issues, see E. Evans-Anfom, *Traditional Medicine in Ghana: Practice, Problems, and Prospects* (Accra, 1986), originally presented—fittingly enough—as the J. B. Danquah Memorial Lectures for 1984.

21. RAGSN WRG 8/1/265, "Psychic and Traditional Healing Association."

22. RAGT NRG 8/12/43, Office of President to Chief Administrator, Ministry of Heath, dd. Accra, 17 July 1962.

23. MRO 1/1/102C, Otumfuo Asantehene to Ag. Principal Secretary, Ministry of Local Government, dd. Kumasi, 8 Nov. 1969; and Evans-Anfom, *Traditional Medicine*, 45–46.

24. Werbner, *Ritual Passage*, 236.

25. Werbner cites Dennis Austin, *Politics in Ghana, 1946–1960* (London, 1964) and Dunn and Robertson, *Dependence*, on 1950s politics. For more recent discussions, see Jean Allman, *The Quills of the Porcupine: Asante Nationalism in an Emergent Ghana* (Madison, 1993), and Richard Rathbone, *Nkrumah and the Chiefs: The Politics of Chieftaincy in Ghana, 1951–1960* (Oxford, 2000).

26. Werbner, *Ritual Passage*, 238. Our evidence suggests a more complicated picture. Although overshadowed in the expanding inter-war ritual marketplace by savanna gods—and in particular by the mobility of their northern rivals—established Bron *abosom* such as Kukuro continued to draw pilgrims: NAG ARG 1/30/1/18, "Kukuro," by W. J. Pitt [n.d. but 1928]; and Dunn and Robertson, *Dependence*, 127. At the same time, new objects of veneration periodically exploded onto the scene: see NAG ARG 1/30/1/18, DC Wenchi to CCA, 8 Feb. 1934, and memorandum by CCA, 14 July 1934. For some discussion of *obosom-brafo* anti-witchcraft shrines in the Brong-Ahafo region in the 1990s, see Jane Parish, "The Dynamics of Witchcraft and Indigenous Shrines among the Akan," *Africa* 69 (1999): 426–48.

27. Field, *Search for Security*, 14.

28. Interview with anonymous visitor in Ewe, dd. Tengzug, 8 Nov. 1999. "Bombed at Kulungulu" refers to an attempt on Nkrumah's life at the northern village of that name on 1 August 1961 as he returned from visiting President Yameogo of Upper Volta (Burkina Faso).

29. John Bawa Zuure is actually the biological son of Tengol's younger brother Zuure, who was his successor as *tengzugnaaba*.

30. Volker Riehl, "The Land Is Ours: Research on the Land-Use System among the Talensi in Northern Ghana," *Cambridge Anthropology* 14 (1990): 36–38.

31. Mahami Salifu, Regional Minister, to Managing Director, Granite and Marble Company, Ltd., dd. Bolgatanga, 17 Aug. 2001 [copy of letter in authors' possession].

32. On similar struggles over the heritage of the sacred Matapos Hills, cf. Ranger, *Voices from the Rocks*, 266–90.

33. See the NCRC site at http://www.ncrc.kabissa.org/savannaCircuit/tongotenzug/tongotenzugHome.html.

34. Tengzug Eco-tourism Committee, "Tongo Hills/Tengzug Shrine, 2002 Pricelist."

35. Ibid.; approximately $1.50.

36. David Bagana Goldaan to All Visitors to Tengzug, dd. Tengzug, 26 Mar. 2002.

37. This became especially clear during various conversations with the late Donald Balagumyetime, MP for Talensi, who had read Fortes's work carefully and sought us out in order to have the opportunity to "set the record straight."

38. We remain indebted to Robert Arbuckle for supporting this event.

Bibliography

Manuscript Sources

Ghana

Akyem Abuakwa State Archives [AASA]
    AASA 1.1. Civil Record Books
    AASA 1.2. Criminal Record Books
    AASA 2. Tribunal Matters
    AASA 3. Stools Chieftaincy and Land
    AASA 8. State Council Matters
Manhyia Record Office, Kumasi [MRO]
    MAG 1. Kumasi Traditional Council and Its Predecessors
    MAG 4. Asantehene/Kumasi Divisional Treasury Records
National Archives of Ghana, Accra [NAG]
    ADM 5. Reports
    ADM 11. Secretary for Native Affairs Papers
    ADM 12. Confidential Dispatches/Reports
    ADM 13. Cabinet Papers
    ADM 23. Saltpond District Records
    ADM 29. Adda District Records
    ADM 32. Kibbi District Records
    ADM 36. Western Akim, Oda District Records
    ADM 51. Kumasi District Records
    ADM 56. Northern Regional Office Records
    ADM 57. Bawku District Office Records
    ADM 58. Bole District Office Records
    ADM 60. Gambaga District Office Records
    ADM 63. Navrongo District Office Records
    ADM 64. Salaga District Office Records
    ADM 68. Zuarangu District Office Records
    CSO 11. Medical and Sanitary
    CSO 21. Native Affairs
    CSO 22. Military
Regional Archives of Ghana, Cape Coast
    ADM 23. Native Affairs Papers
Regional Archives of Ghana, Koforidua
    ADM/KD 29. Regional Administrative Office
    ADM/KD 31. District Administrative Office, Akuse

Regional Archives of Ghana, Kumasi
    ARG 1. Records of the Office of the Chief Commissioner of Ashanti
    ARG 2. Records of the Ashanti Regional Administration Office, Kumasi
    ARG 3. Eastern Provincial Commissioner's Office Records
    ARG 5. Southern Provinces of Ashanti, Obuasi
    ARG 6. Records of the District Commissioner's Office, Kumasi
    ARG 7. Records of the District Commissioner's Office, Kumasi
    ARG 8. Records of the District Commissioner, Juaso
    ARG 9. Records of the District Commissioner, Bekwae
    ARG 10. Records of the District Commissioner, Mampong
Regional Archives of Ghana, Sekondi
    WRG 1. District Administration Office, Takoradi
    WRG 15. Tarkwa District Administration
    WRG 24. Regional Administration Office, Sekondi
Regional Archives of Ghana, Sunyani
    BRG 2. District Administration, Sunyani
    BRG 3. District Administration, Wenchi
    BRG 28. Records of the Western Provincial Commissioner, Ashanti
    BRG 29. Records of Berekum, District Administration
Regional Archives of Ghana, Tamale
    NRG 3. District Administration, Gambaga
    NRG 6. District Administration, Navrongo
    NRG 8. Regional Administration
    NRG 9. Regional Administration, Bolgatanga
    NRG 10. Social Welfare
    NRG 14. Labour Department
    PAT 22. Published Reports
Catholic Mission, Navrongo
    Mission de Notre-Dame de Septs Douleurs, Diary, Vol. 1, 1906–1921
Catholic Mission, Bolgatanga
    Sacred Heart Parish Diaries, 1925–1939, translated by George Apolala
Tengzug Eco-tourism Committee
    "Tongo Hills/Tengzug Shrine, 2002 Pricelist"

Great Britain

Public Record Office, Kew
    Colonial Office Files
    CO 96. Gold Coast, Original Correspondence, 1900–1951
    CO 98. Gold Coast, Sessional Papers, 1900–1956
    CO 343. Gold Coast, Original Correspondence Register, 1900–1951
    CO 445. West African Frontier Force, Original Correspondence, 1898–1926
    CO 820. Military, Original Correspondence, 1927–1951
    CO 879. Africa, Confidential Print, 1848–1961
Rhodes House Library, Oxford
    MSS Brit. Emp. S.344 Harper Papers
    MSS Afr. S.849 Kilby Papers

Royal Anthropological Institute, London
  Rattray Papers MS 109 Field Notes 1928–1930
  MS 298 1 and 2 Fieldwork Reports by Meyer Fortes
Museum of Anthropology and Archaeology, Cambridge University
  Meyer Fortes Photograph Collection

Newspapers

Gold Coast Independent
Gold Coast Times
West Africa Times

Secondary Sources

Addo-Fening, Robert. *Akyem Abuakwa, 1700–1943: From Ofori Panin to Sir Ofori Atta.* Trondheim, 1997.
Akyeampong, Emmanuel Kwaku. *Drink, Power, and Cultural Change: A Social History of Alcohol in Ghana, c. 1800 to Recent Times.* Portsmouth, N.H., 1996.
Allman, Jean. *The Quills of the Porcupine: Asante Nationalism in an Emergent Ghana.* Madison, 1993.
———, ed. *Fashioning Africa: Power and the Politics of Dress.* Bloomington, 2004.
———, and Victoria Tashjian. *"I Will Not Eat Stone": A Women's History of Colonial Asante.* Portsmouth, N.H., 2000.
Anafu, Moses. "The Impact of Colonial Rule on Tallensi Political Institutions, 1898–1967." *Transactions of the Historical Society of Ghana* 14 (1973): 17–37.
Apter, Andrew. "Atinga Revisited: Yoruba Witchcraft and the Cocoa Economy, 1950–1951." In *Modernity and Its Malcontents: Ritual Power in Postcolonial Africa*, ed. Jean Comaroff and John Comaroff, 89–128. Chicago, 1993.
Arhin, Kwame. "Savanna Contributions to the Asante Political Economy." In *The Golden Stool: Studies of the Asante Center and Periphery*, ed. Enid Schildkrout, 51–59. New York, 1987.
———, ed. *The Papers of George Ekem Ferguson: A Fanti Official of the Government of the Gold Coast, 1890–1897.* Leiden, 1974.
Armitage, C. H. *The Tribal Markings and Marks of Adornment of the Natives of the Northern Territories of the Gold Coast Colony.* London, 1924.
Asad, Talal, ed. *Anthropology and the Colonial Encounter.* Ithaca, 1973.
Austin, Dennis. *Politics in Ghana, 1946–1960.* London, 1964.
Austin, Gareth. "The Emergence of Capitalist Relations in South Asante Cocoa-Farming, c. 1916–33." *Journal of African History* 28 (1987): 259–79.
Awiah, Rev. Joseph. "Tongo Festivals, Dances, and Marriage Customs." Mimeograph, n.d.
Baëta, C. G. *Prophetism in Ghana: A Study of Some "Spiritual" Churches.* London, 1962.
Bannerman-Richter, Gabriel. *Don't Cry! My Baby, Don't Cry! Autobiography of an African Witch.* Elk Grove, Calif., 1986.
———. *Mmoetia: The Mysterious Little People.* Elk Grove, Calif., 1987.

———. *The Practice of Witchcraft in Ghana*. Elk Grove, Calif., 1982.

Barnes, J. A. *Three Styles in the Study of Kinship*. London, 1971.

Barnes, Sandra T., ed. *Africa's Ogun: Old World and New*. 2nd ed. Bloomington, 1997.

Barnes, Teresa. "Virgin Territory? Travel and Migration by African Women in Twentieth-Century Southern Africa." In *Women in African Colonial Histories*, ed. Jean Allman, Susan Geiger, and Nakanyike Musisi, 164–90. Bloomington, 2002.

Barry, Boubacar. *Senegambia and the Atlantic Slave Trade*. Trans. Ayi Kwei Armah. Cambridge, 1998.

Baum, Robert M. *Shrines of the Slave Trade: Diola Religion and Society in Precolonial Senegambia*. New York, 1999.

Bayart, Jean-François. *The State in Africa: The Politics of the Belly*. Trans. Mary Harper, Christopher Harrison, and Elizabeth Harrison. Harlow, 1993.

Beecham, John. *Ashanti and the Gold Coast*. London, 1841.

Behrend, Heike, and Ute Luig, eds. *Spirit Possession, Modernity, and Power in Africa*. Oxford, 1999.

Binger, Captain L. G. *Du Niger au Golfe de Guinée: Par le pays de Kong et le Mossi*. 2 vols. Paris, 1892.

Boddy, Janice. "Spirit Possession Revisited: Beyond Instrumentality." *Annual Review of Anthropology* 23 (1994): 407–34.

Bond, George Clement, and Diane M. Ciekawy, eds. *Witchcraft Dialogues: Anthropological and Philosophical Exchanges*. Athens, Ohio, 2001.

Bourdier, Jean-Paul, and Trinh T. Minh-Ha. *African Spaces: Designs for Living in Upper Volta*. New York, 1985.

Bowdich, Thomas E. *An Essay on the Geography of Northwestern Africa*. London, 1821; repr. 1966.

———. *Mission from Cape Coast Castle to Ashantee*. London, 1819; repr. 1966.

Brenner, Louis. "'Religious' Discourses in and about Africa." In *Discourse and Its Disguises: The Interpretation of African Oral Texts*, ed. Karin Barber and P. F. de Moraes Farias, 87–103. Birmingham, 1989.

Carrasco, Davíd. *City of Sacrifice: The Aztec Empire and the Role of Violence in Civilization*. Boston, 1999.

Chernoff, John M. "Spiritual Foundations of Dagbamba Religion and Culture." In *African Spirituality: Forms, Meanings, and Expressions*, ed. Jacob K. Olupona, 257–74. New York, 2000.

Christaller, Rev. J. G. *A Dictionary of the Asante and Fante Language Called Tshi (Chwee, Twi)*. Basel, 1881; 2nd ed., Basel, 1933.

Clifford, James. *The Predicament of Culture: Twentieth-Century Ethnography, Literature, and Art*. Cambridge, Mass.: 1988.

———, and George E. Marcus, eds. *Writing Culture*. Berkeley, 1986.

Colson, Elizabeth. "Places of Power and Shrines of the Land." *Paideuma* 43 (1997): 47–57.

Comaroff, Jean, and John Comaroff. "Occult Economies and the Violence of Abstraction: Notes from the South African Postcolony." *American Ethnologist* 26 (1999): 297–303.

———. *Of Revelation and Revolution*. Vol. 1, *Christianity, Colonialism, and Consciousness in South Africa*. Chicago, 1991.

———, eds. *Modernity and Its Malcontents: Ritual and Power in Postcolonial Africa.* Chicago, 1993.

"Containing Witchcraft: Conflicting Scenarios in Postcolonial Africa." Special issue, *African Studies Review* 41 (1998).

Cruickshank, Brodie. *Eighteen Years on the Gold Coast of Africa.* 2 vols. London, 1853; repr. 1966.

de Craemer, Willy, Jan Vansina, and Renée C. Fox. "Religious Movements in Central Africa: A Theoretical Study." *Comparative Studies in Society and History* 18 (1976): 458–75.

Debrunner, Hans. *The Story of Sampson Opong.* Accra, 1965.

———. *Witchcraft in Ghana: A Study of the Belief in Destructive Witches and Its Effect on the Akan Tribes.* Accra, 1959.

Delafosse, Maurice. *Les frontières de la Côte d'Ivoire, de le Côte d'Or et du Soudan.* Paris, 1908.

Der, Benedict. "God and Sacrifice in the Traditional Religions of the Kasena and Dagaba of Northern Ghana." *Journal of Religion in Africa* 11 (1980): 172–87.

———. *The Slave Trade in Northern Ghana.* Accra, 1998.

———. "The Traditional Political Systems of Northern Ghana Reconsidered." In *Regionalism and Public Policy in Northern Ghana,* ed. Yakubu Saaka, 36–65. New York, 2001.

Douglas, Mary, ed. *Witchcraft Confessions and Accusations.* London, 1970.

Drucker-Brown, Susan. "Notes towards a Biography of Meyer Fortes." *American Ethnologist* 16 (1989): 375–85.

Dunn, John, and A. F. Robertson. *Dependence and Opportunity: Political Change in Ahafo.* Cambridge, 1973.

Duperray, Anne-Marie. *Les Gourounsi de Haute-Volta: Conquête et colonisation, 1896–1933.* Stuttgart, 1984.

Eliade, Mircea. *The Sacred and the Profane.* New York, 1959.

Ellis, Stephen, and Gerrie Ter Haar. *Worlds of Power: Religious Thought and Political Practice in Africa.* London, 2004.

Evans-Anfom, E. *Traditional Medicine in Ghana: Practice, Problems, and Prospects.* Accra, 1986.

Evans-Pritchard, E. E. *Witchcraft, Oracles, and Magic among the Azande.* Oxford, 1937.

Fabian, Johannes. *Time and the Other: How Anthropology Makes Its Object.* New York, 1983.

Fardon, Richard. *Raiders and Refugees: Trends in Chamba Political Development, 1750–1950.* Washington, 1988.

Field, Margaret J. *Akim-Kotoku: An Oman of the Gold Coast.* London, 1948.

———. *Religion and Medicine of the Gã People.* London, 1937.

———. *Search for Security: An Ethno-psychiatric Study of Rural Ghana.* London, 1960.

———. "Some New Shrines of the Gold Coast and Their Significance." *Africa* 13 (1940): 138–49.

Fields, Karen E. *Revival and Rebellion in Colonial Central Africa.* Princeton, 1985.

Firth, Raymond. "Meyer Fortes: An Appreciation." *Cambridge Anthropology* 8 (1983): 52–68.

Fortes, Meyer. "An Anthropologist's Apprenticeship." *Annual Review of Anthropol-*

ogy 7 (1978); reprinted in *Cambridge Anthropology* 8, special issue in memory of Meyer Fortes (1983): 14–51.

———. "Communal Fishing and Fishing Magic in the Northern Territories of the Gold Coast." *Journal of the Royal Anthropological Institute* 67 (1937): 131–42.

———. "Culture Contact as a Dynamic Process: An Investigation in the Northern Territories of the Gold Coast." *Africa* 9 (1936): 24–55.

———. *The Dynamics of Clanship among the Tallensi: Being the First Part of an Analysis of the Social Structure of a Trans-Volta Tribe.* London, 1945.

———. *Oedipus and Job in West African Religion.* Cambridge, 1983.

———. "On the Concept of the Person among the Tallensi." *Colloques internationaux du Centre Nationale de la Recherche Scientifique* 544 (1973): 283–319.

———. "Pietas in Ancestor Worship." *Journal of the Royal Anthropological Institute* 91 (1961): 166–91.

———. "The Political System of the Tallensi of the Northern Territories of the Gold Coast." In *African Political Systems,* ed. Meyer Fortes and E. E. Evans-Pritchard, 239–71. London, 1940.

———. *Religion, Morality, and the Person: Essays on Tallensi Religion.* Ed. Jack Goody. Cambridge, 1987.

———. "Ritual Festivals and Social Cohesion in the Hinterland of the Gold Coast." *American Anthropologist* 38 (1936): 590–604.

———. "Social and Psychological Aspects of Education in Taleland." Supplement to *Africa* 4 (1938): 5–64.

———. "Some Aspects of Migration and Mobility in Ghana." *Journal of Asian and African Studies* 6 (1971): 1–20.

———. "Strangers." In *Studies in African Social Anthropology,* ed. Meyer Fortes and Sheila Patterson, 229–53. London, 1975.

———. "Tallensi Ritual Festivals and the Ancestors." *Cambridge Anthropology* 2 (1974): 3–31.

———. *Time and Social Structure and Other Essays.* London, 1970.

———. *The Web of Kinship among the Tallensi: The Second Part of an Analysis of the Social Structure of a Trans-Volta Tribe.* London, 1949.

———, and S. L. Fortes. "Food in the Domestic Economy of the Tallensi." *Africa* 9 (1970): 237–76.

———, and Doris M. Mayer. "Psychosis and Social Change among the Tallensi of Northern Ghana." *Cahiers d'Études Africaines* 21 (1966): 5–40.

———, and E. E. Evans-Pritchard, eds. *African Political Systems.* London, 1940.

Freeman, R. A. *Travels and Life in Ashanti and Jaman.* London, 1898.

Freeman, Thomas Birch. *Journal of Various Visits to the Kingdoms of Ashanti, Aku, and Dahomi in Western Africa.* London, 1844.

Garrard, Timothy. "An Asante *Kuduo* among the Frafra of Northern Ghana." In *The Golden Stool: Studies of the Asante Center and Periphery,* ed. Enid Schildkrout, 73–79. New York, 1987.

Geschiere, Peter. *The Modernity of Witchcraft: Politics and the Occult in Postcolonial Africa.* Charlottesville, 1997.

Ginzburg, Carlo. *Ecstacies: Deciphering the Witches' Sabbath.* Trans. Raymond Rosenthal. London, 1992.

————. *The Night Battles: Witchcraft and Agrarian Cults in the Sixteenth and Seventeenth Centuries.* Trans. John Tedeschi and Anne Tedeschi. London, 1983.

Gluckman, Max. "Analysis of a Social Situation in Modern Zululand." *Rhodes-Livingstone Papers* 28. Manchester, 1958.

Goody, Esther. "Legitimate and Illegitimate Aggression in a West African State." In *Witchcraft Confessions and Accusations,* ed. Mary Douglas, 207–44. London, 1970.

————, and Jack Goody. "The Naked and the Clothed." In *The Cloth of Many Colored Silks: Papers on History and Society, Ghanaian and Islamic, in Honor of Ivor Wilks,* ed. John Hunwick and Nancy Lawler, 67–90. Evanston, 1996.

Goody, Jack. "Anomie in Ashanti?" *Africa* 27 (1957): 356–63.

————. *Death, Property, and the Ancestors: A Study of the Mortuary Customs of the LoDagaa of West Africa.* Stanford, 1962.

————. *The Expansive Moment: The Rise of Social Anthropology in Britain and Africa, 1918–1970.* Cambridge, 1995.

————. Introduction to *Religion, Morality, and the Person: Essays on Tallensi Religion,* by Meyer Fortes. Cambridge, 1987.

————. "The Over-Kingdom of Gonja." In *West African Kingdoms in the Nineteenth Century,* ed. Daryl Forde and P. M. Kaberry, 179–205. London, 1967.

————. "The Political Systems of the Tallensi and Their Neighbours, 1888–1915." *Cambridge Anthropology* 14 (1990): 1–25.

————. "Population and Polity in the Voltaic Region." In *The Evolution of Social Systems,* ed. J. Friedman and M. J. Rowlands, 535–45. London, 1977.

————. *The Social Organisation of the LoWiili.* London, 1956.

————. *Technology, Tradition, and the State in Africa.* London, 1971.

Gray, Natasha. "The Legal History of Witchcraft in Colonial Ghana: Akyem Abuakwa, 1913–1943." Ph.D. dissertation, Columbia University, 2000.

————. "Witches, Oracles, and Colonial Law: Evolving Anti-witchcraft Practices in Ghana, 1927–1932." *International Journal of African Historical Studies* 34 (2001): 339–64.

Greene, Sandra E. *Sacred Sites and the Colonial Encounter: A History of Meaning and Memory in Ghana.* Bloomington, 2002.

Grier, Beverly. "Pawns, Porters, and Petty Traders: Women in the Transition to Cash Crop Agriculture in Colonial Ghana." *Signs* 17 (1992): 304–28.

Hart, Keith. "The Economic Basis of Tallensi Social History in the Early Twentieth Century." *Research in Economic Anthropology* 1 (1978): 185–216.

————. "The Social Anthropology of West Africa." *Annual Review of Anthropology* 14 (1985): 243–73.

Hawkins, Sean. "The Interpretation of *Naangmin:* Missionary Ethnography, African Theology, and History among the LoDagaa." *Journal of Religion in Africa* 28 (1998): 32–61.

————. *Writing and Colonialism in Northern Ghana: The Encounter between the LoDagaa and "The World on Paper."* Toronto, 2002.

Hill, Polly. *The Migrant Cocoa-Farmers of Southern Ghana: A Study in Rural Capitalism.* Cambridge, 1963.

Holden, J. J. "The Zabarima Conquest of North-West Ghana." *Transactions of the Historical Society of Ghana* 8 (1965): 60–86.

Horton, Robin. "Social Psychologies: African and Western." In *Oedipus and Job in West African Religion*, by Meyer Fortes, 41–82. Cambridge, 1983.

———. "Stateless Societies in the History of West Africa." In *History of West Africa*, vol. 1, ed. J. F. A. Ajayi and Michael Crowder, 3rd ed., 87–128. Harlow, 1985.

Hubbell, Andrew. "A View of the Slave Trade from the Margin: Souroudougou in the Late Nineteenth-Century Slave Trade of the Niger Bend." *Journal of African History* 42 (2001): 25–47.

Hudgens, Jim, and Richard Trillo. *West Africa: The Rough Guide*. London, 1999.

Hunwick, John O., ed. and trans. *Timbuktu and the Songhay Empire: Al-Sa'di's Ta'rikh al-sudan down to 1613, and Other Contemporary Documents*. Leiden, 1999.

Illiasu, A. A. "The Establishment of British Administration in Mamprugu, 1898–1937." *Transactions of the Historical Society of Ghana* 16 (1975): 1–28.

Jahoda, Gustav. "Traditional Healers and Other Institutions Concerned with Mental Illness in Ghana." *International Journal of Social Psychiatry* 7 (1961): 199–215.

Janzen, John M. "Drums of Affliction: Real Phenomenon or Scholarly Chimaera?" In *Religion in Africa*, ed. Thomas D. Blakely, Walter van Beek, and Dennis C. Thompson, 161–81. London, 1994.

———. *Lemba, 1650–1930: A Drum of Affliction in Africa and the New World*. New York, 1982.

———. *Ngoma: Discourses of Healing in Central and Southern Africa*. Berkeley, 1992.

Johnson, Douglas H. "Evans-Pritchard, the Nuer, and the Sudan Political Service." *African Affairs* 81 (1982): 231–46.

———. *Nuer Prophets: A History of Prophecy from the Upper Nile in the Nineteenth and Twentieth Centuries*. Oxford, 1994.

Johnson, Marion, ed. *Salaga Papers*. Institute of African Studies, Legon, n.d.

Kambou-Ferrand, Jeanne-Marie. *Peuples voltaïques et conquête coloniale, 1885–1914: Burkina Faso*. Paris, 1993.

Klein, Martin. "The Slave Trade and Decentralized Societies," *Journal of African History* 42 (2001): 49–65.

Koelle, S. W. *Polyglotta Africana*. London, 1854.

Kopytoff, Igor, ed. *The African Frontier: The Reproduction of Traditional African Societies*. Bloomington, 1987.

Kramer, Fritz W. *The Red Fez: Art and Spirit Possession in Africa*. Trans. Malcolm Green. London, 1993.

Kuklick, Henrika. *The Savage Within: The Social History of British Anthropology, 1885–1945*. Cambridge, 1991.

Kuper, Adam. *Anthropologists and Anthropology: The Modern British School*. 3rd ed. London, 1996.

———. *The Invention of Primitive Society: Transformations of an Illusion*. London, 1998.

Kyei, T. E. *Our Days Dwindle: Memories of My Childhood Days in Asante*. Portsmouth, N.H., 2001.

Ladurie, Emmanuel Le Roy. *Les paysans de Languedoc*. Paris, 1966.

Lance, James. "Seeking the Political Kingdom: British Colonial Impositions and African Manipulations in the Northern Territories of the Gold Coast Colony." Ph.D. dissertation, Stanford University, 1995.

Larbi, Bismark Enoch. "Assiful's Relationship with Nana Tongo." Unpublished ms., May 2002.

Law, Robin. *The Horse in West African History.* Oxford, 1980.

Lentz, Carola. "Colonial Ethnography and Political Reform: The Works of A. C. Duncan-Johnson, R. S. Rattray, J. Eyre-Smith, and J. Guiness on Northern Ghana." *Ghana Studies* 2 (1999): 119–70.

Levack, Brian P. *The Witch-Hunt in Early Modern Europe.* Harlow, 1995.

Levtzion, Nehemia. *Muslims and Chiefs in West Africa: A Study of Islam in the Middle Volta Basin in the Pre-colonial Period.* Oxford, 1968.

Mabogunje, Akin L., and Paul Richards. "Land and People: Models of Spatial and Ecological Process in West African History." In *History of West Africa*, vol. 1, ed. J. F. A. Ajayi and Michael Crowder, 3rd ed., 5–47. Harlow, 1985.

Maier, Donna J. E. *Priests and Power: The Case of the Dente Shrine in Nineteenth-Century Ghana.* Bloomington, 1983.

Manchuelle, François. *Willing Migrants: Soninke Labor Diasporas.* Athens, Ohio, 1998.

McCaskie, T. C. "Anti-witchcraft Cults in Asante: An Essay in the Social History of an African People." *History in Africa* 8 (1981): 125–54.

———. *Asante Identities: History and Modernity in an African Village, 1850–1950.* Edinburgh, 2000.

———. "Komfo Anokye of Asante: Meaning, History, and Philosophy in an African Society." *Journal of African History* 27 (1986): 315–39.

———. "R. S. Rattray and the Construction of Asante History: An Appraisal." *History in Africa* 10 (1983): 187–206.

———. *State and Society in Pre-colonial Asante.* Cambridge, 1995.

McLeod, Malcolm. "On the Spread of Anti-witchcraft Cults in Modern Asante." In *Changing Social Structure in Ghana: Essays in the Comparative Sociology of a New State and an Old Tradition*, ed. Jack Goody, 107–17. London, 1975.

Meyer, Birgit. *Translating the Devil: Religion and Modernity among the Ewe in Ghana.* Edinburgh, 1999.

Mikell, Gwendolyn. *Cocoa and Chaos in Ghana.* New York, 1989.

Miller, Joseph, ed. *The African Past Speaks: Essays on Oral Tradition and History.* Folkestone, 1980.

Mitchell, J. Clyde. "The Kalela Dance." *Rhodes-Livingstone Papers* 27. Manchester, 1956.

Moore, Henrietta L., and Megan Vaughan. *Cutting Down Trees: Gender, Nutrition, and Agricultural Change in the Northern Province of Zambia, 1890–1990.* Portsmouth, N.H., 1994.

Moore, Sally Falk. *Anthropology and Africa: Changing Perspectives on a Changing Scene.* Charlottesville, 1994.

Morton-Williams, Peter. "The Atinga Cult among the South-Western Yoruba: A Sociological Analysis of a Witch-Finding Movement." *Bulletin de l'IFAN* 18 (1956): 315–34.

Nabila, John Sebiyam. "The Migration of the Frafra of Northern Ghana: A Case Study of Cyclical Labor Migration in West Africa." Ph.D. dissertation, Michigan State University, 1974.

Naden, Tony. "The Gur Languages." In *The Languages of Ghana*, ed. M. E. Kropp Dakubu, 12–49. London, 1988.

Olsen, William C. "'Children for Death': Money, Wealth, and Witchcraft Suspicion in Colonial Asante." *Cahiers d'Études Africaines* 167 (2002): 521–50.

Owusu-Ansah, David. *Islamic Talismanic Tradition in Nineteenth-Century Asante.* Lewiston, Mass., 1991.

Parish, Jane. "The Dynamics of Witchcraft and Indigenous Shrines among the Akan." *Africa* 69 (1999): 426–48.

Parker, John. *Making the Town: Ga State and Society in Early Colonial Accra.* Portsmouth, N.H., 2000.

———. "Witchcraft, Anti-witchcraft, and Trans-regional Ritual Innovation in Early Colonial Ghana: Sakrabundi and Aberewa, 1889–1910." *Journal of African History* 45 (2004): 393–420.

Parrinder, E. G. *African Traditional Religion.* London, 1954.

———. "The Prevalence of Witches II." *West Africa,* 26 May 1956, 320.

———. *West African Psychology.* London, 1951.

———. *West African Religion, Illustrated from the Beliefs and Practices of the Yoruba, Ewe, Akan, and Kindred Peoples.* London, 1949.

———. *Witchcraft.* Harmondsworth, 1958.

Peel, J. D. Y. *Religious Encounter and the Making of the Yoruba.* Bloomington, 2000.

Piot, Charles. "Of Slaves and the Gift: Kabre Sale of Kin during the Era of the Atlantic Slave Trade." *Journal of African History* 37 (1996): 31–49.

———. *Remotely Global: Village Modernity in West Africa.* Chicago, 1999.

Ranger, Terence O. *Voices from the Rocks: Nature, Culture, and History in the Matapos Hills of Zimbabwe.* Oxford, 1999.

———, and Isaria Kimambo, eds. *The Historical Study of African Religion.* London, 1972.

———, and John Weller, eds. *Themes in the Christian History of Central Africa.* London, 1975.

Rathbone, Richard. *Murder and Politics in Colonial Ghana.* New Haven, 1993.

———. *Nkrumah and the Chiefs: The Politics of Chieftaincy in Ghana, 1951–1960.* Oxford, 2000.

Rattray, R. S. *Ashanti.* London, 1923.

———. *Religion and Art in Ashanti.* London, 1927.

———. *The Tribes of the Ashanti Hinterland.* Oxford, 1932.

Richards, Audrey I. "A Modern Movement of Witchfinders." *Africa* 8 (1935): 448–61.

Riehl, Volker. "The Land Is Ours: Research on the Land-Use System among the Talensi in Northern Ghana." *Cambridge Anthropology* 14 (1990): 26–42.

Roberts, Richard. *Warriors, Merchants, and Slaves: The State and the Economy in the Middle Niger Valley, 1700–1914.* Stanford, 1987.

Rosenthal, Judy. *Possession, Ecstasy, and Law in Ewe Voodoo.* Charlottesville, 1998.

Saul, Mahir, and Patrick Royer. *West African Challenge to Empire: Culture and History in the Volta-Bani Anticolonial War.* Athens, Ohio, 2001.

Schildkrout, Enid. "The Ideology of Regionalism in Ghana." In *Strangers in African Societies,* ed. W. A. Shack and E. P. Skinner, 183–207. Berkeley, 1979.

———, ed. *The Golden Stool: Studies of the Asante Center and Periphery.* New York, 1987.

Schoffeleers, J. M. *River of Blood: The Genesis of a Martyr Cult in Southern Malawi, c. A.D. 1600.* Madison, 1992.

————, ed. *Guardians of the Land: Essays on Central African Territorial Cults*. Gwelo, 1978.

Schott, R. "Sources for a History of the Bulsa in Northern Ghana." *Paideuma* 23 (1977): 141–68.

Schottner, Michael. "'We Stay, Others Come and Go': Identity among the Mamprusi in Northern Ghana." In *Ethnicity in Ghana: The Limits of Invention*, ed. Carola Lentz and Paul Nugent, 49–67. Edinburgh, 2000.

Schumaker, Lyn. *Africanizing Anthropology: Fieldwork, Networks, and the Making of Cultural Knowledge in Central Africa*. Durham, 2001.

Shaffer, Tanya. "Losing Their Shirts." *Wanderlust*, 1998. http://archive.salon.com/wlust/feature/1998/06/04feature.html.

Sharpe, Barrie. "Ethnography and a Regional System: Mental Maps and the Myth of States and Tribes in North-Central Nigeria." *Critique of Anthropology* 6 (1986): 33–65.

Shaw, Rosalind. "The Invention of 'African Traditional Religion.'" *Religion* 20 (1990): 339–53.

————. *Memories of the Slave Trade: Ritual and the Historical Imagination in Sierra Leone*. Chicago, 2002.

————. "The Production of Witchcraft and Witchcraft as Production: Memory, Modernity, and the Slave Trade in Sierra Leone." *American Ethnologist* 24 (1997): 856–76.

Smith, Jonathan Z. *Imagining Religion: From Babylon to Jonestown*. Chicago, 1982.

————. *Map Is Not Territory: Studies in the History of Religions*. Leiden, 1978.

Stocking, George, Jr. *The Ethnographer's Magic and Other Essays in the History of Anthropology*. Madison, 1992.

Stoller, Paul. *The Cinematic Griot: The Ethnography of Jean Rouch*. Chicago, 1992.

————. *Colonial Memories: Spirit Possession, Power, and the Hauka in West Africa*. New York, 1995.

Tait, David. "Konkomba Sorcery." In *Magic, Witchcraft, and Curing*, ed. John Middleton, 155–70. New York, 1967.

————. "A Sorcery Hunt in Dagomba." *Africa* 32 (1963): 136–47.

Tamakloe, Emmanuel Forster. *A Brief History of the Dagbamba People*. Accra, 1931.

Taussig, Michael. *Mimesis and Alterity: A Particular History of the Senses*. New York, 1993.

Tauxier, Louis. *Le noir de Bondoukou: Koulangos, Dyoulas, Abrons, etc*. Paris, 1921.

————. *Le noir du Soudan: Pays Mossi et Gourounsi*. Paris, 1912.

————. *Nouvelles notes sur le Mossi et le Gourounsi*. Paris, 1924.

Thomas, Roger. "Forced Labour in British West Africa: The Case of the Northern Territories of the Gold Coast, 1906–1927." *Journal of African History* 14 (1973): 79–103.

————. "The 1916 Bongo 'Riots' and Their Background: Aspects of Colonial Administration and African Response in Eastern Upper Ghana." *Journal of African History* 24 (1983): 57–75.

Thurston, Robert W. *Witch, Wicce, Mother Goose: The Rise and Fall of the Witch Hunts in Europe and North America*. Harlow, 2001.

Tonkin, Elizabeth. "West African Ethnographic Traditions." In *Localizing Strategies:*

Regional Traditions of Ethnographic Writing, ed. Richard Fardon, 137–51. Washington, 1990.

Turner, Victor W. *Dramas, Fields, and Metaphors: Symbolic Action in Human Society*. Ithaca, 1974.

———. *The Drums of Affliction*. Oxford, 1968.

———. *The Forest of Symbols: Aspects of Ndembu Ritual*. Ithaca, 1967.

———. *Schism and Continuity in an African Society: A Study of Ndembu Village Life*. Manchester, 1957.

van Binsbergen, Wim. "Regional and Non-regional Cults of Affliction in Western Zambia." In *Regional Cults*, ed. Richard P. Werbner, 141–75. London, 1977.

———. *Religious Change in Zambia: Exploratory Studies*. London, 1981.

———. *Tears of Rain: Ethnicity and History in Central Western Zambia*. London, 1992.

van Dijk, Rijk, Ria Reis, and Marja Spierenburg, eds. *The Quest for Fruition through Ngoma: Political Aspects of Healing in Southern Africa*. Oxford, 2000.

Vansina, Jan. *Oral Tradition as History*. Madison, 1985.

———. *Paths in the Rainforest: Towards a History of Political Tradition in Equatorial Africa*. Madison, 1990.

Verdon, Michel. "Tallensi Kinship or the Rationalism of British Anthropology." *Journal of Anthropological Research* 40 (1984): 109–20.

Ward, Barbara E. "Some Observations on Religious Cults in Ashanti." *Africa* 26 (1956): 47–61.

Warren, Dennis M. "Bono Traditional Healers." In *African Therapeutic Systems*, ed. Z. A. Ademuwagun et al., 120–24. Waltham, Mass., 1979.

Werbner, Richard P. *Ritual Passage, Sacred Journey: The Process and Organization of Religious Movement*. Washington, 1989.

———, ed. *Regional Cults*. London, 1977.

White, Luise. *Speaking with Vampires: Rumor and History in Colonial Africa*. Berkeley, 2000.

Wilks, Ivor. *Asante in the Nineteenth Century: The Structure and Evolution of a Political Order*. Cambridge, 1975.

———. *Forests of Gold: Essays on the Akan and the Kingdom of Asante*. Athens: Ohio University Press, 1993.

———. "The Juula and the Expansion of Islam into the Forest." In *The History of Islam in Africa*, ed. Nehemia Levtzion and Randall L. Pouwels, 93–115. Athens, Ohio, 2000.

———. "The Mossi and the Akan States, 1400 to 1800." In *History of West Africa*, vol. 1, ed. J. F. A. Ajayi and Michael Crowder, 3rd ed., 465–502. Harlow, 1985.

———. *The Northern Factor in Ashanti History*. Legon, 1961.

———. "The Position of Muslims in Metropolitan Ashanti in the Early Nineteenth Century." In *Islam in Tropical Africa*, ed. I. M. Lewis, 318–41. London, 1966.

———. *Wa and the Wala: Islam and Polity in Northwestern Ghana*. Cambridge, 1989.

———, Nehemia Levtzion, and Bruce M. Haight. *Chronicles from Gonja: A Tradition of West African Muslim Historiography*. Cambridge, 1986.

Willis, R. G. "Instant Millennium: The Sociology of African Witch-Cleansing Cults." In *Witchcraft Confessions and Accusations*, ed. Mary Douglas, 129–39. London, 1970.

Worsley, P. M. "The Kinship System of the Tallensi: A Re-evaluation." *Journal of the Royal Anthropological Institute* 86 (1956): 38–75.

Interviews

Adwoa Ankoma, Kofi Obeng, Okomfo Yaa Sekyibiaa, Kwaku Opoku, Efia Nyakoaa, and Isaac Tetteh-Nartey: Tengzug, 8 Nov. 1999
Akankesim, Samsanaab-yiri: Kanjaga, 4 July 2002
Anonymous visitor in Ewe: Tengzug, 8 Nov. 1999
Anurimwazemi: Apuingyire-Samsa, Kanjaga, 4 July 2002
Anyaam: Kpikpaluk, Kadema, 11 June 2001
Asiidem Akanguli: Wiaga, 11 June 2001
Atuli Asamane: Yorogo, 21 Oct. 1999
Atulum Angiaknab and Gariba Angiaknab: Abangyire, Fumbisi-Kasiesa, 4 July 2002
Azabu: Samire, Tengzug, 20 Oct. 1999
Bamibanrib Zandoya: Tengzug, 13 Aug. 1999
Ben Atongnaab Akanisoam: Akannyokyiri, Gbedema, 4 July 2002
Bismark Enoch Larbi: Kokomlemle, Accra, and Abiriw, 17 June 2000
Bo'arana Volemeng: Shia, 17 Aug. 1999
Bo'arnaab Dilimit: Tengzug, 13 Aug. 1999
Boarnii: Tengzug, 12 Aug. 1999
Bosomfo Nii Yaw: Oshieyie, 4 June 2000
Dema'ame and Boarnab Poa: Gundaat, Tengzug, 8 June 2001
Diegire Baa: Shia, 17 Aug, 1999
Golibdaana Malbazaa: Tengzug, 24 July 2000
Goring: Sheaga, Tindongo, 12 June 2001
Isaac Tetteh-Nartey: Tengzug, 7 Nov. 1999
John Bawa Zuure: Tengzug, 23 Aug. 1999, 7 Nov. 1999, 9 Nov. 1999, 24 July 2000, and 24 Aug. 2000.
John Peter Dadson: Kaneshie Estate, Accra, 27 July 2002
Kandiau *tengdaana*: Kandiau, 19 July 2000
Korkor Nartey and Lardje Nartey: Suhum, 13 Nov. 1999
Kumahe: Yinduri, 16 Aug. 1999
Kwame Arhin: Tanoso, 17 June 2001
Kwao Ahoto: Tengzug, 8 Nov. 1999
Lambazaa Naoh: Tengzug, 6 July 2002
Lambazaa Naoh and Zampahi: Tengzug, 14 Aug. 1999
Manyanme, Sapak, Zong, and Azabu: Samire, Tengzug, 11 Aug. 1999
Margaret Azantilo: Sandema, 13 June 2001
Naoh: Tengzug, 9 Aug. 1999
Nayina: Gbezug, Tongo, 5 Aug. 1999
Nii Kofi Akrashie: Oshieyie, 29 July 2000
Okomfo Atta Fordwo: Kukurantumi, 16 June 2000
Okomfo Sika, Okomfo Yaa, and Okyeame Tawia: Tengzug, 8 Nov. 1999 and 9 Nov. 1999
Okomfo Sika and Okyeame Tawia: Kukurantumi, 16 June 2000
Pahinooni and Tengdaana Dukbazaa: Sipaat, 19 Aug. 1999
Paul Assifu: Obretema, 13 Nov. 1999
Piyame, Baa, and Tong: Kpatar, Tengzug, 10 Aug. 1999
Punaar and Mariyama: Kpatar, Tengzug, 8 June 2001

Sandemanaaba Ayita Azantilow: Sandema, 13 June 2001
Senyonwura, Senyon Kupo, and Kulawura: Senyon, 17 July 2000.
Sipaatnaaba, Putehinga, Doabil, Ba'an, and Sapak: Sipaat, 19 Aug. 1999
Tengdaan Dok: Baari, 6 Aug. 1999
Tengdaan Dok: Tamboo, Tengzug, 12 Aug. 1999
Tengdaan Duhibazaa: Shia, 17 Aug. 1999
Tengdaan Kuruk, Kuribil Waadan, and Kpalbil Mebogire: Wakii, 6 Aug. 1999
Tengdaana Bo'anaab Dilimit: Gundaat, Tengzug, 13 Aug. 1999 and 8 June 2001
Tengdaana Pehibazaa and Siikabani: Zubiung, Tongo, 5 Aug. 1999
Tengdaana Zienbazaa: Gbeog, 1 July 2002
Tii Kaha and Kumahe Puhibazaa: Yinduri, 16 Aug. 1999
Tongrana, with Puhik Kambonaba, Kpana, Nabzor, and Zuuran: Tongo, 24 Aug. 1999
Wayanaya Songbazaa: Sakpee, Tengzug, 11 Aug. 1999
Yikpemdaan (or Gorogonaaba) Wakbazaa: Gorogo, 9 June 2001 and 3 July 2002
Yikpemdaan (or Gorogonaaba) Wakbazaa and Chuhiya Doakobik: Gorogo, 21 Aug. 1999
Yiran Boare: Tengzug, 10 Aug. 1999, 23 Aug. 1999, and 24 Aug. 2000
Zimemeh and Yin Kudoog: Yinduri, 16 Aug. 1999

Index

Page references in italics indicate illustrations.

Jean Allman teaches African History and directs the Center for African Studies at the University of Illinois. She has authored and edited several volumes, including *"I Will Not Eat Stone": A Women's History of Colonial Asante* (2000, with Victoria Tashjian), *Women in African Colonial Histories* (2002, with Susan Geiger and Nakanyike Musisi), and *Fashioning Africa: Power and the Politics of Dress* (2004). Her research on gender, colonialism, and social change has appeared in numerous scholarly journals.

John Parker teaches African History at the School of Oriental and African Studies, University of London. He is the author of *Making the Town: Ga State and Society in Early Colonial Accra* (2000) and is currently researching a book on the history of death and burial in Ghana.

CPSIA information can be obtained
at www.ICGtesting.com
Printed in the USA
JSHW030808250921
18930JS00012B/143